In *Christian Spirituality: Lived Expressions in the Life of the Church*, Peter Feldmeier has provided us with a wonderfully readable and clear treatment of the depth and breadth of Christian spiritual traditions. It is informed by the best of recent scholarship.

—Wendy M. Wright, PhD
Professor of Theology
Creighton University

Peter Feldmeier's *Christian Spirituality* is a welcome introduction and guide to the study of Christian spirituality and a companion to the reading of primary texts. Exploration of the terms *spirituality* and *mysticism* is followed by a historical journey from biblical to contemporary interfaith spirituality. Resources include bibliography, Web resources, film, images, short excerpts, questions for discussion, and a glossary that will aid readers who wish to pursue the many topics covered. Feldmeier combines historical, theological, conceptual, and practical perspectives on the many faces of Christian spirituality in a religiously plural, interfaith context.

—Elizabeth Dreyer
Professor Emerita
Fairfield University

This well-crafted survey strikes me as a desirable volume to engage readers with the riches of the Christian spiritual tradition. Well written, adorned with user-friendly pedagogical aids, it is ideal for classroom use.

—Lawrence S. Cunningham
John A. O'Brien Professor of Theology, Emerita
University of Notre Dame

Author Acknowledgments

I'd like to thank several persons who have made this book possible. First and foremost, I am grateful to the folks at Anselm Academic, whom I've found to be the most helpful editorial staff I've ever worked with. I'm particularly grateful to Jerry Ruff who first suggested I write this book and Bradley Harmon who, over the course of several long conversations, helped me conceptualize and organize the chapters in this volume. I am also grateful to Maura Hagarty whose ongoing support and gentle challenges ensured the quality and timely publication of *Christian Spirituality*. Many thanks to Kathleen Walsh and my grad assistant Jim Lethbridge for their careful reads and numerous suggestions for rewrites. They are the behind-the-scenes vital contributors to this book's clarity. Finally, I thank John Sarnecki, the chair of my department, for his constant support.

Publisher Acknowledgments

Thank you to the following individuals who reviewed this work in progress:

Kathleen Fisher, *Assumption College, Worcester, Massachusetts*

Joy Milos, *Gonzaga University, Spokane, Washington*

Raymond Studzinski, *The Catholic University of America, Washington, DC*

Min-Ah Cho, *St. Catherine University, Saint Paul, Minnesota*

CHRISTIAN SPIRITUALITY

LIVED EXPRESSIONS IN THE LIFE OF THE CHURCH

Peter Feldmeier

Created by the publishing team of Anselm Academic.

Cover images: © Denis Radovanovic / Shutterstock.com, © Amanda Carden / Shutterstock.com, © Bill Perry / Shutterstock.com, © Photograph of Thomas Merton by John Lyons. Used with permission of the Merton Legacy Trust and the Thomas Merton Center at Bellarmine University, © Peter Zelei / istock.com, © Florin Stana / Shutterstock.com, © life_is_fantastic / Shutterstock.com, © Steve Mann / Shutterstock.com

Printed in the United States of America

7070

ISBN 978-1-59982-635-6

Contents

1. What Is Spirituality? 7

2. Mysticism 25

3. Biblical Spirituality 42

4. The Spirituality of the Early Church 58

5. Patristic Paths to Union: Four Figures 75

6. Monastic Spirituality East and West 97

7. Eastern Orthodox Spirituality 119

8. Western Medieval Piety 136

9. Carmelite Spirituality 158

10. Ignatian Spirituality 174

11. Spirituality of the Reformers 190

12. Evangelical Spirituality 212

13. Pentecostal Spirituality 229

14. Liberation Spirituality 245

15. Comparative Spirituality 264

16. Three Modern Witnesses 285

Glossary 311
Index 319

131905

What Is Spirituality?

Modern interest in spirituality is big and growing. One needs only to enter a major bookstore to find a plethora of books devoted to the subject. These include works on religious doctrine, the new age movement, mysticism, self-help books, and many other subjects. Many are practical, dealing with such topics as how to pray, how to infuse marriage with religious meaning, or how to develop a twelve-step spirituality. Others are more exotic, promising wisdom from indigenous traditions or esoteric teachings from the East. Still others use the term "spirituality" quite loosely, applying it to such things as optimal golf games or wholesome business strategies. What seems clear from such titles and themes is that the term itself is very unclear. Even trained scholars struggle to agree on a definition. The famous Anglican theologian John Macquarrie considers that spirituality "has to do with becoming a person in the fullest sense." Leading Protestant spirituality scholar Gordon Wakefield says that it "describes those attitudes, beliefs, and practices which animate people's lives and help them to reach out towards super-sensible realities." And finally, former Archbishop of Canterbury Rowan Williams speaks of "each believer making his or her own that engagement with the questioning at the heart of faith."[1]

Each of these definitions has problems. Macquarrie's is a bit vague and assumes a modern bias toward flourishing in *all* dimensions of human life, whereas a number of traditional spiritualities would not see biological health as a necessary component. Regarding Wakefield's definition, many spiritualities, such as Buddhist, might quarrel with the idea that spirituality must involve the pursuit of super-sensible realities. Even Williams's definition can be faulted on the grounds that some persons' "questioning" might be rather superficial.

---

1. John Macquarrie, *Paths in Spirituality* (New York: Harper & Row, 1972), 40; Gordon Wakefield, "Spirituality," in *Westminster Dictionary of Christian Spirituality*, ed. G. Wakefield (Philadelphia: Westminster, 1983), 361; Rowan Williams, *Christian Spirituality: A Theological History from the New Testament to Luther and St. John of the Cross* (Atlanta: John Knox, 1979), 1. See Sandra Schneiders, "Theology and Spirituality: Strangers, Rivals, or Partners?" *Horizons* 13, no 2 (1986): 265–66.

Ewert Cousins, the general editor of the monumental series, *World Spirituality: An Encyclopedic History of the Religious Quest*, after wrestling with the problem, finally settled on this definition: Spirituality is "that inner dimension of the person called by certain traditions 'the spirit.' This spiritual core is the deepest center of the person. It is here that the person is open to the transcendent dimension; it is here that the person experiences ultimate reality."[2] Cousins's definition could be faulted for characterizing spirituality as something solely personal, with little attention to spiritual movements that focus on such goals as social justice or environmental responsibility.

Sandra Schneiders, a leader in the field of spirituality, argues that every spirituality has six analyzable components:

- An understanding of human nature and the human condition from a theological perspective.
- An ultimate horizon. Whether this ultimate horizon is God, union with God, or perhaps Nirvana, there is always something that represents a spiritualty's foundational concern or absolute value.
- A path to that ultimate horizon, a way of life or series of stages that helps aspirants attain the ultimate horizon.
- Typical experiences that represent advancement on the path.
- Integration of the person or community of persons that represents increasingly broad flourishing along the path.
- Specific values that are core and necessary to uphold and pursue.

Many scholars find this framework useful, both for exploring a particular spirituality and for comparing different spiritualities. In my doctoral dissertation, I used Schneiders's strategy fruitfully to compare the spiritualities of sixteenth century mystic John of the Cross and fifth century Buddhist scholar Buddhaghosa. Each of Schneiders's categories helped me comprehensively map their respective understandings of the human person, the respective nature of union with God and Nirvana, how to proceed to that ultimate horizon, what one would typically expect as one proceeded along the path, the kinds of spiritual healing that corresponded to different stages of spiritual growth, and the key values one would have to maintain progress.

Schneiders's account also helpfully exposes the limitations of some spiritualities. For example, twelve-step spiritualities, such as one might find in *Alcoholics Anonymous* and similar recovery models, often prove helpful in addressing addiction, but offer no real sense of who or what God is. Rather,

---

2. Ewert Cousins, "Preface," in *Christian Spirituality*, ed. Bernard McGinn, John Meyendorff, and Jean Leclercq (New York: Continuum, 1988), 1:xiii.

Spiritual but not Religious

Many Americans today say they are "spiritual but not religious." Some who say this mean that they believe themselves spiritually attuned to God or transcendental principle in the universe, but are not members of a religious organization. Others mean that they are committed to specific spiritual practices, typically coming from a religious tradition, but are not formally members of that religion. Others mean that, although they do not participate in religious practices, neither do they consider themselves atheists. Scholars and religious leaders alike often recognize that the "spiritual but not religious" posture sometimes reflects a principled intellectual stance against religious dogma or institutional dysfunction. But the phrase is vague, and sometimes persons use it without actually thinking through what it means to be "spiritual but not religious."

they imagine God only as "a higher power." They also pursue no ultimate goal beyond recovering from addiction and assuming personal responsibility for one's past behavior. Their understanding of the human condition is limited to the recognition of one's powerlessness to resist addiction. In light of the six components, twelve-step recovery programs don't embody a full-fledged spirituality, which involves the whole person in a comprehensive way or contains a clear agenda for pursuing transcendence.

Schneiders's account, however, also has its limitations. Some spiritualities simply do not fit this model very well. Native American spiritualities, for example, do not lay out a clear path with well-defined stages of growth. Daoist and Shinto spiritualities do not have an ultimate horizon. And even the Ignatian spirituality from the Roman Catholic tradition does not seem to fit Scheiders's account well, as explained in chapter 10.

Another helpful framing of the study of spirituality comes from Michael Buckley, who, together with Schneiders, started the first comprehensive doctoral program for spirituality in the United States. Buckley says that every spirituality deals with a theology of God, an understanding about what it means to be human, and ways or means to union with the Divine. To these three concerns, he adds questions related to religious experience:

1. What types of experience gave rise to and foster this spiritual perspective?
2. How were these experiences originally expressed?

3. What theology do these experiences foster?

4. How are such theologies and experiences communicated?[3]

In the academic field of spirituality, many scholars resonate with the approaches of Schneiders and Buckley, in large part because both recognize the crucial importance of experience. Spirituality is simply dominated by the dynamics of religious experience. Both approaches express profound encounters with God, ways of engaging God and the world, and the dynamics of inner transformation. Furthermore, both approaches also recognize the necessity of situating that experience in a structure of theological beliefs and commitments. Every religious experience and path comes with assumptions about how God and nature work, and every experience has to be interpreted. Finally, both approaches emphasize that spirituality is about religious practices and their transformational possibilities. This book will address Christian spirituality mostly through the interpretive lenses of both Schneiders's and Buckley's models. Some spiritualities easily fall into the framing we find in Schneiders's model, and with these her model is most helpful. Others with a less clear path can be best examined with Buckley's framework.

Most contemporary scholarship on spirituality also embraces several other factors, including the understanding that spirituality as such is not necessarily Christian. There are Buddhist spiritualities, Hindu spiritualities, Native American spiritualities, and so on. Because a number of spiritualities can exist even within a given religious tradition, scholars increasingly see spirituality in a less dogmatic or universally prescriptive way. There is no "one-size-fits-all" spirituality that guarantees holiness or can claim to be the only way to become holy. Given such considerations, studies in spirituality overall show less interest in an abstract goal of "perfection" and more interest in ongoing spiritual growth.

Finally, the study of spirituality is invested in everything that gives meaning to human growth and flourishing. Thus the field tends to be holistic, encompassing concerns about the environment, justice, prayer, primary relations, religious community, and so forth. Because spirituality incorporates so many aspects of the human condition, it is also interdisciplinary. Since spirituality involves community, it dialogs with sociology. Since it includes issues of justice, spirituality works with moral philosophy. Since it is concerned with human development, spirituality partners with the field of psychology. Indeed, spirituality has become so interdisciplinary that one can even find books in the field focusing on how quantum theory impacts meditation. Many studies, such as this one, show particular interest in historical and theological issues. Although scholars in spirituality cannot acquire expertise in every relevant field, they tend to have a sound understanding of several fields and apply insights from various disciplines to illuminate their particular areas of inquiry.

---

3. Michael Buckley, "Seventeenth Century French Spirituality: Three Figures," in *Christian Spirituality*, ed. Louis Dupré and Don Saliers (New York: Crossroad, 1991), 3:31–32.

Scholar as Insider

A scholar of spirituality is typically something of an insider, that is, someone who has a personal knowledge of the subject. While it would be inappropriate for the scholar to be essentially working autobiographically, it has become obvious in the field that the most creative and insightful work is done by those who have a participative knowledge of spirituality. Sandra Schneiders writes, "The researcher must know the spiritual quest by personal experience if he or she is able to understand the phenomena of spirituality. . . . A purely disinterested phenomenological approach seems inappropriate if not impossible for spirituality."[4] Schneiders compares spirituality to other fields where participation is critical: "Like psychology, spirituality deals with material that cannot be understood except through analogy with personal experience. It is difficult to imagine that one could understand mysticism, discernment of spirits, or spiritual direction without some personal participation in a spiritual life in which these phenomena or their analogues were experienced."[5]

Christian Spirituality as a Field of Study

History of the Term

In Christianity the term "spirituality" has an interesting and varied history. The English word derives from the Latin *spiritualitas*, which itself is a translation influenced by the Greek noun *pneuma* (spirit). In the New Testament, the term *pneuma* refers both to the Holy Spirit and to the life of God working within the believer. It is this life of God working within that makes someone *pneumatikos* (spiritual). Jesus, in John's Gospel, emphasizes a rebirth in the Spirit and in truth (John 3:2–8; 4:23), and both Luke's Gospel and Acts of the Apostles have the Spirit establishing the community of believers (Luke 4:14; Acts 2:32–33). So integral is the Spirit to the presence of the risen Lord that Saint Paul even identifies the Christ with the Spirit (2 Cor. 3:17). Saint Paul also sees the nature of a Christian as entering the sphere of the Spirit (1 Cor. 6:17), and the indwelling presence of God makes one a "spiritual person" (1 Cor. 2:14–15). In the Vulgate, a late fourth-century Latin translation of

---

4. Sandra Schneiders, "Theology and Spirituality," *Horizons* 13, no. 2 (1986): 268.

5. Sandra Schneiders, "Spirituality and the Academy," *Theological Studies* 50, no. 4 (1989): 694–95.

the Bible, Saint Jerome used the term "spiritual" (*spiritualis*) twenty-two times as a translation of *pneumatikos*. The noun form of the term appeared in a fifth-century letter ascribed to Jerome: "*Age ut in spiritualite perfecias*" (Act in order to grow in spirituality).[6] This is the way the early church typically used the term, and there was no real change in its usage through the first half of the Middle Ages.

In the twelfth century, Saint Thomas Aquinas continued to use *spiritualitas* to mean something like *pneumatikos*, but he also used the term to refer to that which distinguishes humans from other animals. For Aquinas, humans have a "rational soul," that is they have the ability to reflect, pursue morality, and direct their lives to God. Thus they are "spiritual" beings. In contrast, other animals are irrational and have no soul or spirit. In his sixteenth-century *Vocabulary of Theology*, Johannes Altenstaig noted that the adjective "spiritual" referred to ways of acting religiously. It also referenced the kinds of spiritual exercises, such as meditation, that freed the soul from complete dependence on the senses. In the seventeenth century, the term was sometimes used pejoratively. "Spiritual people" were criticized as those who withdrew from the community or thought they were above standard expressions of the faith. By the eighteenth and nineteenth century, "spirituality" tended to be replaced by "devotion" (Catholic preference) or "piety" (evangelical preference) or even "perfection" (Methodist preference). Not until the twentieth century, with the publication of the *Dictionaire de spiritualité* (1932), did the

Acts chapter 2 describes the coming of the Holy Spirit upon the apostles in the form of "divided tongues, as of fire." The artist El Greco has added another traditional image of the Spirit: the dove.

---

6. As cited in Bernard McGinn, "The Letter and the Spirit: Spirituality as an Academic Discipline," in *Minding the Spirit: The Study of Christian Spirituality*, ed. Elizabeth Dreyer and Mark Burrows (Baltimore: Johns Hopkins University Press, 2005), 25–41, at 26.

term "spirituality" return to standard, widespread use. Later that century, journals took up the term. The journal *Révue d'ascétique et de mystique* renamed itself *Révue d'histoire de la spiritualité* in 1972, and in 1978 *Cross and Crown* became *Spirituality Today.*[7]

Emphases in the Study of Christian Spirituality

The study of Christian spirituality has a number of emphases. One emphasis, as noted earlier, is experience. From the beginning, the scriptures depict apostles and other early disciples as having experienced Jesus as risen and among them. They also experienced the Spirit, who both animated their faith in Jesus and guided their lives. Above all, Christian spirituality is interested in making sense of various expressions of God's interaction with persons and communities, and the transformations they have experienced because of it.

Another emphasis is the use of scripture. The Bible provides the core themes, metaphors, and grand narratives out of which Christians make sense of God's revelation in Christ. The Bible, as the first and foremost witness in Christian revelation, serves as a primary source for Christian spirituality.

Theological categories—and in some denominations, church doctrines—keep spirituality grounded in the Christian tradition. Thus theology constitutes another essential emphasis. Important theological themes and doctrines, such as church, grace, the Trinity, and salvation, have become normative and provide central teachings. Christian spirituality is not the study of such themes or doctrines—such as grace,[8] for example—per se, but every Christian spirituality would necessarily deal with grace uniquely as it is experienced in that particular spirituality. Still, an authentic Christian spirituality would be assessed on whether or not its expression of grace proved theologically adequate.

Another emphasis involves history. As the saying goes, "You are your history," and most studies in spirituality investigate classic historical models, whether from the monastic movement, Carmelite spirituality, Ignatian spirituality, or some other source. Even modern day expressions of spirituality tend to have a pedigree in previous historical models, although one cannot simply embrace a given historical model as though the culture from which it came were one's own. Saint Francis of Assisi's spirituality was rooted in many medieval themes, including assumptions about the body and its relationship to the soul, the centrality of Christ's Passion as expressed in the church, and how the incarnation ought to be modeled in the Christian. This spirituality was also culturally contextualized by feudalism and a new burgeoning capitalism, widespread poverty, monarchies, chivalry, and other factors specific to that era. His situation differs

---

7. Ibid., 28.

8. Grace is a theological theme that investigates God's favor and saving presence.

greatly from the contemporary one, so a critical dialog between cultures will comprise a necessary part of any historical study.

Working with historical models tends to involve three major aspects. First, historical studies call for a *thick description* of everything relevant to the spirituality and the culture out of which it emerged—what could be called the "what is it?" phase of the study. Second, *critical analysis* seeks to make sense of it all, including problems and biases of the time that one would not want to export to today. One could call this the "what does it mean?" phase of the study. Third, *constructive interpretation* entails extrapolating the insights and genius of such a spirituality and finding ways to make these relevant to today, or the "what can it mean for us?" phase of the study.

Essential Characteristics of Christian Spirituality

While every Christian spirituality is unique, each contains universal and biblically grounded elements that express core values of Christian identity. Many scholars studying a given spirituality highlight how these elements are expressed in it, and some spiritualities are critiqued when one or more of the following elements is missing.

Christian Spirituality Is a Life of Grace and Faith

Most scholars would agree that the most important theologian in Christianity is Saint Paul. His letters, found in the New Testament, continue to influence both Christian theology and spirituality. Perhaps Paul's most important concern is grace: God's favor and life within us. Paul says that grace justifies Christians before God, making them acceptable to God, and spiritually animates their souls (Rom. 3:9, 22–24). Grace is also a gift. Christians believe that they cannot earn salvation by works, but rather that it comes only by God's gift of himself.

If God's grace is what saves, what is the appropriate human response to it? Paul's answer is "faith." So united are faith and grace that he will even say in shorthand that human beings are "justified by faith" (Rom. 3:28, 5:1). What is faith? Paul does not equate it merely with belief or accepting doctrines about one's religion. Rather, faith represents entrusting oneself to God wholly. It is, from the human side, the dynamism of one's heart and mind to open oneself to God, to trust and follow God. Although faith is sometimes thought of as "belief without evidence," such a perspective is not Christian and would be referred to as "bad faith" or "blind faith." Rather, the experience of the liberating grace of God provides the initial evidence, and one responds to it with one's whole heart.

The life of faith is one of increasing spiritual freedom. Paul says in Galatians, "For freedom Christ set us free; so stand firm and do not submit again to the yoke of slavery" (5:1). Christianity understands human sinfulness as a kind of slavery, while the life of faith represents the true flourishing of a free person. This new kind of freedom is not freedom to do whatever one wants, if what one wants is sin, but rather freedom to love. In Martin Luther's classic, *On Christian Liberty*, he writes, "I shall set down the following two propositions concerning freedom and bondage of the spirit: A Christian is a perfectly free lord of all, subject to none. A Christian is a perfectly dutiful servant of all, subject to all."[9] In this seeming paradox, Luther shows how freedom works. Being truly free means being in the position to serve others and serving, not by compulsion or to prove anything, but because the very nature of freedom is to live the full Christian life of loving care.

Christian Spirituality Is Life in the Spirit

As noted above, Paul believed that being spiritual meant living in the Holy Spirit and attending to the Spirit's influence in one's life: "The fruit of the Spirit is love, joy, peace, patience, kindness, generosity, faithfulness, gentleness, self-control" (Gal. 5:22–23). Here Paul uses this listing to describe the kind of person whose life is infused with the Spirit.

The greatest sign of the animating presence of the Spirit, according to Paul, is the soul's transformation in love. Paul teaches, "Owe nothing to anyone, except to love one another; for the one who loves another has fulfilled the law" (Rom. 13:8). Jesus too taught that all of the Old Testament law could be summed up as love: "You shall love the Lord, your God, with all your heart, with all your soul, and with all your mind. This is the greatest and first commandment. The second is like it: You shall love your neighbor as yourself. The whole law and the prophets depend on these two commandments" (Matt. 22:37–40). Love is, for Jesus, the new and complete commandment (John 13:34; 15:10). Indeed 1 John declares that "God is love" (4:8). So central is this expression of the Christian life that one could safely say that with love one has God within oneself and without love one has no communion with God (1 John 2:10–11).

Christian Spirituality Is Christocentric

A fundamental goal of an authentic Christian spirituality consists of entering into a progressively deeper intimacy with Jesus Christ. Paul even described baptism as being "baptized into Christ" (Rom. 16:3), that is, immersed both in him and "into" him. This intimacy with Christ proves crucial to Christian

---

9. Martin Luther, *On Christian Liberty*, trans. W. A. Lambert (Minneapolis: Fortress Press, 2003), 2.

spirituality. In Jesus' final prayer, he prays, "So that they may all be one, as you, Father, are in me and I in you, that they also may be in us. . . . I in them and you in me" (John 17:21–23).

This Christocentric principle also involves incorporating the fundamental mysteries of Christ. For Christians, the Incarnation of Christ not only creates the condition whereby God and humanity are united in him, it also provides a model for taking on the divine life within oneself. As Saint Augustine said, "God became human that humanity might become God."[10] Here Augustine is not suggesting that humans actually exchange their human nature for the divine nature, but rather that the incarnation allows humanity to participate in God's life radically. The very nature of human existence becomes infused with divine possibilities.

Another fundamental mystery of the Christian faith is the cross. Every Christian spirituality in some way embraces the cross or a kind of personal dying to self. The cross represents God's solidarity with suffering humanity. According to Christian theology, God in Christ literally became united to the very brokenness of the human condition and entered into that darkness with healing love. In Philippians, Paul pleads with community members to take on the mind of Christ, who emptied himself for humanity (Phil. 2:5–8). God's love is revealed here as self-donation. For Christians, the cross can represent a kind of dying to one's sinful self, the self that separates one from God and others. Paradoxically, the very dying to oneself and living for God becomes the condition of finding oneself in God's love.

The cross intrinsically connects to the Resurrection, and authentic Christian spirituality upholds this essential component. Paul proclaims, "If Christ has not been raised, then empty too is our preaching; empty, too, your faith" (1 Cor. 15:14). For Christianity the victory of the Resurrection already empowers believers to new life (Phil. 3:10; 1 Pet. 1:3).

Christian Spirituality Is Trinitarian

Even as Christian spirituality emphasizes Jesus as the "one mediator between God and the human race" (1 Tim. 2:5), it yet maintains an understanding of God as Trinity. A typical expression of this Trinitarian thrust can be seen, for example, in the directive to pray to the Father through the Son in the Holy Spirit. The meaning of the Trinity is difficult to understand. According to the dogmas of the patristic church, Christianity does not believe in three separate beings who all have the divine nature. Nor is there one God who expresses himself in three ways. Rather, the Trinity reflects something of the communal dynamism of the one God.

---

10. Augustine, *Serm.* 13.

Pictures from History / Bridgeman Images

The Trinity is notoriously difficult to represent in art. This beautiful icon by Rublev (ca. 1360–1430) might be misunderstood as suggesting that the three persons are separate beings.

One might consider it thus: the Holy Spirit is the spiritual context through which the risen Lord is known. Christian spirituality is a manifestation of life in the Spirit. The Father represents the eternal source of the Son and Holy Spirit. Augustine, among others, described the Trinity through the dynamic of love. If God is love, then a lover (Father) needs a beloved (Son), and when they share that love, it redounds to the lovers in creative power (Holy Spirit). Love is triune.

The Holy Spirit is the life of the church because the Spirit is the common good of the Father and the Son. The Spirit infuses believers with God's love. The Son, now incarnate, is the very access to the Father, even as intimacy with the Word is conditioned by the Spirit.

Christian Spirituality Is Communal

Paul envisions the community of believers as the Body of Christ, with Christ as the head (Rom. 12:5; 1 Cor. 12:12–13). Although a metaphor, Paul saw it as an apt description of the true nature of Christian identity. During the Second Vatican Council (1962–1965), the Roman Catholic Church described the universal call to holiness as intrinsically communal: "It has pleased God, however, to make men holy and save them not merely as individuals without any mutual bonds, but by making them into a single people, a people which acknowledges Him in truth and serves Him in holiness."[11] The importance of this principle can hardly be overstated. Christianity, by its nature, is a communion of believers, praying together, actively supporting each other's faith, and mutually discerning God's presence in their personal lives and community.

---

11. *Lumen Gentium*, no. 9, *The Documents of Vatican II*, general ed. Walter Abbott, trans. Joseph Gallagher (New York: Guild Press, 1966).

Christian Spirituality Is Just

The communal nature of Christian spirituality means that believers can never reduce the faith to merely "God and me" (and nobody else). Rather, spirituality has to include community and indeed the world, especially with regard to issues of justice. To ignore human suffering is to fail as a Christian, and a spirituality that does not attend to injustice is seriously deficient. As the Letter of James says, "If a brother or sister has nothing to wear and has no food for the day, and one of you says to them, 'Go in peace, keep warm, and eat well,' but you do not give them the necessities of the body, what good is it?" (2:15–16).

This challenge by James is echoed throughout the Bible, particularly with the prophets. Isaiah described the true religious behavior as one of justice (58:1–9), and Jeremiah insisted that the temple would be forever defiled unless oppression against the poor was reversed (7:3–11). Amos even taught that Israel's offerings to God were a blasphemy when justice was not attended to in the land (4:4–5). Justice comprises one of the great themes of the Bible and the Christian tradition.

Christian Spirituality Is Prayerful

The Christian tradition has widely insisted that prayer provides the cornerstone for intimacy with God. Origen, one of the great minds of the patristic era, writes, "Let our whole life be a constant prayer, because the Kingdom of God is established in all who bear the image of the man from heaven."[12] Intimacy with Jesus and solicitude to the movements of the Spirit on one's soul constitute a central aspect of Christian spirituality. The Christian tradition has widely insisted that such intimacy and solicitude are best cultivated through a life of prayer. Praise and worship order the soul to God, who is the source of all good. Petitionary prayer recognizes the universal need for God's blessings. Meditation allows God to work in the soul through reflection on spiritual truths, particularly by using the Bible. Contemplation represents the soul's silent longing for and openness to direct knowledge of God in one's soul. Prayer is simply indispensable to authentic Christian spirituality.

Christian Spirituality Sees Divinization as Its Ultimate Horizon

Sandra Schneiders saw every spirituality as having an ultimate horizon. Christianity's ultimate reference is the triune God. It could be argued, however, that its ultimate horizon, the ultimate end of the path, is actually divinization. The early church called this *theōsis*, which literally means "becoming God." This is not a

---

12. Origen, *On Prayer* 22.5. Translation from *Origen: An Exhortation to Martyrdom, Prayer and Selected Works*, trans. Rowan Greer (New York: Paulist Press, 1979), 125.

literal, metaphysical change from human nature to the divine nature, but refers to living God's life as God lives God's life. Paul considered discipleship as living the very life of Christ within, bearing Christ's likeness and glory, becoming the very holiness of God and being filled with God.[13] The profound goal that Paul foresees is "that God may be all in all" (1 Cor. 15:28).

The First Letter of John also suggests a divinization, where on the last day all will be "like him" (3:2) and become "as he is" (4:17). Perhaps the most explicit description comes from the Second Letter of Peter: "His divine power has bestowed on us everything that makes for life and devotion. . . . Through these, he has bestowed on us the precious and very great promises, so that through them you may come to share in the divine nature" (1:3–4).

The spiritual tradition is replete with descriptions of this radical divine union. Christians do not imagine heaven merely as some *place* to go where one will be in the proximity of God. Rather, it is a full union with God where one lives in and through the Divine. As explored in later chapters, Christians believe that it is possible to experience in *this* life a kind of union that dramatically anticipates this future state.

Putting the Elements Together

The above-mentioned elements may seem quite abstract, but collectively they represent a robust Christian expression. To illustrate how these elements might come together in practice, let us imagine a new and fully engaged adult convert; we might call her Mary. Mary recognized that her life was flat and deeply lacking. She began investigating Christianity and came to see that it could provide direction and meaning—even ultimate meaning—to her life. Mary became baptized and fully took on the Christian faith. Placing her heart and soul in the hands of God felt like a great act of faith, which was both exciting and a little scary. Quite quickly she felt an astonishing inner freedom and communion with God. Mary began to develop a regular prayer life where she often felt close to God. Further, her church became like a second family and a place where she could continue to progress in her faith. Other members of her church also felt blessed by her enthusiasm, and it turned out that she was already ministering to others by her young witness to the gospel. The church was committed to service projects in the city and Mary quickly became conscious of Christianity's insistence of pursuing a just world. Mary's burgeoning Christian spirituality felt like a complete whole: God was filling her with love and her love naturally flowed out to want to help others. As Mary continued to grow in her faith life, her experience of God progressively reflected her truest, deepest self. She was getting a hint of what heaven must be like—living God's life.

---

13. See Rom. 8:14–17; 1 Cor. 15:49; 2 Cor. 5:21; Gal. 2:19–20.

Recurrent Themes in the Spiritual Tradition

When considering the variety of ways of being Christian, regular themes emerge. Each recurrence comes with a different framing or new way of considering a given theme. These include the following:

The Way

A common theme in the Christian spiritual tradition is that Christianity poses a new way of life, one that is daunting, but ultimate. One of the oldest designations for Christians was that they were followers of "the way."[14] Jesus referred to this new way as utterly challenging and yet life-giving: "Enter through the narrow gate; for the gate is wide and road broad that leads to destruction, and those who enter through it are many. How narrow the gate and constricted the road that leads to life. And those who find it are few" (Matt. 7:13–14). Early Christian texts echo this. The *Didache* or *Teaching of the Twelve Apostles* (ca. 90 CE) begins, "There are two ways, one of life and the other of death, and there is a great difference between these two ways."[15] The *Epistle of Barnabas* (ca. 100 CE) concludes part of an exhortation, "This, therefore, is the way of light." The epistle then contrasts it with "the way of the black one," which is "crooked and completely cursed."[16]

One insight in taking the image of "the way" is that the Christian life is something decidedly different from the ordinary road people travel. It is supposed to mean something truly decisive and unique. To be Christian is to think, look, and be different. A second insight is that the way is a road on which one advances. No one should expect to become holy in a day. As one progresses along the path, there will be setbacks, failures, and the realization that spiritual transformation comes slowly. It's a process.

Discipleship

Discipleship emerges as another common theme. The term "disciple" literally means "one who learns," and it refers to a follower. One of the most interesting dynamics in the Gospels is just how much the disciples had to learn from Jesus, and indeed how slow they often were to understand him. Similar to the idea that Christian spirituality is a way on which one progresses, discipleship is an ongoing learning process. Many Christians have reported that meditating on the scriptures or other religious texts through their adult lives gives them ever more to consider and incorporate in their lives. While Christian faith includes learning the

---

14. See Acts 9:2; 19:9; 22:4; 24:19; Heb. 10:20.

15. *Didache* 1.1. Translation from *The Apostolic Fathers*, ed. Michael Holmes, trans. J. B. Lightfoot and J. R. Hamer, 2nd ed. (Grand Rapids: Baker, 1989), 149.

16. *The Epistle of Barnabas* 19–20. Translation from *The Apostolic Fathers*, 185–86.

doctrines and practices within one's Christian tradition, above all it requires learning in terms of being a follower of Christ. Dietrich Bonhoeffer (1906–1945), in his seminal work *The Cost of Discipleship*, offers a telling insight into discipleship:

> Discipleship means adherence to Christ, and, because Christ is the object of adherence, it must take the form of discipleship. . . . Christianity without the living Christ is inevitably Christianity without discipleship, and Christianity without discipleship is always Christianity without Christ."[17]

What Bonhoeffer means here is that discipleship has to be more than just agreeing with doctrines; it must focus on profoundly knowing and following Christ, and at great cost.

The Three-Fold Pattern

A third regular theme is that of the three-fold progression of purgation, illumination, and union. Many classic formulations of interior growth and conversion assume this three-fold progress. The central idea underpinning purgation is that spiritual growth and maturity require moral progress that purges one from disordered attachments and habitual sins. For example, being a heavy drinker or prone to anger profoundly limits the possibilities of spiritual growth. Such sinful dispositions undercut spiritual progress and intimacy with God. Christians regularly claim that opening one's life to God's grace and diligently working to curb these disorders is a necessary foundation. The purged soul then has the freedom and spaciousness to pray more sincerely and with a fuller, purer heart. This provides the context in which one may come to a deeper knowledge of God's indwelling: the illuminative way. Further progress then allows the soul to come to know God in deep experiences of union whereby the soul and God regularly unite—even interpenetrate—and one gains a habitual knowledge of God's presence within: the unitive way.

A Path

Many Christian spiritualities describe the spiritual journey in terms of a specific set of stages. While the three-fold pattern listed above offers a path of sorts, many spiritualities articulate a more detailed series of stages that represent a spiritual course with defined markers. They frame one's ascent to union with God as a step-by-step process. The most famous patristic text describing such a path is Saint John Climacus's (525–606) *The Ladder of Divine Ascent*, in which he describes thirty specific steps to spiritual purification. The first three

---

17. Dietrich Bonhoeffer, *The Cost of Discipleship*, trans. R. H. Fuller (New York: Touchstone, 1995), 59.

reference a skillful decision to embrace the monastic life. The next four have to do with the kinds of virtues a new monk has to cultivate. The ensuing sixteen involve practices one should embrace as a means to undermine inordinate passions, such as anger or lust. The three that follow involve particularly sensitive interior virtues that condition deep contemplative prayer. And the final four reference ever-deepening expressions of prayer, with the final step involving outright union with God. Devotees to this program did not slavishly follow each step with no concern about issues in more advanced steps. Still, Climacus insisted that one has to crawl before one can walk, walk before on can run, and run before one can fly. There is an ordered progression.

Many other expressions of spiritual advancement lay out a relatively stable path. Saint Bernard of Clairvaux (1090–1153) expressed an ever deepening religious life through the metaphor of types of spiritual kisses. Saint Catherine of Sienna (1347–1380) imagined levels of spiritual tears representing the soul's progress. Richard of Saint Victor (d. 1173) described the path of spirituality as involving twelve steps corresponding to the spiritual meaning of the twelve patriarchs in the Old Testament, and John Rusbroeck (1293–1381) describes a *Ladder of Spiritual Love*. The modern period offers no clearer example than Saint Teresa of Ávila's (1515–1582) *Interior Castle*, where she describes seven mansions, each representing more sensitive moral intuitions and a deeper knowledge of God's presence in the soul.

In all these presentations, the spiritual guides posit a series of stages of ascent to union with God that are marked by particular experiences and conditioned by various spiritual practices and virtues. Not all Christian spiritualities have such markings or stages, but many do. Such presentations help spiritual directors and those they guide to recognize particular challenges and possibilities as they progress.

Conclusion

Spirituality is such a widely used term that one might wonder whether it confers much specific meaning. Even in academic circles it can refer to a great many different things and be approached quite variously. Fundamentally, in both popular and academic settings, the term designates something essential—even most essential—about being human. It touches on how humans make sense of themselves in relation to things transcendental. The genius of artists and poets lies in their ability to tap into the heart and soul in ways that elevate human beings beyond conceiving of themselves and their relationships merely in materialistic or utilitarian terms. There is a realm of meaning and truth, a realm of the spirit that cannot be reduced to science or banal cultural exchanges of commerce or politics.

Christian Spirituality as a field of study identifies that realm through history, theology, scripture, and, above all, experience, in ways that both highlight the Christian life and show skillful paths to engage it. The study of spirituality requires a breadth of knowledge in all these fields as well as allied disciplines in the academy. Utilizing this breadth, the study of spirituality provides deep, penetrating insight into Christian understandings of the life of grace and ways to become holy.

Questions for Review

1. *Spirituality* is a difficult term to define. What two theoretical frameworks do scholars use to analyze a given spirituality?
2. What were the origins of the term *spirituality*? How was the term used historically, and how is it used today?
3. What are the main elements of a Christian spirituality?
4. What are the recurring central themes in Christian spirituality?

Questions for Discussion

1. What do you think accounts for the interest in spirituality today?
2. This chapter identifies a number of emphases in Christian spirituality. How would you rank them in order of importance? What is the basis for your ranking?
3. Christian spirituality emphasizes experience. Why do you think that is, and what challenges might a scholar have in assessing religious experience?

Bibliography

Resources with annotations are highly recommended to students interested in further study.

Cunningham, Lawrence, and Keith Egan. *Christian Spirituality: Themes from the Tradition*. New York: Paulist Press: 1996.

> This book offers reflections on particular themes in Christian spirituality, including prayer, solitude, and community life.

Downey, Michael, ed. *The New Dictionary of Spirituality*. Collegeville, MN: Michael Glazier, 1993.

> This collection of articles provides a shorthand expression of a broad range of relevant topics in Christian spirituality.

Dreyer, Elizabeth, and Mark Burrows, eds. *Minding the Spirit: The Study of Christian Spirituality*. Baltimore: Johns Hopkins Press, 2005.

Dupré, Louis, and Don Saliers, eds. *Christian Spirituality: Post-Reformation and Modern*. Vol. 18 of *World Spirituality*. New York: Crossroad, 1991.

Feldmeier, Peter. *The Developing Christian: Spiritual Growth through the Life Cycle*. New York: Paulist Press, 2007

This book addresses various human development models in the social sciences and correlates them with spiritual growth throughout individual challenges in the life cycle.

Holmes, Urban. *Spirituality for Ministry*. San Francisco: Harper & Row, 1982.

This text details how a rightly appropriated understanding of spirituality serves as a necessary resource for pastoral ministry.

Lescher, Bruce, and Elizabeth Liebert, eds. *Exploring Christian Spirituality: Essays in Honor of Sandra M. Schneiders, IHM*. Mahwah, NJ: Paulist Press, 2006.

Locklin, Reid. *Spiritual but Not Religious: An Oar Stroke Closer to the Farther Shore*. Collegeville, MN: Liturgical Press, 2005.

Schneiders, Sandra. "Spirituality in the Academy," *Theological Studies* 50, no. 4 (1989): 676–97.

Schneiders, Sandra. "Theology and Spirituality: Strangers, Rivals or Partners?" *Horizons* 13, no. 2 (1986): 253–74.

Sheldrake, Philip. *Spirituality and History: Questions of Interpretation and Method*. New York: Crossroad, 1992.

This text examines the historical approach to Christian spirituality and how one might extrapolate modern insights from classic spiritual expressions in ways that respect the differences in time and culture.

Vatican II. *The Documents of Vatican II*. Edited by Walter Abbott. Translated by Joseph Gallagher. New York: Guild Press, 1966.

Internet Resources

The Society for the Study of Christian Spirituality. *https://sscs.press.jhu.edu*.

The Society for the Study of Christian Spirituality is widely considered the premier society for the academic study of spirituality. The society also publishes *Spiritus: The Journal of Christian Spirituality*.

Films

Filmsite. "Top 100 Spiritually-Significant Films." *www.filmsite.org/top100spiritual.html*.

A list and description of one-hundred films that have either overt themes in spirituality or deal with issues important to spirituality.

Mysticism

One should not blur the terms *spirituality* and *mysticism*; some spiritual giants and the movements they represent would not be mystical per se. Nevertheless, most spiritualities have mystical elements and many pivotal representatives of various spiritualities were mystics. For this reason, it is essential to understand what mysticism is and how it functions within a spiritual tradition.

What Is Christian Mysticism?

Like *spirituality*, the term *mysticism* is often bandied about with little clarity. In 1975, religious sociologist Andrew Greeley conducted a survey asking Americans if they had ever had an experience that they considered mystical. Just over 40 percent reported that they had. In 1977, Gallup also conducted a poll that asked, "Would you say that you have ever had a religious or mystical experience, that is, a moment of sudden religious insight or awakening?" Here, 31 percent responded that they had. Both studies were problematic in that neither ever defined "mystical."[1]

The English words *mysticism*, *mystery*, and *mystic* all derive from the Greek *mystērion*, which in turn derives from a verb that referred to closing one's eyes. Thus it identified something private. A mystery in this sense refers to something deep, dense, and secretive. For example, Jesus conveyed some things only to his disciples, telling them, "The mystery of the kingdom of God has been granted to you. But to those outside everything comes in parables" (Mark 4:11). Mystical knowledge, then, is something profound and revealed by God. Elsewhere Jesus asked his disciples privately who the crowds say that he is. They reply that some think he is the resurrected John the Baptist, or perhaps Elijah, or another of the prophets of old. Then Jesus asked them who they themselves think he is. "Simon Peter answered, 'You are the Messiah, the Son of the living God.' Jesus replied,

---

1. The Gallup poll blurred the term with religious experience in general and such things as dreams, awakening in nature, and even turning to God at a time of crisis.

"Blessed are you Simon, son of Jonah. For flesh and blood has not revealed this to you, but my heavenly Father" (Matt. 16:13–17). Paul often reminded his Christian readers that they have received the mysteries of God that had not been revealed to unbelievers (Eph. 3:9; Col. 2:2; 1 Tim. 3:16).

The Christian tradition regularly employed the term *mystical* from the second century on. Saint Clement of Alexandria (ca. 150–215) used it to refer to allegorical interpretations of the Bible. Thus the Bible could be read literally as well as mystically. Origen (ca. 185–254), like Clement, used the term to refer to secrets in the Bible when read allegorically. He also used it to refer to the secret presence of Christ in the sacraments, particularly the Eucharist. Finally, he used it for profound experiences of the soul being united with God. This third use of the term became normative for the Christian tradition.

Such experiences of union with God were considered mystical because they transcended the brain's ability to conceptualize God. The logic is thus: The senses and the brain's ability to conceptualize are designed to negotiate the created world. What a person feels and thinks has everything to do with experiencing and making sense of other created things. However, since in the Christian view God is beyond creation, direct experiences with God have to work outside of one's normal feeling and thinking. God, who is radically transcendent of all things, can only be directly known with some other "spiritual faculty," one different from the senses or the normal working of the mind. Thomas Aquinas regularly defined God as Absolute Mystery,[2] and Augustine coined the pithy expression: *Si comprehendis non est Deus,* meaning "If you understand it, it is not God."[3]

Saint Gregory of Nyssa's (335–395) classic spiritual masterpiece *The Life of Moses* describes various levels of spiritual attainment using Moses as a model. Moses' most profound experience of God took place on the top of Mount Sinai where the peak of the mountain was covered in a thick cloud. Gregory called this the "dark cloud where God was."[4] It is not that the soul doesn't know it is experiencing God. Quite the contrary, it recognizes the Divine in an absolute way, but not conceptually. Saint Teresa of Ávila defined mystical theology as "the soul being suspended in such a way that it is completely outside itself."[5] Saint John of the Cross characterizes what is mystical as "secret knowledge of God."[6] As will be seen in upcoming chapters, these

---

2. *De potentia* q.7, a.5, ad 14.

3. *Serm.* 52.16.

4. *The Life of Moses* 2.163. Translation from *Gregory of Nyssa: The Life of Moses,* trans. Abraham Malherbe and Everett Ferguson (New York: Paulist Press, 1978), 95.

5. *The Life of Teresa of Ávila* 10.1. Translation from *The Collected Works of St. Teresa of Ávila,* trans. Kieran Kavanaugh and Otilio Rodriguez (Washington, DC: ICS, 1987), 105.

6. *The Spiritual Canticle* 27.5. Translation from *The Collected Works of St. John of the Cross,* trans. Kieran Kavanaugh and Otilio Rodriguez (Washington, DC: ICS Publications, 1991), 582.

understandings of mystical experiences provide a foundation for understanding Christian spirituality.

Is Mysticism Universal?

Christianity is one of many religions with mystics, adherents who claim to experience the Divine or Ultimate Reality directly. This fact has raised many questions: Is mysticism universal, appearing in all or most religions? Are these mystical experiences the same regardless of one's religion? Is mysticism the height of religious expression? And, finally, because mystical experiences seem to transcend a given religion's doctrine, do they go beyond their own religion?

The earliest and most celebrated studies of mysticism through much of the late nineteenth and twentieth centuries tended to answer "yes" to all of these questions. For the scholars who conducted these studies, mysticism represents a rare form of divine encounter that transcends the particular doctrines or ideas in any particular religion.

This conclusion rests on several assumptions. First, there is only one Ultimate Reality (God). Consequently, all authentic religions pursue, in their own way, that same God. Additionally, since God is beyond all conceptual categories, and since religions are premised on concepts and images, then mysticism represents the transcending of a given religious framing.

Furthermore, these scholars considered mysticism the apex of religious expression. What could be higher than union with God? This position, often termed *perennialism*, claims that all authentic mystical experience is rooted in a single, or universal reality. Many perennialists ranked among the most famous early voices in the comparative study of religion.[7]

Soundings from Various Traditions

A look at representative mystics from various traditions highlights the strong similarities among their descriptions of profound encounters with God. Consider the following examples:

* Plotinus (204–270; Greek philosopher): "Many times it has happened: lifted out of the body into myself; becoming external to all other things and self-encentered; beholding a marvelous beauty . . . acquiring identity with the divine."[8]

---

7. They include William James, Rudolph Otto, Evelyn Underhill, Aldous Huxley, Joseph Campbell, and Walter Stace.

8. *The Enneads* 8.1. Translation from *Plotinus: The Eneads*, trans. Stephen Mackenna (New York: Penguin, 1991), 334.

- Abraham Abulafia (1240–1291; Jewish): "[They] will be united with it [God] after many hard, strong and mighty exercises, until the particular and personal prophetic [faculty] will become universal, permanent and everlasting, similar to the essence of its cause, and he and He will become one unity."[9]

- John of the Cross (1593–1581; Christian): "Having been made one with God, the soul is somehow God through participation. . . . For the will of the two is one will, and thus, God's operation and the soul's are one. . . . A reciprocal love is thus actually formed between God and the soul, like the marriage union and surrender, in which the goods of both (the divine essence that each possesses freely by reason of the voluntary surrender between them) are possessed by both together."[10]

- Jalāl ad-Dīn Muhammad Rumi (1207–1273; Muslim): "The prayer of the holy one is different from other prayers. He has so completely dissolved his ego—nothinged himself—that what he says is like God talking to God. . . . His spirit grows wings, and lifts. His ego falls like a battered wall. He unites with God, alive, but emptied of identity."[11]

- *Prasna Upanishad* (Hindu): "He who knows, O my beloved, that Eternal Spirit wherein consciousness and the senses, the powers of life and the elements find final peace, knows the All and has gone into the All."[12]

- Yan Hui (521–490 BCE; Confucian/Daoist): "I allow my limbs and body to fall away, expel my intellectual faculties, leave my substance, get rid of knowledge and become identical with the Great Universality."[13]

It is striking that these mystics, from highly varied traditions and vastly different times and cultures, describe fundamentally the same experience. These mystics transcend awareness of the body, lose any sense of concepts related to the world, and enter into communion with God. In some sense they *dis*-identify with their ordinary, separate self and *re*-identify with God. They are in one sense fused with God and in another sense in a profound relationship to God. Can one say, then, that the height of Christian experience is the same as the height of the religious experience of other traditions?

---

9. Translation from Moshe Idel and Bernard McGinn, eds., *Mystical Union in Judaism, Christianity, and Islam: An Ecumenical Dialogue* (New York: Continuum, 1996), 30.

10. *The Living Flame of Love* 3.78. Translation from *The Collected Works of St. John of the Cross*, 706.

11. Translation from *The Essential Rumi*, trans. Coleman Barks (New York: HarperSanFrancisco, 1995), 163 [trans. slightly adjusted].

12. *The Upanishads*, trans. Juan Mascaro (New York: Penguin, 1965), 72.

13. Cited in Jordan Paper, *The Mystic Experience: A Descriptive and Comparative Analysis* (Albany, NY: State University of New York, 2004), 91.

Criteria of Universal Mystical Experiences

The similarities among these vastly different religious representatives give weight to the perennialist position. In analyzing such seemingly universal mystical experiences, perennialists have recognized repeated qualities in accounts of mystical union. Mystical union is: (1) direct and immediate, (2) beyond comprehension and ineffable, (3) a conveyer of profound knowledge, (4) an experience of really-real reality, (5) a dis-identification with the conventional self and a re-identification with God, (6) indubitable, and (7) irresistible.

How can one make sense of this list? To describe mystical experiences as direct and immediate encounters with God or Absolute Reality means such experiences do not filter through one's psyche the way all other experiences do. Mystics, then, claim to experience God as God actually is. Because the human brain is structured for the created world, language cannot capture the fullness of experiences that seem to transcend the world. The experiences are ineffable, that is, beyond words and concepts. The normal working of the human mind cannot comprehend them. This does not mean, however, that the mystic knows nothing. On the contrary, mystics would say their experiences communicate a different kind of knowledge. Indeed, some scholars and mystics argue that the soul has a way of knowing the Divine outside of conceptual categories. In fact, they might say that they now see the real reality, whereas the physical world is comparatively a shadow.

In such unitive experiences, the perennialists claim, the kind of self that mystics thought they had vanishes and some sense of identification with God takes place. Such experiences are of the highest order and convey absolute truth, and therefore cannot be doubted. The soul knows what it knows. And finally, mystics broadly claim that such ecstatic experiences happened to them without their being able to resist them.

The mystical experiences described here are categorized as *apophatic*, which comes from the Greek *apophatikos*, meaning "negative." What is negated is any sensory or conceptual data. This is what Gregory of Nyssa meant by the "dark cloud." The counterpart to *apophatic* mystical experience is *kataphatic* experience, from the Greek *kataphatikos*, meaning "positive." Kataphatic mystical experiences engage rather than transcend the senses or mind. Some mystics report that they receive visions; others report that they hear God speaking to them; and still others report gaining profound spiritual insight into their religion. How does one interpret these kataphatic experiences? Evelyn Underhill, in her monumental book *Mysticism* (1911), argued that kataphatic experiences are lesser encounters with the Divine than are apophatic experiences. Her argument is two-fold. First and foremost, many mystics recount experiences of visions and the like occurring early in their spiritual development. As they progressed spiritually, these seemed to give way to reports of radical, direct knowledge of God. Second, experiences mediated through the senses, and thus indirect, are less profound than unmediated, direct experiences of God. Some mystics, such as John of the Cross, argue the very same.

Criticisms of the Perennialist View

Approaches to and conclusions about mysticism began to shift in the mid-1980s. Stephen Katz, a scholar of comparative religion argued that mystical experiences are not all fundamentally the same, and that there simply is no *objective* experience of God or anything else. Every experience necessarily happens to a human subject and therefore must have some *subjective* element to it. How would the psyche even know that it has had an experience unless it was somehow filtered through the psyche?[14]

Katz has argued that removing a given mystic from his or her religious commitments actually violates the experience the mystic claims to have had. Hindu mysticism, for example, includes Hindu training, Hindu theology, and Hindu practices. The Hindu mystic then has experiences that reflect this specific background. In short, Jewish mystics have Jewish experiences, Christian mystics have Christian experiences, Muslim mystics have Muslim experiences, and so on.[15] One could also note that the list of examples above includes no mystical representation from Buddhism, Shintoism, or Native American religions, among others. The perennialist position tends to be selective about what constitutes an authentic apophatic mystical experience.

Katz further argues that just because a number of mystical experiences are considered to be beyond comprehension and ineffable does not mean that they are the same. The respective experiences of, for example, a Hindu and a Christian mystic may be quite different, even if they both transcend concepts or words. Further, the really-real reality they report encountering only means that they themselves believe they encountered something Ultimate. It does not indicate that they actually share the same experience.

Finally, critics fault the perennialist position for taking the mystical experience outside of the religious context, thereby potentially violating the mystic's report of the experience. John of the Cross, for example, believed that he directly experienced the Trinity *as* Trinity—and such kataphatic mystical experiences seem to have supported, not undermined his apophatic experiences.

Scholars today prefer to keep the mystic within his or her own religious identity. At the beginning of his monumental study of Christian mysticism, Bernard McGinn reflects this now-standard approach: "Any remotely adequate contemporary theology of mysticism must begin not from an abstract consideration

---

14. Steven Katz, "The 'Conservative' Character of Mystical Experience," in *Mysticism and Religious Traditions*, ed. Steven Katz (Oxford: Oxford University Press, 1983), 3–60.

15. Steven Katz, "General Editor's Introduction," in *Comparative Mysticism: An Anthology of Original Sources*, ed. Steven Katz (Oxford: Oxford University Press, 2013), 3–22.

of the essential characteristics of mystical experience . . . but rather from an attempt to draw from the decisive stages in the history of Christian mysticism a coherent interpretation that may serve as a ground for a renewed contemporary theory and practice of mysticism."[16] He continues:

> Rather than trying to define mysticism . . . I prefer to give a sense of how I understand the term by discussing it under three headings: mysticism as a part or element of religion; mysticism as a process or way of life; and mysticism as an attempt to express a direct consciousness of the presence of God. . . . No mystics believed in or practiced "mysticism." They believed in and practiced Christianity (or Judaism, or Islam, or Hinduism).[17]

Mysticism as Universal and Unmediated versus Particular and Mediated

Katz: Mystical experiences reveal a *necessary* relationship between the prior education of the mystic and their mystical goal. . . . This means that Sufis are Muslims and that being a Muslim is essential to being a Sufi; that being a Jewish mystic, a kabbalist is inseparable from other fundamental aspects of Judaism; that Christian mystics are formed by Christian teaching; and that Enlightenment (*nirvana*) is unintelligible and not sought as an experience outside of the larger Buddhist worldview.[18]

Underhill: [Mysticism] implies, indeed, the abolition of individuality; of that hard separateness, that "I, Me, Mine" of which makes of man a finite isolated thing. It is essentially a movement of the heart, seeking to transcend the limitations of the individual standpoint and to surrender itself to ultimate Reality. . . . [It is] the science of ultimates, the science of union with the absolute, and nothing else.[19]

---

16. Bernard McGinn, *The Foundations of Mysticism*, vol. 1 of *The Presence of God: A History of Western Christian Mysticism* (New York: Crossroad, 1992), xii.

17. Ibid., xv–xvi.

18. Bernard McGinn, *The Essential Writings of Christian Mysticism* (New York: Modern Library, 2006), xiv.

19. Evelyn Underhill, *Mysticism: A Study of the Nature and Development of Spiritual Consciousness*, 12th ed. (1930; repr., Mineola, NY: Dover, 2002), 71–72.

For McGinn, Christian mysticism is "that part, or element, of Christian belief and practice that concerns the preparation for, the consciousness of, and the effect of what the mystics themselves have described as a direct and transformative presence of God."[20] McGinn's approach will be reflected in future chapters.

Kataphatic Mysticism

Traditionally, scholars of comparative mysticism focused research on apophatic mysticism. One reason is that accounts of apophatic mysticism are easier to compare than accounts of kataphatic mysticism. A second reason is that, like Underhill, many scholars view divine visions, voices, and so on as lesser experiences. Many mystics themselves believe that such experiences serve as preludes to bona fide unitive experiences with God. Teresa of Ávila experienced many kataphatic experiences in her life, including hearing voices, seeing visions, and a number of experiences of levitation in the context of rapture. She believed she experienced these because her soul at the time was not ready for full union, and by the time she did experience full union, many of these experiences had subsided.

The issue of mysticism and its religious meaning, however, remains complex, particularly regarding kataphatic mystical experiences. Catherine of Siena (1347–1380), for example, a Roman Catholic mystic, had only kataphatic experiences. She had visions, heard voices, and received many insights that she reported were infused into her by God. Other mystics, such as Julian of Norwich (1342–1416), had mystical experiences that included seeing and hearing the Virgin Mary. Still others experienced flights into heaven and hell with no experience (direct or otherwise) of God. In studying the spiritualities of these mystics, it will be important to include their accounts of these overwhelming experiences, whether they tell of experiences of God specifically or other profound spiritual realities.

Where does one draw the line on what counts as a kataphatic mystical experience? When investigating Christian mysticism, are only reports of encounters with God considered? Are accounts of experiences of Mary ignored? What about reports of receiving only a kind of supernatural infused knowledge, but with no divine representative at all? How should one evaluate the quality of such experiences? Often several attendees at a Charismatic or Pentecostal prayer meeting claim to have received a prophecy. Should these count too? This text's consideration of mystical experiences—both apophatic and kataphatic—will be limited to accounts of mystics experiencing non-normal states of consciousness that transform the receiver, experiences so extraordinary that they are seared into the mystic's memory.

---

20. Steven Katz, "General Editor's Introduction," in Katz, ed., *Comparative Mysticism: An Anthology of Sources*, 5.

Given these parameters, one could say that a mystical experience is not simply a regular religious experience or even a particularly intense one, but represents something decidedly different from how the vast majority of religious people experiences spiritual reality. So overwhelming is the experience that, in the Christian view, it does something to the soul that is decisive, certain, and part of one's consciousness. Kataphatic experiences also have criteria of authenticity, and these can help us distinguish between bona fide experiences and those produced solely by the psyche. Kataphatic experiences: (1) are profound spiritual experiences, (2) convey deep religious insight, (3) are typically overwhelming, (4) are typically unprompted, and (5) dramatically affect the receiver.

Assessing Kataphatic Mystical Experiences: Two Examples

Examples can prove helpful in evaluating the quality of mystical experiences. A woman I knew in college, call her Jane, had gotten drunk on a particular Saturday night. The next morning, as Jane sat in church feeling deeply ashamed of herself for what she saw as a moral lapse, she heard out of the blue an overwhelming voice that said, "I forgive you." Certain that this was God speaking to her, she felt a rush of power and divine love and knew then and there that she was utterly forgiven. Jane had not expected this experience. She was not prodding it psychologically—in fact she felt that God didn't want to have anything to do with her at the time. The experience did not just inform her of God's forgiveness, it gave her the experience: she *was* forgiven. Jane was still feeling the effects of this experience thirty years later: "I remember it like it was yesterday." Considering the above-mentioned criteria, Jane's appears to have been a true mystical experience. It was profound for her, infusing a deep knowledge of God's compassion. It was spontaneous and unsolicited. It was dramatic, and it was so seared in her memory that she remembered it decades later.

Another friend in college, "Jim," claimed to have had a series of mystical experiences one year. These gave him authority to tell the *real* story of God: how God saw us and what God wanted from us. God told him things he seemed to want to hear. Jim's personal life was not happy, and God told him about God's extraordinary plans for him, plans that made him especially important. Jim had been reading an autobiography of a saint and mystic. A mutual friend began to realize that Jim's mystical experiences mimicked those he was reading about. One night as they prayed together Jim fell into an ecstatic mystical experience. This friend confronted Jim right then and there, and he quickly returned to ordinary consciousness. He told Jim that he questioned these experiences and encouraged Jim to speak to one of the priests on campus. Over the period of several conversations with a priest, Jim conceded that these experiences were self-produced, though earlier he believed they were authentic.

A number of factors suggest that Jim's experiences weren't mystical. The first is that he *wanted* them badly. This certainly primed the pump. Second, Jim had a great many in a short period of time, all quite profound. Even in the autobiographies of the greatest saints and mystics such experiences were rare. Third, rather than humbling him, as one might expect from profound encounters with God, Jim's experiences seem to inflate his ego. Finally, when Jim was confronted by his friend and discussed the experiences with his priest, he was quickly persuaded that they were not real. If they had come from God, Jim would certainly not have been so doubtful.

Four Principles

Regarding mystical experiences, apophatic or kataphatic, four principles prove helpful in discerning authenticity. The first is that anyone can have a mystical experience. Jane was a relatively devout but otherwise ordinary young Christian woman. One can have confidence that she really did have a mystical experience, and this came before much spiritual advancement.

Second, however, mystical experiences tend to be rare and typically come to those who have advanced in the spiritual life. Having a mystical experience at any age is a wondrous thing, but most Christians would not expect to have one and would certainly not expect very many until one's spiritual life had developed and matured.

A third principle highlights the difference between having a mystical experience and being a mystic. Mystics are people who have enough of these extraordinary experiences that they transform the mystic's spiritual horizon. In the Christian view, mystics are those whose experiences have a definitive effect on their soul and their understanding of God and God's engagement with the world.

A fourth principle follows the Latin axiom: *Quidquid recipitur per modum recipitur recipientis,* or "Whatever is received is received according to the mode of the receiver." That is, when God personally and dramatically engages someone, God does so in a way that is understandable to the recipient. For example, if Jesus were to appear and speak to someone, he would not speak Aramaic, the native language of Jesus of Nazareth. He would speak that person's own language and what he said would be relevant to that individual's personal and cultural location. If this were not the case, the experience would be unhelpful. The historical location of a given mystic, then, proves crucially important in interpreting mystical experiences from other times and places. Cultural, theological, and personal factors have an impact upon any mystical experience, and understanding these particular locations helps in making sense of how God worked at that time and in skillfully appropriating insights from those experiences.

Case Study in Kataphatic Mysticism: Juan Diego

This fourth principle, *whatever is received is received according to the mode of the receiver*, is particularly important when examining Christian spiritualities. A given Christian spirituality is historically and culturally located. This does not relegate it to the status of mere historical artifact. However, making contemporary sense of the experience requires fully understanding it in its time.

Consider, for example, the mystical experience that the Catholic Church claims to have happened to Juan Diego Cuauhtlatzin in 1537.[21] In a newly conquered Mexico, the Catholic religion was expanding, but it did so at the expense of honoring the dignity of the Aztec Native Americans. At the time of Juan Diego's mystical experience, the missionary priest Bartolome de las Casas was detailing to the Spanish Catholic world the horrific enslavement of the indigenous peoples and the oppression they endured at the hands of the Spanish Conquistadors. Often the Church was complicit. Certainly, the vast majority of Spanish Catholics had nothing but disdain for the religious life of the Aztecs, and de las Casas even found it necessary to argue that they ought to be understood as full human beings with inherent rights.

This was the context when a poor 57-year-old Aztec widower named Juan Diego approached Tepeyac Hill on his fifteen-mile walk to Mass. He climbed the hill because he heard music and someone softly calling his name: *Juanito! Juanito Dieguito!* (Little Johnny, Little Johnny Diego). There he encountered a young Indian woman wearing traditional Aztec garb, including the black sash around her waist indicating that she was pregnant. She told him that she was the Virgin Mary and wanted a church built there, a place where she could hear her people's weeping and sorrows and could console them.

Mary instructed Juan Diego to inform the bishop of Mexico City. When he did, Bishop Zumarraga shooed away this Aztec native. Mary sent him back, and the bishop again disdainfully sent him away, this time demanding proof by way of a miracle. Returning again to Tepeyac Hill, Mary instructed him to pick roses there and deliver them to the bishop—even though these roses were not indigenous to Mexico and it was not the time of year any rose would be blooming. Juan Diego had nothing to hold them in, so he bundled them into the side of his cloak.

When Juan Diego arrived at the bishop's palace the third time, he opened his cloak to show the roses he had picked from Tepeyac's snowy rocks. On the cloak itself was the image of the very Lady he had met on the hill, an image preserved to this day in the basilica dedicated to her outside Mexico City.

---

21. Some historians have questioned the historicity of this story, pointing to writings from the bishop that failed to mention Juan Diego or the event. On the other hand, a document written in 1548 by respected priests-scholars who knew Juan Diego authenticated the event.

Fascinatingly, his hemp cloak ought to have disintegrated within his lifetime, but both it and the image have continued to be preserved absolutely intact.

There are other interesting elements of this story. Mary came to Juan Diego speaking both Spanish and his native language. When Juan reported this, Bishop Zumarraga could not believe that Mary would speak the "pagan" Nahuatl language. Further, Mary appeared on the small mountain of Tepeyac, the site of veneration of the Aztec goddess *Tonantzin*, the mother goddess who regenerates life. There are also striking features in the figure on the cloak. In the image, the sun radiates out from behind her. The sun was the symbol of the Aztec high god, and the image suggests symbolically that Mary is greater than their Aztec god and covers him, but that he is not extinguished. Rather, he seems to illuminate her from behind. The image of Mary also shows her standing on the moon, which was a lesser Aztec deity. She does not crush it, but stands above it. In Juan Diego's experience, Mary comes from heaven, yet he sees her as familiar. In his dialogue with Mary, Juan Diego calls her *niña mia* (my daughter). Mary says that she is the Mother of the God of Great Truth (*Teotl*). This was

Elements of native Aztec culture and spirituality appear with the Virgin Mary in this image, believed to have been miraculously imparted to the cloak of Juan Diego. Such elements provide the context for understanding Juan's mystical experience.

the name for the local god of the Nahuatls, who had a different designation for the God of Christianity. Thus his mystical experience links the original spiritual life of the Aztecs with the God of Christianity.

What does one make of such a mystical experience? It suggests that God does not demand that Juan Diego abandon his past or utterly reject every part of his Aztec spirituality. Juan Diego is a Christian and Mary is the Mother of Jesus, but only so in the context of the religious life of his people. In this sense, Juan Diego's mystical experience shows him and other Aztec Christians that they can reclaim their past spiritual intuitions even while being wholly

Christian. Mary also demands a kind of new partnership with the Spanish Catholic Church, one in which both Aztecs and Spanish can join together to build a church for the Aztec Christian mother of everyone. The bishop represents the new religion, the religion of Juan Diego, as well as representing something of the oppressive power of the conquering Spanish. Embracing this mystical experience enables the poor natives to reemerge as partners with the Spanish, with the faith of Catholicism, but with wholly Aztec sensibilities. God is on their side.

Conclusion

As noted at the beginning of this chapter, most Christian spiritualities have mystical elements. The mystical experiences of their founders and those who followed them drove them to see a new vision of what was possible, not only with God but also with others. Many who have had mystical experiences report understanding themselves, others, and God differently. The great modern philosopher and theologian Dorothee Soelle writes, "Mystical experience happens when the *I* steps forth from its self-imposed and imagined limits. The *I* leaves the everyday world and, at the same time, leaves itself as the being defined by that world."[22] What Soelle suggests here is that the conventional way one sees oneself and the world disappears in the context of profound encounters with God. Now one has a kind of freedom to see everything differently. Theologian Robert Egan notes that "Mystical experiences are liberating. By providing the direct experience of a reality that transcends and overwhelms the meaning . . . of the reality of everydayness, the mystical experience relativizes conventional judgments about plausibility and frees the person having the experience from conventional definitions of reality. . . . Things do not have to be the way they seem to be."[23]

The history of Christian spirituality is filled with dramatic examples of mystics whose profound religious experiences directed their spiritual life and challenged the world they lived in. Saints Francis and Clare, thirteenth-century founders of religious orders in Assisi Italy, had many mystical experiences that led them to disengage from their society's greed and disregard for the poor. In place, they highlighted the dignity and rights of all and taught a spirituality of humble simplicity and service. The fourteenth-century mystic Marguerite Porete's mysticism challenged France's power structure and its prejudices against

---

22. Dorothee Soelle, *The Silent Cry: Mysticism and Resistance*, trans. Barbara and Martin Rumscheidt (Minneapolis: Fortress Press, 2001), 27 (italics added).

23. Robert Egan, "Foreword," in *Mysticism and Social Transformation*, ed. Janet Ruffing (Syracuse: Syracuse University Press, 2001), x.

women. Saint Ignatius of Loyola, founder of the Society of Jesus (Jesuits), had a mystical experience soon after his adult conversion. In it he saw that everything in the universe flowed from the love of God and was being redirected to return to God healed of its deformities due to sin. From this experience he believed it was his mission to thoroughly immerse himself in the world, finding God through it, and redirect it all back to God. In short, he envisioned a spirituality that joined God's plan of restoration and reunion.

Questions for Review

1. The term *mysticism* is difficult to define and prone to misuse. How has the term been used in the history of Christianity? What are some of the main features of mysticism?
2. Despite having lost prominence in recent scholarship, perennialism remains popular among some scholars and religious believers. What are the main arguments supporting the perennialist position?
3. What are the criticisms of the perennialist position, and how do perennialists respond?
4. The examples of Jane, Jim, and Juan Diego provide concrete examples of likely authentic and inauthentic experiences. What four principles help distinguish valid from false experiences? How do these principles apply to the examples of Jane, Jim, and Juan Diego?

Questions for Discussion

1. Given the discussion of what constitutes a mystical experience, would you say that you have ever had one or know anyone who has? Why or why not?
2. Apophatic mystical experiences have enjoyed higher esteem than kataphatic ones due to the mystic's claim of unmediated contact with the divine. Yet kataphatic experiences have figured prominently in Christianity. Of these two types of mystical experiences, which would you say is more important to Christianity and why?
3. If you believe in God, would you personally rather have an apophatic or kataphatic experience of God? Explain your answer.
4. Presuming that God exists and given what you know about mysticism so far, do the views of perennialists or their critics appear more reasonable to you? Explain your answer.
5. Why is understanding mysticism important to the study of spirituality?

Bibliography

Resources with annotations are highly recommended to readers pursuing further study.

Bernard of Clairvaux. *Bernard of Clairvaux: Selected Works*. Translated by G. S. Evans. Mahwah, NJ: Paulist Press, 1987.

Chan, Wing-Tsit. *A Sourcebook in Chinese Philosophy*. Princeton: Princeton University Press, 1963.

Elizondo, Virgil. *Guadalupe: Mother of the New Creation*. Maryknoll, NY: Orbis, 1998.

Greeley, Andrew. "Mysticism Goes Mainstream." *American Health* 6, no. 1 (1987): 47–49.

Greeley, Andrew, and William C. McCready. "Are We a Nation of Mystics?" *New York Times Magazine* (Jan. 26, 1975): 12–25.

Gregory of Nyssa. *Gregory of Nyssa: The Life of Moses*. Translated by Abraham Malherbe and Everett Ferguson. New York: Paulist Press, 1978.

Idel, Moshe, and Bernard McGinn, eds. *Mystical Union in Judaism, Christianity, and Islam: An Ecumenical Dialogue*. New York: Continuum, 1996.

This volume highlights many striking elements among mystics representing the three great Abrahamic traditions.

John of the Cross. *The Collected Works of St. John of the Cross*. Translated by Kieran Kavanaugh and Otilio Rodriguez. Washington, DC: ICS Publications, 1991.

Katz, Steven. *Mysticism and Philosophical Analysis*. New York: Oxford University Press, 1978.

Katz, Steven, ed. *Comparative Mysticism: An Anthology of Original Sources*. Oxford: Oxford University Press, 2013.

This seminal work provides source material and commentary on major religious traditions.

Katz, Steven, ed. *Mysticism and Religious Traditions*. New York: Oxford University Press, 1983.

Mascaro, Juan, ed. and trans. *The Upanishads*. New York: Penguin, 1965.

McGinn, Bernard. *The Foundations of Mysticism*. Vol. 1 of *The Presence of God: A History of Western Christian Mysticism*. New York: Crossroad, 1992.

This is the first of a six-volume series on Christian Mysticism in the West. The series is seminal in the understanding of Western Christian Mysticism.

McGinn, Bernard, ed. *The Essential Writings of Christian Mysticism*. New York: Modern Library, 2006.

Mommaers, Paul, and Jan Van Bragt. *Mysticism Buddhist and Christian.* New York: Crossroad, 1995.

Origen. *Origen: An Exhortation to Martyrdom, Prayer and Selected Works.* Translated by Rowan Greer. New York: Paulist Press, 1979.

This book is a classic and seminal work on spirituality in the early patristic period.

Paper, Jordan. *The Mystic Experience: A Descriptive and Comparative Analysis.* Albany: State University of New York, 2004.

In this small volume, Paper argues for a universal mystical experience, challenging those who argue against it by drawing on various methodological approaches.

Plotinus. *The Enneads.* Translated by Stephen Mackenna. New York: Penguin, 1991.

Ruffing, Janet, ed. *Mysticism and Social Transformation.* Syracuse, NY: Syracuse University Press, 2001.

Rumi, Jalāl ad-Dīn. *The Essential Rumi.* Translated by Coleman Barks. New York: HarperSanFrancisco, 1995.

Sells, Michael, ed. and trans. *Early Islamic Mysticism.* New York: Paulist Press, 1996.

Soelle, Dorothee. *The Silent Cry: Mysticism and Resistance.* Translated by Barbara and Martin Rumscheidt. Minneapolis: Fortress Press, 2001.

Teresa of Ávila. *The Collected Works of St. Teresa of Ávila.* Translated by Kieran Kavanaugh and Otilio Rodriguez. Washington, DC: ICS Publications, 1987.

Underhill, Evelyn. *Mysticism.* 1930. Reprint, Mineola, NY: Dover, 2002.

This was the first great treatise on mysticism, particularly Christian, for a popular audience.

Woods, James, ed. *Understanding Mysticism.* Garden City, NY: Image Books, 1980.

Zaehner, R. C. *Hindu and Muslim Mysticism.* Oxford: Oneworld, 1960.

Internet Resources

McGinn, Bernard. "What Is a Mystic." *www.youtube.com/watch?v=g7uHZUJ3_VI.*

The foremost authority on Christian mysticism briefly explains what a mystic is (1:35 min.).

Meninger, William. "Contemplative Meditation." *www.youtube.com/watch?v=9mFxhZYn1O4.*

A Trappist monk and leader of a lay-contemplative movement called centering prayer discusses the dynamics of contemplative meditation (46 min.).

Quodlibet Journal. *www.quodlibet.net/articles/foutz-mystic.shtml.*

An on-line journal article that argues for the universality of mysticism and its relation to Christian mysticism.

Films

Into Great Silence [German: *Die Große Stille*]. 2005.

This documentary film portrays the everyday lives of Carthusian monks of the Grand Chartreuse, a monastery high in the French Alps.

Biblical Spirituality

The Bible and God's Revelation in Christ

The central elements and themes of Christian spirituality are grounded in the biblical witness. The Bible is the foundational and indispensable text for Christianity. It is a complex book, though, and its revelatory quality is likewise complex. Christians would say, for example, that the Bible is the *word of God*. They also believe that Jesus is the *Word of God*. Referring to Jesus, John's Gospel begins, "In the beginning was the Word, and the Word was with God, and the Word was God" (1:1). Jesus is the Word of God and the Bible is the word of God, but Jesus isn't the Bible. What is their relationship? Furthermore, the Bible reflects the faith of Judaism (Old Testament) as well as early Christianity (New Testament). Many early Christian texts declared themselves *gospels* or authentic letters from the apostles, but most were not accepted by the larger church. Rather, the church discerned, through its tradition, which represented the authentic faith and which were unacceptable. Why choose the Gospel of Matthew but not the *Gospel of Phillip*, or the Gospel of John, but not the *Gospel of Thomas*? The short answer is that the early church deemed the former Gospels true to the tradition, but not the latter. There is an intrinsic relationship between tradition and text, with *tradition* referring to everything that represents the living church, including the witness of the apostles, the experience of the church, prayer and liturgy, and growing theological commitments.

Ultimately, Christians believe that Jesus is the absolute revelation of God, that the Bible is the written authoritative witness to that revelation, and that the tradition is the context through which the church understands both the Bible and its own existence.[1] The Catholic Church reflects this view, a view broadly shared by Christian academics from Catholic, mainstream Protestant, and evangelical backgrounds, in its document on divine revelation from Vatican II, *Dei Verbum* (*Word of God*):

---

1. One might argue that, even in those denominations that would not choose to formally acknowledge the role of tradition in these terms, tradition does perform this function in practice.

Word of God

To imagine that the Bible is the "word" of God one has to recognize that the term *word* is used as an analogy and metaphor. Language is a human phenomenon, rooted in discursive thought and corporeality. So language cannot be directly predicated to God, who in the Christian tradition is understood as pure spirit and infinite. God transcends language. Language about God can be understood as analogy. For example, people know about love from a human point of view. To say that "God is love" (1 John 4:8) is not to equate human understanding about love to God, but to recognize that human love is analogous to God's love. Another way to think about words referencing God is through metaphor. Metaphors give access to a reality, but in a non-literal way. Christians, for example, refer to "God the Father," in order to engage God as though a father-figure. This is metaphorical language since God is not a male, does not have a body, and does not procreate. Other metaphors for God include Mother, Lover, Companion, and King. Metaphors are superb vehicles for engaging God or other religious truths, but they become problems when they are literalized, thus reducing God to human understandings. Words about God or reported from God cannot be understood in the same way as words about or from other people.

yes!

It pleased God, in his goodness and wisdom, to reveal himself and to make known the mystery of his will. His will was that men should have access to the Father, through Christ, the Word made flesh, in the Holy Spirit, and thus become sharers in the divine nature. . . . The most intimate truth which this revelation gives us about God and the salvation of man shines forth in Christ, who is himself both the mediator and the sum total of Revelation. . . . Hence, Jesus speaks the words of God, and accomplishes the saving work which the Father gave him to do. As a result he himself—to see whom is to see the Father—completed and perfected Revelation and confirmed it with divine guarantees.[2]

As indicated in *Dei Verbum*, revelation is not about certain religious propositions or doctrines. Rather, it is principally about Jesus Christ and encountering

---

2. *Dei Verbum*, nos. 1–4, in *The Documents of Vatican II*, ed. Walter Abbott, trans. Joseph Gallagher (New York: Guild Press, 1966).

him. The Bible then becomes an authentic witness in understanding and experiencing Christ. Saint Jerome coined the pithy saying, "Ignorance of the scriptures is ignorance of Christ." Yet understanding the Bible is no easy task. It contains different perspectives that reflect each author's time, place, circumstances, and theological point of view. One cannot simply take up a given verse, or even a particular teaching, and apply it to today without acknowledging the very different cultural assumptions in the text. The New Testament, for example, assumes a patriarchal worldview where wives are submissive to their husbands.[3] Is this eternal divine revelation for today? Is patriarchy a revelation of God's will? The New Testament also accepts slavery.[4] Is slavery a revelation of God's will? Other biblical quotations include "Cretans have always been liars" (Titus 1:12) and "Blessed is the one who seizes your [the Babylonians'] children and smashes them against the rock" (Psalm 137:9). Most Christians find it impossible to imagine that these lines convey God's revelation.

Biblical scholars have to attend to concerns such as the literary genre (e.g., history, poetry, myth, narrative, instruction) and the historical and cultural horizon from which the text derived. They also strive to understand what the biblical author intended by the text at the time. Finally, they realize that the Bible has a *surplus of meaning*; that is, while respecting the author's intent, they also look to how the text might mediate divine wisdom that goes beyond the author's specific intent and can be meaningful for a contemporary audience. In a sense, two poles need to be kept in creative tension. One pole represents the historical and literary context while the other pole looks to possibilities for a modern appropriation of the text that facilitates both spiritual transformation and encounter with God. Overemphasizing the first pole and neglecting the second results in a dry text that cannot affect the reader, but overemphasizing the second pole to the neglect of the first leads to a kind of ungrounded piety that does not respect the text's original intent.

The Bible Has Authority

Christians broadly understand the Bible as having extraordinary authority, but what does this mean? The word *authority* comes from the Latin *auctoritas*, usually translated as "origination" or "source," and it is related to *auctorare*, which means "to bind." To say that the Bible is *a* or *the* source for Christians and that it has a binding power is significant. One of the few places where the Bible directly speaks of itself is in 2 Timothy 3:16: "All scripture is inspired by God and is useful for teaching, for refutation, for correction, and for training in righteousness." Regarding this authority one needs to ask, "To what domain or domains does

---

3. See 1 Cor. 11:3; Eph. 5:22–24; Col. 3:18; and 1 Pet. 3:1–2.

4. See 1 Cor. 7:22; Eph. 6:5; Col. 3:11; 4:1; 1 Tim. 6:1–2; Titus 2:9–10.

the Bible's authority pertain?" It would not be scientific matters, as the authors did not have access to modern scientific insights. Is the Bible, then, only about religious matters, or could it assist one in crafting wise social policy? Does the text reveal authoritative *data* about things religious or *ways to think* about religious issues? Do some texts do one or the other better than others? When they do, is there anything culturally specific that needs to be considered when converting a biblical perspective to one's own time, place, and culture? How does one skillfully pose questions to the text that it was not originally designed to address, but might bring authoritative wisdom to a modern issue, such as just war or economics and the common good? The Bible serves as an important source, but it can be challenging to use.

The Bible's authority is intimately wedded to its interpretation; discussing one entails a discussion of the other. Some Christians, for example, see the fundamental religious issue as God liberating humans to experience full flourishing in this life and the next. Human dignity and the thriving of all people who are created in the image and likeness of God, then, becomes the lens through which these Christians read the text and appropriate its underlying truth. In this example, certain parts of the Bible become more important than other parts, with all parts read through this vision of liberation. This offers just one example of numerous legitimate lenses through which to read the text. Being conscious of one's assumptions and values and being able to defend them credibly is part of a responsible use of the Bible.

Overarching Themes for Christian Spirituality

The Bible is foundational for an authentic Christian spirituality because it offers patterns, motifs, and core religious framings that structure Christian spirituality. Some themes in the Old and New Testaments dominated the religious horizon of ancient Jews and early Christians. Embracing these themes means taking them up and incorporating them into one's own spiritual horizon. It is as though the Bible were telling believers, "Think *this* way," "Imagine God like *this*," "Relate to each other through *these* values," "Understand your relationship with God like *this*." These themes create the foundations of Christian spirituality and include (1) creation: God made the world good and infused humanity with his image; (2) covenant: God relates to his people personally with binding promises; (3) sin and redemption: the human condition is deeply flawed and God has provided means to heal this; (4) monarchy: God gave Israel a kingdom and Jesus fulfills God's purposes for it; (5) temple and priesthood: God has made a place of worship where he will be particularly present; (6) sacrifice: reparation of sin and communion with God comes through sacrifice; (7) prophecy: God has announced his will through holy men and women; (8) wisdom: the laws of God and the presence of God can be known through wisdom that has infused creation; (9) law and grace: God's favor and blessings can be experienced in the law and later in Christ who completes the law; (10) the reign of God: the justice and goodness of God is experienced through his rule; and (11) prayer: faithful followers can praise and know God intimately.

The theme of covenant, for example, offers a framework for seeing and appreciating God's desire to enter into a relationship with his people. Rather than make an impersonal contract with them, whereby each party fulfills individual obligations, the Bible tells of God binding himself to Israel by covenant, an intimate relationship. Covenants are more than terms and obligations; they create a kind of unity between parties. In three places the Bible portrays God as articulating a covenant with Abraham, the father of Jewish and Christian faith.[5] God promises the land of Canaan (Israel) and innumerable descendants, and he demands that Abraham be circumcised as a covenantal sign and that he "walk in [God's] presence and be blameless" (Gen. 17:1). God makes another covenant with the people of Israel through Moses on Mount Sinai (Exod. 20 and 24). He promises to be God to his people, to protect them and assure their flourishing in the land of Canaan, and he also demands that they follow his law. Failure to do so will result in their demise. God makes a third covenantal engagement with King David and his successors.[6] God promises that David's kingdom will be everlasting, that he will bless the monarchy, and that no matter the circumstances God will never remove his protection. He also warns that if the successors to David sin, he will punish them. Finally, the prophets Jeremiah (31:31–34) and Ezekiel (37:25–26) anticipated a new and everlasting covenant, one where the law would be written on the people's hearts, where God's dwelling would be among them.

Israel understood herself, above all, as a covenant community that loved God and was particularly loved by God. When things got bleak, they appealed to God and the covenants he made with them. The prophets also regularly challenged Israel when Israel proved unfaithful to the covenant. They warned Israel using the very threats God made when first establishing these covenants. Being a people of the covenant molded Israel's self-understanding and spirituality. It inspired and challenged them.

In the New Testament, Jesus appeals to this covenantal identity. He promised to fulfill the covenantal law (Matt. 5:17), he was recognized as an anointed figure who would be a new kind of David or messiah (Matt. 16:16; 21:4–9), and he created the anticipated new and eternal covenant with his sacrifice on the cross (Matt. 26:26–29). Paul would later teach that the eternal covenant in Jesus fulfilled the covenant God made with Abraham (Gal. 3:15–29), thus linking the most ancient covenant with the new and eternal one.

---

5. Gen. 12:1–3; 15:1–21; 17:1–11.

6. 2 Sam. 7.

Thus the motif of covenant serves as one of the great driving forces in Jewish and Christian spirituality. To imagine oneself as a Jew or Christian is to think of oneself as having a covenantal relationship with God, a relationship of intimacy, filled with promises and expectations. Biblical spirituality draws on this and many other great themes as a way to define and mold a believer's identity.

Biblical Spirituality: Ways of Proceeding

It is possible to approach biblical spirituality from a variety of perspectives, each one engaging a different biblical worldview and way of being holy within it.[7] It is possible to discern, however, three basic understandings of biblical spirituality: (1) spiritualities expressed in the Bible, (2) a pattern of Christian life deeply imbued with the spiritualities of the Bible, and (3) the transformative process of personal and communal engagement with the biblical text. Biblical spirituality seeks to recapture the experience of God reflected in the text. This is sometimes understood as entering into the spiritual imagination that gave rise to the text. It also involves seeing how the text might create a transformative possibility in oneself or one's community. The text creates a kind of proposed world where the believer can enter and be challenged and inspired. This proposed world enlarges the soul, and experiencing the text prompts the reader to consider his or her life differently.

All three meanings of the term "biblical spirituality" encompass the many spiritualities found in the Bible. To be responsible for a biblical spirituality means to be attentive to the many ways the Bible presents God and faithfulness. They do not cohere nicely into some kind of collective whole, but each comprises part of the biblical witness and regularly draws on the same themes in different ways. The New Testament functions as the interpretive foundation for a Christian making sense of the Old Testament, but the Old Testament represents much more than an addendum. There are also numerous spiritualities in the Old Testament, and Christians must incorporate these also into a responsible biblical spirituality.

---

7. By way of illustrating possible approaches, one might consider the fifteen-volume series, *Messages of Biblical Spirituality*, edited by Carolyn Osiek: Kathleen O'Connor (vol. 5, *The Wisdom Literature*) writes about the sphere of life where humans expect to meet God and the stance they ought to take in life; John Endres (vol. 2, *Temple, Monarchy and Word of God*) sees the text as witnessing healthy ways to live one's faith life, based on a world-view and self-understanding in relationship to God; Toni Cravin (vol. 6, *The Book of Psalms*) sees biblical spirituality as an attempt to articulate who God is and what it means to be faithful; and Thomas Tobin (vol. 12, *The Spirituality of Paul*) investigates the spirituality that Paul himself had: his own experiences, values, and method in making sense of the faith tradition.

An Example of Gospel Spirituality

Every report is an interpretation. This is true of today's documentaries, news reports, and histories, and it is true of ancient accounts such as the Gospels. In providing a narrative of Jesus' ministry, the Gospel writers drew on a multitude of stories about the deeds and sayings of Jesus and tried to make sense of it all in light of their own interpretive lens as well as the perspective of the communities for which they wrote. As will appear in the following brief exercise, the texts provide different ways of engaging expressions of a biblical spirituality. While they reference the same Jesus and his ministry, they are not the same.

Christian tradition associates the four "living creatures" of Revelation 4:6–8 with the four Gospels, as in this page from the ninth-century Book of Kells. The fourfold iconography acknowledges that each Gospel presents a distinctive interpretation of Jesus.

The Spirituality of the Gospel of Matthew

Matthew begins his Gospel by showing God's providence throughout salvation history. He lists Jesus' genealogy from Abraham to Joseph—three sets of fourteen generations that outline Israel's history. Jesus is the very embodiment of Israel. His family dwells in Bethlehem, King David's city, and his birth draws in the nations. As Israel is "light to the nations" (Isa. 49:6), so a star calls wise men from the Gentile world with gifts. But King Herod, a sort of new pharaoh, seeks his destruction, and the holy family flees to Egypt, just as Israel was once in exile. Jesus will become the new Moses. In his first sermon, Jesus climbs a mountain much as Moses did on Sinai to receive the law, and he reflects what the new reign of God will look like. This kingdom will be for the poor in spirit, for those who mourn, who are humble, who hunger and thirst for righteousness, who are merciful, who are pure of heart, who are peacemakers, and who will be persecuted for righteousness.[8]

---

8. Matt. 5:3–12.

Jesus assures his listeners that he hasn't come to abolish Moses' law but to fulfill it. While the law warns against murder and adultery, Jesus warns against even angry or lustful thoughts. Everything is about interior transformation. Every kind of hypocrisy, every kind of self-advancement at the expense of others, every kind of religious show must be reversed.

Most shockingly, the kingdom is for everyone who is willing to be transformed. It is for the Roman centurion, the pious synagogue ruler, the tax collectors and public sinners. Jesus' message is about hearing and doing: "Not everyone who says to me, 'Lord, Lord,' will enter the kingdom of heaven, but only the one who does the will of my Father in heaven" (7:21); "Therefore, I say to you, the kingdom of God will be taken away from you and given to a people that will produce its fruit" (21:43). Jesus identifies with both the authority of God and humanity at large. In one of his most provocative teachings, he says that the nations will be gathered on the last day and separated for eternal life or eternal damnation. To those who will be given life he will say, "For I was hungry and you gave me food, I was thirsty and you gave me drink, I was a stranger and you welcomed me, naked and you clothed me, ill and you cared for me, in prison and you visited me" (25:35–36). When, they will ask, did they do these things for Jesus? Jesus will reply, "Whatever you did for one of these least brothers of mine, you did for me" (25:40). And to those who will be damned he will say, "What you did not do for one of these least ones, you did not do for me" (25:45).

To understand the spirituality of Matthew's Gospel one must grasp the ancient Jews' vision of God. This Gospel's message exhibits extraordinary continuity between God's providential love for Israel and the fulfillment of that love in the ministry of Jesus. God had promised a new covenant, one of true interior holiness, not as a replacement but as a completion of his law. The Hebrew word usually translated as "law" is *Torah*, which can also mean "direction" or "instruction." *Torah* is all about doing acts of holiness. God wants the whole self involved. Holiness without engagement in acts of love and service is no holiness at all. It is also the case that an engaged life of service without a pure heart and transformed inner life is still a life of sin. Jesus calls his listeners to become and live the Torah of the new covenant.

The Spirituality of the Gospel of Mark

The world of Mark is a dark one; forces of evil and power reign unresisted. Mark begins his Gospel with Jesus bursting on the scene announcing an imminent kingdom that demands a response: "This is the time of fulfillment. The kingdom of God is at hand. Repent, and believe in the gospel" (1:15). Almost immediately thereafter, Jesus exorcises an evil spirit. The evil spirit yells out, "Have you come to destroy us?" (1:24). Yes, this is certainly the case. The first half of the Gospel is filled with testimony of Jesus curing those who are ill, releasing those who are controlled by evil spirits, and extending God's forgiveness by his own authority.

But along with the message of the kingdom comes resistance: "The Pharisees went out and immediately took counsel with the Herodians against him to put him to death" (3:6). Now the kingdom fights not only against supernatural evil, but also the religious and political leadership.

The second half of the Gospel turns darker still as Jesus travels to Jerusalem. His way is a way of self-offering. Peter *rebukes* Jesus when he hears such news, but Jesus responds, "Get behind me Satan!" (8:33). Then to the crowds he declares, "Whoever wishes to come after me must deny himself, take up his cross, and follow me" (8:34). The disciples do not understand and are as spiritually blind as those whom Jesus physically heals. Discipleship is hard and the powers of the anti-kingdom are strong. However, Jesus is stronger, and he promises that those who follow him will have the strength of his Spirit: "They will hand you over to the courts. You will be beaten in synagogues. You will be arraigned before governors and kings because of me, as a witness before them. . . . When they lead you away and hand you over, do not worry beforehand about what you are to say. But say whatever will be given to you at that hour. . . . You will be hated by all because of my name. But the one who perseveres to the end will be saved" (13:9–13).

The end of Mark's Gospel is odd and abrupt.[9] It describes how Mary Magdalene, Mary, the mother of James, and Salome went to the tomb where they find a young man inside who tells them that Jesus has been raised. He orders them to tell the disciples to go to Galilee to meet the risen Lord, and "then they went out and fled the tomb, seized with trembling and bewilderment. They said nothing to anyone, for they were afraid" (16:8). This is a very dark Gospel indeed.

Many scholars believe that the Gospel of Mark originated in Rome at a time when the church suffered great persecution at the hands of the Roman authorities.[10] The church had already witnessed the martyrdom of many of its members, including Peter and Paul. In 64 CE, a great fire in Rome destroyed a large segment of the city. The Emperor Nero blamed the Christians for it, and they were broadly suspected and hated by the populous. To be a Christian at that time and place was dangerous. Fully appreciating the spirituality of Mark means seeing how the message and ministry of Jesus engage powers of evil and conflict. To understand Mark's spirituality is to understand Jesus as mightier than any of these powers even as one might fall victim to them. Christ has

---

9. The ancient manuscripts have two or possibly three endings of Mark that do not cohere. In the longer second ending Jesus appears to several of his disciples and then to the apostles, commissioning them to preach to the whole world. After this, they see him ascend into heaven. A possible third ending has the resurrected Jesus working through the disciples in preaching the word. The first and shortest ending is, according to scholars, almost certainly the one Mark originally penned.

10. The other popular theory is that this Gospel originated in the vicinity of Palestine, possibly Syria, at about the time of the Jewish War (66–73). See Francis Moloney, *The Gospel of Mark: A Commentary* (Peabody, MA: Hendrickson, 2002), 11–15.

ultimately conquered them. In Mark's Gospel, faith is perseverance especially in
times of trial, and confidence that even in one's suffering the victorious Christ
walks with the faithful.

The Spirituality of the Gospel of Luke

In a famous speech in Luke's Gospel, Mary praises God:

> My soul proclaims the greatness of the Lord; and my spirit rejoices
> in God my savior. For he has looked upon his handmaid's low-
> liness. . . . His mercy is from age to age to those who fear him. He
> has shown might with his arm, dispersed the arrogant of mind and
> heart. He has thrown down the rulers from their thrones but lifted up
> the lowly. The hungry he has filled with good things; the rich he has
> sent away empty. He has helped Israel his servant, remembering his
> mercy, according to his promise to our fathers, to Abraham and to his
> descendants forever. (1:46–55)

Mary's extraordinary praise to God encapsulates much of this Gospel's spirituality. God has remembered his covenant and Jesus has now arrived to fulfill God's
promises and bring salvation to his people. This salvation is especially marked by
a reversal of fortunes, such as feeding the hungry and raising the poor while putting down the arrogant and those rulers unconcerned for the least among them.

Like Matthew, Luke places Jesus' birth in Bethlehem, though he describes
his family as poor pilgrims who have come to register for a census. There is no
problem with Herod, no wise men, no flight into Egypt. Rather, Jesus is born
in a humble stable, attended by poor shepherds. Throughout Jesus' ministry,
Luke shows him as the champion of the poor and a public challenger to all the
social, political, and religious conventions that have kept them marginalized.
The differences between Matthew's version of Jesus' great sermon and Luke's
highlight this shift in emphasis. In Matthew, Jesus proclaims, "Blessed are the
poor in spirit, for theirs is the kingdom of heaven. . . . Blessed are they who
hunger and thirst for righteousness, for they will be satisfied" (5:3, 6). In Luke,
Jesus proclaims, "Blessed are you who are poor, for the kingdom of God is
yours. Blessed are you who are now hungry, for you will be satisfied. Blessed
are you who are now weeping, for you will laugh" (6:20–21). And he continues,
"But woe to you who are rich, for you have received your consolation. But woe
to you who are filled now, for you will be hungry. Woe to you who laugh now,
for you will grieve and weep" (6:24–25). While Matthew's Gospel focuses on
spiritual transformation, Luke's addresses those who are literally poor, hungry,
and suffering.

Not only does Luke's Gospel include more parables than appear in Matthew and Mark, they have a different slant. Many describe the kingdom of God

elevating the lowly. The poor need only believe in God's mercy, while the well-off are expected to embrace solidarity with the poor. Jesus did not demand that everyone become poor or indicate that being poor was a good thing. Moreover it seems clear that Jesus wanted both rich and poor to repent. The Gospel emphasizes, however, the plight of the poor as of utmost concern in God's kingdom.

In Luke, the Holy Spirit dominates the scene. John the Baptist proclaims, "I am baptizing you with water, but one mightier than I is coming. . . . He will baptize you with the holy Spirit and fire" (3:16). When John baptized Jesus, "heaven opened and the holy Spirit descended upon him" (3:21–22). Thereupon, Jesus, "filled with the holy Spirit, . . . returned from the Jordan and was led by the Spirit into the desert for forty days" (4:1–2). In his first act of public ministry Jesus declares: "The Spirit of the Lord is upon me, because he has anointed me to bring glad tidings to the poor. He has sent me to proclaim liberty to captives and recovery of sight to the blind, to let the oppressed go free" (4:18).[11] This shows a perfect combination of the role of the Spirit in Jesus' life and the mission of the kingdom to uplift the poor and oppressed.

To become imbued with the spirituality of Luke is to look for God's presence and blessings among the poor. A spirituality based on Luke's Gospel sees their plight; indeed, it looks for it. This spirituality demands a careful examination of personal values, priorities, and decisions. It proclaims that one's very faith, and even eternal life, depends on taking their side, identifying with them and their needs.

The Spirituality of the Gospel of John

Who is God and what does God look like? These questions dominate John. This Gospel shows no interest in the infancy of Jesus, preferring to focus on the nature of Jesus as the human face of God. John starts his Gospel this way:

> In the beginning was the Word, and the Word was with God, and the Word was God. He was in the beginning with God. All things came to be through him, and without him nothing came to be. What came to be through him was life, and this life was the light of the human race; the light shines in the darkness and the darkness has not overcome it. . . . And the Word became flesh and made his dwelling among us. . . . No one has ever seen God. The only Son, God, who is at the Father's side, has revealed him. (1:1–18)

Right away the narrative suggests that Jesus is something like the Old Testament Wisdom through whom God created the universe and ordered it.[12] He is both

---

11. Jesus is applying to himself a quotation from Isa. 61:1.

12. See Wis. 7–8.

with God and identified as God. Interestingly, John's prologue ends with the Son *revealing* the Father. John uses the word *exēgeomai*, the meaning of which is closer to "interpret." Jesus is the interpretation of God. So to decide about Jesus is to decide about God. There is no half-measure in discipleship. Throughout the Gospel, Jesus distinguishes between light and darkness, truth and falsehood, spirit and flesh, being children of God or children of the devil. The dramatic language demands a decision: Which will you choose?

The Gospels of Matthew, Mark, and Luke present the cross as a necessary place of self-offering that is daunting and unnerving. One might think of it as Satan's imagined place of victory, with the Resurrection symbolizing God's reversal and ultimate victory. In each of these Gospels, Jesus suffers at the thought of the cross.[13]

John's Gospel stands in stark contrast. Here Jesus sees his crucifixion as "bread . . . for the life of the world" (6:51). Through it he will reveal his own and the Father's glory: "When you lift up the Son of Man, then you will realize that I AM" (8:28). The cross here is a place of glory (17:5, 22, 24), a place where Jesus "will draw everyone" to himself (12:32). Jesus reveals the divine life as a free self-offering in love, saying, "No one has greater love than this, to lay down one's life for one's friends" (15:13). The theme of love dominates this Gospel: "I give you a new commandment; love one another. As I have loved you, so you also should love one another. This is how all will know that you are my disciples, if you have loved one another" (13:34–35).

Such a loving self-offering provides deep communion. To believe in Jesus and to love as he loves is to have intimacy with him and his Father, as well as with other believers. Before his arrest Jesus prays: "I pray . . . so that they may all be one, as you, Father, are in me and I in you, that they also may be in us, that the world may believe that you sent me. And I have given them the glory you gave me, so that they may be one as we are one, I in them and you in me, that they may be brought to perfection as one" (17:20–23).

The spirituality of John is a spirituality of decisiveness: Are you in or are you out? John's Gospel unmasks lukewarm faith. One cannot be *sort of* Christian or an *average* Christian or a *modest* churchgoer. John presents a spirituality that is all or nothing—and being "all in" means offering oneself unreservedly. The paradox is that this very self-emptying to God in love reveals the divine life working within. In and with Jesus one can be an icon of the Father and enjoy extraordinary love and intimacy with God and others, but the cost is everything.

---

13. "My soul is sorrowful, even to death," he tells his disciples. He prays, "My Father, if it is possible, let this cup pass from me; yet not as I will, but as you will" (Matt. 26:38–39). Luke even reports that "his sweat became like drops of blood" (22:44).

Making Sense of Gospel Spirituality

One might wonder which of these versions of the gospel represents the "real," meaning "historical," Jesus. The Gospel writers intended to represent the real Jesus, although the rules at the time for being historical certainly allowed for some narrative license. However, the Gospels are not documentaries, and even documentaries involve interpretation. Neither do they resemble photographs. In some sense, they more closely resemble collages of portraits, even impressionistic paintings. Claude Monet's panels of water lilies, like Vincent van Gogh's wheat fields, may be less accurate than a photograph, but they are utterly beautiful and true. They draw the viewer into the wonder of lilies and wheat fields like no photo could. In that sense, their impressionistic style is more true than any photo could be.

Another false start might consist of asking which spirituality is most authentically Christian? An authentic biblical spirituality cannot isolate one Gospel to the neglect of others. They are all about Jesus—who he was, his message, and the meaning of his life. To see the horror of the crucifixion is to see how sin disfigures the human condition and to understand the cost of discipleship. It means recognizing the forces of the anti-kingdom at work. To see crucifixion as a place of triumph is to see how self-offering really is a secret glory.[14]

A skillful biblical spirituality draws on various spiritual postures in the Bible at different times or for different reasons. As noted in chapter 1, spiritualities follow a path; a person does not become holy in a day. One sees this dynamic in the Gospels with the growing faith of the disciples as they had to rely on and be taught by the Holy Spirit. Luke focuses on the Spirit in his Gospel. His second volume, Acts of the Apostles, emphasizes this even more. The church and even individual disciples grow and learn and need to be led by the Spirit. Acts demonstrates how discipleship can be a long, slow process. This truth, however, need not undermine the demand in John for absolute faith. This latter truth challenges one to confront any mediocrity in the soul. To one who experiences joy in the Spirit, the good news in Matthew and the flourishing that Jesus promises celebrate this. To one who suffers persecution, Mark's emphasis on perseverance and faith in Jesus becomes true solace. To one whose sense of justice is atrophied, Luke's Gospel offers a challenge to rethink personal values and priorities.

There is far more to the Gospels than this small experiment in biblical spirituality provides. Jesus himself seemed to have his own spirituality, and one could approach the Gospels collectively in order to derive a portrait of that. This is different, albeit related, to the spirituality he strove to imbue in his disciples, which could be another way to engage the Gospels collectively. Finally, it is important to remember that the Gospels themselves only make up part of the Bible.

---

14. Mother Teresa of Calcutta embodied this paradox. She experienced decades of spiritual darkness and interior poverty, but in this very context the world saw a radiant saint, an icon of Jesus.

Conclusion

The Bible is the core Christian text. It informs, guides, and teaches like no other Christian resource. Broadly speaking, Christian theology and spirituality are deeply informed by the Bible, and the forthcoming chapters will show that it has a decisive presence in the major movements and schools of spirituality. In another sense, it is a document that itself is filled with spiritualities. And, as noted above, this plurality of biblical spiritualities do not combine to a single vision. Rather, they reflect the time, place, and lived experience out of which they emerge. The challenge for Christians who are serious about the Bible is to hold these various spiritualities in a kind of creative tension, knowing how and what to draw on in fruitful ways. For example, the books of Deuteronomy and Leviticus are suspicious of the cultures around them, while the wisdom literature, such as Proverbs or Wisdom, is very open to the spiritual and moral insights of non-Jews. This needn't be a contradiction if one can develop the prudence and religious savvy to know when to be doubtful and when to be hospitable to other religious points of view.

Understanding the Bible, its various witnesses to God's presence and activity in the life of Israel and particularly its witness to the message and ministry of Jesus, cannot be overstated in importance for Christian spirituality. Saint Jerome's dictum, "Ignorance of scripture is ignorance of Christ," is not merely a pithy saying to get Christians to read the Bible. Rather it reflects the importance of the Bible as Christianity's central resource.

Questions for Review

1. What precautionary suggestions from the chapter should be kept in mind when interpreting a biblical text?
2. According to the chapter, what does it mean to say that the Bible has "authority"?
3. What is a covenant and what role have covenants played in the Bible?
4. What are the distinctive features of each Gospel's spirituality?

Questions for Discussion

1. As discussed, a number of interpretive lenses can be used in reading the Bible, for example, liberation theology. What interpretive lens do you think is most useful? How might different lenses provide different interpretive results?
2. The Bible has many literary genres, such as poetry, history, and myth. How might readers come to incorrect or unsupported interpretations if they fail to keep these genres in mind?

3. How might the differences in how the Gospels present the story of Jesus be helpful to modern readers? What challenges might the discrepancies between Gospel accounts pose for a contemporary audience?

4. Keeping in mind the different emphases of the Gospels, if a non-Christian wanted to learn about Jesus and Christianity, which Gospel would you recommend first and why?

Bibliography

Resources with annotations are highly recommended to students interested in further study.

Bowe, Barbara. *Biblical Foundations of Spirituality: Touching a Finger to the Flame.* Oxford: Rowman & Littlefield, 2003.

> This volume offers a great synopsis of many predominant themes through the Bible as well as attention to Jesus in the Gospels and Paul in his letters.

Brown, William, ed. *Engaging Biblical Authority: Perspectives on the Bible as Scripture.* Louisville: Westminster John Knox, 2007.

> This book is a collection of essays that demonstrate the many ways that the Bible is understood as authoritative and how such perspectives affect one's interpretation of the text.

Craven, Toni. *The Book of Psalms.* Collegeville, MN: Michael Glazier, 1992.

Endres, John. *Temple, Monarch, and Word.* Collegeville, MN: Michael Glazier, 1988.

Furnish, Victor Paul. *The Moral Teaching of Paul: Selected Issues.* 2nd ed. Nashville: Abingdon Press, 1985.

Grech, Prosper. *An Outline of New Testament Spirituality.* Grand Rapids: Eerdmans, 2011.

> This book focuses on biblical spirituality as a response to central themes, such as the kingdom of God.

Johnson, Luke Timothy. *Prophetic Jesus, Prophetic Church: The Challenge of Luke-Acts to Contemporary Christians.* Grand Rapids: Eerdmans, 2011.

Jones, Cheslyn, Geoffrey Wainwright, and Edward Yarnold, eds. *The Study of Spirituality.* New York: Oxford University Press, 1986.

Lescher, Bruce, and Elizabeth Liebert. *Exploring Christian Spirituality: Essays in Honor of Sandra Schneiders.* New York: Paulist Press, 2006.

Lohfink, Gerhard. *Jesus of Nazareth: What He Wanted, Who He Was.* Translated by Linda Mahony. Collegeville, MN: Michael Glazier: 2012.

> This may be the best, small study on the historical Jesus and his message available in English.

O'Conner, Kathleen. *The Wisdom Literature*. Collegeville, MN: Michael Glazier, 1988.

Perkins, Pheme. *Reading the New Testament: An Introduction*. New York: Paulist Press, 1978.

Schneiders, Sandra. "Biblical Spirituality." *Interpretation* 56 (April 2002): 133–42.

Schneiders, Sandra. *The Revelatory Text: Interpreting the New Testament as Sacred Scripture*. New York: HarperSanFrancisco, 1991.

This volume examines how scripture can be both a scholarly pursuit and vehicle for personal transformation.

Schneiders, Sandra. "Scripture and Spirituality." In *Christian Spirituality*, edited by Bernard McGinn, John Meyendorff, and Jean Leclercq, 1:1–20. New York: Continuum, 1988.

Smith, Christian. *The Bible Made Impossible: Why Biblicism Is Not a Truly Evangelical Reading of Scripture*. Grand Rapids: Brazos Press, 2011.

This book examines the problem of biblical fundamentalism, and why few if any scholars in any part of Christianity are fundamentalists.

Tobin, Thomas. *The Spirituality of Paul*. Collegeville, MN: Michael Glazier, 1987.

Films

The Gospel of John. 2003.

The story of Jesus' life as recounted by the Gospel of John using a word-for-word transcript of the *Good News Bible*.

Jesus of Nazareth. 1977.

A British-Italian television miniseries directed and co-written by Franco Zefferelli, dramatizing the birth, life, ministry, crucifixion, and Resurrection of Jesus.

The Passion of the Christ. 2004.

Depicts the Passion of Jesus largely according to the Gospels and other traditional devotional writings, by Anne Catherine Emmerich. The dialogue is entirely in reconstructed Aramaic and Latin with English subtitles.

Chapter

The Spirituality
of the Early Church

During the apostolic era, the period of church history from the time of the apostles to the early second century, the church emerged as a bona fide religion, with a set of relatively secure doctrines, church order, a stable liturgical life, and an early Christian spirituality. The "patristic era" designates the period from the second century to the end of the sixth. During this period, the church exhibited both continuity and significant changes and developments, as this chapter will show.

The Spirituality of the Apostolic Church
From the Bible to the Apostolic Church

The primitive church was decidedly Jewish, as seen particularly in Matthew's Gospel. Jesus was Jewish, as were his apostles and followers. Saint Paul did not see himself as leaving Judaism for another religion called "Christianity." Rather, he and his fellow believers understood Jesus as the fulfillment of God's covenants and the one to usher in the new messianic age, that is, a kingdom of God that fulfilled the Old Testament prophetic expectations of the people of Israel. By the end of the first century, however, faith in Jesus had indeed become a new religion. Knowing something of the history behind this transition facilitates a better understanding of the spirituality of the early church.

One of the most decisive events in first century Judaism was the destruction of the Temple in Jerusalem in 70 CE, during the Jewish War, a Jewish rebellion against Roman control. This development ended all but one of the various factions of Jews: the Pharisees.[1] Consequently, following the war, the Pharisees'

---

1. The other three factions were armed resistance movements (e.g., the Zealot party), the Essenes, and the Sadducees. The resistance movements were devastated in the war. The reclusive, separatist Essenes did not participate directly in the revolt, but were destroyed by the Romans nonetheless. The Sadducees, whose power base consisted of the elite, priestly families and worship in the Temple, ceased to exist when the Temple was destroyed.

understanding of the Jewish faith, centered around *Torah*, the law, came to dominate. Modern Judaism finds its roots in the Pharisees' revision, what is now called "Rabbinic Judaism."

The Pharisees, along with the majority of Jews, did not believe Jesus was the Jewish messiah (anointed one), much less the savior of the world. In Palestine, if not more widely, they excluded Jews who believed Jesus was the messiah from participating in synagogue worship, and this exclusion forced believers to create a new identity. One can see hints of this in the Gospel of John (ca. 90). In chapter 9, Jesus heals a blind man in Jerusalem. The Pharisees question this newly healed man and then his parents, but his parents do not cooperate, saying, "'Ask him, he is of age; he can speak for himself.' His parents said this because they were afraid of the Jews, for the Jews had already agreed that if anyone acknowledged him [Jesus] as the Messiah, he would be expelled from the synagogue" (9:21–22). Jews did not expel people for this reason until many decades after the time of Jesus. Throughout John's Gospel Jesus uses language that distinguishes his followers from *the Jews*, even though he and his disciples were also Jews. The account depicts the experience of late first-century believers who were in fact being excluded from the synagogue and were breaking away from their Jewish identity. Further, these Jewish believers in Jesus met on Sunday with their fellow believers; they were shifting communities and loyalties.

A second reason that Christianity became distinct from its Jewish identity has to do with the membership requirements of the new-found faith. Accounts throughout the Acts of the Apostles and Paul's letters indicate that Gentiles (non-Jews) were coming to the faith. The question emerged: Did they then have to abide by the *Torah* or law? Acts 15 describes a meeting of the elders of the faith where they decided that Gentiles did not have to take on the law, but were acceptable to God without it. The law represented Jewish identity and piety, and it constituted the covenant that allowed them to fulfill the command, "Be holy, because I am holy" (Lev. 11:45). Now holiness had been divorced from the law. In Galatians, Paul even says, "For through the law I have died to the law, that I might live for God. I have been crucified with Christ; yet I live, no longer I, but Christ lives in me" (2:19–20). This breaking away from the law as a core framing of one's faithfulness is not only theological, but also spiritual. Christ is the center. Living in and through him is now all that matters.

A third reason, no less important, is that sociologically the new-found faith in Christ increasingly became a Gentile religion. If the community of the apostles was virtually entirely Jewish with a few Gentiles joining them, the community of believers in the latter part of the first century was primarily Gentile. In terms of numbers, Christianity was becoming a Gentile religion. The Romans saw it the same way. It would even be more accurate to say that the Romans saw Christianity somewhere between superstition and cult. Judaism was a tolerated religion in the Roman Empire as a longstanding tradition, and because of their objection to worshipping other gods, Jews were not required to offer sacrifice to the emperor. Christians, however, were persecuted for nonobservance of this duty. The Roman law was clear: *Non licet esse Christianos* ("It is against the law to be a Christian").

Apocalypticism

The book of Revelation reflects the persecuted church. As noted in chapter 3, the Emperor Nero found in the Christians the perfect scapegoats for the fire in Rome. Anyone who publicly admitted to being a Christian risked torture and martyrdom for the faith. The book of Revelation describes the young Christian church as being attacked by political and supernatural evils, both working together. It notes, for example, the "mark" of the "beast" who works for Satan in persecuting the faith: "Wisdom is needed here; one who understands can calculate the number of the beast, for it is a number that stands for a person. His number is six-hundred and sixty-six" (13:18). This reference makes use of numerology, which assigns numbers to letters. The Hebrew letters that make up Caesar Nero are: qoph: 100; samekh: 60; resh: 200; nun: 50; resh 200; vav: 6; nun: 50, for a total of 666.

The book of Revelation was not intended to be a fortune-telling text about the historical specifics of the end of the world, despite the fact that some use it that way.

This fifteenth-century woodcut depicts the four horsemen of the Apocalypse (Rev. 6:1–8), who will rain terror on an unrepentant world in the end times.

It is above all a book of spirituality. To a persecuted church, one under brutal attack, Revelation offers this assurance: know that despite the plight you now endure God is on your side. While horrors come at you from all sides and your enemies work for evil, they will not prevail. The Lord is coming soon; hold on. There is even now a celebrated victory in heaven (4–5) and the final victory will conclude with a heavenly wedding between Christ the groom and his church the bride (19). After this, there will be a new heaven and a new earth, a paradise where the just will live in peace, love, and union with God (21). The persecuted early church embraced a spirituality of suffering with the crucified one, of clinging to him in the midst of the horrors of abuse, and, above all, of trust that God was with them and would deliver them gloriously.

The apocalyptic text the *Shepherd of Hermas* (ca. 100) reflects much the same spirituality. In one place, the Christian Hermas has a vision in which he is invited to a banquet table but not allowed to sit on the right (favored) side, which is reserved for martyrs "who have already pleased God and have suffered for the sake of the Name. . . . 'What,' I asked, 'have they endured?' 'Listen,' she said. 'Scourgings, imprisonments, severe persecutions, crosses, wild beasts, for the sake of the name. This is why the right side of Holiness belongs to them, and to whoever suffers because of the Name.'"[2] Later Hermas is offered symbols of spiritual comfort, but with a warning: "Only you must keep your house clean. . . . If, therefore they find your house pure, they [angels] will remain with you. But if the slightest impurity turns up, they will leave your house at once."[3] The spiritual life implied here is one of moral rigor, undaunted by the possibility of suffering for the faith, for God comforts and strengthens those who would embrace such a life, and promises glory, honor, and table-intimacy to those who suffer the most.

Moral Rigor

Moral rigor is one of the marks of apostolic-era Christianity. As cited in chapter 1, the great early church text the *Didache* (ca. 90) begins: "There are two ways, one of life and the other of death, and there is a great difference between these two ways."[4] The text goes on, in the voice of Jesus to his apostles, demanding (not just encouraging) the love of enemies, the prohibition against murder, adultery, corruption of others, promiscuousness, stealing, magic, sorcery, abortion, coveting possessions, lying, speaking evil, holding grudges, greed, hypocrisy, anger, jealousy, lust, and practicing astrology or magic (or even being interested in such activities). The *Letter of Barnabas* (ca. 100) reiterates the command to be upright both inwardly and outwardly: "This, therefore, is the way of light."[5]

---

2. *The Shepherd of Hermas* 9–10. Translation from *The Apostolic Fathers*, trans. J. B. Lightfoot and J. R. Harmer, 2nd ed. (Grand Rapids: Baker Book House, 1989), 201. All quotations from *The Shepherd of Hermas* come from this source.

3. Ibid., 113.

4. *Didache* 1.1, from *The Apostolic Fathers*. All quotations from the *Didache* come from this source.

5. *Barnabas* 19, from *The Apostolic Fathers*.

Being a Christian meant something: it meant that the old self died in baptism and that one's new life in the Holy Spirit was decidedly different. One wasn't just to act differently, but was to *be* different. Christian life was marked by urgency: Christ was returning soon. While they did not know when, Christians still presumed it to be imminent. The *Didache* ends with, "Watch over your life: do not let your lamps go out and do not be unprepared, but be ready. . . . The Lord will come, and all his saints with him. Then the world will see the Lord coming upon the clouds of heaven."[6] Interestingly, the Eucharistic prayer found in that text also ends with an Aramaic imperative: *maranatha* [Come Lord!].[7]

Communal Identity and the Eucharist

While the spirituality of early Christianity was one of moral severity, it was also deeply communal, with a central focus not only on the soul, but on the church, the mystical body of Christ. Despite being persecuted from without, the community understood itself as infused with the Holy Spirit. Baptism did not simply indicate personal conversion to Jesus as Lord, but entrance into a holy body, a living expression of the kingdom of God. This precluded any sort of exclusiveness based on social distinctions. Jesus regularly taught that one received the kingdom as a child,[8] that is, as one without social standing, and he directly

Catacombs of San Callisto, Rome, Italy / Bridgeman Images

This fresco of the last supper was found in the catacombs of Rome and dates to the third century, when Christianity was illegal and Christians sometimes had to worship literally underground.

---

6. *Didache* 16.

7. Ibid., 10.6.

8. Mark 10:15.

contrasted discipleship with lording over others. Rather, being a servant of all is the mark of the true disciple.[9]

The community of Christians was Eucharistic. They met on Sunday for fellowship and participated in the Lord's Supper, or Eucharist, which represented communion with one another and communion with Christ himself. Saint Ignatius of Antioch (d. 115) referred to the Eucharist as "the flesh of our Savior Jesus Christ" and "the medicine of immortality."[10] The Eucharist constituted the future messianic banquet here and now. It was the spiritual event par excellence, and those who refuse to come to the Eucharistic table, Ignatius predicts, will "perish in their contentiousness."[11]

The Eucharist created and reflected church unity: "Take care, therefore, to participate in one Eucharist (for there is one flesh of our Lord Jesus Christ, and one cup which leads to unity through his blood; there is one altar, just as there is one bishop, together with the presbytery and the deacons, my fellow servants), in order that whatever you do, you do in accordance with God."[12] For Ignatius, the Eucharist aligns with the bishop, presbyters, and deacons, who represent a kind of ministerial hierarchy. Rather than standing in contrast to a community that eschewed "lording over others," this hierarchy was thought to represent the very structure that assured unity: "Thus, it is proper for you to act together in harmony with the mind of the bishop, as you are in fact doing. For your presbytery, which is worthy of the name and worthy of God, is attuned to the bishop as strings to a lyre. Therefore in your unanimity and harmonious love Jesus Christ is sung."[13] Throughout Ignatius's letters one can discern the theme of church unity being created and sustained by the bishop and his assisting ministers of presbyters (elders) and deacons (servants/ministers). He writes, "Flee from divisions, as the beginning of evils. You must all follow the bishop, as Jesus Christ followed the Father, and follow the presbytery as you would the apostles; respect the deacons as the commandment of God. Let no one do anything that has to do with the church without the bishop. Only that Eucharist which is under the authority of the bishop . . . is to be considered valid."[14]

---

9. Mark 10:42–45.

10. Ignatius of Antioch, *Smyrnaeans* 6 and *Ephesians* 20, from *The Apostolic Fathers*. All quotations from Ignatius of Antioch come from this source.

11. Ignatius of Antioch, *Smyrnaeans* 7.

12. Ignatius of Antioch, *Philadelphians* 4.

13. Ignatius of Antioch, *Ephesians* 4.

14. Ignatius of Antioch, *Smyrnaeans* 8. Ignatius wrote his letters while on his way to Rome to face martyrdom.

Eucharistic Understanding Today

Until the Protestant Reformation in the sixteenth century, Christians broadly believed that the Eucharist or Lord's Supper represented the body and blood of Jesus in the sacramental form of consecrated bread and wine. Today this belief is known widely as the *real presence*. While there may be differences of understanding about the nature of the real presence, Roman Catholic, Eastern Orthodox, and Anglican Christians still hold strongly to this belief. Martin Luther affirmed the real presence of Jesus, though he challenged the Roman Catholic use of Aristotelian philosophy to explain it. For him, the real presence was in and through the consecrated elements. John Calvin, another leading Reformer, believed in the real presence in the sense of experiencing the risen Christ in the context of communion. In contrast, Reformer Ulrich Zwingli challenged the real presence and understood the Eucharist as a memorial meal. Since then, many Protestant Christians understand it as something of a symbol of Christ without any objective presence, while other Protestants retain belief in the real presence. Evangelical Christians typically understand the Eucharist as a memorial meal commemorating the Last Supper, and most celebrate it infrequently.

Developments in Patristic Spirituality

The Church as the Center of Life

Patristic-era Christians continued to be decidedly communal in their identity, with the sacraments, especially the Eucharist, as their center and the bishop as their guide. Saint Augustine (354–430) wrote, "A man possesses the Holy Spirit in the measure in which he loves the Church."[15] Augustine serves as a fine example of this. He was ordained against his will, but because he believed that sacraments were authentic conveyers of grace and because his bishop demanded it and the people desired it, he saw no moral option except to embrace his ordination fully for the good of the community. In a sermon commemorating his ordination, Augustine preached, "Where I am terrified by what I am for you, I am given comfort by what I am with you. For you, I am a bishop; with you, after

---

15. Augustine, *Treatise on the Gospel of John* 32.8.

all, I am a Christian. The first is the name of an office undertaken, the second a name of grace; that one means danger, this one salvation."[16]

Christians regularly gathered together daily for prayer before and after the workday, which today is called the *Liturgy of the Hours* or *Divine Office*. They sang hymns, chanted psalms (or at least a repeated verse called an antiphon), and offered prayers. Because the people were largely illiterate, they memorized standard hymns and antiphons. The psalms reflected the time of day. Morning Prayer typically included psalms that expressed trust in God, hymns (canticles), a Gloria, intercessions of the community, and a blessing and dismissal by the bishop. Evening Prayer began with a ritual lighting of lamps, symbolizing Christ as the light of the community, followed by psalms that sought God's protection through the night, incense, representing prayers rising to God, more hymns and antiphons, intercessions, and a blessing and dismissal. Gathering in community marked the day for many Christians.

In one sense, the church, particularly in the absence of persecution, settled in. More people converted to the faith, and by the fourth century it could even be advantageous to be a Christian. In another sense, the church did not lose its commitment to high standards of moral behavior. For example, committing a serious sin (such as adultery) barred a Christian from receiving the Eucharist. Rather, one would sit in church with others who had seriously sinned in what was called the *Order of Penitents*. Only after a lengthy period of penitence would the bishop allow them to return to normal Eucharistic fellowship. A second serious sin would likely result in permanent excommunication. This practice even led some Christians to forego baptism until later in life, for fear of sinning twice and being excluded not only from the church but, presumably, from salvation itself. Like the apostolic church, the patristic church believed that Christian life was a truly new life in the Spirit; a Christian was supposed to reflect this.

Asceticism and *Apatheia*

Perhaps the biggest difference between apostolic spirituality and patristic spirituality came in the popular Christian understanding of the body. Many Christians turned to a highly ascetical life. Asceticism generally means "discipline," but in this context it meant more than merely a structured, accountable life. Rather, many used deprivation as a means to increase in moral purity and interior openness to God. They wanted to free themselves from the passions of the body and mind.[17] Passions, in this sense, were inordinate desires that caused a

---

16. Augustine, *Serm.* 340, as cited in *The Works of Saint Augustine: A Translation for the 21st Century*, ed. John E. Rotelle, trans. Edmund Hill (Brooklyn, NY: New City Press, 1990), 292–94.

17. In English, to be passionate about something might mean that one is dedicated to it or zealous about it. One can be passionate about football or perhaps even passionate about social justice. The etymology of the word, however, includes the sense of "suffering"—as in the "Passion" of the Lord—which is how the patristic church understood it.

person to suffer. For example, if one were hungry, one should eat. But gluttony or being obsessed with food would be an inordinate desire, one that controlled one's heart and by which one suffered. The remedy was found in striving for *apatheia* or "no suffering." This constituted a mind and heart that was unattached to its experience.

What if one made choices based only on what is objectively best, without taking into account whether it was easy or hard, comfortable or uncomfortable? Often decisions about how to act have much to do with how something makes a person feel. Is this not an example of being controlled by the pleasure-pain principle? Many church leaders believed that, unless freed both by God's grace and an ascetical life, a person would remain a prisoner of his or her passions. *Apatheia* meant freedom.[18] To achieve a certain amount of *apatheia* meant loving others purely for their own sakes and not as means to secure some personal pleasure or comfort. It did not dull one's love for others, but rather enlivened and purified it. Consider the minister of a church who regularly meets pastorally with members. If a member has a pleasant personality, the minister is likely to spend a good deal of time with that person because it is enjoyable. But if the parishioner has an abrasive personality, such pastoral presence is likely to be far shorter. Ministers may even try to avoid such difficult parishioners. But shouldn't the minister's attention and time be geared toward those who would benefit most from his or her ministry, regardless of whether they are pleasant to be around?

Apatheia aimed not only to assure right relationships, but also to purify the soul in order to discover God. It is the pure soul, both spacious and at rest, that allows for communion with God. It is a precondition before entering deep contemplation. Synthesizing this patristic agenda, the great spiritual giant Maximus the Confessor (580–662) saw four degrees of *apatheia*: (1) abstain from sin, (2) train the thoughts not to consent to sin, (3) make all affections subject to reason, and (4) purify the mind to be a mirror of divinity.

Virginity

Associated with suspicion of the passions was the emerging value attached to virginity or lifelong celibacy. While most Christians married and lived standard family lives, many devout Christians embraced a celibate life. It was a life imagined to be wholly dedicated to service and the knowledge of God. Saint Paul reflects this value: "Now to the unmarried and to widows, I say: it is a good thing for them to remain as they are, as I do, but if they cannot exercise self-control they should marry, for it is better to marry than to be on fire" (1 Cor. 7:8–9). Later in the same chapter, he explains:

---

18. The English cognate for *apatheia* is "apathy," but this word does not capture the meaning of the term as used in the early church.

"I should like you to be free of anxieties. An unmarried man is anxious about the things of the Lord, how he may please the Lord. But a married man is anxious about the things for the world, how he may please his wife, and he is divided. An unmarried woman or a virgin is anxious about the things of the Lord, so that she may be holy in both body and spirit. A married woman, on the other hand, is anxious about the things of the world, how she may please her husband. I am telling you this for your own benefit, not to impose a restraint upon you, but for the sake of propriety and adherence to the Lord without distraction. If anyone thinks he is behaving improperly toward his virgin, and if a critical moment has come and so it has to be, let him do as he wishes. He is committing no sin; let them get married. The one who stands firm in his resolve, however, who is not under compulsion but has power over his own will, and has made

Saint Margaret (d. ca. 304) was a virgin and ascetic. According to legend, Satan assumed the form of a dragon and attempted to devour her. He could not harm such pure devotion, however; he burst asunder, and Margaret emerged unscathed.

up his mind to keep his virgin, will be doing well. So then, the one who marries his virgin does well; the one who does not marry her will do better" (1 Cor. 7:32–38).

While Paul thought that the Lord would come very soon—"the time is running out" (7:29)—he also clearly believed that the unmarried state (celibacy or perpetual virginity) was best suited to utter focus on the Lord. Of course, it has to be freely chosen, and the other apostles were, in fact, married.[19]

Even though Paul does not use such a term as *apatheia*, it seems clear that, at least in 1 Corinthians, he associates virginity or celibacy with freedom from

---

19. Later in 1 Corinthians Paul remarks, "Do we not have the right to take along a Christian wife, as do the rest of the apostles, and the brothers of the Lord, and Cephas [Peter]?" (9:5).

sexual passions. He frames marriage as something of a concession. While clearly not a sin, Paul seems to reserve it for those who are on fire with the sexual passions. If the situation proves overwhelming, then one ought to marry and keep the sexual passions ordered to one's spouse. However, the one who is "not under compulsion, but has power of his own will" does better in that he can remain unreservedly devoted to the Lord.

The church fathers, as well as most Greek philosophers, imagined sex as not only the prime example of the passions, but also as the most egregious way to lose one's self-control and spiritual energy. They even thought that human physiology worked to this end. Having intercourse brought one's blood to a boil, turning the blood into a foam of semen. The great church father Tertullian (160–225) asks, "Do we not feel something of our very soul go out from us?"[20] In contrast, abstinence from sex was the best way to purify and free the soul, "Let us look at our own inner world. Think of how a man feels in himself when he abstains from a woman. He thinks spiritual thoughts . . . it fills his whole being with enjoyment; if he exorcises a demon, he does so confident in his own strength."[21]

This chapter began with a discussion of how believers in Jesus moved from a sect in Judaism to having their own separate religion. They retained the Hebrew Bible, still understood Jesus as the fulfillment of God's promises to Israel, and continued to see justice and moral rectitude as central to faithfulness. Even their leadership took on a priestly identity modeled both after the Jewish Levitical priesthood and the teaching authority of the rabbis. Still, the church increasingly diverged from its roots. The church's concern about sensual pleasures—whether inordinate comfort, rich foods, or particularly sex—marked a decided shift away from its Jewish heritage. The rabbis did not idealize the ascetic who shuns the world and its pleasures, but extolled the one who knows how to live in moderation and how to take pleasure in the fullness and richness of the divine creation. In fact, they declared that on judgment day each person would be destined to give account to God for all the good things God provided that one *did not* partake of. As the Talmud says, "He who indulges in fasting is called a sinner."[22] Judaism understood marriage itself as a prerequisite for spiritual fulfillment: "A person who is without a wife is without joy, without blessing, without good. . . . A man without a wife is not a complete man."[23] This stands in stark contrast to a typical reflection by Pope Gregory the Great:

> The custom of the Romans [Church in Rome] from antiquity has always been, after sexual intercourse with one's spouse, both to cleanse

---

20. Tertullian, *De anima* 27.5, as cited in Peter Brown, *The Body and Society: Men, Women, and Sexual Renunciation in Early Christianity* (New York: Columbia University Press, 1988), 18.

21. Tertullian, *De ieiunio* 5.1, as cited in Brown, *The Body and Society*, 78.

22. *Taanit* 11a, as cited in Ben Zion Bokser and Baruch Bokser, "Introduction," in *The Talmud: Selected Writings*, trans. Ben Zion Bokser (New York: Paulist Press, 1989), 46.

23. *Yevamot*, as cited in Bokser and Bokser, *The Talmud: Selected Writings*, 132.

oneself by washing and to abstain reverently from entering the Church for a time. In saying this we do not intend to say that sexual intercourse is sinful. But because every lawful sexual intercourse between spouses cannot take place without bodily pleasure, they are to refrain from entering the holy place. For such pleasure cannot be without sin.[24] *Yikes!*

Besides the values of asceticism and *apatheia*, and the suspicion of pleasure, consecrated virginity had a kind of Christian cultural supremacy for another reason: it freed women from the oppressive control of a patriarchal culture and opened the way for their greater participation and leadership in the community. Greco-Roman culture considered a wife subordinate to her husband in all things and her social location, generally speaking, derived solely from her role as wife and mother. In order to be seen as an authentic member of society, a woman had to be married, and this often occurred at the median age of fourteen. While *hmm* many women were glad to be married and felt blessed to have and raise children and, indeed, typically loved their husbands and were loved by them, theirs was a culturally restricted existence. Perpetual virginity for the sake of the kingdom challenged the social structure of the day. It opted for a different image of social cohesion, and in this regard, Christianity was counter-cultural. Instead of a society being formed by the bonds of marriage, virginity provided a more ecclesial and eschatological social arrangement. It was a sign of kingdom. As Jesus taught, "At the resurrection they neither marry nor are given in marriage but are like the angels in heaven" (Matt. 22:30).

Virginity, especially for women, offered freedom from the rigid social constraints of the Roman world. Virgins were mobile. They were allowed to mix with men and even exercise roles in leadership. They took on an authority otherwise unavailable to women.

While it is uncontroversial to see an authentic Christian spirituality as one freed from inordinate desires, many contemporary scholars have criticized both *apatheia* and the supposed link between holiness and virginity. For them, these values amount to disdain for natural pleasure and the reduction of sexuality to something spiritually dangerous. Most scholars and Christian leaders today would celebrate the sacramental value of sexuality in marriage, and it would be hard to imagine many seeing it as somehow polluting, as Gregory the Great did.

Veneration of the Saints

A final characteristic of the spirituality of the patristic church is reverence of the saints, particularly those who died for the faith. Augustine's *Confessions* include a curious reference to his mother, Monica (331–387): "In accordance with my mother's custom in Africa, she had taken to the memorial shrines of the saints

---

24. *Epistolarum liber* 9.64.

cakes and bread and wine."[25] Apparently the Christian custom was to celebrate a memorial meal with others and offer some of the bread and wine to the saint on his or her grave. The bishop, Ambrose (340–397), forbade this as it looked too much like heathen superstition. Monica obeyed, but it was apparently a widespread practice that even this future saint found virtuous.

Who were the saints and what was their purpose in the Body of Christ now that they were dead and buried? The patristic church considered the saints heroes who witnessed to the extraordinary grace of God. This was particularly the case with martyrs, who had been tortured and killed for the faith. Two of the most famous were Perpetua and Felicity, whose account of bravery was celebrated throughout the whole church. Saints manifested God's presence and transformational possibilities. Further, even in heaven, they continued to be members of the mystical body of Christ, still active in the church, still interceding for the church. In this sense, they united heaven and earth, and their tombs functioned like poles where heaven and earth met. The fourth-century Greek historian, Eunapius of Sardis, mocked Christians, writing, "For they collected the bones and skulls of criminals . . . [and] made them out to be gods, and thought that they became better by defiling themselves at their graves. *Martyrs* the dead men were called, and ministers of a sort, and ambassadors with the gods to carry men's prayers."[26] In this description by a pagan outsider looking in, one can see an extraordinary veneration of the saints, vigils and services at their graves, and the belief that these saints could intercede on one's behalf.

The graves of saints were themselves believed to be holy. Saint Jerome (347–420) remarks, "When I am angry or had some bad thought . . . I do not dare to enter the shrines of the martyrs. I quake with body and soul."[27] The shrines were considered holy because the relics, those very remains that represented them in this life and will be transformed in the resurrection of the dead, remained somehow part of them. Saint Gregory of Nyssa (335–395) taught that the relics were still heavy with the fullness of the beloved saint. In *City of God* Augustine defends the resurrection of the body, in contrast to the opinions of Plato or Cicero, who saw the body as a weight or imprisonment for the soul. Augustine's evidence includes the miracles performed at the local shrines of Saint Stephen at Hippo and Uzalis.[28]

In many ways, saints became a kind of spiritual version of Roman patrons, wealthy persons who took less privileged others under their wing and financed their undertakings. This might be an artist who otherwise would not be free to

---

25. Augustine, *Confessions* 6.2, Translation from Augustine, *Confessions*, trans. Henry Chadwick (Oxford: Oxford University Press, 1991).

26. Cited in Peter Brown, *The Cult of the Saints: Its Rise and Function in Latin Christianity* (Chicago: University of Chicago Press, 1981), 7.

27. Jerome, *Contra vigilantium* 12, cited in Brown, *The Cult of the Saints*, 11.

28. See Augustine, *City of God* 22.8.

pursue the craft or perhaps a very bright child who would otherwise not get an education. As patristic scholar Peter Brown remarked, "The saint was the good *patronus*: he was the *patronus* whose intercessions were successful, whose wealth was at the disposal of all, whose *potentia* [power] was exercised without violence and to whom loyalty could be shown without restraint."[29]

Veneration and the plea for intercessions of the saints mark an important part of patristic spirituality. Saints were relied upon and remembered on feast days, which celebrated the heroism, spiritual transformation, and active ministry of the saints among Christians still. Perhaps most importantly, veneration of the saints celebrated the extraordinary possibilities of God's grace.[30]

Saints in Modern Christianity

The practice of canonizing and venerating saints has been part of Christianity from the early ages. Because saints were believed to be in heaven, Christians also held that the saints could intercede for them in a powerful way. Veneration of the saints became controversial during the Protestant Reformation, particularly as the more extreme Reformers removed all icons and statues of saints. Many Protestants accused Catholics of worshipping saints or, at best, engaging in pious practices that tended to reduce Christ's direct mediation. For Protestants, all Christians are saints (made holy) by their baptism, and the practice of highlighting particular holy people after death ignored this truth. Catholic and Orthodox Christians affirm the holiness of all Christians, but still believe that saints continue to act powerfully in the church, particularly by their intercessions.

Conclusion

The apostolic church was imbued with a spirituality it thought both consistent with its time and place and faithful to the essential message of the Lord. As a persecuted church it saw itself as vulnerable to political, social, and spiritual abuse. It was a church whose spirituality imagined the outside world as hostile,

---

29. Brown, *The Cult of the Saints*, 41.

30. As the fifth century *Decretum Gelasianum* declared: "We must include also [for public reading] the deeds of the saints in which their triumph blazed forth through the many forms of torture that they underwent and their marvelous confession of faith. For what Catholic can doubt that they suffered more than is possible for human beings to bear, and did not endure this by their own strength, but by the grace and help of God?" *Decritum Gelasianum*, as cited in Brown, *The Cult of the Saints*, 79.

but which felt assured that God's grace would protect it, either in the present or on the last day. Ultimately, early Christians believed that God would win, and they saw themselves as victors even in persecution. In their eyes, their vulnerability to exterior evil stood in sharp and happy contrast to the unity of love they experienced within the community. They saw themselves less as a group of individual Christians and more as a corporate body that shared the life of the Spirit. To be a member of such a body was challenging. Being dead to sin but alive in Christ meant that they could give no quarter to sin. Not only were they to abstain from wrong-doing, they were also to be transformed within. Their souls, and not just their behavior, had to be Spirit-driven.

These represented their ideals, their theology, and what would constitute their spiritual identity. Was this standard always met? It does not seem to be the case. Ignatius, for example, wrote his letters to challenge those who believed other than what he considered the authentic doctrine. And it is clear that there were divisions in the churches to which he wrote.[31]

That these spiritual values did not get lived out completely, or even well in some cases, should come as no surprise given the human condition. Still, in appealing to these values and striving to live them, the apostolic church survived persecution and even thrived.

As the church developed, it lost its apocalyptic urgency, but not its belief that it represented an eschatological reality. The eschaton refers to the end or finality of history. Even if Christ would not return soon, his covenant was still understood as the final and complete one. The patristic church expressed this commitment by its virginity for the sake of the kingdom and by the daunting demands inherent in being a Christian. Such a demanding witness was celebrated in martyrs and saints and by disciplined practices to become free of all attachments so that one might be available to love God and neighbor utterly. At least in vision, the church saw herself as the ark of salvation, a unique presence of God's grace.

Questions for Review

1. Why did Christianity come to be viewed as its own distinct religion rather than continuing to be seen as a sect within Judaism?

2. What were the distinguishing characteristics of the apostolic church and how were they understood?

3. How were the apostolic and patristic eras in the church similar? What developments distinguished the patristic communities?

---

31. Similarly, Saint Clement of Rome wrote an apostolic letter to the Corinthian church (ca. 96) to address a dispute within the community. Not only had the Corinthian church been unruly in Paul's day (see 1 Cor. 11:1), it also struggled later. They appealed to Clement to settle a disagreement about whether they could throw out their current leadership and start over.

4. What role did *apatheia* play in the life of the Christian in the patristic era?

5. How did the church understand virginity and what factors contributed to that understanding?

Questions for Discussion

1. Early Christianity was marked by a sense of urgency, at least in part because many Christians then believed Christ would return soon. Given that Christ has not returned yet, do you believe it is possible for the modern church to retain a sense of urgency? Why or why not?

2. Early Christianity put an emphasis on the idea of Christianity as a communal enterprise, centering on the Eucharist and common life of the Spirit. How do various contemporary denominations align or not align with these conceptions of the church? Given your answer, how would you summarize modern Christianity in this regard?

3. Many trends that emerged in the patristic era have made their way down to the contemporary church. Which do you think play the most important role in the spiritual life of the modern Christian?

4. What do you think of the rigorous conception of sexuality in the patristic era? What are the assets and liabilities of their position for a modern Christian spirituality?

Bibliography

Resources with annotations are highly recommended to students interested in further study.

Augustine of Hippo. *City of God*. Translated by Henry Bettenson. New York: Penguin, 1984.

> This is Augustine's great interpretation of salvation history and his understanding of the relationship between the church and Roman Empire.

Augustine of Hippo. *Confessions*. Translated by Henry Chadwick. Oxford: Oxford University Press, 1991.

> This is Augustine's autobiography, particularly as it regards his conversion.

Brown, Peter. *The Body and Society: Men, Women, and Sexual Renunciation in Early Christianity*. New York: Columbia University Press. 1988.

> This classic study examines the role that celibacy played in the early church and how the patristic church understood the relationship between the spiritual life and the body.

Brown, Peter. *The Cult of the Saints: Its Rise and Function in Latin Christianity.* Chicago: University of Chicago Press, 1981.

Brown, Peter. "The Notion of Virginity in the Early Church." In *Christian Spirituality*, edited by Bernard McGinn, John Meyendorff, and Jean Leclercq, 1:427–43. New York: Continuum 1988.

Holmes, Michael, ed. *The Apostolic Fathers.* Translated by J. B. Lightfoot and J. R. Harmer. 2nd ed. Grand Rapids: Baker Book House, 1989.

This collection provides primary material from the early second century of the church.

Sullivan, Francis. *From Apostles to Bishops: The Development of the Episcopacy in the Early Church.* New York: Newman Press, 2001.

Taft, Robert. *The Liturgy of the Hours in East and West: The Origins of the Divine Office and Its Meaning for Today.* Collegeville, MN: Liturgical Press, 1986.

Tugwell, Simon. "The Apostolic Fathers." In *The Study of Spirituality*, edited by Cheslyn Jones, Geoffrey Wainwright, and Edward Yarnold, 102–8. New York: Oxford University Press, 1986.

Zizioulas, John. "The Early Christian Community." In *Christian Spirituality*, edited by Bernard McGinn, John Meyendorff, and Jean Leclercq, 23–43. New York: Continuum 1988.

Internet Resources

Beliefnet. "Embracing the Jewishness of Jesus." *www.beliefnet.com/Faiths/2000/06/Embracing-The-Jewishness-Of-Jesus.aspx#.*

An article on the Jewishness of Jesus in order to contextualize his message for the apostolic church.

Levine, Amy-Jill. "The Jewishness of Jesus." Interview with Chris Yaw. 2012. *www.youtube.com/watch?v=QfiA2xFl_Io.*

Describes how Christians misinterpret Jesus and offers ways to better engage Jewish-Christian dialogue (52 min.).

New Advent. "The Fathers of the Church." *http://www.newadvent.org/fathers/.*

Site offers a massive number of primary readings of church fathers.

Films

A.D. NBC.

Miniseries attempts a fictionalized portrayal of the apostolic church from the Resurrection of Jesus to the formation of the early church.

Patristic Paths to Union: Four Figures

This chapter investigates the paths to union with God as found in four spiritual giants of the patristic age: Origen, Augustine, Gregory of Nyssa, and Pseudo-Dionysius. Their spirituality, like that of the patristic era in general, was highly ecclesial, ascetical, committed to virtue, and interested in a just society with special concern for the poor. In addition to embracing these major currents of early Christian spirituality, they provide something that is otherwise relatively rare in the patristic age: mystical paths to union with God. Their influence in Christian spirituality can hardly be overstated. Many Christian spiritualities going forward rely on their assumptions about where to find God and *how* to find God most profoundly.

As noted in chapter 1, Christian spirituality often follows a recurring pattern of purgation, illumination, and union. Purgation refers to purifying the soul from inordinate desires and aligning it to a life of prayer and service. Illumination is the experience of God working within the soul. Union is direct encounter with God, referred to in chapter 2 as *apophatic* mysticism. The patristic-era writings by theologians and church leaders contain a large body of material on the purgative way, which is where most Christians find their lives. Expressions of the illuminative way appear less frequently, as it is rarer in Christian experience. The unitive way represents the rarified air enjoyed by very few Christians. It is difficult to describe as it transcends concepts and language. Because it is so profound and even so extraordinarily private, there is simply less discussion of it. These four figures offer some of the most interesting, explicit, and influential understandings of its nature and how to attain it.

Intellectual Life in the Patristic Era

Many of the most influential theologians and spiritual giants of the patristic age were intellectuals. They were highly educated in Greco-Roman culture, rhetoric, poetics, philosophy, history, political theory, and so on. They shared many of the assumptions of the other well-educated individuals of the day. They shared their cultural milieu, and while this milieu was not originally Christian, it had spiritual and intellectual resources that Christian leaders found valuable. For example, Christians disagreed with Stoics regarding the gods and fate, but agreed with them in regard to *apatheia* and the need to perform one's duty in a posture of freedom and care. The notebook of the Stoic philosopher and emperor Marcus Aurelius[1] (121–180), *Meditations*, contains wisdom to which many Christians could assent:

> Perceive at last that you have within yourself something stronger and more divine than the things which create your passions and make a downright puppet of you. What is my consciousness at this instant? Fright, suspicion, appetite? Some similar evil state? First, do nothing aimlessly nor without relation to an end. Secondly, relate your action to no other end except the good of human fellowship.[2]

Christians did not encounter the ideals of Stoicism, such as *apatheia*, and then decide to Christianize them. Rather, such values were simply in the intellectual air they all breathed. The same can be said of the philosophy of Plato. Plato believed that there was an absolute spiritual world in which the rest of the created world, especially human souls, participated. He taught that God created through his *Logos*, which means "word" or "reason." Christians thought likewise, as John's Gospel begins, "In the beginning was the Word (*Logos*) and the Word was with God and the Word was God. He was in the beginning with God. All things came to be through him" (1:1–2). Indeed the great Christian apologist Saint Justin tried to explain the Christian faith to Roman rulers through many concepts Roman intellectuals already had.[3] Saint Clement of Alexandria once remarked, "For what is Plato but Moses speaking in Attic Greek?"[4] Augustine was even more enthusiastic, imagining that Plato and his followers would have been Christians if they lived in a Christian era: "So if these men could live their lives again today . . . with the change of a few words and sentiments, they would become Christians, as many Platonists of recent times have done."[5]

---

1. Note that Marcus Aurelius was no friend of Christians, and in fact some were martyred by his orders.

2. Marcus Aurelius, *Meditations* 12.19–20. Translation from *Meditations*, ed. and trans. S. S. L. Farquharson (New York: Alfred A Knopf, 1946).

3. Justin's most famous were his *First Apology* to Emperor Antonius Pius and the senate, his *Second Apology* to the elite of Rome, and his *Dialogue with Trypho*, a Jewish intellectual.

4. Clement of Alexandria, *Stromata* 1.22. Translation at *www.earlychristianwritings.com/text/clement-stromata-book1.html*.

5. Augustine, *On True Religion* 7. Translation from *Augustine: Earlier Writings*, trans. John Burleigh (Philadelphia: Westminster Press, 1953), 229.

While early Christianity and the pagan intellectual world of the time shared a broad understanding of morality and even some philosophical principles, Christianity was influenced outright by the philosophy of Plato and the Platonic school. For example, while still an unbeliever Augustine travelled to Milan to take on a high profile position in the empire. He was skeptical about Christianity and the Bible, but then learned that it could be interpreted differently than many of Christianity's critics understood it. Augustine became interested in the faith and sought instruction, so the bishop of Milan, Saint Ambrose (340–397), assigned his priest Simplicianus to teach him. The first thing Simplicianus did was have Augustine read Platonic philosophy. Simplicianus's thinking was this: before engaging the mysteries of the faith, first think about the spiritual and physical world like Plato and his school. Platonism opened Augustine's eyes.

The Platonic School

Plato (428–348 BCE) was one of the great philosophers of the classical Greek period. He was taught by Socrates and his favorite pupil was Aristotle. Plato had a strong interest in a true and virtuous society, which was the focus of his famous book *The Republic*. He believed that virtue had to come from knowledge of the true, the good, and the beautiful. How then, he wondered, could a person come to such knowledge? He observed the created world and the perceptions one has of it: both are changing and unreliable. Pure knowledge had to come from somewhere else. Plato thought that pure truth emanated from God, the source and creator of all. Knowledge first emanated from God's reason and order, God's *Logos*. The *Logos* created a world of eternal forms and ideas, which represented a sphere of the universe that was purely spiritual and perfect. Everything that exists in the physical world, then, participates in these forms. A tree, for example, is a tree because it is a physical instance of the universal form of *treeness*. A human being is an instance of the universal form of *humanness*. If one were to open the curtain, so to speak, and encounter the universal form, then one could know how best to be human; it would be based on living out *humanness* most authentically.

To illustrate the human condition, Plato created the famous image of a cave. He asked his listeners to imagine that they all exist chained up in a cave with firelight behind them and the shadows of puppets being cast against the wall. Those inside the cave believe that this is reality as it truly is, despite it being a mere shadow of the real thing. What if one escaped the cave? That is, what if one could see reality as it really is? An escapee would initially be blinded by the light of the sun, but after a while would see reality clearly. Upon returning to the cave, the escapee finds that sharing such knowledge meets with little enthusiasm from the other prisoners. They are so deluded that they do not even realize they are prisoners, much less that what they see is not, in fact, reality as it is. Such is the life of the populace. They are convinced they live in the real world, yet

Laura Stone / Shutterstock.com

Platonic thought conceives of the individual as essentially a soul "imprisoned" within the body. In this early American tombstone engraving, a soul, released from its bodily prison by death, wings its way heavenward.

it is but a shadow of true reality. The one who sees the truth of the world, the essence, would then be fit to rule; he would be a philosopher king.

In Plato's allegory of the cave, not only are most people unaware of the real world, but they seem to prefer to stay both ignorant and chained. Their bodies bind them to the physical world, and they identify with it. Plato thought of the body as little more than a mask of the soul and, in one sense, a prison for it. The soul was the person's truth, the essence of the person, and a purified soul could most easily participate in its eternal form. The physical world was not bad per se, but it was a poor mediator of the spiritual world. Those who became attached to it, particularly through the passions, could not participate well, if at all, in the spiritual world.

Plato's philosophy was highly influential among intellectuals, and became more so with the resurgence of his school in the third century of the Common Era. The most important voice in this resurgence, called middle-Platonism, was Plotinus (205–270), who accepted Plato's metaphysics and even sharpened it a bit. Plotinus believed that everything emanated from God, whom he called One, and was destined to return to God. One could briefly return to the Source even in this life, something Plotinus experienced on a number of occasions. Chapter 2 included an expression of this that bears repeating: "Many times it has happened: lifted out of the body into myself; becoming external to all other things and self-encentered; beholding a marvelous beauty . . . acquiring identity with the divine."[6] The account seems strange. Plotinus was lifted out of the body *into* himself. That is to say, he left consciousness of his body and the whole physical world, all of which would get in the way of union with God. In doing so, he was actually attentive to his soul's center. It is here that Plotinus finds God, described as "a marvelous beauty" and here that he recognizes his eternal identity (in some manner) with God.

Plotinus had a spiritual program for returning to God, the Source. The first stage involved being convinced of the baseness of the physical world. While not necessarily evil, the physical world was no mediator for spiritual enlightenment. Second, one had to undergo extensive training in spiritual purification, which required rigid asceticism and the acquisition of virtue. One had to be spiritually and morally pure. Third, after attaining such purity one moved to deep contemplation of one's soul. This involved not only participation in the eternal forms but even a participation in God as the soul's origin. The true contemplative could actually encounter God quite directly. This encounter is ecstatic, taking one outside oneself, and is characterized as a kind of simplification. Here all vestiges of the created world and its complexity vanish. The soul, in its essence, meets its eternal source. In such an encounter the soul loses normal consciousness, even of itself, and takes on the mode of "knowing" the One. Plotinus considers contemplation the very essence of the soul's authentic activity: "All things come from contemplation and are contemplation."[7]

Common Assumptions among Greek Philosophers and Christians

Platonism believed that the created universe was a poor mediator of the spiritual world because it only constituted vague and changing expressions of the eternal forms. Further, knowing the *form of the Good* that comes from the *Logos* (divine word or reason) allows one to become virtuous. Aristotle taught that human souls (*psychē*) functioned well only according to the end to which they were created. One becomes a morally developed person through the unremitting practice and balance of virtues, such as prudence, justice, fortitude, and courage. Stoics held that passions (inordinate desires) derived from false judgments and imprisoned the soul. By divesting any attachment to the passions one could become spiritually and morally free.

---

6. Plotinus, *Enneads* 4.8.1. Translations of Plotinus are from Plotinus, *The Enneads*, trans. Stephen Mackenna (New York: Penguin, 1991).

7. Ibid., 3.8.7.

The church fathers did not believe that the soul was eternal or that the soul was imprisoned by the body. They believed that God created the soul in time and that the body would be resurrected in some way. Like the Platonists, though, they saw the universe as emanating from God and held that the physical world only mediated God's presence modestly. They recognized how being caught up in or even distracted by the senses could compromise the soul's progress. They also shared a common belief that God dwelt most profoundly in the center of the soul and that one could attain experiences of union with God through contemplation.

Origen (185–254)

Origen was born to a Christian family in Alexandria, Egypt, in 185. At that time, Emperor Septimius Severus was persecuting Christians; Origen's father was martyred for the faith when Origen was seventeen years old.[8] He was already gaining notoriety in the church as a brilliant Christian thinker, and he supported his mother and siblings through his teaching. By age nineteen, Origen was named head teacher of the Alexandrian catechetical school, one of the great theological centers in Christianity. He became famous throughout the church, traveling to Athens, Arabia, and even Rome at the behest of the emperor's mother, Julia Mamaea, to expound the Christian doctrine at the imperial court (his safety being assured). At one point, his activity in the larger church brought him to Caesarea, Palestine, where the bishop implored him to be ordained. He consented and then returned to Alexandria and to his furious bishop, Demetrius, who thought it presumptuous of him to be ordained by another. Demetrius sent him back to Palestine, where he ministered for the rest of his life as a priest. During the persecution of Christians by the Emperor Decius in 250, Origen was arrested and beaten viciously. He was not martyred, but many believe that this torture hastened his death just a few years later.

Origen is one of the most important theologians in Christianity, particularly in the East. His works were read widely during and after his life, and his influence can be seen in the great architects of orthodoxy, such as Saints Athanasius, Gregory of Nyssa, Basil the Great, and Gregory of Nazianzus. He is also credited as being a major force in developing a spirituality that grounded monasticism, which will be discussed in the next chapter. It may then seem surprising that the church roundly condemned him at the Second Council of Constantinople (553). Two major charges were leveled against him: he believed in universal salvation and in the pre-existence of souls.

---

8. According to the historian Eusebius of Caesarea, Origen wanted to join his father by publically claiming his faith in front of the Roman authorities, but his mother hid his clothes and his modesty kept him inside the house.

Origen held that everything God created would ultimately return to him; that is, Origen embraced the belief, known as *apokatastasis*, that every soul is ultimately saved. The purification of great sinners and those who were temporally damned would be severe, but since God "wills everyone to be saved and to come to knowledge of the truth" (1 Tim. 2:4) and since even sin cannot thwart God's providence, then somehow God will save even the worst of sinners: "We believe that the goodness of God through Christ will restore his entire creation to one end, even his enemies being conquered and subdued."[9] Origen, following Plato, also believed that souls existed with God before the creation of the physical world. Persons attained bodies after the fall, with the physical world supporting these bodies. Unlike Plato, Origen believed in the resurrection of the body, which he envisioned as something of a spiritualized body with no functional resemblance to the earthly one.[10] Whether or not Origen could have defended himself successfully or modified his theology adequately by the sixth century is impossible to know. He was condemned after three hundred years in the grave, but not without having had a massive influence on theology and spirituality.

Origen's Mystical Path

Origen believed that the original creation was a spiritual one of solely spiritual beings who were all created equal after the pattern of the true image of God, the *Logos*. Each "intellect" had a spiritual body and lived a joyous life contemplating God, "a pure and perfect reception of God into itself."[11] This was a kind of preexistent church, under the preexistent Christ, bonded in love. One of the most important qualities of these spiritual beings is freedom, and this freedom allowed for the possibility of the fall. What precipitated this fall from perfect contemplation? Origen answers, "Sloth and weariness of taking trouble to preserve the good, coupled with disregard and neglect for better things, began the process of withdrawal from the good."[12] Angels represent those spiritual beings who retained a good deal of their contemplative interest, while humans fell much farther because of neglect. Demons, then, represent those who fell the farthest, because they became not only slothful, but contentious to the good.

---

9. *De Principiis* 1.6.1. Translation from Bernard McGinn, *The Foundations of Mysticism: Origins to the Fifth Century* (New York: Crossroad, 1992), 115.

10. This may not differ all that much from St. Paul's teaching: "There are both heavenly bodies and earthly bodies, but the brightness of the heavenly one is one kind and that of the earthly another. . . . So also is the resurrection of the dead. It is sown corruptible; it is raised incorruptible. . . . It is sown a natural body; it is raised a spiritual body (1 Cor. 15:40–44).

11. *De Principiis* 4.4.9. Translation from McGinn, *The Foundations of Mysticism*, 113.

12. Ibid., 2.9.2.

Through physical creation, then, God created a possibility of human recovery. The physical world allowed for a kind of educational opportunity for the soul. In this sense, matter is not only good but necessary to return to God. However, matter is a limited good; its sole purpose is to help intellects ascend above it to a pure vision of God.

Origen imagined the human being as consisting of two parts. The spirit (*pnuema*) or soul (*psychē*) represents the deepest self, the intellect capable of participating in the life of the Holy Spirit and contemplating God. The body (*sōma*) provides the possibility of the spirit to ascend back to God or fall deeper into withdrawal. Most everything about Origen's spirituality connects back to the journey of the spirit or soul back to God in its original state of contemplation. Jesus Christ, as preexistent Lord, represents both God and the mediator to the divine. In his incarnate state, Origen taught, Jesus never lost perfect contemplation of God and thus became the model and teacher for all. Jesus, the incarnate Word (*Logos*), entered into the fallen state, without himself having fallen, to rescue and guide souls back to contemplative union.

How does one attain such a union? As noted earlier, a rigorous moral life is fundamental. Origen preached, and indeed lived, a highly ascetical life. He believed that *apatheia* was crucial to rediscovering one's original freedom. Like other Christians of the patristic era, he was suspicious of the passions, particularly sexual passions. Eusebius reports that, in order to allay these sexual passions, Origen even castrated himself. This may or may not have been the case, though many scholars trust this account. However, it underscores how the fathers understood *apatheia* as a kind of psychological disposition that freed them for more authentic love and service. This certainly comprises part of Origen's spirituality and biography. While he wrote, studied, and prayed assiduously, he also served as a priest with great vigor; contemplation and action complemented each other. The deeper one prayed, the more one's soul was charged with divine love. This love, of course, was not only for God but for others. So prayer laid a foundation for service. Service, too, assisted one in purifying the soul and helped one gain greater *apatheia*. For Origen and so many others, an actively engaged life not only tried one's soul, but stretched it.

Ultimately, however, union comes from contemplation, which represents the soul's most authentic activity and reason for its existence. Like Plotinus, Origen believed that one had to enter within. So the journey upward was really a deeper descent into the soul to find God. Contemplation is, above all, the discovery of God's presence at the core of one's soul.

Unlike Plotinus, Origen believed in a personal God, a God who loved him. While he considered physical sexual passions distracting at best, he used the metaphors of sexual love to describe God's nature and the nature of union. The term *eros* ("love") is often associated, both then and now, specifically with sexual love. Perhaps one might say that it is love as drive-for-union. The term "erotic" reflects this sense. God reveals himself as Eros, a passionate lover of the soul who desires union. Authentic love for God is a drive-for-union as well. Origen explains in his *Commentary on the Song of Songs*, itself a biblical erotic love poem, "We understand not anything corporeal (physical sexual love), but only that which is found first in God and in the powers of the soul—it follows that the only laudable love is that which is directed to God and to the powers of the soul."[13] Origen wrote about being wounded in divine love (smitten by God), the kiss of lovers (ecstatic encounters with God), and the embrace of the beloved (union with God).

What does such language mean? First, Origen and his readers would clearly interpret this language as metaphorical. How might humans talk about a relationship that only has, at best, analogues among human relationships? One uses metaphors, realizing that they ought not be taken literally. Second, however, one could also imagine that Origen took his literal sexual energy and redirected it to a spiritual end. After all, everything ultimately came from God and, in a purified form, must return to God who is the source and life of all that is good.

Gregory of Nyssa (335–395)

Gregory of Nyssa belonged to the third generation of an aristocratic Christian family in Cappadocia (modern Turkey). His older sister, Macrina, became a famous saint, and his brother Basil was one of the great saints and theologians of the church. In fact, of his nine siblings, four were made saints. Gregory, along with Basil, was classically trained in literature, philosophy, and rhetoric (the art of public speaking), as well as theology. His father was a well-known and well-paid teacher of rhetoric, and he followed his father's footsteps by marrying and entering public life. Influenced by his brother Basil and sister Macrina, he subsequently entered a monastery, as did his wife. Basil, a metropolitan bishop and influential in selecting bishops in that part of Cappadocia, chose Gregory to become the bishop of the town of Nyssa in 372. Gregory proved to be an exemplary bishop and a superb theologian. Along with his brother, he took a prominent part in the First Council of Constantinople (381). In his later years, Gregory wrote less about speculative theology and more about the spiritual life. During this time he wrote perhaps his most famous book, *The Life of Moses*, in which the Exodus account of Moses' encounter with God, from the burning bush to receiving the Law on Sinai, becomes an allegory of the soul's ascent to God.

---

13. Origen, *Commentary on the Song of Songs*. Translation from McGinn, *The Foundations of Mysticism*, 121.

Gregory's Mystical Path

By the second century, the Bible was read on various levels. One could read it literally, that is, typically as history. Reading it in terms of morality represented another level of appropriation. While the text might not be overtly about moral guidance, a deeper meaning sometimes revealed truths about the purgation of the soul. The text could also be understood as mystical, with characters and situations representing allegorical types that reflected deeper spiritual meanings. Another mystical appropriation, sometimes called the *anagogical* meaning, saw the text as reflecting the end times or the soul's full union with God. Together, these approaches constituted the fourfold method of interpretation: the literal teaches readers what to know, the moral guides what to do, the allegorical says what to believe, and the anagogical shows what to hope for. Some texts were understood as including all levels of interpretation, although that would be rare. Other passages, even if framed in a historical narrative, were meant to be understood allegorically. Regarding the Exodus story, for example, Gregory found it morally impossible that God literally killed the firstborn of all the Egyptian citizens and their livestock. He understood this as referring to human sinfulness. Before actually sinning, one first has evil thoughts and the intention of sinning. So killing off the firstborn really refers to the necessity of vanquishing those thoughts immediately.[14]

Gregory's classic work *The Life of Moses* sketches out his understanding of the spiritual ascent to union with God. In Gregory's understanding, Moses was a good man, someone God could rely on. God calls Moses from the burning bush at Sinai to lead his people from slavery into the promised land. Moses comes to Pharaoh to ask freedom for the people of God, but God hardened Pharaoh's heart, so God had to send plagues upon Egypt in order to break Pharaoh's resolve. In one plague, for example, God makes the waters of Egypt polluted and red like blood, and in another case God sent a plague of frogs that infested Egypt and made the people sick. Finally, with the plague of the destruction of Egypt's firstborn, Pharaoh releases the Hebrews and they depart from Egypt, but not without taking with them many jewels and fine things that the people gave the Israelites on their way out; this event is known as the despoiling of the Egyptians. After they left, Pharaoh changed his mind and sent his army to attack Israel and take them back into slavery, but God sent the Egyptians a cloud of confusion and allowed Israel to cross the Red Sea. Even after this escape into freedom, the Israelites rebelled against God and Moses. Yet God fed them with manna and protected them in wars. The high point of the Exodus story occurs when Moses ascends Mount Sinai to receive the law and encounters God directly while Sinai is covered by a dense cloud.

---

14. Gregory of Nyssa, *Life of Moses* 2.90. Translations of this work are taken from *The Life of Moses*, trans. Abraham Malherbe and Everett Ferguson (New York: Paulist Press, 1978).

What could all this mean? Gregory believed that much of the Exodus account happened quite literally and historically, but its mystical meaning had everything to do with the dynamics of the Christian spiritual life. Moses represents a *type* of the baptized Christian and the story can be interpreted allegorically. When Moses encountered God in the burning bush, God told him to take off his sandals. This, Gregory teaches, refers to the animal skin of sense perception. God as a transcendent being can only be encountered profoundly by withdrawing one's vision from the perceptible world. One first experiences God as light, as in the burning bush. God offers enlightenment and can be known in some way through the intellect. Pharaoh represents the will. God did not literally harden Pharaoh's heart, since this would be counter to God's nature and the natural freedom of the will. The problem, Gregory says, lies in Pharaoh's failure to acknowledge God and in his inclination to evil. Thus one must train the will to incline always to the good. The plagues represent the work of the passions. Evil presuppositions corrupt the clear waters of life and frogs represent evil in the heart. They are the beasts of passion, which bring illness.

Finally, the Israelites depart, which stands for the transience of life itself. Moses' command to the Israelites on the night of Passover to eat with sandals on their feet and their cloaks tightly drawn by a belt symbolizes how life is a journey that must be taken with the virtue of prudence (the belt). Moses had also commanded the Israelites to eat with their staff in hand, which represents the virtue of hope by which to gain support against the weariness of the spiritual journey. The Passover food itself represents faith, and the fire that heats it is the life of the Holy Spirit within.

The despoiling of the Egyptians represents pagan learning, something with which Gregory himself was intimately familiar. It is not Christian per se, but can be of help. So it is acceptable to take the wisdom of the pagans as long as it is beautified by the riches of reason and protected through understanding its goods in light of Christian doctrine. As the Israelites departed from Egypt with the protective cloud that both held the Egyptian army in check and guided them on the way, so the Holy Spirit guides Christians too. The crossing of the Red Sea, according to Gregory, represents baptism, in which one escapes the slavery of unbelief for the true faith. And just as the Egyptian army was drowned in the Red Sea, so everything contrary to the Gospel must be drowned in the waters of baptism. Here Gregory gets specific: "Those who pass through the mystical water in baptism must put to death in the water the whole phalanx of evil—such as covetousness, unbridled desire, rapacious thinking, the passion of conceit and arrogance, wild impulse, wrath, anger, malice, envy, and all such things."[15] The manna that the Israelites ate in the desert is the Word of God that nourishes the soul, and the strength of Israel's army in winning several battles against its enemies refers to the strength gained through deeper contact with the Spirit.

---

15. Gregory of Nyssa, *Life of Moses* 2.125.

The most profound religious expression in the Exodus story is that of Moses ascending Mount Sinai to receive the law. Here Moses experienced God as directly as one could in this life. The top of the mountain is covered in a thick cloud, which Gregory calls the *dark cloud*. At the beginning of the spiritual journey, God typically reveals himself as light. He can be seen, that is, known, through enlightening experiences of his truth. But such experiences are limited. God cannot be seen or known *as* God through any concept or perception; God transcends them all. To the created intellect, God is absolutely incomprehensible.[16] Gregory is not saying that the soul does not know it is experiencing God, but rather that one has *spiritual senses* that can perceive what the natural intellect cannot. There is a faculty of the soul that has the ability to know the Divine, even if one's conscious intellect cannot. This faculty knows God for what God really is.

Gregory believed that every concept related to God is, in the end, a false likeness, even an idol. Of course, one must use language to talk about God and one can do so skillfully, keeping in mind that all words and concepts fall short in the end. In one sense, Gregory thought of God as good—as infinitely good, thus exceeding anything that can be known or said about the good. Thus, understanding God as good is apt, even if God's goodness is unimaginable. In another sense, Gregory believed that God is so *other* that even speaking about God at all ultimately proves problematic; God is incomprehensible. While not wrong, revelation—God's revealing himself in images and concepts—cannot do justice to the reality of God.

Gregory thought that, since God is infinite, one can never engage God fully, even in the most radical *apophatic* experience. Rather, one continues to penetrate the inexhaustible divine life. In his *Commentary on the Song of Songs* he writes, "The bride (soul) never ceases going in or going out, but she rests only by advancing towards that which lies before her and by always going out from what she has contemplated."[17] This remains true eternally. Heaven, for Gregory, is not simply dwelling with God, but an ongoing eternal penetration into the infinite God who has no boundaries. It is a kind of rest, but a paradoxical rest by eternal advancement.

Both Christians and Jews believe humanity was created in the divine image and likeness (Gen. 1:26). Gregory understood this to mean that God is the archetype of the human being. If God is incomprehensible, then so too is the soul. Gregory also thought that the human being was made to be the very mirror of God, both in this life and in the life to come. The final perfection of the human being is a state of deification whereby one shares the divine fullness by grace. And yet, such a sharing is an eternal project.

---

16. In an interesting contrast, Origen's favorite image for mystical knowledge is light, while Gregory's is absolute darkness.

17. Gregory of Nyssa, *Commentary on the Song of Songs* 5.6. Translation from McGinn, *The Foundations of Mysticism*, 141.

Augustine of Hippo (354–430)

As Origen is one of the most influential intellects in the Orthodox Church, so Augustine is one of the most influential in Western Christianity. He was born in Thagaste (Eastern Algeria) to a pagan father, Patrick, and a Christian mother, Monica, who later became a saint. His father was a minor local official, and they belonged to what one perhaps might call the middle class. Augustine was clearly a prodigy, and with the support of a patron, Romanian, he studied Greek and Latin, Greco-Roman history, politics, philosophy, and literature. With the exception of Greek, which he never mastered, he excelled as a student. At seventeen years old, he traveled to Carthage for further studies, and at twenty began his career as a teacher in Carthage. At about this time, Augustine encountered a text from the philosopher Cicero called *Hortensius* (now lost). In it, Cicero urged the reader to pursue wisdom at any cost and to abandon any other ambition. Augustine was hooked, and for the next ten years he searched for a religion he found intellectually compelling.

Initially, he thought he found answers to his questions in the Manichean religion, which explained the nature of good and evil, creation, and the relationship of the soul to the body, but soon began to question aspects of Manichean belief.[18] In 384, he moved to Rome and became part of a circle of intellectuals, none of whom were Christian. He impressed everyone. The emperor, whose court had been in Constantinople (Istanbul) for over fifty years, tasked the leader of this group of intellectuals, Symmacus, to choose an orator for the empire, someone who would speak at official functions about the nature of Roman law and society. The position was part publicist and part propagandist for the empire, and Symmacus chose Augustine, who then moved to Milan, the intellectual center of the Latin world. Augustine immediately became famous and wealthy.

Milan was decidedly Christian, and its bishop and former governor was the famous Ambrose (340–397). Augustine was impressed by Ambrose's holiness and intelligence. He had never heard Christianity expounded with such intellectual vigor, and he began to think that his Roman friends had not really understood Christianity at all. He became interested in the Christian faith, and Ambrose assigned his priest Simplicianus to mentor Augustine. The first thing Simplicianus did was have Augustine read Platonic philosophy. From this intellectual starting point, Augustine began to learn the Christian faith and to immerse himself in the Bible.

In one sense, Augustine had a moral conversion when he read Cicero's *Hortensius*, in that he directed his life to the pursuit of truth. He had an intellectual conversion as he came to believe that Christianity, in fact, held that truth. He wavered, however, over the cost of committing himself to Christianity and

---

18. Augustine had particular difficulty with the Mancheans' commitment to astrology and their account of how their dualistic world could have actually been created that way.

receiving baptism. Augustine saw this as an all or nothing proposition; deciding to be baptized was also deciding to purify himself from all his passions and to pursue Christian holiness as profoundly as he could. In his mind, this meant that he would have to abandon any interest in even modest worldly success. In a famous passage he describes his angst: "Tomorrow, tomorrow. Why not now? Why not an end to my impure life in this very hour? As I was saying this and weeping in bitter agony of my heart, suddenly I heard a voice from the nearby house chanting as if it might be a boy or a girl (I do not know which), saying and repeating over and over again 'Pick up and read, pick up and read.'" Augustine had with him a collection of Paul's letters, and he opened it up to the passage from Romans (13:13–14): "'Not in riots and drunken parties, not in eroticism and indecencies, not in strife and rivalry, but put on the Lord Jesus Christ and make no provision for the flesh in its lusts.' I neither wished nor needed to read further."[19]

Augustine submitted to baptism and returned to Africa and to the city of Hippo. He had intended to lead a monastic lifestyle of prayer, asceticism, study, and writing, but he did not lead this life for long. The bishop of Hippo pressured him to receive ordination; he subsequently became bishop of Hippo, a position he would hold for the next thirty-six years.

Augustine's Mystical Path

Augustine's spirituality, like that of so many others, was wholly ecclesial. He believed that "a man possesses the Holy Spirit in the measure in which he loves the Church."[20] As bishop, he worked tirelessly to teach, comfort, and guide the people under his charge. He was particularly interested in alleviating poverty in Hippo. He also created a kind of monastery for his priests, many of whom became bishops in other parts of northern Africa. Augustine also practiced asceticism in the sense that he embraced celibacy, slept little, never drank wine, and lived on a vegetarian diet. He did everything according to reason, however. Augustine did not consider abusing one's body a virtue. For example, he believed that the point of fasting is to purify the soul's inordinate attachments to food; it can never be an expression of abuse of the body. If one is exhausted, one must rest; if hungry, one must eat. The body is good and has to be cared for. Augustine never thought that *apatheia* was wholly achievable. He believed that the effects of original sin (a term he coined) were so great that no one could ever fully attain *apatheia*. One could only hope to minimize the drive of the passions, not supersede them.

---

19. Augustine, *Confessions* 8.12. Translation from Augustine, *Confessions*, trans. Henry Chadwick (Oxford: Oxford University Press, 1991), 153. All quotations from Augustine's *Confessions* come from this source.

20. Augustine, *Treatise on the Gospel of John* 32.8.

Augustine was also a man of prayer, who spent many hours both in liturgical prayer and private prayer. He charged both his people and his priests to be Christians of prayer as well. What makes Augustine's spirituality particularly interesting, however, is his mystical life. Like Origin and Gregory, Augustine believed in the human capacity for union with God in this life. In his treatise, *On Seeing God*, he writes, "The Lord is spirit, and so whoever adheres to the Lord is one spirit [with him]. Hence, the person who is able to see God invisibly can adhere to God incorporeally."[21] Two passages in his *Confessions* offer particular insight into Augustine's mysticism. The first passage tells of an experience he had with his mother Monica just before she died.

Augustine and Monica were sitting on a ledge, overlooking a garden:

> We asked what quality of life the eternal life of the saints will have. . . . The conversation led us towards the conclusion that the pleasure of the bodily senses, however delightful in the radiant light of this physical world, is seen by comparison with the life of eternity to be not even worth considering. Our minds were lifted up by an ardent affection towards eternal being itself. Step by step we climbed beyond all corporeal objects and the heaven itself, where sun, moon, and stars shed light on the earth. We ascended even further by internal reflection and dialogue and wonder at your works, and we entered into our own minds. We moved beyond them so as to attain to the region of inexhaustible abundance where you feed Israel eternally with truth for food. . . . And while we talked and panted after it, we touched it in some small degree by a moment of concentration of the heart. And we sighed and left behind us the first fruits of the Spirit.[22]

Both Augustine and his mother speculate and yearn for knowledge of God and eternity. Interestingly, the experience starts with them looking at the beauty of the created world. The beautiful garden only makes them desire absolute beauty beyond physical things. Then their imaginations move through the greatness of creation only to let such considerations go, as God is greater still. From here, they enter into their own minds or souls where they believe God is most profoundly present, and finally with a degree of concentration of their hearts, they "touch it" ("it" being either God or God's inexhaustible abundance).

In the second passage from the *Confessions*, Augustine reports an even deeper experience, which occurred before he became a Christian:

> By the Platonic books I was admonished to return into myself. . . . I entered and with my soul's eye, such as it was, saw above that same

---

21. Augustine, *Epistle* 147.15.37. Translation from McGinn, *The Foundations of Mysticism*, 232.

22. Augustine, *Confessions* 9.10.

eye of my soul the immutable light higher than my mind—not the light of every day, obvious to everyone, nor a larger version of the same light. . . . It was not that light, but a different thing, utterly different from all our kinds of light. It transcended my mind. . . . It was superior because it made me, and I was inferior because I was made by it. The person who knows the truth knows it, and he who knows it knows eternity. Love knows it. Eternal truth and true love and beloved eternity: you are my God. . . . What I saw is Being . . . I trembled with love and awe . . . and heard as if it were a voice from on high: "I am the food of the fully grown; grow and you will feed on me. And you will not change me into you like the food your flesh eats, but you will be changed into me."[23]

This is an extraordinary mystical account because it appears to have both apophatic qualities, in which the soul directly meets God, and kataphatic qualities, which engage one's ability to conceptualize or imagine. In the kataphatic part of the experience, Augustine's soul heard God tell him to feed on God so as to become transformed into God, which is an expression of divinization. In Augustine's ascent to God he clearly follows the Platonic threefold pattern of withdrawal from the sense world, interior contemplation into the depths of the soul, and elevation to the vision of God. He even mentions this specifically in the passage. He refers to this elsewhere as well: "I passed beyond myself that I might touch him."[24]

Augustine's experience has many of the marks of apophaticism. Like Origen and unlike Gregory, he depicts God as light, but carefully explains that this is not like the light as we know it only infinitely greater. It is "utterly different from all our kinds of light." In his *Homily on Psalm 99*, he writes, "Before you had the experience, you used to think you could speak of God. You begin to have the experience, and there you experience that you cannot say what you experience."[25] He also identifies God as love, which is typical of Christianity. Then he goes a step further by saying, "Love knows it." That is, one knows God and has a vision of God in the context of love. The soul's response to union is both awe and love. This is where Christianity breaks from Platonism, which would neither see God as love nor the soul's encounter with God as a loving one. For Plato and Plotinus, God was impersonal, and the soul's knowledge of God and union with God is purely intellectual and impersonal. Augustine is clear: love meets Love.

What then, is the path to union with God? For Augustine, it must be grounded in love from the start. Even before he became a Christian he

---

23. Augustine, *Confessions* 7.10.

24. Augustine, *Homily on John* 20.11. Translation from McGinn, *The Foundations of Mysticism*, 241.

25. Augustine, *Homily on Psalm 99*. Translation from McGinn, *The Foundations of Mysticism*, 241.

recognized God as love: "I was astonished to find that I already loved you [God]."[26] Augustine did not view the spiritual life as merely including love along with other practices and virtues. It is fundamentally about love from start to finish: "When, as someone who is like him, you begin to draw near to and to become fully conscious of God, you will experience what to say and what not to say insofar as love grows in you, because 'God is Love.'"[27]

Pseudo-Dionysius (Fifth or Sixth Century)

No biography of this patristic author of the mystical path exists. He wrote under the name of Dionysius, supposedly the man converted by Saint Paul's speech at the Areopagus in Athens (Acts 17:34), and thus has been known as Dionysius the Areopagite. Some patristic and medieval authors doubted this, especially since he was not noted by any other of the patristic giants and first cited only in 533. Others, however, imagined him to be the very same biblical figure. Saint Maximus the Confessor (580–662) embraced his writings completely, and Saint Gregory of Palamas (1296–1379) addressed his theology and spirituality as though authentically ancient. In the West, such greats as John Scotus Erugena (810–877) drew on him heavily, and Thomas Aquinas even wrote a commentary on his works. It is possible, however, to date and locate him, even if provisionally. He relied on Gregory of Nyssa and references liturgical practices only used since the fifth century. He also approached his theological themes in ways that reflect the monophysite controversy of the fifth century, which debated whether Jesus had one nature or two. This controversy raged particularly in Syria. Thus many scholars now believe that he lived in Syria in the late fifth or early sixth century. Because most dispute that the author is the Dionysius of Acts, they often refer to him Pseudo-Dionysius. Along with several letters ascribed to him, Dionysius authored *The Divine Names*, which presents a philosophical interpretation of the many names of God found in the Bible; *Mystical Theology*, which summarizes Dionysius's understanding of how one would come to spiritual knowledge; *The Celestial Hierarchy*, which discusses the types of angels or celestial beings and how they reflect both God and spiritual progress; and *The Ecclesiastical Hierarchy*, which addresses the hierarchy and sacraments within the church as an expression of the divine life.

Dionysius's Mystical Path

A central theme in all of Dionysius's writings is the Neoplatonic framing of creation and redemption as an *exitus* and *reditus*, that is, coming from God and

---

26. Augustine, *Confessions* 7.16.

27. Augustine, *Homily on Psalm 99*. Translation from McGinn, *The Foundations of Mysticism*, 241.

returning to God. How do human beings understand themelves as having come from God? What kind of participation does created reality have with the Uncreated? How does one return to God, given the answers to these first two questions? Such issues dominate all of Dionysius's writings.

Dionysius was convinced that if everything came from God, including the church and its structure and worship, then these are real manifestations of God and reveal a way of knowing him. Dionysius saw hierarchy everywhere. For example, in *The Celestial Hierarchy* Dionysius borrows New Testament texts to posit nine classes of celestial beings or versions of angels: Along with many biblical texts referring to seraphim, cherubim, archangels, and angels, the Pauline Epistles mention five more that came to be interpreted as separate classes of angels.[28] Dionysius sees the whole spiritual world as one of a hierarchy of triads: (1) seraphim, cherubim, and thrones; (2) dominations, powers, and authorities; and (3) principalities, archangels, and angels. *The Ecclesiastical Hierarchy* presents a hierarchy of (1) liturgical expressions of anointing, Eucharist, and baptism; (2) bishops, priests, and deacons; (3) monks, laity, and those Christians not fully in communion.

All of these created things symbolize and manifest God's truth and presence in the world. They teach human beings about God and provide means of transcending their created quality to encounter the uncreated God. Dionysius believed, like the other exemplars in this chapter, that God is invisible, ultimately imperceptible, and incomprehensible. These symbols, along with the names of God, draw the soul into the truth of God. God is both similar to them as they manifest the Divine, as well as dissimilar in that they can never actually address God as God really is. One begins with the perceptual appearances of symbols to rise higher to their conceptual meaning. Yet, Dionysius insists, even the conceptual meaning has to be transcended:

> Sometimes the mysterious tradition of the scriptures represents the sacred blessedness of the transcendent Deity under the form of "Word," "Mind," and "Being." It shows thereby that rationality and wisdom are, necessarily, attributes of God, that he is also to be deemed a true subsistence and the true cause of the subsistence of every being, and that he may also be represented as light and hailed as life. Now these sacred shapes certainly show more reverence and seem vastly superior to the making of images drawn from the world. Yet they are actually no less defective than this latter, for the Deity is far beyond every manifestation of being and of life; no reference to light can characterize it; every reason or intelligence falls short of similarity to it.[29]

---

28. Eph. 1:21; 3:10; 6:12; Col. 1:16; 2:11, 15.

29. Pseudo-Dionysius, *The Celestial Hierarchy* 140C. Translations of Pseudo-Dionysius are taken from *Pseudo-Dionysius: The Complete Works*, trans. Colm Luibheid (New York: Paulist Press, 1987).

As one engages God's revelation, one becomes imbued in contemplation of its truth. From the perceptual, such as liturgical rites, one can experience the truth they manifest. Encountering their truth more fully requires negating their perceptual limitations and experiencing them on the conceptual or immaterial level. This becomes a deeper appropriation of their truth. Yet the conceptual is itself still a problem, for God is not only similar to them but also dissimilar. The conceptual has to be transcended. Dionysius's final goal is union with God, a God beyond and in some way dissimilar to everything one can say or think about him.

Dionysius's treatises express both kataphatic theology, affirming true revelation about God, and apophatic theology, negating any perceptions about God, who is beyond concepts. Such a negation brings the soul into the silence of the Divine.

> The fact is that the more we take flight upward, the more our words are confined to the ideas we are capable of forming; so that now as we plunge into the darkness which is beyond intellect, we shall find ourselves not simply running short of words but actually speechless and unknowing. . . . When it has passed up and beyond the ascent, it will turn silent completely, since it will finally be at one with him who is indescribable.[30]

Dionysius believed that even these negations must be negated. Pure negation would imagine God as unrelated to the world.[31] God is real and related to the created world, but God is not merely the infinite expression of truth, God is also radically unique. Dionysius's theology holds a kind of "both-and" in tension. God is both the absolute expression of the good, true, and so on, and different from what one can consider about it.

For Dionysius, theology and spirituality are not disciplines to acquire knowledge about God, but means to experience that which surpasses all understanding. His spirituality entails embracing God's manifestations and using them to ascend even higher. Unlike a purely "negative way," his ascent takes seriously God's self-manifesting descent into the world. His school of contemplation fully embraces the created world and gifts of the church, all the while using them to discover the divine incomprehensibility that ultimately grounds their meaningfulness.

Conclusion

The spiritual perspectives and agendas of these four great patristic representatives create something of a legacy for Christian spirituality. Origen and Gregory's use of the Bible as representing levels of interpretation and meaning

---

30. Pseudo-Dionysius, *Mystical Theology* 1033B–C.

31. "The Cause of all is . . . not inexistent, lifeless, speechless, mindless." Pseudo-Dionysius, *Mystical Theology* 1040D.

remained mainstays of biblical interpretation throughout the Middle Ages and into the modern period. The fourfold method of interpretation allowed Christians to envision numerous possibilities for biblical interpretation and inspiration. Dionysius's understanding of celestial and church hierarchies gave Christians levels of understanding on how to recognize and engage truths about God through creation and the very nature of the church. In his sacramental vision physical realities were experienced as dense with spiritual meaning. And Augustine's emphasis on love continues to dominate Christian spirituality today.

Above all, these representatives provide a way to see the possibilities and limitations of the created world. They give roadmaps to union with God that honored but also transcended the world so as to encounter God who transcends creation. More recently, many scholars have criticized their over-emphasis of leaving behind creation, particularly their bodies, as something too Platonic and too dualistic. For these scholars, the patristic legacy needs to also acknowledge these consequential liabilities.

Questions for Review

1. What recurring Platonic ideas did these four Christian figures use in their theologies?
2. How did each Christian figure diverge from Platonic ideas?
3. What different types of biblical interpretation did Gregory of Nyssa put forth? Explain each one.
4. In what ways did Pseudo-Dionysius construe reality as consisting of hierarchies?

Questions for Discussion

1. Greek philosophy provided some intellectual foundations that these four Christian figures used to understand Christian truths. In your opinion, how well does this work? Is there anything that you think would not fit well in a modern Christian worldview? Is there anything that you think fits exceptionally well?
2. Given that Origen held views that the church later deemed heretical, do you think it is appropriate when Christians treat Origen as a model for Christian spirituality? What parts of his understanding do you think make a positive contribution to the discussion of spirituality, and what parts do not?
3. What do you think of Gregory of Nyssa's interpretation of Exodus? Is there any reason a modern Christian would find his interpretive methods problematic?

4. Pseudo-Dionysius's mysticism balanced apophatism and kataphatism. Is this balance a positive contribution to Christian spirituality? Explain your answer.

Bibliography

Resources with annotations are highly recommended to students interested in further study.

Augustine of Hippo. *Augustine of Hippo: Selected Writings*. Translated by Mary Clark. New York: Paulist Press, 1984.

Augustine of Hippo. *City of God*. Translated by Henry Bettenson. New York: Penguin, 1984.

Augustine of Hippo. *Confessions*. Translated by Henry Chadwick. Oxford: Oxford University Press, 1991.

One of Augustine's most famous books, it details his life and how he makes sense of the Christian revelation, both philosophically and theologically.

Aurelius, Marcus. *Meditations*. Edited and translated by S. S. L. Farquharson. New York: Alfred A. Knopf, 1946.

Brown, Peter. *Augustine of Hippo*. Berkeley: University of California Press, 1967.

This is the most authoritative biography of Augustine in English.

Brown, Peter. *The Body and Society: Men, Women, and Sexual Renunciation in Early Christianity*. New York: Columbia University Press. 1988.

Brown, Peter. *The Cult of the Saints: Its Rise and Function in Latin Christianity*. Chicago: University of Chicago Press, 1981.

Burns, J. Patout. "Grace: The Augustinian Foundation." In *Christian Spirituality*, edited by Bernard McGinn, John Meyendorff, and Jean Leclercq, 1:331–49. New York: Continuum, 1988.

Gregory of Nyssa. *Gregory of Nyssa: The Life of Moses*. Translated by Abraham Malherbe and Everett Ferguson. New York: Paulist Press, 1978.

Lossky, Vladimir. *The Mystical Theology of the Eastern Church*. Translated by the Fellowship of St. Alban and St. Sergius. Crestwood, NY: St. Vladimir's Seminary Press, 1976.

Louth, Andrew. "Denys the Areopagite." In *The Study of Spirituality*, edited by Cheslyn Jones, Geoffrey Wainwright, and Edward Yarnold, 184-89. New York: Oxford University Press, 1986.

Louth, Andrew. *The Origins of the Christian Mystical Tradition: From Plato to Denys*. 2nd ed. Oxford: Oxford University Press, 2007.

This text examines patristic mysticism, particularly as it aligns with Greek philosophical assumptions.

McGinn, Bernard. *The Foundations of Mysticism: Origins to the Fifth Century.* New York: Crossroad, 1992.

This is the first of a six-volume series, seminal in the understanding of Christian mysticism in the West.

Origen. *Origen: An Exhortation to Martyrdom, Payer and Selected Works.* Translated by Rowan Greer. New York: Paulist Press, 1979.

Plotinus. *The Enneads.* Translated by Stephen Mackenna. New York: Penguin, 1991.

Pseudo-Dionysius. *Pseudo-Dionysius: The Complete Works.* Translated by Colm Luibheid. New York: Paulist Press, 1987.

Rorem, Paul. "The Uplifting Spirituality of Pseudo-Dionysius." In *Christian Spirituality*, edited by Bernard McGinn, John Meyendorff, and Jean Leclercq, 1:132–51. New York: Continuum, 1988.

Sullivan, Francis. *From Apostles to Bishops: The Development of the Episcopacy in the Early Church.* New York: The Newman Press, 2001.

Internet Resources

Clergy.asn.au.: Australian Confraternity of Catholic Clergy. "The Father of Christian Mysticism." *www.clergy.asn.au/journal/november-2010/st-gregory-of-nyssa-father-of-christian-mysticism/.*

Lengthy presentation of the dominant role of Gregory of Nyssa for Orthodox mysticism.

Roots of Western Mysticism Resources. *pegasus.cc.ucf.edu/~janzb/mysticism/.*

University of Central Florida's professor Bruce Janz's web-page with numerous resources regarding mystical union, particularly in the early church.

Films

Restless Heart: The Confession of St. Augustine. 2013.

Details the entire life of Saint Augustine, who was the most influential theologian in Western Christianity.

Monastic Spirituality East and West

Patristic spirituality was marked by asceticism, prayer, and a preference for celibacy. These characteristics were understood as mutually enriching. Celibacy allowed for an undistracted life and, in the patriarchal society of the day, could mean freedom and even empowerment for women. Women could often express real spiritual leadership in the church rather than be merely subordinate wives to their husbands. Asceticism freed one from the domination of one's inordinate desires or passions, and both celibacy and asceticism led to possibilities of greater interiority and a unified spirit for prayer. Syrian and Egyptian Christians in particular embraced these principles with unusual rigor and, independently from each other, developed a tradition of monasticism.

Monachos in Greek means "solitary," and is the root from which derives the word "monk." Around 324 the term *monachos* began to appear in Egyptian papyri. These devout men and women were believed to be particularly holy. They prayed, fasted, slept little, and served as models of the spiritual life. The papyri described *monachoi* (plural) as offering blessings and interceding before God on behalf of the people. They were portrayed as living saints with spiritual power. While no documentation of them prior to the early fourth century exists, it is clear that they existed prior to this time, as can be seen from the biography of Saint Antony.

Particular expressions of early monasticism varied. In Syria, fraternities of monks lived in their own huts, but prayed together and performed ministry in the neighboring villages. In Palestine, a system developed whereby monks lived in huts or caves close enough to each other so that they could regularly join one another in prayer. Sometimes their modest housing even encircled an area where they met in the middle for prayer and support. In Egypt many monks lived quite alone, though they might periodically visit one another for support or to meet a senior monk, an *abba*, for guidance.

Before Emperor Constantine's decision to allow freedom of religion in the Roman Empire, particularly after his defeat of Licinius in 323, martyrdom was considered the greatest expression of holiness. Ignatius of Antioch wrote letters to different churches while on his way to Rome to be martyred. He eagerly desired martyrdom, and begged the Roman church not to intercede on his behalf.[1]

After Constantine, this "red" martyrdom—a baptism in blood—had been replaced by a "white" martyrdom, in which Christians died to themselves heroically in order to live purely for Christ. Instead of combating the evil of the Roman Empire and beasts of the coliseum, these Christians engaged in a lifelong combat with the evil of their own sinfulness and the beasts of the demons who assaulted them in the lonely solitude of the desert.

Harlots of the Desert

The great historian Benedicta Ward has collected a number of stories that circulated in early monastic circles. These all feature women and repentance, and they became models of early monastic piety. They express something of the ethos of the early spirituality of the desert.

Saint Mary of Egypt

The story of Saint Mary of Egypt exists in several versions. It begins with a holy priest named Zossima, who was out on pilgrimage in the deserts of Palestine. After twenty days of journeying, he discovered a monk in a cave and called out to him. This monk, Mary, said that she was a woman and naked, so she could not reveal herself, even to Zossima the holy priest. He was stunned that she knew his name. Throwing his cloak into the opening of the cave, he begged her to come out and bless him. She did and then told him her story.

She had been a prostitute in Alexandria. "For nearly seventeen years I lived as a fire for public depravity but not at all for the money. I wanted to do it and did it for nothing."[2] One day she decided to join pilgrims on a journey to Jerusalem, seducing many of them along the way. She continued her life as a prostitute in Jerusalem until the Feast of the Veneration of the Holy Cross.

---

1. "I am writing to all the churches and am insisting to everyone that I die for God of my own free will—unless you hinder me. I implore you: do not be 'unseasonably kind' to me. Let me be food for the wild beasts, through whom I can reach God. I am God's wheat, and I am being ground by the teeth of the wild beasts, that I might prove to be pure bread. . . . I am passionately in love with death as I write you." Ignatius of Antioch, *Rom.* 4.7. Translation from *The Apostolic Fathers*, ed. Michael Holmes, trans. J. B. Lightfoot and J. R. Harmer, 2nd ed. (Grand Rapids: Baker Book House, 1989).

2. Benedicta Ward, *Harlots of the Desert: A Study of Repentance in Early Monastic Sources* (Kalamazoo, MI: Cistercian Publications, 1987), 26–56. Ward's account combines several original sources.

She decided to attend services at the Church of the Holy Sepulcher, but an invisible force kept her from entering. Suddenly she was filled with contrition for her life and prayed to Mary, the Mother of the Lord, for help. The next day she found she could enter the church, and she venerated the cross. Later that same day she left Jerusalem and entered the desert with nothing but the clothing she wore and a little bread. That was forty-seven years ago. Mary told Zossima that she had been able to eat of that same original loaf for the past forty-seven years and mostly fed on the mercy of God. "Have you suffered?" he asked her. She responded that she had suffered for seventeen years with the wild beasts of irrational desires, but since then had found a place of peace and refuge.

A year later, Zossima prayed that he would see this holy woman again and was directed by the Spirit to the banks of the Jordan. Mary arrived on the other side, appearing radiant, and walked on the water to cross it. "Indeed," he thought, "God does not lie when he promises we shall be like him insofar as we have been purified." Some years later he found the woman's body lying on the ground with a great lion standing over it. Then he saw the lion make a sign of the cross, dig out a grave, and lovingly place her in it.[3]

This strange and fantastic story is but one of many featuring a deeply sinful woman who has a striking moment of repentance and adopts a heroically ascetical lifestyle in the desert. If taken literally, these stories stretch the imagination and hardly seem like an attractive spiritual possibility; however, when monks heard them as expressions of repentance, they resonated deeply. In some of the stories the woman, usually a harlot, hears a word from the Bible, and God convicts her of her sinfulness. In other stories, she encounters a holy man or woman who can read her soul and who exposes the state of her soul to her. In this story, it was the holiness of the church on the site where Jesus was said to have died and rose, and which held the relic of the original cross, that forbade her entrance. In many of these stories, the repentant harlot places herself in the hands of the holy man or woman that she has encountered to guide her to salvation. The vehicle to her salvation is deep repentance, a repentance that lasts a lifetime.

In this story, Mary was "on fire" with her passions and continued to be disturbed by them for many years. Cool refreshment came paradoxically from the arid, hot desert where she could still her passions. She ate little food, but fed on God's mercy all the while. She moved from the city, where passions flow, to the desert, where she could meet God and fully confront her soul.[4]

---

3. Ibid.

4. Along with many other points of this story, the lion cannot be taken literally. Rather, it is a symbol for God (Gen. 49:9; Hos. 5:14; Rev. 5:5).

Model for Monks

These stories give a sense of what early monastic life felt like. Monks desired solitude. Mary lived in a cave and only came out to converse with Zossima after much persuasion. Unlike a broader Christian spirituality, which is marked by community life and the authority of the institutional church, particularly guided by the bishop, this kind of piety is highly individualistic. The early monks rarely celebrated the Eucharist or any other sacraments. They respected the institutional church—Mary did, after all, recognize Zossima as a holy priest—but that was about it. In fact, Zosimma, the church representative, marvels at the monk's holiness and begs for Mary's blessing. The story suggests that Mary's austerity led to her transformation. Many early monks believed that, by God's grace, they could return to a kind of pre-fallen state of harmony and perfection, a kind of unification of body, mind, and soul that Adam and Eve enjoyed before they sinned.

It is also significant that Mary's whole life was one of repentance. Typically, Christian repentance is thought of as a moment of conversion (or ongoing conversion) that leads from sin to a life of grace. One repents and then moves on. These stories, in contrast, depict monastic existence as a constant state of repentance. It is not that Mary refused to believe she was forgiven for her past life, but rather that repentance was a life-long spiritual posture. The monks called it *penthos*, compunction or spiritual sorrow. They understood this as a kind of godly sorrow that is simultaneously an experience of God's mercy. It was paradoxically aligned with thanksgiving.

Origen taught that each sin is like a wound. The wound will heal, but the scar, an imprint of the sin, remains in the soul. One cannot but be saddened by them, even after the wounds have healed. Further, monastic life was one of deep self-awareness. As Abba Matoes said, "The nearer a man draws to God the more he sees himself as a sinner."[5] Compunction should be one's life posture: "A brother said to Abba Matoes, 'Give me a word.' He said to him, 'Restrain the spirit of controversy in yourself in everything and weep, have compunction, for the time is drawing near.'"[6] While it may seem strange to contemporary readers, early monks seemed to enjoy confessing their sins to each other. They did not see this as a kind of scrupulosity or neurosis, but a way to feed on God's mercy; it brought them joy.

---

5. Cited in Benedicta Ward, ed. and trans., *The Sayings of the Desert Fathers: The Alphabetical Collection* (Kalamazoo, MI: Cistercian Publications, 1975), 143.

6. Ibid., 145. Similarly, Abba Ammonas once said, "Fear [of the Lord] produces tears, and tears joy. Joy brings strength, through which the soul will be fruitful in everything." Saint Ammonas, *Letter* 2.1. Translation from Irenee Hausherr, *Penthos: The Doctrine of Compunction in the Christian East* (Kalamazoo, MI: Cistercian Publications, 1982), 142.

Ammas in the Desert

Women in the desert were not merely models of repentance, they often acted as great authorities. These were the *ammas*, or mothers, of the monastic movement. As noted above, freedom from marriage often afforded women possibilities of spiritual leadership. This was nowhere better expressed than in the desert. Women often served as spiritual guides of other women ascetics and even guides of some men. In the early fifth century, Palladius of Galatia archived the lives of early Christian monks. In this seminal text he mentions almost three thousand women living in the desert, including many *ammas*.[7] What we find is an array of women leaders whose authority, like that of the men, rested not on church office but on their reputation for holiness and wisdom. Two of the most well-known are Amma Sarah and Amma Syncletica, whose sayings were authoritative enough to be included in *The Sayings of the Desert Fathers*.

Sayings of the Ammas

Amma Sarah: "Then the spirit of fornication appeared corporeally to her and said, 'Sarah, you have overcome me.' But she said, "It is not I who have overcome you, but my master, Christ" (no. 2); "If I prayed God that all men should approve of my conduct, I should find myself a penitent at the door of each one, but I shall rather pray that my heart may be pure towards all" (no. 5); "I put out my foot to ascend the ladder, and I place death before my eyes going up it" (no. 6).

Amma Syncletica: "In the beginning there are a great many battles and a good deal of suffering for those who are advancing towards God and afterwards, ineffable joy. It is like those who wish to light a fire; at first they are choked by the smoke and cry, and by this means obtain what they seek. . . . So we also must kindle the divine fire in ourselves through tears and hard work" (no. 1); "Just as the most bitter medicine drives out poisonous creatures so prayer joined to fasting drives evil thoughts away" (no. 3); "Imitate the publican, and you will not be condemned with the Pharisee. Choose the meekness of Moses and you will find your heart which is a rock changed into a spring of water" (no. 11).

---

7. We also know of the lives of many women saints of the desert from the *Lives of the Desert Fathers* (*Vitae Patrum*).

Antony (251–356)

The greatest representative of early monasticism is Saint Antony of Egypt, whose life story was chronicled in *The Life of Antony*, written by Saint Athanasius (296–373). This biography spread across the Christian world and influenced many. In fact, when Augustine was considering converting to Christianity, his priest-mentor Simplicianus told him an edifying story of two imperial court officials who read the account and immediately abandoned their comfortable posts to become monks. Augustine was profoundly impressed.

Athanasius writes that when Antony was eighteen or twenty his wealthy parents died, leaving him in charge of his sister and family possessions. One day in church, while considering ways to make his life more radically pure, he heard the Gospel verse, "If you wish to be perfect, go, sell what you have and give to the poor, and you will have treasure in heaven" (Matt. 19:21). It struck him as though God were speaking to him directly. He made provisions for his sister and sold the rest of his family's belongings, giving them to the poor. Antony sought direction from an elderly solitary man who lived in a simple hut outside the village. Here he gave himself to manual work and prayed constantly, even while working. He often held vigil long into the night, fasted assiduously, and slept on the ground. He also consulted others who were adept in prayer. The devil regularly tempted Antony to abandon his life: "First he attempted to lead him away from the discipline, suggesting memories of his possessions, the guardianship of his sister, the bonds of kinship, love of money and of glory, the manifold pleasure of food, the relaxations of life, and finally, the rigor of virtue, and how great the labor is that earns it."[8] The monastic life is daunting, too hard to fully embrace on one's own. To persevere one has to rely on the strength of God's grace.[9] This may be part of the purpose of monasticism: finding an ascetical way of life that demonstrates personal weakness so as to learn full dependence on God.

Antony's next step consisted of moving away from the town completely and living among the tombs of the cemetery. Friends periodically brought him food, and he gave himself wholly to prayer. There demons tried any means to dissuade him; one night they beat him so badly that he almost died. The next day a friend happened to come by to bring him bread and carried him back to the village church. While lying on the church floor, Antony had a vision whereby the roof of the church vanished and a beam of heavenly light bore down on the demons who were surrounding him. They quickly vanished. Antony complained, "'Where were you? Why didn't you appear in the beginning, so that you could

---

8. Athanasius, *The Life of Antony* 5. Translation from Athanasius, *Athanasius: The Life of Antony and the Letter to Marcellinus*, trans. Robert Gregg (New York: Paulist Press, 1980).

9. "Working with Antony was the Lord, who bore flesh for us, and gave to the body the victory over the devil, so that each of those who truly struggle can say, *It is not I, but the grace of God which is in me* [1 Cor. 15:10]." Athanasius, *The Life of Antony*, 5.

stop my distresses?' And a voice came to him: 'I was here, Antony, but I waited to watch your struggle. And now, since you persevered and were not defeated, I will be your helper forever.'"[10]

Antony moved even further into the Egyptian desert and for the next twenty years lived along the Nile delta in an abandoned fortress. When he did finally emerge, he appeared to his friends not only as radiant, but as though he had not aged at all. Finally, he went to live on a mountain close to the Red Sea. People flocked to him because of his reputed ability to heal infirmities and to read their souls so as to offer spiritual direction. Even though he lived a solitary life, Antony was a gracious host who fed guests from his garden and housed them in a second hut he built just for visitors.

Antony was an *anchorite* or a hermit. His life exemplifies the ideal of early Egyptian monasticism. He was a man convicted by God to seek *perfection* (as Christians at the time understood it). He did not then simply become a hermit, but was mentored by elders who understood the way of prayer and asceticism. He progressively moved to more remote places as he was also progressively tested and tempted by the devil or other evil spirits. As he grew in the monastic life he gained interior strength for the hardships of a life of rigorous prayer and solitude, and such a life paid spiritual dividends. He became deeply holy and attained spiritual gifts for the service of others. Although he lived mostly alone, he modeled holiness for the church at large and served members of the church as a spiritual master. Antony also witnessed a kind of harmony as a result of his rigorous life. After his twenty-year foray into the desert, his friends still found him youthful and vigorous. Indeed, he lived to the age of 105 years. His biography makes clear that Antony lived in total dependence on God's grace. The healthiest of monks did not think themselves profoundly strong, but profoundly weak, and in their weakness they quite dramatically experienced God's strength.

Eastern Cenobitism

The term for monks who lived together is *cenobite,* from the Greek *koinos* ("common") and *bios* ("life").[11] In what may seem something of a contradiction in terms, these were *monks* (solitaries) who lived together in community. As noted above, many of the earliest monks in Syria and Palestine also lived communally. They prayed together and supported each other. In Syria, they also performed ministerial works in nearby towns. Egyptian monasticism eventually embraced such a communal life.

---

10. Ibid., 10.

11. A solitary monk is termed an *anchorite.*

Pachomius (290–346)

Pachomius entered the military as a young man. He was not a Christian, but was profoundly impressed by a group of Christians he met at Thebes, Egypt. One story goes that his troop, which had just succeeded in a battle and were taking prisoners through Thebes, were met by some Christians who came out and ministered equally to the wounded soldiers and the prisoners. They showed universal love and tenderness. After his release from the army, Pachomius was baptized and took on the solitary life under the direction of the great *abba* Palemon.

Pachomius trained successfully under Palemon for six or seven years as an anchorite, but he also saw the potential dangers inherent in the life of an anchorite. Some hermits had become less holy than neurotic. While there were many famous and holy spiritual masters, both men and women (*abbas* and *ammas*), there were also bad or perhaps even unstable spiritual guides. There was nothing to keep such personalities in check. A solitary life could also fall prey to self-delusion. One could imagine oneself holy, but without the presence of other brothers and sisters, self-deception was always possible. One could also envision oneself as a kind of spiritual warrior, where one's fasting and prayers produced more pride than humility, more self-dependence than dependence on God.

Sophy Ru / Shutterstock.com

The sixth-century monastery of Saint Catherine, at the foot of Mt. Sinai, Egypt, is one of the oldest working Christian monasteries in the world. It is a classic representative of Egyptian desert monasticism.

Pachomius saw the two biggest problems as spiritual pride and lack of discretion.[12] Without some kind of obedience to an authority a monk could fall into vain-glory. Fasting is good, but destroying the body is hardly a virtue. Long vigils are necessary, but lack of sleep could not support deep prayer. Discretion meant being able to read one's heart. It meant not being rigid and knowing in the moment the best course of action for oneself or for another. Monastics called it *second sight:* "A man can spend his whole time carrying an axe without succeeding in cutting down the tree; while another, with experience of tree-felling brings the tree down with a few blows. . . . That axe is discretion."[13]

Pachomius founded nine monasteries to provide the kind of support and balance that he thought would allow monasticism to flourish—seven for men and two for women—and set up a common rule that they could follow. By around 330, as many as nine thousand monks lived under his rule. They lived with other monks under the supervision of a superior, while Pachomius served as the superior of all of the communities. In one monastery, which he built like a fortress, almost five thousand monks lived together. Although it may have seemed ironic to the anchorites, these monks left the city with its noise and distractions only to enter another kind of city, sometimes also rather busy.

Basil (330–379)

As mentioned in the last chapter, Basil was the brother of Gregory of Nyssa and the bishop of Caesarea in Cappadocia (Turkey). Like his brother Gregory, Basil initially desired to take up a secular profession, in his case politics. Also like Gregory, his sister Macrina convinced him to whole-heartedly embrace a life of Christian service. Basil toured monasteries in Syria, Palestine, and Egypt before being ordained a priest. After the death of the bishop of Caesarea, Basil took his place. He quickly founded several monasteries and regarded the cenobitic life superior to the anchoritic life. For Basil, Christian life necessarily involved a Christian commitment to loving service of others. This would be expressed in mutual support of other monks. Loving, serving, and sharing spiritual gifts were, for him, essential to a healthy spiritual life. Basil also believed that monasteries should be centers of support for the church at large. While Pachomius's monasteries flourished in the desert, Basil's monasteries were more typically located on the edge of towns and cities and sometimes even within the cities themselves. Basil's monasteries often included schools and orphanages and served as places of hospitality for the sick and needy.

---

12. Indeed, many of the sayings of the desert fathers address both of these problems.

13. Translation from Ward, *Sayings of the Desert Fathers,* 174, slightly adjusted.

Basil wrote a rule for monks that, from the patristic period to today, remains standard.[14] By contemporary standards, they seem harsh. A monk gives up "ties of physical relationship, human friendships and . . . repudiates all worldly affections. . . . He will deem all possessions foreign to him [and be] crucified to the world."[15] "Leanness of body and pallor produced by the exercise of continency mark the Christian . . . making a sparing and frugal use of necessities, ministering to nature [by eating] as if this were a burdensome duty, and begrudging the time spent on it."[16] One is to embrace "complete abstinence from all that tends to harmful pleasure . . . [realizing that] filling the stomach to satiety, burdening it with food, is an act deserving of malediction."[17] Interestingly, in the monastic community, Basil's rules were known for their gentleness and reasonability. He wanted balanced monks who had the strength and the fortitude to live long, healthy lives, and who had the energy to care for each other and the church at large.

Evagrius of Pontus (345–399)

Anchoritic, or solitary monks, were typically simple and in most cases unlettered. For the most part, the *Life of Antony* and the sayings of the desert fathers do not include the kind of mystical speculation that marked the intellectual mysticism discussed in the last chapter. Those who could read perhaps had a few collections of sayings and some biblical texts. Monks typically memorized the psalms as well as other parts of the Bible. There is a story of a monk who went to the hut of another monk to have a spiritual conversation and share dinner, which consisted of a small loaf of bread. The host asked his guest to offer a prayer, and he began to recite Psalm 1. So enraptured by the word of God, he continued throughout the whole psalter. When he had finished with Psalm 150 his host thanked him for such a blessing, and then proceeded to recite the whole of the Gospel of Mark. When he had finished, they realized that it was already morning, so the guest monk thanked his host and returned home, fed only on the word.

This constituted their lives and their ideals: they prayed the scriptures, particularly meditating on the Psalms, and they reflected over and over again on advice or a sentence an *abba* gave them to consider. They worked, often weaving baskets and selling these in the nearest town.

---

14. Basil actually wrote two: the *Shorter Rules* and the *Longer Rules*, the *Longer Rules* acting as a commentary on the *Shorter Rules*.

15. *Longer Rules*, 8. Translations of this work are from *St. Basil: Ascetical Works*, trans. Monica Wagner (New York: Fathers of the Church, 1950).

16. Ibid., 17.

17. Ibid., 19.

Much of this lifestyle would change for those monks who lived in community, who were taught to read, and who often prayed together in the community chapel. This new way of life would be changed also by a progressive intellectualism that became part of the monastic heritage. The most influential theologian of the monastic spiritual life was Evagrius, who hailed from the town of Pontus in early Cappadocia, and was a disciple of both Basil and Gregory of Nazianzus. Evagrius also studied the writings of Origen. In 383, he went to the monastic center of Nitria, Egypt, and then deeper into the desert to Kellia, where he stayed until his death in 399. Later, the church grew suspicious of Origen and, by association, Evagrius, who embraced Origen's radical Neoplatonism; the church condemned Evagrius in the late sixth century. His writings, however, circulated during and after his life, and they continued to be read long after his condemnation.

Evagrius divided the soul's journey into three stages, the *praktikē*, *physikē*, and *theologia*. The *praktikē* represents the development of the virtues. It consists of struggle with the demons and overcoming the passions, or *apatheia*. This kind of purgation was thought to bring stillness to the soul and allowed for deeper prayer. The *physikē* represents the practice of natural contemplation, which involves recognizing the divine presence in the created world. Because everything proceeds from God and exists in participation with God, everything manifests God to some degree. *Theologia* represents supernatural contemplation of God as God is. "*Apatheia* gives birth to love, love is the door to natural knowledge which leads to *theologia* and final bliss."[18] Prayer, for Evagrius, was not so much an activity, but a state of being. As one progresses, knowledge of God and intimacy with God become something that one has; one becomes prayer.

Evagrius is particularly known for his attention to demons. As seen in the *Life of Antony*, monks were thought to be particularly troubled by demons because their dramatic expression of spiritual purity made them such a threat to the demons. Evagrius taught that demons were limited and could not know the contents of the heart, but they could attack the imagination. They decide on a given monk's weak points by his behavior. Evagrius identified eight types of evil thoughts, representing either eight different demons or a given demon who attacked variously. They are: gluttony, fornication, avarice, grief, anger, listlessness, vainglory, and pride. The key to defending oneself lies in self-knowledge and recognizing these demons as they attack so as not to give them any leverage. The remedy is patience, avoiding any kind of judgmentalism, and continued chanting of Psalms. A modern person might interpret these not as supernatural beings attacking the monk's mind, but simply as the way the psyche operates. Of particular interest is Evagrius's understanding of how these thoughts work. As seen here, he was a master psychologist:

---

18. Evagrius, *Praktikos* 81. Translation from *Evagrius Ponticus: The Praktikos and Chapters on Prayer*, trans. John Eudes Bamberger (Kalamazoo, MI: Cistercian Publications, 1981).

The demon of *acedia* (listlessness)—also called the noonday demon—is the one that causes the most trouble at all. He presses his attack upon the monk about the fourth hour and besieges the soul until the eighth hour. First of all he makes it seem that the sun barely moves, if at all, and that the day is fifty hours long. Then he constrains the monk to look constantly out the window, to talk outside the cell, to gaze carefully at the sun to determine how far it stands from the ninth hour, to look now this way now that to see if perhaps one of the brethren appears from his cell. Then too he instills in the heart of the monk a hatred for the place, a hatred for his very life itself, a hatred for manual labor. He leads him to reflect that charity has departed from among the brethren, that there is no one to give him encouragement.[19]

Like the exemplars in the last chapter, Evagrius was certain that God transcended all images and concepts, something like Gregory of Nyssa's dark cloud. Evagrius framed this as a kind of supernatural ignorance.[20] Thus, if one was deeply prayerful and had conquered the lower demons, a last temptation was to imagine seeing God when one has not, in fact, seen God: "When the mind prays purely and impassibly, then the demons no longer come from the left but from the right. And they represent to him the glory of God as a certain form which delights the senses so that he thinks he has attained perfectly the end of prayer."[21] The remedy consists of constantly reminding oneself that such images have no place in real contemplation.[22]

Western Monasticism

Monasticism was quickly adopted in the West. It took off in Italy and Gaul (France), and some bishops, including Ambrose and Augustine, required that their priests take up a quasi-monastic existence of community living and prayer, and take vows of poverty and celibacy. Augustine's monastic formation proved so influential that many of the bishops of Latin North Africa came from his diocese. It represented a new form of monasticism that was intimately connected to priestly pastoral service. Like Pachomius, Saint Martin of Tours (317–397) left the life of a soldier and adopted the monastic life. He had lived with Saint Hilary of Poitiers (300–368) in a semi-anchoritic community before being named

---

19. Ibid., 12.

20. "Blessed is he who has reached the ignorance that is inexhaustible." Evagrius, *Kaliphalia gnostika* 3.88. Translation from *The Mind's Long Journey to the Holy Trinity: The Ad Monachos of Evagrius Ponticus*, trans. Jeremy Dricoll (Collegeville, MN: Liturgical Press, 1993).

21. Evagrius, *On Prayer* 73. Translation from Bamberger, trans., *Evagrius Ponticus*.

22. Images and shapes belong to the lower reaches of mental activity. Ibid., 85.

bishop of Tours. Martin established many monasteries in France and these often housed an educated, upper class. Monasteries became a center of culture and learning, and many bishops were chosen from among their ranks. Saint Cesarius (468–542) became the bishop of Arles in 502 and founded a monastery for men and another for women under the leadership of his sister Cesaria. He wrote a rule for both communities, which other monasteries quickly embraced.

John Cassian (360–435)

Saint John Cassian came from a Latin-speaking province in the East, now Romania. For ten to twelve years he visited monasteries in Palestine and Egypt. He was particularly attracted to the eremitical (anchorite) form of monasticism, though he also spent a great deal of time in cenobitic monasteries. Cassian and his friend Germanus were ordained in Constantinople under Saint John Chrysostom (Cassian as a deacon and Germanus as a priest) and served under him for several years. When the emperor deposed Chrysostom because of his unremitting advocacy of the poor, Cassian and Germanus traveled to Rome to appeal to the bishop of Rome. This was in 405, and Cassian stayed in Rome ten years. He then traveled to Gaul and founded two monasteries in Marseilles, one for men and one for women. There he wrote the *Institutes*, which described the way of monastic life and various practices of Eastern monasticism. This text was widely read and had an enormous influence on how monasteries were run. By far his most influential book was the *Conferences*, which constitutes a large collection of teachings from the monks in Egypt. Unlike the typical sayings of the desert fathers, which are short and pithy, the *Conferences* are lengthy citations. They would begin with a question, such as, what is perfect prayer? And then an *abba* would offer a long teaching, sometimes interrupted by another figure or two who were also present. This book constituted, for the West, a compendium of wisdom on how to think about being a monk.

One might ask how, after two decades, Cassian could have remembered these teachings so well that he could compile them as actual quotes. People of the time, particularly monks, had impressive memories. In addition, in the ancient world, and indeed in subsequent cultures up until the modern period, it was considered acceptable for writers to present their own words as though they were the words of others. Reporting was considered accurate so long as it represented the kinds of things the subjects would have actually said or did. Cassian, however, probably didn't quote the monks accurately all the time, and he was certainly capable of putting his own spin on their words. For example, Cassian insisted on absolute obedience to one's religious superior. *Discretion* was the developed spiritual gift that allowed a monk to determine the wisest course of action, but Cassian interprets this to mean virtually the opposite. In contrast to imagining the virtue as helping one respond creatively to life's challenges, in the *Conferences* it means *not* trusting one's own judgment, but rigorously following the advice of others, the rule of the house, and the unquestioned authority of one's superior, particularly the *abbot* or head of the monastery. This was the monastic way of the West. Another anonymously circulated monastic rule, the *Regula Magistri* or *Rule of the Master*, calls on monks to hand over to the abbot complete responsibility for their souls. At the final judgment, the abbot will be held to account for every decision he made for the monastery and its inhabitants; the monks will be judged only on whether they obeyed his command.

Cassian also shows the enormous influence of Evagrius and others by focusing on contemplation for the purpose of union as the primary goal. This continues to mark a real divergence from the spirit of the earliest monks. In commenting on the biblical story of the hardworking Martha complaining that her sister Mary only wanted to sit by the Lord's feet, Cassian writes, "You will note that the Lord establishes as the prime good contemplation, that is, the gaze turned in the direction of the things of God. Hence we say that the other virtues, however useful and good we may say they are, must nevertheless be put on a secondary level, since they are all practiced for the sake of this one."[23] Cassian describes four kinds of prayer: supplication for beginners; good resolutions for those making progress; intercession for others; and thanksgiving that comes from contemplation of God's goodness. But he also believes that prayer can be a mystical union. In his chapter on prayer he quotes the famous Abba Isaac:

> Yet, sometimes the mind . . . conceiving all of these at one and the same time and rushing through them all like a kind of ungraspable and devouring flame, pours out to God wordless prayers of the purest vigor. These the Spirit itself makes to God as it intervenes with unutterable groans, unbeknownst to us, conceiving at that moment and pouring forth in wordless prayer such great things that they not only—I would say—cannot pass through the mouth but are unable even to be remembered by the mind later on.[24]

Benedict of Nursia (480–547)

The most famous legislator of monasticism in the West is Saint Benedict, whose life-story is known through Pope Gregory the Great's *Dialogues*. Gregory describes a man who radiated love and wisdom and who was gifted with powers of healing and prophecy. Benedict was born in the Nursia region, northeast of Rome, to a prosperous family. He was educated in Rome, but abandoned his life of privilege and embraced an anchorite existence on Mount Subiaco. There

---

23. *Conferences* 1.8. Translations from this work are from John Cassian, *The Conferences*, trans. Boniface Ramsey (New York: Paulist Press, 1997).

24. *Conferences* 9.2.

Lori Goltz c/o www.holyimagesicons.com

Saint Benedict is shown here with his sister, Saint Scholastica, who was abbess of a monastery for women. The artist has placed the two saints on a par, comparable in venerability. In monastic life, women could rise to great prominence and authority.

he gained the reputation of being extraordinarily holy. The monks of Vicovaro asked him to be their abbot, which proved to be disastrous. Benedict was strict while the monks of Vicovaro were not. The monks were so frustrated by him that they tried to poison him, but a miracle thwarted their plans. Benedict returned to Mount Sabiaco and started over, though this time with disciples in large numbers. Soon Benedict established twelve monasteries, each with its own abbot, and he directed another one that was intended for novices who would feed into these other monasteries. The highlight of his monastic career was his final three foundations. The first was on the hills above Cassino, about eighty miles south of Rome. He also built a nearby monastery for women whose abbess was Saint Scholastica, his sister, and the final one about thirty miles away at Terracina. The monastery at Cassino would become the most famous monastery in Western Christendom, and it was there that Benedict wrote his rule. The *Rule of Benedict* became the standard for the whole Latin church, and by the year 800 it was the required rule for all monasteries in the West.

Like all rules, his depicts a particular spirituality. The rule included the usual expectations of obedience to the abbot and rules for fasting, prayer, and work. He also included his famous twelve steps of humility: (1) fearing God, (2) leaving one's desires and renouncing one's will, (3) submitting to a superior,

(4) embracing suffering silently, (5) laying out one's conscience fully to the abbot, (6) being content with low treatment, (7) being convinced one is inferior to all, (8) doing only what is endorsed in the rule, (9) controlling the tongue, (10) not giving in to laughter readily, (11) speaking briefly and soberly, (12) keeping one's head bowed and eyes cast down.[25] This indeed laid out a serious monastic life.

Benedict's Steps for Humility Today?

On first glance, Benedict's steps for humility seems outmoded at best and neurotic at worst. It is, however, possible to see great wisdom in these steps even for today. In *A Guide to Living the Truth*, Benedictine scholar Michael Casey shows how each step constitutes greater interior freedom and availability to others and to God. Consider, for example, steps six and seven.[26] On the surface, they appear self-denigrating. Rightly appropriated, Casey argues, they become the foundation for living in the community peacefully and joyously. He writes, "Nobody contributes less to the common life than those who constantly make demands or attribute absolute importance to their individual desires over the needs of the community as a whole. . . . If I am satisfied with a lower place, it is only to give honor to another. Yielding to others is a concrete means of demonstrating respect and love. . . . The most important element of the sixth step of humility is not the lowly status of the monk, but his contentment."[27]

One of the dramatic shifts in the rule was its leniency and practicality. Given Benedict's own history as a disciplined ascetic and strong, perhaps tyrannical, leader, his rule was surprisingly moderate. It was also flexible, allowing a great deal of freedom in regard to the organization of the monastery, work, and relations among members of the community.

Benedict's rule is filled with a sacramental spirit. The dictum, "the medium is the message," is never truer than in *The Rule of Benedict*. The rule, which is extraordinarily short, is filled with metaphor, most of which imagines the property, life, and people as real mediations of God's grace. Think of the monastery,

---

25. *Rule of Benedict*, 7.

26. I.e., being content with low treatment and being convinced one is inferior to all.

27. Michael Casey, *A Guide to Living the Truth: Saint Benedict's Teaching on Humility* (Liguori, MO: Liguori Press, 2001), 141–43.

the *Rule* teaches, as a school to learn the Lord's service, or as a workshop to build holiness, or as a very altar of God.[28] Consider, the goods of the monastery as though they are vessels of the altar.[29] What would it mean to be working in the field and imagine that one's very pitchfork is as holy as a chalice at Mass? Who is Christ and where is he to be found? The *Rule* answers that he is found in the members of the community, in the abbot, and in any visitor who may come to the monastery.[30] The famous Benedictine hospitality, which still thrives today, is grounded in a spiritual perspective that a visitor is not someone who obstructs the community's silence and prayer, but someone who is Christ before us. The world, which Basil seems to find burdensome and distracting, can be a sacramental place for the monk who looks for holiness everywhere. The monastery is less a place for deep private contemplation away from others than a place for sacramental encounters.

The monastic Liturgy of the Hours consisted of coming to chapel many times a day. Here monks chanted the scriptures, especially the psalms, and listened to classical readings of the monastic spiritual life. An average day in the life of a monk was one of *ora et labora* (prayer and work). Monks rose before dawn for *matins*, which consisted of a lengthy spiritual reading. They then returned to their rooms (cells) to pray. Then they entered the chapel for the first full Liturgy of the Hours, principally chanting the Psalms (*prime* or *lauds*). Then, after breakfast they worked, often in the fields or whatever job they had been assigned to do. Then back to chapel for more scriptural prayer (*terse*); then to work; then to chapel (*sext*); then to lunch and work; then to chapel (*none*); then to work; then to chapel (*vespers*); then to a meal and private reading or prayer; and finally to chapel again (*compline*).

What might seem like an annoying call to chapel again and again, as well as an incredibly inefficient work day, was for them a balanced life where scriptural prayer was ever in their consciousness. The times in chapel during the workday (*terse, sext, none*) were not long and might be considered the monastic version of an extended coffee break. What would life look like if one marked every part of the day as holy with prayer, and continued that prayerful spirit throughout work? For them, it looked grace-filled.

Finally, it is notable that the *Rule* makes no mention of contemplation, mystical union, mystical prayer, or *theoria*. Prayer for Benedict was *lectio divina* (divine reading). Here the vehicle for communion with God does not consist of going beyond concepts and images, but of finding God through them. The Word (Jesus) is encountered in the word (Bible). For them, it was to be enough. This is not to say that there were no mystics in Benedictine monasticism or that

---

28. Ibid., Prologue, 4, 31.

29. Ibid., 31.

30. Ibid., 4, 53.

the monks never knew anything about *aphophatic* prayer. Still, such mysticism does not seem to be a significant part of this monastic culture.

The twelfth-century Carthusian monk Guigo II (d. 1189) describes a way of considering *lectio divina* that does lead to contemplation. This fourfold method of prayer is considered Benedictine, though it does not appear in the *Rule*. One begins by reading the biblical text prayerfully (*lectio*). Then one probes the text and mulls it over, often asking God to move the soul through the biblical word (*meditatio*). Presumably such meditation on the word has indeed moved one to respond to God (*oratio*). Finally, it could be that in communing with God via the word one lets go of thoughts and simply remains with God (*contemplatio*). Guigo II describes it like this:

> Reading comes first and it is as it were a foundation; it provides the subject matter which we must use for meditation. Meditation considers more carefully what is to be sought after; it digs as it were for the treasures which it finds and reveals, but since it is not in meditation's power to seize upon the treasure, it directs us to prayer. Prayer lifts up to God with all its strength and begs for the treasure which it longs for, which is the sweetness of contemplation. Contemplation, when it comes, rewards the labors of the other three; it inebriates the thirsting soul with the dew of heavenly sweetness. Reading is an exercise of the outward senses, meditation is concerned with the inward understanding, prayer is concerned with desire, contemplation outstrips every faculty. The first degree is proper for beginners, the second to proficients, the third to devotees, the fourth to the blessed.[31]

Conclusion

Monastic spirituality dominated the East and to a lesser extent the West by the fifth century. It became the model for what a heroic Christian life should look like. Ordinary Christians marveled at monks' self-control, their silence, and their depth of prayer. They also received ministry from monasteries located near cities. People saw the monastery as the true place where one could meditate on scripture, perform penance, and know God profoundly. While the beginnings of the movement were virtually anti-institutional, the monastery soon became one of the firm cornerstones of institutional Christianity. As noted in chapter 4, the church practiced morning and evening prayer in cathedral churches. The pattern continued for lay Christians. Priests and bishops adopted the monastic

---

31. Guigo II, *The Ladder of Monks: A Letter on the Contemplative Life and Twelve Meditations,* trans. Edmund Colledge and James Walsh (Garden City, NY: Doubleday Image Books, 1978), 92–93.

Liturgy of the Hours, praying the Psalms and other scriptures throughout the day. Monks served as their model. Even today, while priests in the Eastern Orthodox Church can be married, its bishops are only chosen from the ranks of celibate monks. The Eastern Orthodox still think of it as the holiest life and the one from which their highest leaders should come. In the West, a monastic style of life was considered the best training ground and lifestyle for pastoral ministry. Not only did celibacy become the norm for priests, and was demanded by many bishops, but a quasi-monastic life also became common in some dioceses.

This transformation in the spirituality of the church had a downside. People came to see the church as composed of two different kinds of Christians—those who thoroughly embraced the pursuit of interior perfection (monks), and those lay Christians who lived a conventional life. Although challenged at different points in history, this two-tiered framing of the Christian life stuck in Christian imagination until the Reformation of the sixteenth century. While it was acknowledged that anyone, monk or layperson, could become extraordinarily holy, monastic life became the model even for lay people. It was considered the surest means to sanctity.

Questions for Review

1. In what ways does the story of Saint Mary of Egypt serve as a model for those who opted for the monastic lifestyle?
2. What is the difference between anchoritic and cenobitic monasticism? Discuss a figure who exemplifies each type and his contribution to monasticism.
3. How did monasticism develop from its earliest forms to the rules of Basil and Benedict? In what ways did it show continuity and in what ways did it change?

Questions for Discussion

1. Circumstances played a major role in shaping the ideal life for Christians, from martyrdom to monasticism. What forms of the ideal Christian life are particularly striking in the modern period?
2. Monasticism tended to morph from anchoritism to cenobitism. Which form do you think better allows one to achieve the goals of monasticism? Why?
3. The *Life of Antony* highlights one of the goals of monasticism, namely, the quest to encounter one's inherent weakness and thus depend on the strength of Christ. How could this ideal be addressed today?

4. Evagrius saw the harassment of demons in qualities that today would be identified with the human psyche. Do you think that there are demons who harass human beings? How would one distinguish between a psychological trial and a supernatural trial?

5. Given monasticism's rigor, moral purification, and attention to prayer, it seems inevitable that it would take on a kind of elitism. Do you think this is fair or justified? Is monasticism the best lifestyle for the pursuit of Christian spirituality? How would you argue each way?

Bibliography

Resources with annotations are highly recommended to students interested in further study.

Athanasius. *Athanasius: The Life of Antony and the Letter to Marcellinus.* Translated by Robert Gregg. New York: Paulist Press, 1980.

Athanasius's biography of Antony served the patristic church with a model of eremitical monasticism.

Basil of Caesarea. *Saint Basil: Ascetical Works.* Translated by Monica Wagner. New York: Fathers of the Church, Inc., 1950.

This volume contains Basil's fundamentals of the spiritual life as well as both his longer and shorter monastic rules.

Benedict of Nursia. *The Rule of St. Benedict.* Translated by Timothy Fry. Collegeville, MN: Liturgical Press, 1982.

Casey, Michael. *A Guide to Living in the Truth: Saint Benedict's Teaching on Humility.* Liguori, MO: Liguori Press, 2001.

This text follows the twelve steps of humility in Benedict's rule and shows how they can be appropriated today in a healthy, modern manner.

Cassian, John. *The Conferences.* Translated by Boniface Ramsey. New York: Paulist Press, 1997.

This is a lengthy collection of the teachings of the Egyptian monastic fathers. It served as inspiration for Western monks.

Cassian, John. *The Institutes.* Translated by Boniface Ramsey. New York: Newman Press, 2000.

Chryssavgis, John. *In the Heart of the Desert: Spirituality of the Desert Fathers and Mothers.* Bloomington, IN: World Wisdom, 2008.

Earle, Mary. *The Desert Mothers: Spiritual Practices from the Women of the Wilderness.* New York: Morehouse, 2007.

Gribomont, Jean. "Monasticism and Asceticism: Eastern Christianity." In *Christian Spirituality*, edited by Bernard McGinn, John Meyendorff, and Jean Leclercq, 1:89–112. New York: Crossroad, 1988.

Guigo II. *The Ladder of Monks: A Letter on the Contemplative Life* and *Twelve Meditations*. Translated by Edmund Colledge and James Walsh. Garden City, NY: Doubleday Image Books, 1978.

Hausherr, Irenee. *Penthos: The Doctrine of Compunction in the Christian East.* Kalamazoo, MI: Cistercian Publications, 1982.

This small volume examines the Greek monastic understanding of cultivating *penthos* or sorrow for one's sins.

Healey, Charles. *Christian Spirituality: An Introduction to the Heritage.* New York: St. Pauls, 1999.

Leclercq, Jean. *The Love of Learning and the Desire for God: A Study of Monastic Culture.* Translated by Catharine Misrahi. New York: Fordham University Press, 1961. This study examines the role of literacy and education in Western monasticism.

Leclercq, Jean. "Monasticism and Asceticism: Western Christianity." In *Christian Spirituality*, edited by Bernard McGinn, John Meyendorff, and Jean Leclercq, 1:113–31. New York: Crossroad, 1988.

Louth, Andrew. *The Origins of the Christian Mystical Tradition: From Plato to Denys.* Oxford: Oxford University Press, 2007.

McGinn, Bernard. *The Growth of Mysticism: Gregory the Great through the Twelfth Century.* New York: Crossroad, 1994.

Merton, Thomas. *The Wisdom of the Desert.* New York: New Directions, 1970.

Palmer, G. E. H., Philip Sherrard, and Kallistos Ware, eds. and trans. *The Philokalia.* 4 Vols. London: Faber and Faber, 1979–1995.

These four volumes constitute the premier collection of sayings of the desert fathers as well as the spiritual teachings of Orthodox bishops.

Regnault, Lucien. *The Day-to-Day Life of the Desert Fathers in Fourth-Century Egypt.* Petersham, MA: St. Bede's Publications, 1999.

Swan, Laura. *The Forgotten Desert Mothers: Sayings, Lives, and Stories of Early Christian Women.* Mahwah, NJ: Paulist Press: 2001.

Tugwell, Simon. *Ways of Imperfection: An Exploration of Christian Spirituality.* Springfield, IL: Templegate, 1985.

Ward, Benedicta. *Harlots of the Desert: A Study of Repentance in Early Monastic Sources.* Kalamazoo, MI: Cistercian Publications, 1987.

This book examines the stories of women converts who took on a monastic life. Their conversion biographies stood as exemplars for the early monastic ethos.

Ward, Benedicta, ed. and trans. *The Sayings of the Desert Fathers: The Alphabetical Collection.* Kalamazoo, MI: Cistercian Publications, 1975.

Internet Resources

The Denver Post. "Photos: Ancient Christian Monastery near Cairo, Egypt.". *http://photos.denverpost.com/2013/04/18/photos-ancient-christian-monastery-near-cairo-egypt/#1.*

> Photographs of an ancient monastery of Saint Anthony, southeast of Cairo, Egypt.

Evangelical Monasticism. *www.prayerfoundation.org/dailyoffice/evangelical_monasticism.htm.*

> Website detailing practices and lifestyles regarding "Evangelical Monasticism."

Funkystock. "Photos and Pictures of Meteora Monasteries, Greece." *www.funkystockphotos.com/PICTURES-OF-GREECE/METEORA-MONASTERIES-GREECE-PICTURES-PHOTOS-IMAGES.html.*

> Photographs of ancient Greek monasteries.

"Monks of the Desert—Meet the Monks of the Desert." *www.youtube.com/watch?v=U5YY684ZXDE.*

> A Sony documentary of an isolated American monastery (9 min.).

Peters, Gregg. "The New Monasticism Gets Older." *www.firstthings.com/web-exclusives/2014/03the-new-monasticism-gets-older.*

> Article describing new versions of monasticism for Protestant Christians and even their families.

Films

Into Great Silence [German: *Di Große Stille*]. 2005

> A documentary portrayal of the everyday lives of Carthusian monks of the Grande Chartreuse, a monastery high in the French Alps.

Of Gods and Men. 2005.

> A true story of the Benedictine monks of Atlas, Algeria who were fully integrated into their Islamic town and beloved by the community, but were tragically killed by Algerian terrorists.

Eastern Orthodox Spirituality

There was a great deal of cohesion among Christian spiritualities until the Protestant Reformation of the sixteenth century, even though not all Christians were in communion with each other. For example, in the patristic era the Assyrian and Coptic churches broke communion over theological disputes, and in 1054 the Greek Church and the Latin Church broke communion over issues of jurisdiction. Nevertheless, when one looks at these various churches' spiritualities, one finds great similarities. The greatest differences among these various communions have to do with emphases. This chapter intends to highlight the emphases in the Eastern Orthodox Church, which developed rich traditions in art, liturgy, and prayer.

What particularly marks Orthodoxy is a holistic sense of religion. The Orthodox make little separation between theology, spirituality, liturgy, mysticism, and piety; they all imply and mutually inform each other. To the Orthodox, the Eucharist, for example, is a ritual of theology. It is a theology of the incarnation, because in the Eucharist the Orthodox experience Christ and commune with his incarnate body. It is a theology of salvation (soteriology), because by that very communion one gains something of the life of heaven and progresses toward divinization by assimilating oneself to Christ. Finally, it is a theology of the church (ecclesiology), for through the sacrament the church expresses its deepest nature, a living body of Christ.

This chapter will explore the spiritualities of icons, liturgy, devotion to Mary, and forms of prayer particularly important to the Orthodox. Roman Catholicism as well as those ancient churches who broke off during the patristic era share all of these spiritual impulses, much of the theology behind them, and many similar practices. The aim here is to focus on the particular way the Eastern Orthodox Church engages them.

Icons: Channels of Divine Encounter

The incarnation of God in Jesus Christ is central to the Christian message. Such a message is inconceivable from the perspective of Platonic philosophy, in which the created world is at best a poor mediator of the divine and at worst a burden and a problem. In contrast, Christianity proclaimed that the Uncreated God united himself to the created world in Jesus. The body, and indeed all physical realities, could mediate the divine. Admittedly, the passions posed a problem; thus *apophatic* mysticism sought to transcend the limits of the created world. Still the world and the body were gifts, and through them one could encounter God's grace.[1]

As noted in chapter 5, Dionysius believed that one could engage a concrete expression of the faith and use it to move beyond the physical toward the conceptual, and then transcend even that to the spiritual. He saw this represented in the nature of the church, in the sacraments, and even in contemplating the created world. Dionysius represented a broad Christian understanding. Couple this conviction with the ultimate witness of God made human in Jesus, and the church saw sacramental possibilities everywhere. One of the most important was in iconography. An icon (Greek: *eikōn*) is an image, and the early church used icons that represented Christ, the saints, and even the Eucharist.

One might imagine that any icons of God would be forbidden for Christians because of the second commandment.[2] During the icon controversy that ebbed and flowed between the eighth and ninth centuries, some argued that Old Testament archetypes had been fulfilled in the person of the incarnate Son and therefore this restriction no longer applied. God himself had lifted the proscription. God had become visible in the Son and thus could be represented in graphic form.

In some ways the icons from the patristic age reflected the art of the time. Both pagan and Christian art looked flat and two-dimensional. Saints and Jesus had halos like those that pagans gave to their gods. Christians, however, developed new style. The art of antiquity strove to represent their subjects as accurately as possible, using shading and a rather sophisticated sense of light. Christian iconographers avoided this, opting instead for symbolic use of colors with an emphasis on depicting harmony and inner stillness. Icons were not meant to evoke an emotional response, but rather to cultivate contemplation. Looking at the facial expressions of icons, one might think that the person depicted in the image was emotionless. The image does not seem to communicate joy. Christians use icons in a specific way. One contemplates the icon, goes through it, and enters the realm of contemplation that the icon intends to facilitate. Any emotionally charged expressions would compromise such a contemplative approach.

---

1. Saint John of Damascus wrote, "I do not worship matter. I worship the Creator of matter who became matter for my sake, who willed to take his abode in matter, and through matter wrought my salvation." John of Damascus, *On the Divine Images* 1.16. Translation from John of Damascus, *On the Divine Images*, trans. David Anderson (Crestwood, NY: St. Vladimir's Seminary Press, 1980), 23.

2. "You shall not make for yourself an idol or a likeness of anything in the heavens above or on the earth below or in the waters beneath the earth; you shall not bow down before them or serve them" (Exod. 20:4–5).

Icons generated controversy in the Eastern Church during the Middle Ages. An iconoclastic (literally "breaking images") movement emerged full-force during two periods (730–787 and 813–843). Some objected that icons were idols. A second objection draws more on Christian Platonism. As seen in Origen, some Christians believed that a wide gulf separated spirit and matter. The material world was an obstacle to prayer, something one had to overcome and transcend. One achieved such transcendence not by going through the material world to the spiritual, as Dionysius believed, but by setting aside the material world altogether. This argument gains additional credence from the works of the some of the great apophatic mystical writings of the church fathers.

The issue of icons had broad implications. If icons were permitted, should they be venerated? Could one offer incense or light candles before them? Could one carry them in procession and even kiss them? These were not abstract questions, but pertained to the actual practices of Christians, which iconoclasts claimed were inappropriate.

In 787 the Seventh Ecumenical Council (Nicaea II) defended icons, and the *iconodule* position (from *eikōn*, "icon," and *doulia*, "service, veneration"). The council distinguished between worship (*latreia*), which is only given to God, and veneration (*douleia*), which can be offered to persons or objects associated to God, including images of Christ and the saints. The council first pointed out that icons have been part of Christianity from the start. Thus iconography is a decided part of the apostolic tradition.[3] Second, the council described icons as fruitful in facilitating true veneration toward what they represent:

> The more frequently they are seen in representational art, the more are those who see them drawn to remember and long for those who serve as models, and to apply these images the tribute of salutation and respectful veneration. Certainly this is not the full adoration in accordance with our faith, which is properly paid only to the divine nature, but it resembles that given to the figure of the honored and life-giving cross, and also to the holy books of the gospel. . . . Further, people are drawn to honor these images with the offering of incense and lights, as was piously established by ancient custom. Indeed, the honor paid to an image traverses it, reaching the model and he who venerates the image, venerates the person represented in that image.[4]

---

3. Nicaea declares: "The tradition of making painted images . . . existed already in the time of apostolic preaching. . . . The holy fathers witness to it, and the historians whose writings have been preserved until our times, confirm it." Translation from Leonid Oupensky, "Icon and Art," in *Christian Spirituality*, ed. Bernard McGinn, John Meyendorff, and Jean Leclercq (New York: Crossroad, 1988), 1:382–94, at 382–83.

4. Translation from Christopher Bellitto, *The General Councils: A History of the Twenty-One Church Councils from Nicaea to Vatican II* (New York: Paulist Press, 2002), 32.

These two main arguments by Nicaea II do not fully address the spirituality of icons. Nicaea does hint at the theological issue: "[Icons] guarantee that the incarnation of God the Word is true and not illusory."[5] What it addresses here is part of a Christian doctrine of creation. The materiality of the human being is spiritually potent, but so too is the Spirit-bearing potential of all material things directed to God. Humans are not saved *from* the material world, but *with* the material world. Further, humans are the pinnacle of this creation, and thus depiction of humans in a spiritual manner is particularly laudable. As Saint Theodore the Studite, one of the great supporters of iconography, insisted, "The fact that the human person is made in the image and likeness of God means that the making of icons is in some way a divine work."[6]

Writing an Icon

Artists who create icons typically do not refer to their work as *painting* an icon, but rather as *writing* an icon. The practice is called *iconography* (Greek, *eikōn*—image and *graphein*—to write). For them, icons act as meditations on and interpretations of deep truths of the faith. We might consider it a part of the gospel narrative in visual form. As one Russian monk reflected, "Icons are not civil paintings. They are not for museums. They are not decorations. They are a reflection of God that has become man. Icons carry the real feeling and teachings of Orthodoxy."[7]

Traditionally, Iconographers fast and pray for days before beginning their work. When they create icons ideally they are not so much expressing their own personal piety or idiosyncratic creativity as they are articulating the shared faith of Orthodoxy. They consider themselves something as co-creators with God and their tradition. As Iconographer Nicusor Dumitru reflects, "The art of painting comes from God, who alone can guide the painter's hand to give form to the mysteries of God. . . . Painting an icon is a liturgical work."[8]

---

5. Translation from Kallistos Ware, "The Spirituality of the Icon," in *The Study of Spirituality*, ed. Cheslyn Jones, Geoffrey Wainwright, and Edward Yarnold (New York: Oxford University Press 1986), 196.

6. Theodore the Studite, *On the Holy Icons* 3.2.5. Translation from *On the Holy Icons*, trans. C. P. Roth (Crestwood, NY: St. Vladimir's Seminary Press, 1981), cited in Ware, "The Spirituality of the Icon," 197.

7. See *http://www.stlukeorthodox.com/html/iconography/iconhistory.cfm*.

8. Ibid.

Icons do not merely serve as visual aids in Orthodox spirituality. They work like sacramental channels of divine encounter. Icons invite the worshipper to enter into the dimensions of sacred space and time and thus commune with the mystery they depict. They are instruments and vehicles of prayer, just like the rites of the sacraments. Orthodox Christians commonly speak of two ways of praying, one iconic and the other imageless. These do not represent two exclusive paths, but mutually enriching possibilities; each deepens the other.

Liturgical Prayer

[handwritten: = The Work of the ppl in public → Sacraments that Present reality]

Historically, the most important activity Christians performed was liturgy. The Greek term *leitourgia* refers to a work or action that people performed in public. The ancient Greek version of the Old Testament (Septuagint) uses *leitourgia* to refer to public religious services offered to God by priests in the temple. In the church, they refer to the sacraments, particularly the Eucharist.

What Are Sacraments?

In brief, sacraments are liturgical rites that use symbols, which in the Christian view mediate divine realities. Here a symbol does not merely represent or point to ultimate realties, but *presents* those realities. Symbols not only disclose sacred truth, but enable participants to enter into the presence of God's grace through them. They serve as divine models or archetypal forms that participants ritually engage and that allow them to experience the very realities represented.

Typically, sacraments involve a series of symbols and activities that reach back to saving events in the past in order to experience the same grace of the events here and now. This is not simply recalling a past event and praying to God that these events could be renewed. The technical term, *anamnēsis* (literally "remembering" or "recalling") in this context means to *re-member*. That is, it brings *membership* to those involved with the very event or saving dynamic being celebrated. Through liturgy, participants enter into the original event here and now and experience its transforming power. The following two examples of Eastern Orthodox liturgical prayer could also be prime examples of Roman Catholic liturgy. In both churches these rituals embody each tradition's core essence. The purpose here is to highlight these two sacraments in the particular way that the Orthodox celebrate them.

Baptism

Baptism, the initiation rite that makes a person a Christian, is a chief example of Christian liturgy. The Orthodox baptismal liturgy is complex and the prayers used in it are long. The following is a shorthand explanation of the liturgy of baptism.[9] It begins with the priest coming from the altar to the back of the church where the baptismal font is located. He offers incense around the altar and then blesses the water, ultimately praying, "O Loving King, be present now also through the descent of your Holy Spirit and hallow this water." If the one baptized is an infant, then the godparents articulate the faith on behalf of the child. They "renounce Satan, and all his angels, and all his works, and all his pride" and they promise on behalf of the child to unite to Christ. They then profess the Nicene Creed on behalf of the child and the child is formally named and received into the church. The godparents are then given a lit candle to hold, representing the light of Christ. The church expects the baptized person to bring this same candle to church for major events, such as marriage.

The infant is then anointed with blessed oil on the breast and back for healing of body and soul; on the ears for hearing the faith; on the feet so as to walk the path of God; and on the hands recognizing God as one's creator. The infant is baptized in the naked state by three immersions: "The servant of God (name) is baptized in the name of the Father [first immersion]. Amen. And of the Son [second immersion]. Amen. And of the Holy Spirit [third immersion]. Amen."

The practice in the Orthodox Church is that all those initiated receive the sacraments of Baptism, Confirmation, and Eucharist at the same service. Orthodox call Confirmation *Chrismation*, which refers to being anointed. Thus there is a second anointing with oil, this to "seal" or "confirm" the newly baptized with the Holy Spirit and preserve this new life of faith. At one point the priest prays:

> Compassionate King of all, bestow upon her also the seal of Your omnipotent and adorable Holy Spirit, and the Communion of the Holy Body and Most Precious Blood of Your Christ; keep her in Your sanctification; confirm her in the Orthodox faith; deliver her from the Evil One and all his devices; preserve her soul, through Your saving fear, in purity and righteousness, that in every work and word, being acceptable before You, she may become a child and heir of Your heavenly kingdom."

Following this prayer, the priest anoints the eyes, nostrils, mouth, ears, breast, hands, and feet. At each anointing he says, "The seal of the gift of the Holy Spirit, Amen."

The child is dressed in a new white garment, signifying a new life in Christ, and the priest and godparents circle the baptismal font three times while the choir sings, "As many of you as have been baptized into Christ, have put on

---

9. The following texts and explanations come from "The Sacrament of Holy Baptism in the Orthodox Christian Church," *www.orthodoxchristian.info/pages/Baptism.htm*, and "Zoe Eliza Tzanis: Baptism," *view.officeapps.live.com/op/view.aspx?src=http%3A%2F%2Fwww.tzanis.org%2Fzoe%2FBaptism %2FGREEK%2520ORTHODOX%2520BAPTISM-final3.doc.*

Christ. Alleluia." At this point of the liturgy, the priest reads a selection from Romans (6:3–11), where Paul describes baptism as entering the tomb of Christ so as to be united to him in his Resurrection. Then he reads from the Gospel of Matthew (26:16–20), where Jesus commands his disciples to baptize and make disciples of all nations. Initiation ends with the ritual of "tonsure," whereby the priest cuts four locks of hair from the child's head in the form of a cross. It is considered a first-offering to God.

The *anamnēsis* here—what is being re-membered—consists of many layers. The prayers and pronouncements of the priest reference Jesus' baptism in the river Jordan. After Jesus' baptism, according to the Gospels, he heard God proclaim, "You are my beloved Son; with you I am well pleased" (Luke 3:22). Jesus' divine sonship was proclaimed and realized at this moment. So too upon baptism, understood sacramentally, one realizes one's status as a son or daughter of God, co-heir with Christ himself (Rom. 8:17). Baptism is also an experience of the tomb and Resurrection. In Baptism, one takes on a new identity.

The candle given to the one baptized is bestowed with the words, "Receive the light of Christ," and the anointing with oil serves as an additional identification with Christ, for the term *Christ* means "Anointed One." This ritual identification with Christ comes by entering into his ministry and saving death and Resurrection. The newly baptized is now clothed in Christ.

The emphasis in the Orthodox Church holds particular interest. In the Latin tradition, the prayers of the priest emphasize being freed from original sin, the burden of sin inherited from Adam and Eve. Orthodox spirituality, particularly in its more ancient expressions, includes no mention original sin. Rather, it emphasizes becoming a new creation. Although Saint Cyril of Jerusalem does mention the sin of Adam and Eve in his teaching on baptism, he does so only to contrast Adam's shame with a Christian's purity:

> You were stripped of your clothing, and this is an image of the putting off the old man with his deeds. Having stripped yourselves, you were naked; in this also imitating Christ who was naked on the cross, and in his nakedness spoiled principalities and powers and openly trampled them on the tree. . . . Oh marvel, you were naked before all, and you were not ashamed. For, in truth, you were in the image of the first man, Adam, who was naked in paradise and not ashamed."[10]

Focused on the new life in the Spirit, the ancient Greek Church referred to the baptismal font as a *womb* out of which a newly reborn person emerges.

---

10. Cyril of Jerusalem, *Mystagogical Catechesis* 2.2, Translation from Paul Meyendorff, "Liturgy and Spirituality: Eastern Liturgical Theology," in McGinn et al., eds., *Christian Spirituality*, 1:350–63, at 355.

Eucharist

Orthodox Christians, as well as Roman Catholics and many other Christian denominations, consider the Eucharist the premier sacrament. In the Eucharist, the *anamnēsis* is many-layered. On one level, it represents entering into the dynamics of the Last Supper. In the Gospel accounts, Jesus drew his disciples together during the Passover (Seder) supper, the Jewish celebration of God's liberating love as experienced in their Exodus from slavery. During this highly symbolic meal Jesus announced his new and eternal covenant. Now, instead of simply addressing liberation from slavery, this covenant would liberate one from sin and death and formally inaugurate the kingdom of God.

Jesus takes bread and identifies it with his body; then he takes wine and identifies it with his own blood. In doing so, he anticipates his sacrifice on the cross the very next day. The covenant with Moses was ratified with the slaughtering of sacrificial animals and with their blood being splashed on the people.[11] In contrast, this covenant would be ratified with Jesus' own blood. Here he becomes both priest and victim. Jesus has the disciples eat the bread and drink from the cup, his Body and Blood, as an expression of communion with him and with his covenant. He also implicates them in his self-offering, for they are to follow his way and offer themselves to God.[12]

Understood thus, the new covenant is both Christ's (and his disciples') self-offering and God's definitive victory, leading to the participants' radical communion with one another and with Christ. Such a victory was definitively caused by Jesus' Resurrection and guarantees the fullest communion with God in heaven. So the communion they share also offers a foretaste of the heavenly union with God; it marks a real uniting here and now even as it anticipates the fullest union in the afterlife.

Orthodox Christians, emphasizing that in the Eucharist heaven and earth have merged, engage in a kind of heavenly liturgy. The church buildings themselves are designed to draw one into such a spiritual posture.[13]

Entering an Orthodox church can be a dazzling experience. The dome above the gathering space typically has an enormous painting of Jesus as *pantocratōr* (ruler of all), sometimes surrounded by angels and saints. Icons of saints are everywhere. The sanctuary, where the altar is located, is separated from the main church by a series of icons called the *iconostasis*. From the pews, one can see into the sanctuary but only above the icons, or as the Orthodox might say

---

11. "This is the blood of the covenant which the Lord has made with you" (Exod. 24:8).

12. Matt. 10:38; Mark 8:34; Luke 17:33; John 12:25.

13. To cite one example, in 988 Prince Vladimir of Kiev sent ambassadors to Constantinople on a formal visitation. They observed the Eucharist being celebrated at the great cathedral church *Hagia Sophia* (Holy Wisdom). They reported that they did not know whether they were still on earth or in heaven. According to the *Russian Primary Chronicle,* it was this very experience that led the Russians to adopt the Orthodox faith.

An iconostasis in an Orthodox church in Jerusalem. It depicts saints surrounding the sanctuary while the congregation partially sees around them and "through" them to the altar reserved for clergy and acolytes.

through the icons. The iconostasis separates the laity from the priest at the altar, but does not block their view of him.

The sanctuary works like a kind of holy of holies, that sacred place in the ancient Jewish temple reserved for the Ark of the Covenant. So holy was this space that ancient Jews tied a rope around the high priest who entered it just in case he had an absolute encounter with God and died. Who would want to retrieve the body in this circumstance? With the rope at least they could drag him out. While this circumstance never came to pass, ancient Jews considered the holy of holies an awesome place that could overwhelm. An Orthodox sanctuary has the same kind of spiritual impact. It is particularly holy, an overwhelming meeting place between God and the church. Indeed, the whole building's architecture and art underscores the fact that one has entered into a space with profound divine possibilities.

The most common liturgy is the rite of Saint John Chrysostom.[14] The liturgy opens with a series of prayers and hymns, each led by the deacon, with the people chanting a response, and the priest offering a concluding prayer. All of these have been memorized by the congregation and so function like a kind of sung dance of prayers between the deacon and the people. It is highly rhythmic and meditative.

---

14. The Liturgy of St. John Chrysostom, *www.ocf.org/OrthodoxPage/liturgy/liturgy.html*. All subsequent quotations come from this source.

In the next part of the liturgy the priest and servers carry the book of the Gospels in procession. The priest then offers a prayer that emphasizes that just as God is glorified by the heavenly hosts so Christians glorify him before the altar. Heaven and earth start to merge here. The priest recognizes that all are sinners, but reminds God that they have been redeemed. Even so, as a preparation for the authentic worship, he asks God to forgive their sins that they might worship him purely. Following this prayer, an epistle and Gospel are read and a sermon (homily) given. More litanies and prayers follow.

The initial entrance of the priest with the book of the Gospels is called the "Little Entrance." The next procession, following the scripture proclamation, is known as the "Great Entrance." This consists of a much more elaborate procession of the priest, deacons, and servers throughout the church. They carry the bread and wine to be consecrated as well as incense and fans, which represent the wings of the attending angels before God. The lengthy prayers are designed to prepare the heart of the community members for the Eucharist proper.[15]

The word *Eucharist* means "thanksgiving," and the main Eucharistic prayer thanks God for all the ways God has saved the human race through Jesus Christ. The prayer moves to the consecration of the bread and wine with the words believed to be those of Jesus himself:

> Take, eat, this is my Body which is broken for you for the forgiveness of sins. . . . Drink of it all of you; this is my Blood of the new Covenant which is shed for you and for many for the forgiveness of sins.

The prayer continues with the request for the Father to send the Holy Spirit upon the people gathered and the gifts so they may be changed for the sake of the people: "Make this bread the precious Body of Your Christ. And that which is in this cup the precious Blood of Your Christ. . . . So that they may be to those who partake of them for vigilance of soul, forgiveness of sins, communion of Your Holy Spirit, fulfillment of the kingdom of heaven, confidence before You, and not in judgment or condemnation."

The Eucharistic prayer continues by honoring Mary and the saints, and commemorating all who have died. It further prays that such worship advance the salvation of all. Throughout the prayer, the people chant (or say) responses in due order, so that they not only silently pray with the priest, but also participate actively in the prayer. The community then collectively prays the Lord's Prayer and lines up to receive communion, while the congregation (or choir) sings, "We have seen the true Light; we have received the heavenly Spirit; we have found the true faith, worshipping the undivided Trinity; for this has saved us."

---

15. One particularly striking prayer reads, "We who mystically represent the Cherubim sing the thrice holy hymn to the life giving Trinity. Let us set aside all the cares of life that we may receive the King of all invisibly escorted by the Angelic Hosts. Alleluia!"

Further prayers and blessings conclude the service, and people leave after receiving blessed (but not consecrated) bread to be eaten for the journey back into the world. It communicates the idea that they are leaving heaven. The elaborate and intentionally other-worldly liturgy typically takes one and a half to two hours to perform.

The Eucharist stands at the center of Orthodox spirituality. Members celebrate and evermore become what they are and are meant to be, that is, fully members of the mystical body of Christ and sharers in the divine life.

Devotion to Mary

One Protestant critique of Roman Catholics has to do with devotion to the saints, particularly Mary. Protestant Reformer Ulrich Zwingli considered the Roman Catholic veneration of Mary and the saints heretical and blasphemous. Yet devotion to the saints and especially to Mary is even more elaborate among the Orthodox, for whom Mary has a central place as a figure or type of the church and an archetype of one's very soul.

PavleMarjanovic / Shutterstock.com

While the Latin Church always had a love for Mary and saw her as both exemplar and intercessor par excellence, large-scale devotion to Mary came relatively late.[16] In contrast, from early on Orthodox writers devoted a great deal of space and energy to Mary.

The Orthodox see Mary as related to Christ's work in every way. She is the archetypal recipient of the Word-made-flesh, the model for everyone's reception of Christ in their own souls. Many ancient liturgical hymns depict Mary as the "bride of God."

A mosaic icon of Mary and Jesus at the Hagia Sophia Cathedral in Istanbul, Turkey. The abbreviations on either side of Mary identify her as *Matēr Theou*, "Mother of God."

During the feast of the Entry of the Theotokos [God Bearer] into the Temple,

---

16. Augustine's *Confessions*, for example, includes no reference to her, which seems odd given that the book is all about his conversion, new faith, and important discussions about an authentic life of Christian piety.

one strikingly beautiful prayer reads, "O Virgin, fed in faith by heavenly bread in the temple of the Lord, thou hast brought forth unto the world the Bread of Life, that is, the Word; and as his chosen temple without spot thou was betrothed mystically through the Spirit, to be the Bride of God the Father."[17]

Theological themes in the patristic era include an increasing parallel between Mary and Eve. While Eve's disobedience brought a curse into the world that led to death, Mary's obedience brought life into the world that leads to salvation. The Orthodox appeal to Mary repeatedly in virtually all rituals and many prayers and consider her to be utterly integral to how God blesses the world. In fact, there is more Orthodox iconography of Mary than of any other saint, even more than Jesus himself. She is not merely an exemplar, but a virtual feminine expression of God's love. The Orthodox do not confuse Mary with the Trinity or bypass the Trinity because of her. They would frame it this way: Mary intercedes for us and is our patron. God wills this because he wants to bless us through her presence in the mystical body of Christ. For the Orthodox, one does not properly love God without also venerating Mary, and those who venerate Mary properly find that she always leads to her Son. Many liturgical texts, in fact, refer to her as "Light-Bearer." She enlightens the way to the Trinity.

Prayer and Contemplation
Standing before God Unceasingly

The great nineteenth-century Russian bishop, spiritual director, and eventual hermit, Theophan the Recluse, once wrote, "What God asks for is the heart; and it is enough that we should stand before Him with reverence. Standing before God with reverence is unceasing prayer: such is its exact description."[18] From this short piece of wisdom, Theophan makes three central points of the Orthodox spirituality of prayer. First, prayer is standing before God, meaning that prayer does not necessarily entail asking for things or even speaking. Prayer is a meeting between the soul and God: one does not necessarily stand, but one places oneself immediately before God, face to face as it were. Second, Theophan refers to the heart. In the Orthodox view, the heart has always represented the deepest center of one's existence, not just one's emotions. Third, prayer ought to be unceasing. Such an aim follows Saint Paul's exhortation: "Pray without ceasing" (1 Thess. 5:17).

Orthodox Christians have tried to take this quite literally, not by considering everything prayer, but by doing everything in a spirit of constant communion with God. The great spiritual master John Climacus wrote, "Let the

---

17. See *www.pravoslavie.ru/english/66118.htm.*

18. Translation from Igumen Chariton and Timothy Ware, eds., *The Art of Prayer: An Orthodox Anthology,* trans. E. Kadloubovsky and E. M. Palmer. (London: Faber and Faber, 1997), 83.

remembrance of Jesus be present with your every breath."[19] This lofty goal cannot be attained quickly or easily. But, they argued, it can indeed be cultivated and attained. As Theophan wrote,

> When he who prays is wholly concentrated within his heart and mentally contemplates God, present to him and within him . . . he experiences the feelings corresponding to such a state—fear of God and worshipful admiration of Him in all his greatness; faith and hope; love and surrender to his will; contrition and readiness for every sacrifice. He who prays thus for a long time and in the proper way will enjoy such a state more and more frequently until it may finally become permanent: then it can be called walking before God, and constitutes unceasing prayer.[20]

The Jesus Prayer

One of the most popular expressions of prayer, and one that leads to unceasing prayer, is the *Jesus Prayer*. By the thirteenth century, it had become a method of contemplation. First, one sat with head and shoulders bowed, with the gaze of the eyes toward the place of the heart. One attempts to physically symbolize what the ancient Greek monks called the "descending of the mind into the heart," where intellect, emotions, and soul unite. Second, the one praying would slow down the speed of breathing and coordinate the Jesus Prayer to his or her inhalation and exhalation. The inhalation of the breath is imagined as a physical exercise of having the mind descend into the heart. Beginners start by using words, but as prayer intensifies or as one gets more used to the prayer, it becomes a silent prayer coming from one's center. While the words vary in the tradition, a typical version would consist of repeating the words "Lord Jesus Christ" on the inhalation and "have mercy on me" on the exhalation.

This prayer has four elements: the invocation of the name of Jesus, in itself considered spiritually powerful; the appeal to God's mercy, accompanied by a spirit of *penthos*, or compunction; the repetition of the words as with each slow breath, the prayer is repeated again and again, sometimes for hours at a stretch; the eventual movement to non-discursive, non-conceptual apophatic prayer, as at a certain point, one becomes the prayer.

The most famous modern expression of this prayer is the anonymous Russian classic, *The Way of the Pilgrim*. This tells the story of a humble peasant who wishes to become a man of prayer, but finds himself filled with distractions. He visits a spiritual elder who teaches him this prayer. At first, the master instructs

---

19. John Climacus *The Ladder of Divine Ascent*, trans. Colm Luibheid and Norman Russell (New York: Paulist Press, 1982), 270.

20. As cited in Chariton and Ware, eds., *The Art of Prayer*, 85.

him to say this prayer 3,000 times a day. For the first several days, the pilgrim finds this very difficult, almost impossible. However, he gets used to it and starts to find his mind and heart becoming increasingly centered, and his love for God increasing. On the next month's visit, the master tells him to recite it 6,000 times a day. He soon learns how to achieve this. On the third visit, he is instructed to pray this 12,000 times a day. He exhorts the pilgrim to get up earlier and go to bed later, and it turns out that the prayer itself is so centering and subtly energizing that he needs less sleep. Finally, it is as though his heart is praying this prayer constantly. "I stopped vocalizing the prayer and began to listen attentively as the heart spoke."[21]

According to the pilgrim, the prayer bears fruit in three ways: in the spirit, in the emotions, and in revelations.

> In the spirit one can experience the sweetness of the love of God, inner peace, purity of thought, awareness of God's presence, and ecstasy. In the emotions a pleasant warmth of the heart, a feeling of delight throughout one's being, joyful bubbling of the heart, lightness and courage, joy of life, indifference to sickness and sorrow. And in revelation, one receives the enlightenment of the mind, understanding of Holy Scripture, knowledge of speech of all creatures, renunciation of vanities, awareness of the sweetness of the interior life, and confidence in the nearness of God and his love for us.[22]

Conclusion

As mentioned in the beginning of this chapter, the Orthodox have a particular gift in unifying theology and spirituality. They often repeat a dictum from Evagrius: "If you are a theologian you truly pray. If you pray you are a theologian."[23]

In the Orthodox understanding of icons, while God's beauty cannot be seen, it can be engaged through representations that take one beyond what is being depicted to the realm of spirit, where the soul experiences divine beauty itself. The Orthodox do not say that someone "painted" an icon. Rather, they say that one "wrote" an icon, in the same way that the Bible is written. Icons represent revelation in art. Orthodox understanding of sacraments is rich with layers of theology, piety, and even mysticism. They literally ritualize their identity, their understanding of the church's relationship to God, how one becomes

---

21. *Way of the Pilgrim.* Translation from *The Way of the Pilgrim* and *The Pilgrim Continues His Way,* trans. Helen Bacovcin (New York: Image Books: 1992), 26.

22. Ibid., 41.

23. Evagrius, *Chapters on Prayer* 60. Translation from Evagrius Ponticus, *The Praktikos and Chapters on Prayer,* trans. John Eudes Bamberger (Kalamazoo, MI: Cistercian Publications, 1981), 65.

holy, and even how one could participate in a foretaste of heaven while still here on earth. Devotions to saints, particularly Mary, reveal their understanding of what discipleship ought to look like and how Christ graces the church through the mediation of his mother. Finally, for them prayer is transformative. The Pilgrim, an unlettered peasant, discovers a deep, profound understanding of scripture because of his union with God. Further, he understands the created world more profoundly through this union. Bishop Kallistos of Diokleia describes Orthodox spirituality in the following exhortation: "Become what you are. Become consciously and actively, what you already are potentially and secretly, by virtue of your creation according to the divine image and your re-creation at baptism."[24]

Questions for Review

1. What role do icons play in the spirituality of the Eastern Orthodox Church?
2. What complaints were raised against icons and how did their defenders respond?
3. How do the Eastern Orthodox understand the Eucharist, and what are some distinct features of their understanding?
4. What role does Mary play in Eastern Orthodoxy?

Questions for Discussion

1. The debates between the iconoclasts, those who forbade images, and the iconodules, those who supported images, still arise today. Which side of the controversy do you find more compelling? Explain your choice.
2. Some consider the Eastern Orthodox devotion to Mary an excellent expression of Christian spirituality, while others find it disconcerting. How do you view this devotion?
3. What do the ornate liturgies of the Eastern Orthodox Church have to say about the role of beauty in coming to know God?
4. Do you think it is a good spiritual exercise, or even possible, to *pray unceasingly*, as is the goal in the Eastern Orthodox "Jesus Prayer"?

---

24. Kallistos Ware, *The Power of the Name: The Jesus Prayer in Orthodox Spirituality* (Oxford: SLG Press, 1986), 3.

Bibliography

Resources with annotations are highly recommended to students interested in further study.

Bacovcin, Helen, trans. *The Way of the Pilgrim* and *The Pilgrim Continues His Way*. New York: Image Books: 1992.

> This classic autobiography of a nineteenth-century Russian peasant describes how he embraced the Jesus Prayer as a primary spiritual practice and how it transformed him. It also includes discussion on how his experiences reflect the patristic and medieval understanding of prayer.

Bellitto, Christopher. *The General Councils: A History of the Twenty-One Church Councils from Nicaea to Vatican II*. New York: Paulist Press, 2002.

Bilaniuk, Petro. "Eastern Christian Spirituality." In *The New Dictionary of Catholic Spirituality*, edited by Michael Downey, 330–50. Collegeville, MN: Michael Glazier, 1993.

Chariton, Igumen, and Timothy Ware, eds. *The Art of Prayer: An Orthodox Anthology*. Translated by E. Kadloubovsky and E. M. Palmer. London: Faber and Faber, 1997.

> This collection of primary texts expresses various values, descriptions, and theologies of Orthodox prayer.

Climacus, John. *The Ladder of Divine Ascent*. Translated by Colm Luibheid and Norman Russell. New York: Paulist Press, 1982.

> One of the most famous books in Orthodoxy, it describes thirty steps of spiritual progress. Though thoroughly monastic, it has become a classic spiritual treatise for lay Orthodox Christians.

John of Damascus. *On the Divine Images*. Translated by David Anderson. Crestwood, NY: St. Vladimir's Seminary Press, 1980.

> This is a lengthy argument for the role of icons in the Orthodox Church.

Joncas, Jan Michael. "Eastern Christianity." In *The Christian Theological Tradition*, edited by Catherine Cory and Michael Hollerich, 194–210. Upper Saddle River, NJ: Pearson, 2009.

Lossky, Vladimir. *The Mystical Theology of the Eastern Church*. Translated by the Fellowship of St. Alban and St. Sergius. Crestwood, NY: St. Vladimir's Seminary Press, 1976.

> This volume offers a deep analysis of the theology of the Orthodox Church and how Orthodox spirituality infuses its doctrine.

McGinn, Bernard, John Meyendorff, and Jean Leclercq, eds. *Christian Spirituality*. Vol. I, *Origins to the Twelfth Century*. New York: Crossroad, 1988.

Palamas, Gregory. *The Triads.* Translated by Nicholas Gendle. Mahwah, NJ: Paulist Press, 1983.

Ponticus, Evagrius. *The Praktikos and Chapters on Prayer.* Translated by John Eudes Bamberger. Kalamazoo, MI: Cistercian Publications, 1981.

Ware, Kallistos. *The Orthodox Way.* Rev. ed. Crestwood, NY: St. Vladimir's Seminary Press, 1995.

Ware, Kallistos. *The Power of the Name: The Jesus Prayer in Orthodox Spirituality.* Oxford: SLG Press, 1986.

Ware, Kallistos. "The Spirituality of the Icon." In *The Study of Spirituality,* edited by Cheslyn Jones, Geoffrey Wainwright, and Edward Yarnold, 195–98. New York: Oxford University Press, 1986.

Wybrew, Hugh. "The Byzantine Liturgy from the *Apostolic Constitutions* to Present Day." In *The Study of Liturgy,* edited by Cheslyn Jones, Geoffrey Wainwright, and Edward Yarnold, 209–19. New York: Oxford University Press, 1978.

Internet Resources

Bauman, Steven. "The Spirituality of Early Christianity." Interview with Ted Nottingham. *www.bing.com/videos/search?q=spirituality+of+the+early+church +videos&FORM=VIRE5#view=detail&mid=F284F303DE 432D45AD48F284F303DE432D45AD48.*

Father Bauman reflects on current Orthodox teachings and their relevance throughout the history of the church (26 min.).

Skedros, James, and Demetrios Katos. "The Early Church—Discovering Orthodox Christianity." Interview with Stacy Spanos. *www.bing.com/videos/search ?q=spirituality+of+the+early+church+videos&FORM=VIRE15#view=detail &mid=948D4EAA55B5A9502A9E948D4EAA55B5A9502A9E.*

A wide-ranging discussion on the continuity of the early church as it is expressed in Orthodox spirituality (31 min.).

8

Chapter

Western Medieval Piety

The last chapter discussed central elements of Eastern Orthodox spirituality—elements that were not missing from the West, but were uniquely framed in the East. The West also developed spiritual traditions in ways that represent its unique history and culture. Most important was its feudal culture.

In the Early Middle Ages, the West became a feudal society, taking on many of the cultural assumptions of the Germanic peoples who began to dominate. Feudalism was premised on the assumption that large landowners wielded broad control over their realms. Wealthy landlords believed everything under their realm was also their responsibility. They built churches and monasteries, and they typically thought they had the right to control them. Bishops and abbots often functioned more as vassals of the lord than independent leaders. Peasants owed part of their produce to their lord, and the lord had an obligation to protect all those under his patronage.

This system tended to concentrate wealth among lords, and their understanding of money and goods would not have looked like the capitalism of today. It has sometimes been called a "gift economy." Commerce existed, but goods and services were often exchanged without specific, calculated values attached to them. Prestige, power, and honor were expressed in gifts that made ties with others and obliged the recipient to counter-gifts.

Although the move from a gift economy to a clearer profit economy would take centuries, it was surely under way by the eleventh century. Europe was experiencing relative peace, which allowed the culture to grow and begin to flourish. Money began to serve as a more calculated standard of value in the market. Further, the balance of trade between East and West began to favor the West, particularly in southern Europe with its greater trading access. Improved farming practices also had a dramatic impact upon the developing of markets. Finally, the West saw the formation of banks and companies that allowed merchants to trade more freely. Previously, trading had been hazardous. Large exchanges required one to carry enormous amounts of money, and the possibility of getting robbed or of losing the money (for example, in shipwreck) was high. Now a letter of credit from a bank could suffice. Money became a tool rather than a treasure.

The development of a profit economy led to the establishment of large cities with well-organized markets. These cities derived wealth and political power from trade. The cities expanded dramatically as peasants and tradesmen flocked there. Towering cathedrals and great municipal buildings were erected, and urban schools began to replace monastic foundations as centers of education. This marked the beginning of the great universities in Europe.

Not everyone benefitted, however. Any major cultural and economic shift usually involves winners and losers, and many peasants were losers. While some migrated to the cities to establish a trade, others were forced to the cities because the lord no longer wanted them on his land. Taking responsibility for them ceased to make financial sense. Lords also no longer needed a coterie of knights and vassals; they could simply pay mercenaries to defend their property. Cities became centers both of great wealth and massive poverty.

Before, when life was simple and fixed, morality was considered unchanging, as were people's possibilities. As medieval culture took on a capitalist air, morality had to be considered in the context of social mobility and of money-making. Interestingly, among the traditional seven deadly sins (pride, envy, anger, sloth, greed, gluttony, and lust), pride had always been described as the chief deadly sin. Now, greed had taken its place. Of particular moral concern was the act of making money on money. How could one morally make money without producing goods or services? To some, this seemed immoral.

Responding to the Crisis: Hermits and Heretics

The religious responses to the economic and cultural shifts were many. The eleventh and twelfth centuries saw the beginnings of anchoritic monasticism in the West. In a fully feudal worldview, monasticism was constitutive of the social order. Education and high culture tended to revolve around monasteries, not towns. The monks exemplified the gift economy; their wealth was consumed, displayed in sanctuaries, or given to the poor. As the economic landscape changed, they played a central part of the developing market system, garnering income and savings for the monastery. In short, they began to be players in the market economy.

Saint Peter Damian (1007–1072) is perhaps the classic monastic example of reacting against the new cultural shift. When he abandoned his life of luxury to become a monk, he resisted entering a conventional Benedictine monastery, which he considered just another bastion of wealth. He ended up in a hermitage, from which he preached a monastic life of radical poverty and disengagement from society. Many followed his lead, and numerous other monastic communities developed. The Carthusians, started by Saint Bruno of Cologne in

1084, created a new rule that required monks to live as semi-hermits far from urban centers, thereby discouraging visitors. Saint Norbert founded the Premonstratensians in 1120 in France. While it consisted of parish priests serving local communities, the order required that its members live in common without personal property and follow an austere lifestyle. All of these new orders of monks and priests emerged as a prophetic contrast to a church that they saw as falling into the clutches of wealth and entitlement.

Other religious groups also preached a new austerity. A group of priests and laymen called the Humiliati traveled from town to town throughout Italy preaching what they called "apostolic simplicity." In addition to preaching, their mission included serving the poor, many of whom had suffered because of the shift in the economy. The Waldensians organized in 1170 in France as a group of laymen also living in radical poverty. They saw themselves as prophets challenging the worldliness of the clergy. Rome tried to suppress them for preaching without the bishop's approval. The fact that women Waldensians preached as well as men also alarmed the church. Finally, there emerged a collective group that historians refer to as the Cathars. This preaching movement consciously divorced itself from the church and taught a kind of dualism between matter and spirit, believing all matter, particularly the body, was tainted by evil. All these groups critiqued the church, her priests, her wealth, and the very culture that produced such wealth.

Dominican Spirituality

The Order of Preachers (Dominicans) was founded by a Spanish priest, Dominic Guzman (1170–1221) in 1216. Saint Dominic was a highly educated and deeply pious priest of the Toulouse diocese who, along with his bishop, responded to the various preaching initiatives that challenged the church. Where the church was worldly, he preached simplicity. However, Dominic saw the mostly uneducated Christian populace and the many poorly educated priests as the main problem. Dominic believed that the Cathars, despite their radically dualistic theology, exerted such influence because they were not checked by an authentic, intellectually compelling response by the church.

Dominic sent his friars out in pairs to preach, imitating Jesus' own mission.[1] Dominicans adopted a life of "evangelical poverty." These priests had no salary and carried no money. Rather, as they went from town to town they begged. They, like the Franciscans discussed below, were called *mendicants*, literally "beggars."

---

1. "After this the Lord appointed seventy-two others whom he sent ahead of him in pairs to every town and place he intended to visit. He said to them, 'The harvest is abundant but the laborers are few. . . . Carry no money bag, no sack, no sandals'" (Luke 10:1–4).

As Dominic saw, the fact that many priests were illiterate posed a real problem. At this point in history, virtually everyone was illiterate. Unless one was a priest in a high profile city church, the possibilities for an education were quite limited. Dominic insisted that his priests be well-trained before they preached. He created Dominican houses of study and recruited members from universities. Within one hundred years, Dominicans could boast of having some of the best and the brightest theologians of the church, including Saints Albert the Great (ca. 1200–1270) and Thomas Aquinas (1225–1274).

From the very beginning of the order, study was an essential element of the life of Dominicans. Every Dominican house had a resident theologian and many were themselves centers of theological study. Dominic's successor, Jordan of Saxony (d. 1237), wrote a circulated letter to Dominican houses in 1233 that warned them of Christian souls in danger of the true faith by the brothers' lack of rigorous study. Certainly, such devotion to study was not simply for study's sake, rather, they considered it the necessary condition to preach and teach well. The fifth superior of the order, Humbert of Romans (1200–1277), insisted that those who have the grace to preach should prefer it to all other spiritual exercises, including prayer, sacraments, and spiritual reading. Leading souls to Christ by preaching is a hallmark of Dominican spirituality.

Because of their focus on study and preaching, the original mendicancy or begging that marked the earliest years of the order simply could not be sustained. Daily begging took too much time and energy away from study and preaching. Given their focus on preaching and teaching, Dominican life was known as highly flexible. This would constitute one of the greatest shifts from other religious orders, which, until then, had clearer rules of community discipline and specific spiritual practices. Dominicans were likewise less austere than religious orders that preceded them. The demands of a busy preaching or academic life made it virtually impossible to practice the austerities that marked other vowed religious.

It is difficult to articulate a Dominican spirituality as neither Dominic nor his successors advanced a particular lifestyle or systematic advancement in prayer. As Dominican scholar Simon Tugwell wrote, "Dominicans were generally unoriginal."[2] Humbert's *Letter on Religious Life*, a classic expression of the spiritual life in the Order, is principally derived from other sources of piety with no discussion on how Dominican spirituality is distinctive. In Dominican spirituality, for example, nothing addresses how the purgative, illuminative, and unitive stages work and nothing is said about particular ways of imaging Christ or unique Christian lifestyles. But this, for Dominicans, is not considered a lack. Rather, it may very well represent something of the heart of Dominican spiritual character.

---

2. Simon Tugwell, "The Mendicants: The Spirituality of the Dominicans," in *Christian Spirituality: High Middle Ages and Reformation*, ed. Jill Raitt (New York: Crossroad, 1989), 23.

The Dominican tradition by and large rejects the idea of "grades" of prayer or necessary heroic expressions of the faith. "Perfection," for Thomas Aquinas, consisted of perfect love. And this love should be expressed in everything that one did. Attending to one's prayers with devotion and love represented true spirituality, whether one experienced the presence of God or not. Performing one's tasks with willingness and dedication was de facto spiritual, whether one felt spiritually elated or not. Compared to other spiritualities, Thomas Aquinas gives what appears to be a rather tepid definition of prayer: "Petition, a rational response to our total dependence on God and an expression of our readiness to subject our will to his."[3] For the Dominicans, such a definition fits well. The focus is twofold: on one's heart's readiness to do God's will, and actually *doing* it. This emphasis follows Dominic's prime directive: "Do whatever is useful for souls."

Aquinas's definition includes something else that might appear rather dry. He calls prayer a *rational* response. For Dominicans, faith is highly connected to the intellect. They insist on the union of faith and reason. For Aquinas, with the exception of Moses and Saint Paul, who experienced supernatural raptures outside of their intellects, the supernatural life did not contradict the working of the intellect. Unlike the apophatic mysticism that exceeds the intellect and the natural use of one's faculties, Aquinas believed that any phenomenon from God ought to align with natural powers. Contradiction to the intellect, he supposed, did not come from God but from the devil.

Franciscan Spirituality

Understanding the cultural shifts in the medieval world is, if anything, more essential in comprehending Franciscan spirituality. Saint Francis of Assisi (1181–1226) was a man of his time. His father, a prosperous cloth merchant, took advantage of the emerging capitalistic economy of Europe. Not of noble class, he was nonetheless part of what might today be called the *nouveau riche*. Francis was raised in comfort and received a fair education.[4]

Francis grew up with his six siblings in comfort and popularity. He and his friends loved to drink wine and sing the songs of the troubadours about courtly love and the nobleman's life. Although he had the reputation of being a lover of pleasure, accounts of his early life include a report of his encounter with a beggar while tending his father's booth in the marketplace. In this story, Francis concluded the business deal he was involved in, abandoned the booth, and ran after

---

3. *Summa Theologica* 2a.2ae q.83.

4. Much of what is known about Francis comes from a time when his order, the Friars Minor ("Little Brothers"), was debating the nature of the order. Consequently, authenticating the most popular elements of his biography proves difficult. The following is a relatively broadly agreed-upon story of his life.

the beggar, giving him everything in his pocket. In 1201, at the age of twenty, he joined a military expedition against a neighboring city-state at war with Assisi and spent a year as a captive. This was a decisive year. He returned in 1203 a different man, though he had not completely given up his previous carefree life. In 1204 he endured a serious illness that led to a deepening disillusionment with the world of luxury. By 1205, Francis underwent a conversion experience, which he described as follows:

> The Lord granted to me, Brother Francis, to begin to do penance in this way: While I was in sin, it seemed very bitter to me to see lepers. And the Lord Himself led me among them and I had mercy upon them. And when I left them that which seemed bitter to me was changed into sweetness of soul and body; and afterward I lingered a little and left the world.[5]

Francis then gave away all of his possessions and lived as a penitent doing charitable works for lepers and beggars around Assisi. According to later biographers, his father initially locked him in the house, but eventually took him to the bishop. Francis publically stripped and gave his father his clothes, the last thing that associated him with his family. The bishop then put his mantle over Francis as a sign of the church's sponsorship. Francis prayed, served, and lived radical poverty, owning only "a miserable tunic and cord." While meditating in a broken-down chapel, *San Domiano*, Francis heard Jesus speak from the crucifix, "Francis, rebuild my church." Initially, he believed that this divine command instructed him to rebuild *San Domiano*, realizing only later that the "church" was not the chapel, but the Catholic Church as a whole.

Soon Francis had attracted companions interested in living a similar life of poverty, prayer, and service. He and his companions entered the Church of Saint Nicholas in Assisi and made use of the *sortes apostolicae*, a Christian version of an ancient divinatory rite. In the context of prayer, they opened the Bible three times at random and read, "If you wish to be perfect, go, sell what you have and give to the poor, and you will have treasure in heaven" (Matt. 19:21); "Take nothing for the journey" (Luke 9:3); and "Whoever wishes to come after me must deny himself, take up his cross and follow me" (Matt. 16:24). Collectively, these verses fortified their initial intuitions and guided their lifestyle of absolute poverty, total dependence on God (including perpetual begging), and self-denial or asceticism.

With the approval of Pope Innocent III in 1209, they preached penance and simplicity as the core of the Christian life. The early order seems to have had two missions or *apostolates*. Like the Dominicans, one focused on preaching

---

5. Francis of Assisi, *The Testament* 1. Translation from *Francis and Clare: The Complete Works*, trans. Regis Armstrong (New York: Paulist Press, 1982), 154.

and the second on service to the poor and sick. By 1217 the general chapter of the brothers decided to send missions outside of Italy and throughout Europe. Francis himself went to Egypt in 1219 to try to convert the Sultan. After his return, and in failing health, he resigned his position as leader of the order.

A painful tension existed between Francis's original vision of apostolic spontaneity and radical simplicity and the institutional demands for a robust, organized religious order. In contrast to Dominic, Francis imagined a ministry of traveling troubadours for Christ, preaching evangelical simplicity without the need for theological learning. He also personally practiced extraordinary asceticism. He ate little, slept little, and wore virtual rags. When the community drew up a rule for the order and sent it to Rome in 1221, it simply proved too rigorous and unworkable. A second modified rule in 1223 was approved, much to Francis's sadness. Francis's original vision for his community really was too much, on two levels. First, not everyone could be Francis. Such radical poverty and penance, if indeed a grace, is a rare one. Some of it was physically unhealthy; Francis's lifestyle probably contributed to his early death. Second, it was impossible to function without some kind of institutional structure. New brothers had to be trained in novitiates, preaching without theological training turned out to be naïve, and missions could not be carried out well when one is forbidden to carry money.

The Canticle of the Creatures

Toward the end of Francis's life he penned one of the most inspiring poems in Christian literature, known as "The Canticle of the Creatures."

> Most high, all-powerful, all good, Lord! All praise is yours, all glory, all honor, and all blessing. To you, alone, Most High, do they belong. No mortal lips are worthy to pronounce your name. All praise be yours, my Lord, through all that you have made. And first my lord Brother Sun, who brings the day; and the light you give to us through him. How beautiful is he, how radiant in all his splendor! Of you, Most High, he bears the likeness. All praise be yours, my Lord, through Sister Moon and Stars; in the heavens you have made them, bright and precious and fair. All praise be yours, my Lord, through Brothers Wind and Air, and fair and stormy, all the weather's moods, by which you cherish all that you have made. All praise be yours, my Lord, through Sister Water, so useful, lowly, precious and pure. All praise

Continued

The Canticle of the Creatures *Continued*

be yours, my Lord, through Brother Fire, through whom you brighten up the night. How beautiful is he, how gay! Full of power and strength. All praise be yours, my Lord, through Sister Earth, our mother, who feeds us in her sovereignty and produces various fruits with colored flowers and herbs. All praise be yours, my Lord, through those who grant pardon for love of you; through those who endure sickness and trial. Happy those who endure in peace, by you, Most High, they will be crowned. All praise be yours, my Lord, through Sister Death, from whose embrace no mortal can escape. Woe to those who die in mortal sin! Happy those she finds doing your will! The Second death can do no harm to them. Praise and bless my Lord, and give him thanks, and serve him with great humility.[6]

While seemingly sentimental, this canticle is actually theologically and spiritually dense. The Canticle falls into five parts. In the first Francis deals with God. Everyone and everything must praise God, even as "no mortal lips are worthy to pronounce your name." The next stanzas represent his cosmological section. The sun expresses the divine light and goodness, and the entire cosmos reflects God's beauty. The next four stanzas describe what was believed to be the four main elements in the universe: air, water, fire, earth. The world is a theophany, a manifestation of God's presence and glory. The next two stanzas refer to fundamental postures of Francis's spirituality. Finally, the last part of the Canticle is *eschatological*, referring to death and final judgment. Sister death is praised as the vehicle for union with God. Those who do God's will have nothing to fear. They have understood the true meaning of praise.

The most dramatic part of Francis's life story happened the year before he died while Francis spent forty days in retreat on Mount Alverna.

While he was praying on the mountainside, Francis saw a Seraph [angel] with six fiery wings coming down from the highest point in the heavens. The vision descended swiftly and came to rest in the air near him. Then he saw the image of a man crucified in the midst

---

6. Francis of Assisi, *St. Francis of Assisi: Omnibus of Sources*, ed. Marion Habig, trans. Raphael Brown et al., 4th ed. (Chicago: Franciscan Herald Press, 1983), 130–31.

The mother church of the Franciscan Order, the Basilica of San Francesco d'Assisi in Assisi, Italy, was built immediately after Francis died. Francis is buried in a crypt underneath the lower level.

of the wings, with his hand and feet stretched out and nailed to a cross. . . . Eventually he realized by divine inspiration that God had shown him this vision in his providence, in order to let him see that, as Christ's lover, he would resemble the fervor of his spirit. As the vision disappeared, it left his heart ablaze with eagerness and impressed upon his body the miraculous likeness. There and then the marks of nails began to appear in his hands and feet. . . . His right side seemed as if it has been pierced with a lance and was marked with a livid scar which often bled, so that his habit and trousers were stained.[7]

This describes Francis's experience receiving the *stigmata*, the wounds of Christ. The stigmata serve as the pinnacle of his life. Francis believed that the poverty and Passion of Christ represented the premier expressions of Christ's gift to humanity. Francis had spent his ministry identifying with this suffering, poor Christ who was filled with compassion for the world. Francis too lived in humility and poverty, serving lepers and the poorest of the poor. In this experience he came to the insight that, in order to become Christ's lover, he must resemble Christ perfectly. These wounds were, in this sense, sweet to him, just as giving all he had to the leper, something that before had seemed horridly distasteful, was now sweet. Francis retained the wounds of Christ for the rest of his

---

7. Bonaventure, *Major Life* 3. Translation from Habig, ed., *St. Francis of Assisi*, 730–31.

short life. It is said that these wounds, which bled daily, never showed infection, nor did the flesh around them deteriorate.

Common Themes in Franciscan Spirituality

This rather lengthy biography is necessary to understand the Franciscan spiritual path, for Francis himself stands at the core of Franciscan spirituality. The most important theme of Franciscan spirituality is embracing Francis as a model, thinking like Francis, imagining the world like Francis, and taking on Francis's personal spiritual principles.

One key component is the idea of a reversal of attractions. Before his conversion Francis had a deathly aversion to lepers and enjoyed the life of the young, wealthy troubadour, yet he developed a disdain for the life of comfort. He grew to love poverty so much he referred to that state as "Lady Poverty," as though she were a courtly noblewoman. So, too, lepers now were sweet to him, as he was filled with compassion for them and identified with them. He even identified them with the abject Christ. Two of Francis's biographers tell the same story, albeit somewhat differently, about how as a wealthy young man he rode by a leper who was begging. He jumped off his horse, gave the leper his coat and money and kissed him on the mouth. This last act filled him with extraordinary joy. Upon riding away, he looked back only to see the leper had transfigured into an apparition of Christ.

Another great Franciscan theme holds that one can know Christ most clearly in humility and vulnerability. Nothing speaks more clearly of the meaning of Christ's incarnation than the poor baby Jesus, born in a stable and surrounded by animals and simple shepherds. It is to Francis that one can trace to beginnings of the nativity scene.

Though less prominent in contemporary expressions, medieval Franciscan spirituality emphasized penance and asceticism, even to the detriment of the body. Francis himself wrote,

> Many people, when they sin or receive an injury, often blame the Enemy [devil] or some neighbor. But it is not right, for each one has the real enemy in its own power; that is, the body through which he sins. Therefore, blessed is that servant who, having such an enemy in his power, will always hold him captive and wisely guard himself against him.[8]

Finally, Franciscan spirituality is marked by poverty and obedience. Poverty and obedience went together. Francis saw poverty as an expression of total vulnerability to and trust in God. To cease clinging opens the soul to anyone and

---

8. Francis of Assisi, *The Admonitions* 10. Translation from Armstrong, trans., *Francis and Clare*, 30.

everything. The writings of Saint Francis address the theme of obedience more often than any other virtue. There is no self-promotion or self-protection. For Francis, obedience did not restrict the soul, but freed it.

Medieval Feminine Affective Piety

In many respects, the patristic world looked very Platonic. Monastic spirituality, particularly in the East, found its highest expression in apophatic mysticism; the spirituality of the four great figures discussed in chapter 5 was also Platonic. Christians saw the world as sacramental, but in the monastic view sacramentality led the soul to encounter God beyond the created world and even beyond any conceptualizations of God himself. Even icons and the liturgy were intended to use physical imagery to take the soul beyond the visual and conceptual to God. The body, although taken seriously, could, according to this way of thinking, only go so far as a mediator of grace.

While the Western Medieval world accepted much of this, and certainly had its own apophatic mystics, its spiritual locus was far more sacramental, with less a need to transcend the created world. In Benedictine monasticism, the community, the abbot (or abbess), and visitors were regarded as real experiences of Christ. Even the tools of the monastery were imagined sacramentally. The Franciscan worldview also saw the world as reflecting and mediating Christ. Although many medieval saints, including Francis, abused their bodies by their asceticism, these bodies could act as real spiritual metaphors. If you asked Augustine or Gregory of Nyssa if fasting was of value, they would probably say that it was, insofar as it supported one's stripping oneself of inordinate desires (the passions) and the attainment of *apatheia*, a kind of stillness of mind and spirit that came from not being controlled by one's experience. If you asked a medieval saint, he or she would certainly agree that fasting was morally valuable, but might also add that fasting was the body's expression of the soul's hunger and thirst for holiness. In contrast to a more Platonic Christianity, where the body or even the whole created world served as a modest mediator of grace, a medieval Christianity would far more likely imagine both body and world as extraordinary mediators. The body becomes not only the context, but even the content of spiritual insight.

Sexual Stereotypes

Typical modern stereotypes of gender characterize men as less emotional, more rational, less relational, and more introspective; women are characterized as less rational, more relational, more emotional, and more nurturing. These stereotypes existed in the patristic and medieval worlds as well. However, while the patristic world found these feminine qualities an obstacle to a deep spiritual life, the medieval world found them profoundly important. The patristic master Gregory of Nyssa offered this unhappy assessment: "For the material and passionate disposition to which human nature is carried when it falls is the female form, whose birth is favored by the tyrant [the devil]. The austerity and intensity of virtue is the male birth."[9] He clearly sees bodily existence and an emotional disposition as liabilities.

In a similar vein, when Augustine cried at his mother's death, he acknowledged, "I slipped towards weeping. . . . I was reproaching the softness of my feelings."[10] Augustine did not feel ashamed that he felt sorrow—he thought it natural—but he still considered it weak: "I could be reproached for yielding to that emotion of physical kinship."[11] Augustine considered himself inordinately attached to his mother, as evidenced by his grief at her death. He did not have adequate *apatheia*, for any suffering and sorrow represented some kind of attachment.

Augustine's reaction differs markedly from that of the medieval great Saint Catherine of Siena (1347–1380), for whom suffering and sorrow increased in her proportion to her love for Christ and the church. In one mystical encounter with Christ he exhorts her, "Bring, then, your tears and your sweat, you and my other servants. Draw them from the fountain of my divine love and use them to wash the face of my bride. I promise you that thus her beauty will be restored . . . through peace and through the constant and humble prayers and sweat and tears poured out by my servants with eager desire."[12] Here tears are not an obstacle, but the very condition for praying for and suffering for the restoration of the church. Catherine even relates a mystical experience where God the Father teaches her about different kinds of tears, each representing a stage of spiritual growth. There are the tears of fear regarding one's sins, the tears one weeps when one has arisen from sin, the tears of those who have attained perfection in loving their neighbors without self-interest, and finally the tears one sheds in perfect union with God. God not only recommends but demands emotions and suffering (even vicarious suffering for others).

The stereotype of women stressed vulnerability, which is exactly how medievals saw Christ. If the patristic church emphasized Christ as the glorious victor, the medieval church emphasized the vulnerability of the Incarnation. To imitate Christ was to be poor, exposed, and weak, like the infant in the crib of Francis's nativity scene. Christ took on a feminine quality.

---

9. Gregory of Nyssa, *Life of Moses* 2.2. Translation from in *Gregory of Nyssa: The Life of Moses*, trans. Abraham Malherbe and Everett Ferguson (New York: Paulist Press, 1978).

10. Augustine, *Confessions* 9.12. Translation from *Confessions*, trans. Henry Chadwick (Oxford: Oxford University Press, 1991).

11. Augustine, *Confessions* 9.13.

12. Translation from Catherine of Siena, *Catherine of Siena: The Dialogue*, trans. Suzanne Noffke (New York: Paulist Press, 1980), 54.

Jesus as Mother

Femininity, and the relational, nurturing, compassionate, and emotional associations with it, became a key access point for encountering God and expressing authentic spirituality during the medieval period. Many of the great spiritual leaders of the day imagined God as Mother and Jesus as Mother as well. Such representations appear in the works of Saint Bernard of Clairvaux (d. 1153), Aelred of Reivaulx (d. 1167), Guerric of Igny (d. 1157), Isaac of Stella (d. 1169), Saint William of St. Thierry (d. 1148), and Saint Anselm of Canterbury (d. 1109). For Anselm, Jesus who rules is Jesus the father, and Jesus who loves is Jesus the mother. Anselm writes,

> But you, Jesus, good Lord, are you not also a mother? Are you not that mother who, like a hen, collects here chickens under her wings? Truly, master, you are a mother. For what others have conceived and given birth to, they have received from you. . . . It is then you above all, Lord, God, who are mother. . . . Christ, mother . . . your warmth resuscitates the dead, your touch justifies sinners. . . . May your injured one be consoled by you; may he who of himself despairs be comforted by you.[13]

The theme of the motherhood of God appeared in the writings of females as well. One of the most celebrated, the English mystic Julian of Norwich (1342–1416), wrote, "And so I saw that God rejoices that he is our Father, and God rejoices that he is our mother"; "For the almighty truth of the Trinity is our Father, for he made us and keeps us in him. And the deep wisdom of the Trinity is our Mother, in whom we are enclosed"; "How we are brought back by the motherhood of mercy and grace into our natural place in which we were created by the motherhood of love, a mother's love which never leaves us."[14] This kind of language shocked no one at the time.

For Bernard of Clairvaux, the feminine image of Jesus has everything to do with divine nurturing, particularly suckling. Breasts, for Bernard, served as a symbol of nurturance and care. He writes, "Suck not so much the wounds of as the breasts of Christ. He will be your mother, and you will be his son."[15] Bernard saw not only Christ as mother, but believed that spiritual leaders, particularly abbots of a monastery, were also called to be mothers to those in their care. A number of his sermons include imagery of the abbot as having breasts that feed and comfort those in his charge. One need not imagine some sort of

---

13. Anselm, *Opera Omnia* 3.33. Translation from Caroline Walker Bynum, *Jesus as Mother: Studies in the Spirituality of the High Middle Ages* (Berkeley: University of California Press, 1982), 114.

14. Julian of Norwich, *Showings* 52, 54, 60. Translation from Julian of Norwich, *Showings*, trans. Edmund Colledge and James Walsh (New York: Paulist Press, 1978).

15. Bernard of Clairvaux Letter 1. Translation from Bynum, *Jesus as Mother*, 117.

sexual perversion or a fascination with breasts per se. The medieval world was, in this sense, freer with their religious metaphors than many people are today. The point here is that femininity and all that goes with it became a model for an authentic spiritual life.

Feminine Sexual Mysticism

Sex is one of the most powerful metaphors for union with God. The Genesis account of the creation of Adam and Eve depicts this well: "That is why a man leaves his father and mother and clings to his wife, and the two of them become one body" (2:24). The "clinging" here refers to sexual intercourse. Old Testament prophets also used the nuptial union metaphor to reflect Israel's relationship to God.[16] When Israelites worshipped other gods, prophets denounced them as unfaithful wives, even harlots.[17] In this context, God called them back to a nuptial life.[18] In the New Testament, Paul even referred to Christ as husband of the church.[19]

The imagery here is powerful. From the patristic period on the church used this metaphor, and it became standard to interpret the Old Testament Song of Songs as an allegory for the church's nuptial relationship with God. Christian writers also saw it in personal terms. Not only is the church the bride to Christ's groom, so is the individual soul. The medieval mind began to use this metaphor more literally. This is to say, medieval authors did not see it merely as a way of speaking about union, but as having something to do with the content of the relationship between the soul and God. This, one might say, reflects a full use of the metaphor, an actual way of engaging the spiritual life.

A classic example is Bernard of Clairvaux's sermons on the Song of Songs. The Song of Songs begins, "Let him kiss me with the kisses of his mouth." Bernard spends many sermons just on this one verse. He theologizes on the nature of the Trinity, the nature of the Incarnation, the state of the soul, the experience of mysticism, and even the stages of spiritual growth—all associated with kissing. In Sermon 1 he writes, "This sort of song only the touch of the Holy Spirit teaches, and it is learned by experience alone. Let those who have experienced it enjoy it; let those who have not burn with desire. . . . It is a wedding song indeed, expressing the embrace of chaste and joyful souls, the concord of their lives and the mutual exchange of love."[20]

---

16. "For as a young man marries a virgin, your Builder shall marry you; as a bridegroom rejoices in his bride so shall your God rejoice in you" (Isa. 62:5).

17. Ezek. 16; Hos. 1–3.

18. "On that day—oracle of the Lord—You shall call me 'My husband.' . . . I will betroth you to me forever" (Hos. 2:18, 21).

19. 2 Cor. 11:2; Eph. 5:32.

20. Bernard of Clairvaux, *Sermons on the Song of Songs* 1. Translation from *Bernard of Clairvaux: Selected Works*, trans. G. R. Evans (New York: Paulist Press, 1987).

Bernard and other medieval mystics and theologians were not merely taking sexual imagery and applying it to the spiritual life. They were fully engaging their sexual energy and sublimating it for spiritual purposes. Sublimation is a modern psychological term for taking raw biological energy and directing it to a different purpose. Sexual energy is part of an individual's drive for physical sexual intercourse. Medieval writers drew on that same energy and directed it toward union with God. In some respects, God was their divine lover. Medievals were not so naïve as to think that God was somehow having spiritual sexual intercourse with them. God is, after all, pure spirit and utterly transcendent. But neither did they simply use sexuality as an analogy. The individual took on the role of bride to groom, beloved to divine lover. Interestingly, this metaphorical relationship understands the Christian soul of both men and women as feminine; while God could take on the image of the divine feminine, and thus model femininity, here God is masculine and the soul models the feminine.

Perhaps the greatest example of medieval nuptial mysticism comes from the thirteenth century mystic Hadewijch of Antwerp: "The beloved and lover penetrate each other in such a way that neither of the two can distinguish oneself from the other. . . . They abide in one another in fruition, mouth in mouth, and soul in soul, while one sweet divine nature flows through them both, and they are both one thing through each other."[21]

Authoritative Women

Given the patriarchy of the church and indeed the patriarchal society, one of the most striking aspects of the High Middle Ages is the emergence of authoritative women's voices. While women held no church offices, many of them had great influence due to their extraordinary spiritual authority. Like the ammas of the desert, these women were respected and listened to because they were experienced as being particularly close to God.

Hildegard of Bingen

One such figure was Hildegard of Bingen (1098–1179). Saint Hildegard was born near the German town of Alzey. When she was just eight she was brought to a women's hermitage at a Benedictine monastery to be raised and spiritually trained by Jutta, a daughter of a local count. Her early education was limited. She learned to read, but only so she could pray the Psalter in Latin and take part in the monastic life. Other women came to join Jutta and Hildegard,

---

21. Hadewijch, *Letter* 9. Translation from Hadewijch, *Hadewijch: The Complete Works*, trans. Columba Hart (New York: Paulist Press, 1980), 66.

so their life gradually expanded to become a small Benedictine convent on the men's monastery grounds. When Hildegard was fifteen, she formally took vows to become a Benedictine nun. At thirty-eight years old Hildegard was elected leader or *magistra* of the community, though it was still under the administration of the monks.

Throughout her life, starting from childhood, Hildegard received numerous mystical visions. Initially, she saw these visions as something more of a distraction from her prayer and devotion. By the time she gained leadership of her community, however, she came to believe that they represented something of a divine education. She believed that these visions gave her a depth of understanding so that she could interpret the scriptures, theologians, and even philosophers in a wholly new way.

As Hildegard's reputation as a visionary grew, she gained confidence with her inner authority. This authority was confirmed by the Benedictine monks on whose monastery the convent sat. It was also confirmed by others. In 1146, she wrote to Bernard of Clairvaux, the most important monastic figure in the Benedictine reform

In this fourteenth-century painting, Hildegard looks heavenward while receiving the divine inspiration that guided her work.

movement. Bernard assured her that he thought her experiences were genuine. By now Hildegard had written her first major visionary work, *Scivias*, a book discussing Christian revelation represented in visionary form. Her book was presented at the Trier Synod of 1147–1148, presided over by Pope Eugenius III. Eugenius authorized Hildegard to publish all that she learned from her visions.

Soon after, Hildegard was told by God in a vision to leave the convent with her sisters and found a new community in Bingen. During the early years of forming her own monastic house she wrote three more books: Natural History (*Physica*), a study of the natural world, *Causes and Cures* (*Causae et curae*), a study on the workings of the human body, and *Book of Life's Merits* (*Liber vitae meritorum*), a second visionary book. In 1163, Hildegard began her third visionary book, the *Book of Divine Works* (*De operatione Dei*), where she addressed the relationship between God and creation. Hildegard not only produced medical and visionary texts, she also wrote biblical commentaries, theological tracts, biographies, and a play. Finally, she is author to seventy-seven songs, both text and music.

In 1158, she set out on a preaching tour to the towns and villages along the River Main. Over the next twelve years, despite frequent periods of illness, Hildegard made three more preaching tours within a radius of 120 miles of Bingen. Frequently she preached to clergy and monks in chapter houses, but she also preached publically to lay people.

Catherine of Siena

Saint Catherine of Siena (1348–1380) serves as another striking example of an authoritative woman who lived in the medieval period. Catherine was born the twenty-fourth of twenty-five children to a successful merchant in the city-state of Siena. Dominican influence dominates her life. Her family lived close to San Domenico, a church and Dominican chapter house, and her first spiritual director was a Dominican priest, the brother of her brother-in-law. Also active in Siena were the *mantellate*, lay-women who were affiliated with the Dominican Order. These represent what is called *Third-Order* Dominicans.

When Catherine was seven years old she vowed perpetual virginity to God. Despite this, her parents pressed her to marry at the age of fifteen. To thwart their plans, she cut off her hair to make her unmarriageable. At eighteen she became a Third-Order Dominican and a hermit in her parents' house. Her solitary life of prayer came to a climax at twenty when she had a mystical experience where she was "espoused to Christ."

From this point on, Catherine began ministry to the poor and sick. Her notoriety for holiness grew and, when she was not praying or serving the poor, she gathered with other women in ministry as well as Dominican priests who taught her theology and sought her spiritual wisdom. In 1368, Catherine met Dominican priest and theologian, Bartolomeo de' Dominici, who would become her second spiritual director and lifelong friend. During this time she had been experiencing numerous mystical visions and locutions (voices from God).

Catherine's most famous work is the *Dialogue*, in which she relates ecstatic encounters with God who taught her various spiritual truths. Dominican scholar Suzanne Noffke, in assessing Catherine's masterpiece, writes, "Theologically, there is nothing new or original. Catherine is completely immersed in the main current of Catholic teaching. . . . What is original in Catherine is her capacity for fresh and vivid expression of the tradition. . . . Her pages are studded with metaphors and compounded metaphors. She repeats, yet always with some new layer of relationship. She explodes into ecstatic prayer. She teaches. Always she teaches."[22]

Because of Catherine's reputation as a visionary and saint, she held a great deal of authority in the Church. On several occasions she was pressed to mediate controversies in Italian politics and religion. In 1375, for example, she used her influence to sway the leaders of the cities of Pisa and Lucca to remain loyal to the pope as anti-papal forces were gaining momentum. In 1376, leaders in Florence sought her help in mediating a conflict between Florence and the papacy (which was then located in Avignon, France). During this time, she also used her authority to press Pope Gregory XI to return the papacy to Rome, which he did. Later in 1378, Catherine was again in Florence, now by the insistence of Pope Gregory, to mediate the continuing conflict. Historically speaking, Catherine was not an extraordinary ambassador, either for the Florentines or for the pope. Nevertheless, both sides saw this unmarried, uneducated, lay woman as a daunting figure. Her authority was solely due to the spiritual depth they found in her.

The Beguines

A final example of women's authority in the medieval period comes not from a given woman saint but from a women's movement: the Beguines. Every religious movement emerges from a cultural context. As noted above, some religious groups, such as the Humiliati, Waldensians, and Cathars, developed in response to the changing circumstances of the twelfth and thirteenth centuries. These were principally lay groups who claimed authority in contrast to that of the institutional church. They sought to implement what has been called the *vita apostolica*, a lay spirituality of poverty, celibacy, and often service to the poor. Many of these lay groups publically preached as well, thus usurping the role of the clergy, who held exclusive prerogative to preach.

The Beguine movement arose in this milieu. As an alternative to joining a convent, where personal freedoms were curtailed, many women in northern Europe gathered together to form houses of mutual support, prayer, and apostolic service. Each community was independent with no centralized structure. Some houses were small, having somewhere between three and twenty women, while other communities were so large they eventually constituted independent parishes with their own priests to serve them. Some of the Beguine communities were known for their apostolic work. The women would pray and study scriptures together, and serve the needy in the towns and cities where they were located. Others were far more contemplative, and resembled an urban

---

22. Suzanne Noffke, "Introduction," in *Catherine of Siena: The Dialogue*, trans. Suzanne Noffke (New York: Paulist Press, 1980), 10.

expression of monasticism. Many of these women were known for extraordinary religious experiences, like those that Hildegard and Catherine enjoyed. Some of these experiences represented a sharp critique of the wealth and control of the clergy. For example, the great Beguine, Mechtild of Magdeburg's mystical work, *The Flowering of the Godhead*, is filled with denunciations against the abuses of the church and the laxity of the clergy. Her ridicule, she believed, came directly from God.

The institutional church was in many ways supportive of the movement, particularly reform-minded clergy. Who could complain about women joining each other in prayer and service? They even gained quasi-legal recognition with the Pope Gregory IX's papal bull, *Gloriam Virginalem*, where they received church and civic protection. On the other hand, many church leaders were suspicious of them—they simply did not fit the model of religious orders and were deemed unmanageable. In 1274, the great Franciscan theologian and preacher, Gilbert of Tournai, railed against the Beguines in his *De Scandalis Ecclesiae* (On the Scandal of the Church). He challenged their use of scriptures in the vernacular (not the official Latin text), and their claimed authority to interpret the Bible. Bishop Bruno of Olmutz in 1273 condemned them for lacking proper approval, failing to place themselves under the obedience of the local clergy, and failing their duty as lay women to marry.

By the end of the thirteenth century, most Beguinages were forced to become convents ruled by a women's religious order. The church hierarchy's suspicions of them surely were connected to the issue of authority. They did not fit the pattern of vowed religious life, and claimed the ability to live out the gospel in the way they saw fit. Modern scholar of Christian spirituality, Philip Sheldrake writes,

> They offered something new—an organized way of life for lay women which was informal and not constrained by the canonical regulations of traditional life. . . . They managed to create an alternative life-style, in line with many of the values of the *vita apostolica*, which gained patronage and support from sufficient reforming clerics that it could live in the mainstream of the Church. . . . Their spirituality fitted the needs of the thirteenth century in that women could live an apostolic life and seek perfection while remaining free of strict enclosure.[23]

---

23. Philip Sheldrake, *Spirituality and History: Questions of Interpretation and Method* (New York: Crossroad, 1992), 154–55.

Conclusion

The spirituality of the medieval world was less a break from the patristic world than a development of it. The values, practices, and spiritual impulses in patristic Christian life also appear in medieval spirituality. Consequently, one shouldn't make stark distinctions between the two. Nevertheless, one can see important shifts. The medieval mind began to see the created world, including the body, as having extraordinary possibilities for divine encounter. The created world did not have to be transcended so much as engaged dramatically, particularly in its lowliness. Christ continued to be the glorious Lord who conquered sin and was raised victor, but he was also the lowly one, whose sharing in the human condition united grace with poverty and humility. Christ was the Suffering Servant, the compassionate one, who nurtures and cares for her children as a mother. He was one they could know profoundly in and through their own humanity, in their bodies, in their emotions, in their sexuality, even in their own vulnerability. This is the spiritual context from which the dominant themes of the divine feminine and the human feminine emerge. As mother, God completely accepts and nurtures the soul. As bride, the soul unites to her divine lover.

Questions for Review

1. In what ways did Europe change as it transitioned from a feudal society to a more capitalist one?
2. How did Saint Dominic and the Dominican Order deal with the new movements in the church and the wealth of its institutional forms?
3. What are the characteristics of Franciscan spirituality and how was it modeled on the life of Saint Francis?
4. How did medieval thinkers use feminine stereotypes metaphorically to depict the relationship between humans and God?

Questions for Discussion

1. Francis was an extreme figure whose own spirituality proved difficult to emulate. Which parts of his life do you think form a healthy spirituality and which do you think are better left unpracticed?
2. Do you think it is appropriate to use human metaphors for God? Does the use of human metaphors also pose problems?
3. Do you think that it is possible to engage the metaphor of God or Jesus as the soul's lover or spouse? If so, how would this really work? If not, does that mean that all metaphors should be relegated to the status of symbols?

Bibliography

Resources with annotations are highly recommended to students interested in further study.

Bernard of Clairvaux. *Bernard of Clairvaux: Selected Works.* Translated by G. R. Evans. New York: Paulist Press, 1987.

Bynum, Caroline Walker. *Holy Feast and Holy Fast: The Religious Significance of Food to Medieval Women.* Berkeley: University of California Press, 1987.

This classic study addresses medieval women's engagement with food, particularly rigorous fasting, as ways of cultural empowerment, vicarious suffering, and spiritual encounter.

Bynum, Caroline Walker. *Jesus as Mother: Studies in the Spirituality of the High Middle Ages.* Berkeley: University of California Press, 1982.

This study looks at the variety of medieval expressions of femininity as models, both divine and human.

Catherine of Siena. *Catherine of Siena: The Dialogue.* Translated by Suzanne Noffke. New York: Paulist Press, 1980.

Fatula, Mary Ann. *Catherine of Siena's Way.* Collegeville, MN: Michael Glazier, 1987.

Francis of Assisi. *St. Francis of Assisi: Omnibus of Sources.* Edited by Marion Habig. Translated by Raphael Brown et al. 4th ed. Chicago: Franciscan Herald Press, 1983.

Francis and Clare of Assisi. *Francis and Clare: The Complete Works.* Translated by Regis Armstrong. New York: Paulist Press, 1982.

Hadewijch. *Hadewijch: The Complete Works.* Translated by Columba Hart. New York: Paulist Press, 1980.

Hildegard of Bingen. *Hildegard of Bingen: Mystical Writings.* Edited by Fiona Bowie and Oliver Davies. Translated by Robert Carver. New York: Crossroad, 1995.

Julian of Norwich. *Showings.* Translated by Edmund Colledge and James Walsh. New York: Paulist Press, 1978.

Sheldrake, Philip. *Spirituality and History: Questions of Interpretation and Method.* New York: Crossroad, 1992.

Ward, Benedicta. *Miracles and the Medieval Mind: Theory, Record and Event 1000–1215.* Rev. ed. Philadelphia: University of Pennsylvania Press, 1987.

This text examines the medieval mindset, particularly regarding the development of patron saints.

Internet Resources

Anonymous 4. "The Origin of Fire." *www.youtube.com/watch?v=qU7mQylKgqQ*. One of the best of the recordings of music composed by Hildegard of Bingen (105 min.).

Martin, James. "Who Cares about the Saints? St. Francis" *www.youtube.com /watch?v=kw1LDSV23zA*. Shares the history and spirituality of Saint Francis (8 min.).

Panciera, Silvana. "The Beguines." *www.youtube.com/watch?v=toJp9c-LXys*. Discussion of the history and impact of the Beguine movement (31 min.).

Films

Brother Sun, Sister Moon. 1972. A biopic of Saint Francis of Assisi by Franco Zefferelli with inspiring sound track.

Catherine of Siena: Reforms from a Mystic. 2006. A four-disc DVD on the life and ministry of Catherine.

Vision: From the Life of Hildegard Von Bingen [German: *Aus dem Leben der Hildegard von Bingen*, with subtitles]. 2009. A highly rated film depicting Hildegard as a leader, mystic, and artist.

9

Chapter

Carmelite Spirituality

Thus far this book has discussed a number of spiritual values and expressions in Christianity. Some represent spiritual postures and principles that most Christians readily embrace: prayer, a sacramental life and other pious practices, a commitment to the body of Christ, and to service, or what has come to be called corporal acts of mercy. Most Christians experienced God's grace as mediated through the church's liturgical life; Christian art, especially icons; and the ministry of and devotion to the saints, particularly Mary. The exemplars of Christian spirituality in the medieval period, discussed in chapter 8, reflected broad Christian sensibilities.

On the other hand, Christian spirituality historically has been susceptible to a kind of elitism. Some considered monasticism, and the learning that often went along with it, the best way to live out the Christian life. Few Christians understood apophatic mysticism, and only some monks ever experienced it. Even the kataphatic mystical life, such as that of Catherine of Siena, was rare. While most Christians appreciated some degree of asceticism, the examples of ascetical living discussed to this point did not reflect the experience of the majority of Christians. Most Christians lived short and difficult lives, and their faith was fixed on life's essentials. Religion was local and tied to the normal events and fears of a peasant existence: baptisms and funerals, marriage, attending Mass, offering tithes, fasting on penitential days, and abstaining from sex during Lent. Few could read, and Christianity was simply inculturated into the spiritual horizons of the peoples who converted. This often included a good deal of superstition.

Carmelite spirituality, the topic of this chapter, also reflects the tendency toward elitism found in certain spiritualities. The premier representatives of Carmelite spirituality, Saints Teresa of Ávila and John of the Cross, are both doctors of the church, that is, their teachings are considered substantive and of perennial value and authority in Catholicism. While their writings reflect a perennial wisdom and are widely extolled, they express the rarified realms of the Christian mystical life. In them one can see the culmination of asceticism, contemplation, kataphatic mysticism, apophatic mysticism, nuptial spirituality, a vivid description of union with God, and paths to that union.

John of the Cross's Poem *The Dark Night*

One of John of the Cross's most famous poems is *The Dark Night*

One dark night,
Fired with love's urgent
    longings
—ah, the sheer grace!—
I went out unseen,
My house being now
    all stilled.

In darkness, and secure,
By the secret ladder, disguised,
—ah, the sheer grace!—
In darkness and concealment,
My house being now
    all stilled.

On that glad night
In secret, for no one saw me,
Nor did I look at anything
With no other light or guide
Than the one that burned in
    my heart.

This guided me
More surely than the light
    of noon
To where he was awaiting me
—him I knew so well—
There in a place where no one
    appeared.

O guiding night!
O night more lovely than the
    dawn!
O night that has united the
    Lover with his beloved,
Transforming the beloved in
    her Lover.

Upon my flowering breast,
Which I kept wholly for him
    alone,
There he lay sleeping,
And I caressing him
There in the breeze from the
    fanning cedars.

When the breeze flew from
    the turret,
As I parted his hair,
It wounded my neck
With its gentle hand,
Suspending all my senses.

I abandoned and forgot myself,
Laying my face on my Beloved;
All things ceased; I went out
    from myself,
Leaving my cares
Forgotten among the lilies.[1]

This poem depicts union of the soul and God in imagery that is both apophatic and kataphatic. As apophatic, the soul leaves behind all thoughts or concepts toward pure union with the divine. Here the soul is lost in divine transcendence. As kataphatic, this very leaving seems to include deep nuptial imagery.

---

1. John of the Cross, *The Dark Night*. Translation from *The Collected Works of St. John of the Cross*, trans. Kieran Kavanaugh and Otilio Rodriguez (Washington, DC: ICS Publications, 1991), 358–59.

Who Are the Carmelites?

The history of the early Carmelites is relatively unknown. They began in the thirteenth century as a small group of lay Christians who immigrated to Palestine when it was under the control of the Crusaders. They lived on Mount Carmel in small hermitages that surrounded a chapel. It was a highly ascetical expression of monasticism, much like that found in the early church. Key practices included contemplative prayer, fasting, and long vigils. The central formation document, *The Institution of the First Monks*, portrayed Carmelite spirituality as withdrawing from the preoccupations of the world and entering into solitude for the purification of the heart. Personal, direct experience of God was the ideal.

As the community grew, some Carmelites returned to Europe and devised a rule, which Pope Innocent IV approved in 1247. When Christians definitively lost political control of the Holy Land in 1291, the Carmelites there all immigrated back to Europe. The rule had been devised by two former Dominicans who had joined the order, and the life took on some of the Dominican structure, including a common refectory where they ate and an organized Liturgy of the Hours that they prayed together daily.

This new structure led to a new identity for the former hermits and a rapid expansion of the order in Europe. It also led to a clericalization of the order and a full community life. They ceased to be lay hermits who lived alone and joined each other in a common chapel. Instead, they lived together, and many of the ordained members offered pastoral ministry to Christians in neighboring towns. In many respects, the Carmelites looked like Dominicans. Given this radical transition away from their original intent and the way the order developed, there was (and still is) a tension within the order between living a life of contemplative solitude and exercising ministerial service to the church at large.

In 1432, the rule changed again, relaxing the obligations pertaining to fasting, solitude, and contemplation even more. Far from being an expression of corruption, this new Rule reflected the desire to reconcile the original spirit of the community with the pressures of ministry. In 1452, the papal bull *Cum nulla* approved the reception of women in the order, which paved the way for the establishment of female Carmelite monastic foundations. Within a century, though, the women's monastic life also lost its focus on contemplation, the order's original spirit (*charism*). The men's monastic lifestyle was relatively rigorous, but the order continued to struggle with the tension between the original purpose of contemplative prayer and solitude and the call for pastoral ministry. Eventually, Teresa of Ávila initiated a reform of the women's order that was embraced by John of the Cross.

Teresa of Ávila (1515–1582)

Her Life

Teresa de Capeda y Ahumada was born in Ávila, Spain. Her father, a prosperous man, bought a knighthood and successfully assimilated into the noble class. She was raised with a modest education and was quite interested in medieval and Renaissance literature. Teresa has been described as somewhat of an extrovert, cheerful, and happy, and, above all, quite religious. At the age of sixteen, her father (her mother now deceased) entrusted her to the care of Augustinian nuns in Ávila. This would have been something of a boarding school and preparation for married life. At the age of twenty she entered the Carmelite monastery of the Incarnation in Ávila. Some one hundred and fifty nuns, along with a number of servants, lived at this large monastery. While monastic life there was relatively austere, it was not highly contemplative, nor was it a strict enclosure. That is, sisters could come and go as could visitors. This circumstance gave rise to Teresa's later interest in reforming the rule to require greater separation.

Spanish piety was extraordinarily active during the sixteenth century, and Spanish Catholics testified to many extraordinary religious experiences. Prophets, mystics, and spiritual visionaries seemed to be everywhere. The Catholic Church, while supportive of deep devotion, was often suspicious of such experiences and claims, and for good reason. Traditionally, deep contemplative prayer aimed to move one from any form of conceptualization to non-conceptual spiritual union with God, who transcends the mind's normal operations. Images of God, mental or otherwise, were considered limiting to a robust contemplative experience of God. In contrast, Spanish piety was filled with wild claims of ecstatic experiences of visions, messages from God, and so on.

Teresa, in fact, had many such mystical experiences, most of them visions and voices. Several spiritual directors over the years instructed her to disincline from these and even suspect them as purely illusionary. Some suggested that they might even be a product of supernatural evil, and Teresa often suffered from scrupulosity, fearing these experiences could be counterfeit. Only later did Teresa gain certainty that her experiences were authentic. Teresa noted in her autobiography that the more she resisted these supernatural favors the more they arose. She also later realized that the use of images, prayers, biblical scenes in prayer, and even devotion to the humanity of Christ, did not suppress deeper experiences of apophatic union and even sometimes stimulated them. In addition, Teresa overcame her fear of the devil:

> I don't understand these fears, "The devil! The devil!" when we can say "God! God!" and make the devil tremble. . . . Without a doubt I fear those who have such great fear of the devil more than I do the devil himself, for he can't do anything to me. Whereas these others, especially if they are confessors, cause severe disturbance; I have undergone

some years of such great trial that I am amazed now at how I was able to suffer it."[2]

Teresa continued throughout her life to have profound kataphatic and apophatic experiences, often combined. One of her most celebrated experiences is depicted in Lorenzo Bernini's sculpture called *The Ecstasy of Teresa*, which sits in the Church of Santa Maria della Vittoria in Rome. Teresa describes the experience in her autobiography:

> I saw close to me toward my left side an angel in bodily form. . . . . saw in his hands a large golden dart and at the end of the iron tip there appeared to be a little fire. It seemed to me that angel plunged the dart several times into my heart and that it reached deep within me. When he drew it out, I thought he was carrying off with him the deepest part of me; and he left me all on fire with great love of God. The pain was so great that it made me moan, and the sweetness this greatest pain caused me was so superabundant that there is no desire capable of taking it away; nor is the soul content with less than God. . . . The loving exchange that takes place between the soul and God is so sweet that I beg Him in His goodness to give a taste of this love to anyone. . . . It seems the Lord carries the soul away and places it in ecstasy.[3]

Teresa's experiences of ecstasy periodically included *rapture*, where she was lifted into extraordinary union with God. It is said that these were so powerful that her body sometimes levitated, even during public prayer. This itself caused many problems for her, as the last thing she wanted was to be a public spectacle.

In 1562, with the support of Church leaders in Rome, Teresa created a reformed Carmelite Order and wrote a new Constitution. She wanted to return to the original impulse of the hermits on Mount Carmel, though really the reform only took the revised order back to the ideals of the rule of 1247. Still, it succeeded in guaranteeing a monastic life much more deeply committed to silence, solitude, and contemplation. Teresa ended up personally founding sixteen convents and supported the opening of a number of men's monastic houses that embraced her reform.

The Interior Castle

Teresa's masterpiece is her *Interior Castle*, where she maps the spiritual development of the soul. The castle represents the soul itself and contains a series of

---

2. Teresa of Ávila, *Autobiography* 25.22. Translation from *The Collected Works of St. Teresa of Ávila*, trans. Kieran Kavanaugh and Otilio Rodriguez (Washington DC: ICS Publications, 1987), 1:223.

3. Teresa of Ávila, *Autobiography* 29.13–14. Translation from Teresa of Ávila, *Collected Works*, 1:252–53.

concentric levels, each with many rooms, with God dwelling in the center. For Teresa, the spiritual journey is also a journey of self-discovery as one progressively moves deeper and deeper into the recesses of the soul. *Interior Castle* works like a spiritual stage theory, where one progressively moves from sin to greater knowledge of and devotion to God.

First Dwelling Place

Teresa describes the first dwelling place as self-knowledge. She challenges her readers to recognize their absorption in worldly affairs, their pursuit of superficial things, such as wealth or comfort, and their propping up of their egocentricity. In this stage one begins to see mortal sin more clearly and learns to fear it. One also learns something of the greatness of God. The first step consists of feeling humility and sorrow for one's sins. This dwelling place also represents a conscious embrace of a serious spiritual path.

Second Dwelling Place

This dwelling represents those souls who pray regularly, but are not resolute enough to avoid sin. The central issue concerns the will: do I really want a holy life and will I ardently strive for it? The virtue most needed in this dwelling is simply effort. Habits are strong and replacing old habits with new ones proves difficult. Teresa believes that one ought to seek God at this time through exterior things. She recommends meditating on the goodness and beauty of creation as well as scripture, sermons, and inspiring religious books, as they mediate God's wisdom and something of God's presence. On the one hand, she advocates great perseverance. On the other hand, she also notes that souls will fall often at this time and that one needs to be gentle with oneself.

Third Dwelling Place

Teresa believes that souls who attain the third dwelling place are surely saved because they now habitually avoid venial (small) sins. This dwelling represents souls committed to prayer and a holy lifestyle. Having restrained bad habits and cultivated spiritual ones, they find that prayer becomes much easier. Although souls here may experience some aridity in prayer, Teresa explains that this typically comes from themselves and their lack of ardent desire. Greater initiative in prayer and loving service to others tends to solve any problems with a dry prayer life.

Fourth Dwelling Place

To this point the soul's experience of God has been mediated; God's grace is experienced in relationships, the created world, images, sermons, scripture, and so on. In the third dwelling place, the soul becomes practiced in the art of prayer, perhaps praying with scriptures, reflecting on the truths of the faith, and so forth. Actively using the mind to imagine one's faith experience is traditionally called *mental prayer*. In the fourth dwelling place, one transitions from mental prayer to the *prayer of recollection*. The soul advances by thinking less and by being mentally silent before God. The first three dwelling places prepare the soul for this. Teresa affirms that God is really present in experience and that one can recognize God's presence in it. Scripture and sermons can do more than just inspire or provoke thought; they can mediate grace. In the prayer of recollection, however, thinking itself gets set aside. From such a posture, one could even attain what she calls the "prayer of quiet" and experience God moving the soul quite directly. Teresa says that God enlarges the heart by his *touches* and is experienced with extraordinary sweetness.

Fifth Dwelling Place

Teresa describes this dwelling place as by far the largest and as having the most rooms. Most of the sisters in her communities attained this dwelling place. In it God addresses the soul quite directly and prayers of recollection and quiet occur regularly. Beginning in the fourth dwelling and now flowering in the fifth, the soul deeply encounters God outside of the natural use of the mind. Since God transcends concepts, this rather direct experience of God also transcends any thoughts or forms. In this dwelling Teresa introduces the *prayer of union*, a profound experience that overwhelms the soul in love. Such an experience can only last a short time, and the soul feels certain that it is God.[4] The prayer of union is completely absorbing and its after-effects can be as well. Teresa, herself a great extrovert, admits that it could be difficult, even painful, to dialogue with anyone after experiencing the prayer of union. The soul only thinks about and wants God. This is not to say, however, that the soul loses love for others. Quite the contrary: the soul now loves others much more deeply because God's love transforms it.

Sixth Dwelling Place

While Teresa regularly describes the fifth dwelling as a kind of falling in love with God on a profoundly deep level, she insists at that stage they have yet to fully "betroth" themselves (become engaged) to one another. The sixth dwelling is the betrothal. During this time of dwelling the soul experiences great raptures from God, but also greater trials. The soul often endures long

---

4. "Union is always short. . . . God so places Himself in the interior of that soul that when it returns to itself it can in no way doubt that it was in God and God was in it. This truth remains with it so firmly that even though years go by without God's granting that favor again, the soul can never forget nor doubt that it was in God." *Interior Castle* 5.1.9. Translation from Teresa of Ávila, *Collected Works*, 2:339.

experiences of seeming abandonment from God as it becomes even more purified. Unlike the aridity of the third dwelling place, which came from immaturity, the dryness of this dwelling is extraordinary and initiated by God. It stretches the soul to love God for God's sake and not for comfort or spiritual sweetness. On the other hand, the soul in this stage can also experience God quite dramatically and overwhelmingly. Teresa's experience of the angel's dart belonged to this stage. Teresa calls it a *wound of love*, which so overwhelms the soul that it both becomes utterly elated and sweetly pained. In this dwelling no pleasures of the world entice the soul, which becomes constantly preoccupied with God. This dwelling place can include experiences of visions, voices, and spiritual insights infused by God. It represents the highest form of kataphatic mysticism.

Seventh Dwelling Place

If the soul had fully fallen in love with God in the fifth dwelling and become betrothed in the sixth, in the seventh she is mystically married to her divine spouse. Teresa says that a direct knowledge of the Trinity accompanies the transition between the sixth and seventh dwelling. The seventh dwelling represents full union with God, a condition whereby the soul perpetually experiences God's ongoing presence in the soul's operations. Teresa says that the "lower part" of the soul continues to engage the world normally, but the "spiritual part" of the soul constantly communes with God. This dwelling includes no more raptures. One might imagine that these would come even more regularly, but raptures should be thought of as something of a defect. In the sixth dwelling these experiences of union painfully and beautifully stretch the soul. Now union becomes the standard or normal experience of the soul.

Teresian Spirituality

The Roman Catholic tradition views Teresa of Ávila as a mystic of the highest sort. The outline of her mystical stages expresses something of her own biography. However, she does not merely witness to a mystical union with God. The Catholic Church considers her teaching perennial because she highlights the regular development that she saw in other sisters and that the Church has recognized well beyond the walls of Carmel. Her writings include several regular themes. The first is the role of self-knowledge; the deeper the soul enters into God the more the soul knows itself and the more acutely one recognizes one's sinfulness. A second theme is humility. Not only is it humbling to see the depths of one's own sin, the soul becomes increasingly humbled by deeper and more intimate experiences of God. Teresa explains that the soul feels utterly unworthy of the great gifts God bestows on it. Finally, Teresa regularly discusses the importance of the role of suffering. The soul suffers greatly in recognizing its sinfulness. Additionally, the soul suffers variously in encountering God, who overwhelms the soul painfully, purifying it and expanding it to hold divinity itself. Teresa also regularly teaches that the soul longs to suffer for God, a theme discussed also in the last chapter in conjunction with both Catherine and Francis. All of them find something salutary in the soul's ability to suffer on behalf of Christ.

John of the Cross (1542–1591)

His Life

Juan de Yepes was born in a small Castilian town of Fontiveros in 1492. As a child, and after his father had died, his family moved to Medino del Campo, where he entered a school for the poor and received an elementary education. At seventeen, with the sponsorship of the school's administrator, he was enrolled for four years at a Jesuit school, whose foundation was philosophy and humanities. In 1563, when he was twenty-one years old, John entered the Carmelite order and a year later began formal studies at the University of Salamanca. Even while a student, John was serious and ascetical. Reports attest to his devotion; when not attending lectures he would sit at his desk engrossed in studies during the day and spend a large part of every night in prayer. He also fasted assiduously.

The very day of his ordination, John met Teresa of Ávila. He had actually been considering leaving the Carmelites and entering the Carthusian order of semi-hermits, but Teresa encouraged him to consider joining her reform movement instead. His decision to do so created severe tensions among the Carmelites and even led to him being captured and held prisoner in a monastery for at least six months. Lines of authority regarding the Spanish renovation of religious orders were unclear at this time. The Spanish Church authorities did not think the men's community needed reform. Rome, however, supported Teresa's reform, which resulted in a new order. Instead of the Order of Carmelite (OCarm.), they became the Order of Carmelite Discalced (OCD). This was a controversial development at the time; to many of his contemporaries John looked like a renegade.

During the twenty-three years of John's work in the newly reformed Carmelite order he took on numerous, highly responsible jobs, from creating monasteries to acting as a religious superior, to novice director, and so on. Ironically, while he joined Teresa's reform with the intention of pursuing a more contemplative existence, the men's reform did not achieve this well. It continued, even in the earliest years, to wrestle with the tension between a solitary life of contemplation and one of pastoral service.

The Path to Union

Saint John argues that the body and mind can help in negotiating the created world. Thus everything a person does, thinks, or prays about is based on the way human beings naturally understand and experience the world. But if God is not just another object of the universe, and if one's final end is a supernatural union with this Transcendent One, such an approach is limited and even distorting. To know God directly and to be purified utterly, John argues, requires somewhat of a bypass of this natural way.

> To reach satisfaction in all, desire satisfaction in nothing.
> To come to possess all, desire to possess nothing.
> To arrive at being all, desire to be nothing.
> To come to the knowledge of all, desire the knowledge of nothing.
> To come to enjoy what you have not, you must go by a way in which you enjoy not.
> To come to the knowledge you have not, you must go by a way which you know not.
> To come to possession you have not, you must go by a way in which you possess not.
> To come to be what you are not, you must go by a way in which you are not.[5]

John describes contemplative prayer—and one's whole spiritual progress—as going the way one knows not, has not, and is not.

Beginners and the Active Night of the Senses

He starts with those he calls *beginners*, though they are hardly that. These would be Christians, typically monks, who are zealous in faith and prayer. They could correspond to Teresa's third dwelling. While beginners know and love God to a degree, they experience God through their natural orientations. And because they are not yet purified, their piety tends toward seeking spiritual satisfaction, that is, they perform those pious practices that make them feel good. John's analysis of beginners highlights their attachment to both themselves and their experiences. Beginners must practice what John calls "the active night of the senses." They must seek greater asceticism, imitate the crucified Lord, and seek only those things devoted to the honor and glory of God. He intends it to be daunting: "Endeavor to be inclined always: not to the easiest, but to the most difficult, not to the most delightful, but to the most distasteful . . . not to what means rest for you, but to hard work . . . not to the highest and most precious, but to the lowest and most despised, not to wanting something, but to wanting nothing."[6]

---

5. *Ascent of Mount Carmel* 1.13.11. Translation from St. John of the Cross, *Collected Works*, 150–51.
6. Ibid., 149.

Passive Night of the Senses

The prayer life of beginners is typically traditional, through rote prayer or, more commonly, meditation or mental prayer. When God begins to infuse a contemplative knowledge of himself, however, God ceases to communicate through the senses or natural functioning of the intellect; one's meditational life dries up. One key to determining whether this is the kind of aridity of Teresa's third dwelling place or something generated by God is the soul's deep longing and solicitude toward God. Often dryness merely points to spiritual sloth or some kind of spiritual depression, but if this dryness comes from God then the soul actually finds itself quite devoted, even if a bit lost. The soul simply wants to be with God in simple loving awareness without particular mental considerations. This brings one into what John terms "the passive night of the senses." God draws the soul away from its sensory way of praying.

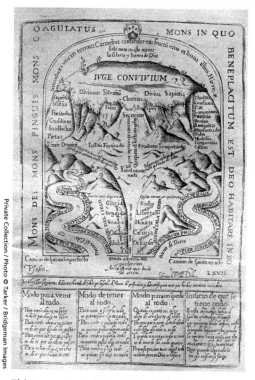

The passive night of the senses marks the beginning of the contemplative life and an increasing awareness of God's general loving presence. The transition from the active night of the senses to the passive night of the senses shifts one from being a beginner to being what John calls a "proficient." The soul lives in this stage for many years, becoming increasingly liberated. One readily finds within the heart a serene, loving contemplation and spiritual delight. What had at first been a vague awareness of God slowly grows to a developed knowledge of God's indwelling and can even flare into quite intense experiences, similar to Teresa's fourth and fifth dwelling places. Interestingly, John would have been critical of the soul seeking mediated forms of meditation at this stage, the very kind that Teresa of Ávila continued to practice.

This seventeenth-century engraving is based on John's sketch of Mt. Carmel, his image of the soul's ascent to union with God. The byways lead to dead ends, but the center path—complete self-emptying to God—leads directly to the summit.

Active Night of the Spirit

While all spiritual progress results from God's initiative, one must properly dispose the soul in order to progress. The beginner cultivated asceticism and detachment from physical things; the proficient must actively practice spiritual detachment. Saint John refers to this as "the active night of the spirit." One empties the self, or loses the self in faith, hope, and love. Detachment focuses not on physical gratifications—this is assumed—but on self-identity, with a naked disinterest in spiritual consolations, even from any image of God.

These three virtues—faith, hope, and love—come from 1 Corinthians 13:13, where Paul writes, "So faith, hope, love remain, these three; but the greatest of these is love." Theologians and spiritual writers throughout the tradition have termed these the "theological virtues," and John follows Augustine, who associated them with the three parts of the psyche or soul. Faith aligns with the intellect, hope aligns with the memory, and love aligns with the will. John writes that the normal expression of these corresponds to how the psyche works in a *natural* way. Faith embraces the revelation of God and the God known through revelation. Hope looks to the future in a manner that corresponds to expectations derived from the past. And love is the will's operation toward something known and desired. In the active night of the spirit one lets go of this natural way so as to allow God to act supernaturally. Here faith blinds the intellect from its natural operations, and one approaches God in darkness, much like Gregory of Nyssa, as discussed in chapter 4. While an individual can only *naturally* hope in what derives from prior experience, in preparing for the supernatural operations of God one lets go of any expectations and blindly hopes in God's graces beyond anything the mind can imagine. And love, naturally expressed, cannot help but be somehow attached to what it loves. The soul can easily love the favors of God rather than God himself, but now the will cultivates emptiness of any self-interest.

The active night of the spirit is a gentle but relentless embrace of the spiritual path. Principally, a person cultivates this kind of self-emptiness in contemplative prayer, by letting go of any thoughts, expectations, and self-interest. However, Saint John ultimately intends the whole of one's life to be both recollected and emptied of self. So how does he define contemplative prayer? John provides no specific technique. He writes, "The contemplative soul must be content simply with a loving and peaceful attentiveness in God."[7] The soul sits before God, empty of self but alive in spirit, and in a posture of openness and deep, gentle love. One does not conjure up an emotion of love here. Rather, one has been given a deep love for him who dwells within, and one simply attends to God in love.

Passive Night of the Spirit

The active night of the spirit prepares for the passive night of the spirit, in which God purges and illuminates the soul most directly and radically. This

---

7. *Dark Night of the Soul* 1.10.6. Translation from St. John of the Cross, *Collected Works*, 382.

active night comprises the transition from being a proficient to entering into union with God. As a passive night, it is really the work of the Divine. God paralyzes the natural operations of the soul. Now, the very virtues of faith, hope, and love that the soul cultivated in the active night of the spirit become infused supernaturally. Through faith, one's intellect now knows God supernaturally, even if not conceptually. Through hope God releases one of all expectations, and one becomes supernaturally inclined to what is beyond all expectations. Through love, the will is taken over that one might love as God loves.

This stage of interior growth also involves the most intense and difficult period of the journey, sometimes called the dark night of the soul. As seen in Teresa's sixth dwelling, God strips the soul of everything, and the soul often feels utterly abandoned by God. During this stripping period the soul paradoxically engages in contemplation to a high degree. It receives a kind of spiritual knowledge that cannot be objectified by the mind.

Saint John describes this part of the path as both painful and sublime. It is painful because in it one has lost one's natural moorings in life. Cut off from any props, attachments finally get ripped out at their roots. Ironically, it is also painful because God can be overwhelming here, as seen with Teresa's raptures.

Union

Like Teresa, Saint John often refers to union as a spiritual marriage. One moves from glory to glory; from being saved and knowing the forgiveness of God to being invited into a direct knowledge of the indwelling love of God. This also represents the divinization of the soul where the soul lives the divine life with God by his grace: "Accordingly, the intellect of this soul is God's intellect; its will is God's will; its memory is the memory of God; and its delight is God's delight; and although the substance of this soul is not the substance of God, it has become God through participation in God, being united to and absorbed in him, as it is in this state."[8] Using the image of the flame for the soul's love of God and the flame of God's love for the soul, he writes that the two flames now become a single fire.

Conclusion

This chapter has highlighted only two of the numerous saints in the Carmelite tradition. These two representatives of Carmelite spiritual life have had an enormous effect on Roman Catholic spirituality. For example, the most widely revered Catholic spiritual presentation in the modern era, prior to the Second Vatican Council (1962–1965), Reginald Garrigou-Lagrange's *The Three Ages of*

---

8. *Living Flame of Love* 2.34. Translation from St. John of the Cross, *Collected Works*, 671.

the Interior Life, is an extension of the writings of Teresa and John. In what was traditionally known as "spiritual theology," discussions of the prayers of recollection, quiet, rapture, and union, the dark night of the soul, mystical marriage, and so on, all rely on the writings of these two. They prove particularly valuable because they not only vividly describe religious experience, but also map out the spiritual journey. Those who find themselves on such a path can consult their work for guidance in interpreting their experience and what would be most appropriate during a given stage.

The regularity of such a stage theory turns out to be a bit of a liability as well. As noted in chapter 1, modern study of spirituality recognizes a number of Christian spiritual expressions, and one size does not fit all. The Carmelite path as laid out either by Teresa or John tends to be highly individualistic and monastic. While some lay Christians living in the world have certainly found themselves on this path, it is far from typical. If holiness is a universal call, and if this Carmelite way to union represents the only path to holiness, the universal call appears quite restrictive. Saint John might ask, however, which is better: a direct experience of God or an indirect one, an immediate experience of God or a mediated one, loving God through loving others or loving others precisely because one has been transformed into God's very love? Such a framing makes a persuasive point.

On the other hand, simply because Teresa and John's full-blown mystical paths to union with God are rare, this does not mean that the spiritual values on which they concentrate are necessarily lost on those not called to "mystical marriage." Many scholars in spirituality as well as spiritual directors draw on a wide variety of insights from classic Carmelite writings, particularly Teresa and John's. These scholars describe skillful ways to attend to various kinds of spiritual darkness, how to work with different kinds of desires, how to recognize authentic expressions of inner freedom, how to negotiate the relationship between an understanding of God one could conceptually know and God who transcends all thoughts, and so on. Some scholars have aligned Carmelite spirituality with the "centering prayer" movement for a broadly-based lay contemplative practice, while others have even shown alignments among Carmelite insights and modern depth psychology. Carmelite mysticism is a rare experience, but Carmelite spirituality has values and insights that can be far more widely engaged.

Questions for Review

1. How did the Carmelite Order develop from its thirteenth-century origins and what did it look like by the fifteenth century, before Teresa of Ávila and John of the Cross?
2. What impact did Teresa have on the rule of the Carmelite Order?

3. What are the essential aspects of each of Teresa's "dwelling places" in her *Interior Castle?*

4. What are the central stages of development in John of the Cross's map of spiritual development? What are the significant progressions among them?

Questions for Discussion

1. Teresa saw an affinity between her kataphatic experiences of God and her apophatic experiences of union. Do you think these ought to go together, given the discussion in chapter 2 that distinguished them?

2. John of the Cross claims that the end of the spiritual journey represents becoming so united to God that one ends up participating in God's very life as God experiences it. Is such a goal achievable?

3. Where do you think most Christians would be placed in Teresa's seven stages? Do you think more Christians would actively pursue spirituality if they felt that, by following Teresa's stages, they really could achieve a higher level?

Bibliography

Resources with annotations are highly recommended to students interested in further study.

Burrows, Ruth. *Ascent to Love: The Spiritual Teachings of St. John of the Cross.* Denville, NJ: Dimension Books, 1987.

Collings, Ross. *John of the Cross.* Collegeville, MN: Michael Glazier, 1990.

Egan, Keith, ed. *Carmelite Prayer: A Tradition for the Twenty-First Century.* New York: Paulist Press, 2003.

This edited text provides insights on Carmelite prayer for the modern Christian that are both attentive to the classical texts and accessible to the modern spiritual life.

Garrigou-Lagrange, Reginald. *The Three Ages of the Interior Life.* Translated by M. Timothea Doyle. 2 vols. St. Louis: Herder, 1947–1948.

John of the Cross. *The Collected Works of St. John of the Cross.* Translated by Kieran Kavanaugh and Otilio Rodriguez. Washington, DC: ICS Publications, 1991.

Matthew, Iain. *The Impact of God.* London: Hodder & Soughton, 1995.

This small book provides a synopsis and reflection on the spirituality of John of the Cross as it could be appropriated by modern sensibilities.

Payne, Steven. *John of the Cross and the Cognitive Value of Mysticism: An Analysis of Sanjuanist Teaching and Its Philosophical Implications for Contemporary Discussions of Mystical Experience.* Boston: Kluer Academic Publishers, 1990.
This represents one of the finest expositions on the mystical doctrine of John of the Cross in English.

Payne, Steven, ed. *John of the Cross.* Carmelite Studies 6. Washington, DC: ICS Publications, 1992.

Ruiz, Federico, ed. *God Speaks in the Night: The Life, Times, and Teaching of St. John of the Cross.* Translated by Kieran Kavanaugh. Washington, DC: ICS Publications, 1991.
This is the best English biography of John of the Cross. It includes many photos of the sites of John's monasteries and places of ministry.

Teresa of Ávila. *The Collected Works of St. Teresa of Ávila.* Translated by Kieran Kavanaugh and Otilio Rodriguez. 3 vols. Washington, DC: ICS Publications, 1976–1985.

Welch, John: *The Carmelite Way: An Ancient Path for Today's Pilgrim.* New York: Paulist Press, 1996.

Welch, John. *Spiritual Pilgrims: Carl Jung and Teresa of Ávila.* New York: Paulist Press, 1982.

Welch, John. *When Gods Die: An Introduction to John of the Cross.* New York: Paulist Press, 1990.

Internet Sources

Carmelitana Colletion. "Carmelite Spirituality and History." *carmelitanacollection. com/spirituality.php.*
Site is devoted to Carmelite spirituality, including a number of resources for prayer according to the Carmelite tradition.

"'Spiritual Canticle' by St. John of the Cross." *www.youtube.com/watch?v=k 0ZHDI8kKhs.*
Stanzas from John of the Cross's poem *The Spiritual Canticle* set to "May It Be" from *The Lord of the Rings* soundtrack (4 min.).

Films

Thérèse: The Story of Saint Thérèse of Lisieux. 2004.
This film depicts the biography and spirituality of the short life of modern Carmelite mystic Saint Thérèse of Lisieux.

10

Chapter

Ignatian Spirituality

The beginning of the last chapter discussed the general tendency of some forms of Christian spirituality toward elitism. Much of it was highly mystical, which itself tends to be rare even among the most devout Christians, and many spiritualities highly valued celibacy. On the one hand, any Christian could adopt many of the principles and counsels in these spiritualities. In fact, John of the Cross originally wrote his classic *The Living Flame of Love* for a lay woman he thought could attain mystical union. On the other hand, fully embracing a Dominican, Franciscan, or Carmelite spirituality seemed best suited for those willing to adopt a life of poverty, chastity (celibacy), and obedience. These three "evangelical counsels" were contrasted to the "commandments." Ordinary Christians followed the commandments, but God's "virtuosos" entered religious communities and embraced the counsels. Broadly speaking, Christians of the time assumed that everyone should strive for holiness, regardless of life commitments, but in general most believed that spending one's entire life focused explicitly on prayer and pastoral service gave one a spiritual advantage.

Ignatian spirituality counters this tendency within Christian spirituality to split Christian spiritual life into two camps: the great ways of the few and the mediocre ways of the many. This spirituality strives quite consciously and even systematically to discover God's presence in the day-to-day. It tries to *find God in all things* and learn how to become a *contemplative in action*. These are two core expressions of Ignatian spirituality. Appropriating them in one's life requires great detachment from all disordered desires and a perpetual availability to God, but anyone can do it. Once, while having lunch with a seminarian and a spiritual director, the seminarian asked whether I would advise taking on quite a serious fasting regime for the upcoming Lenten season. I responded much like John of the Cross would: "It depends on how holy you want to be." The spiritual director, trained in Ignatian spirituality, interjected, "No, it depends on what the Holy Spirit is moving your soul to do at this time." Herein lies the difference between these two spiritualities.

Ignatius and the Early Jesuits

Saint Ignatius of Loyola (1491–1556) was born to a noble family in the Basque village of Loyola in what is today northern Spain. He spent much of his early life as a soldier striving to promote himself in the royal court. He took up arms for the Duke of Nájera in 1509 and for over ten years was a successful soldier. But in 1521, while storming the fortress of Pamplona, a cannonball shattered his leg. He returned to his family's castle in Loyola to convalesce. Prior to his injury

Georgios Kollidas / Shutterstock.com

and convalescence he had been inspired by many chivalrous stories of romantic glory. During his recovery he only had religious literature to read, such as the Gospels and lives of the saints, but they kindled within him the same kind of enthusiasm. He noticed that the tales of chivalry and heroism that had energized and inspired him for a time quickly left him dry and dissatisfied. But when he read the lives of the saints, he not only felt inspired, he experienced a prolonged satisfaction and inner joy that the models of chivalry did not provide. Ludolph of Saxony's *The Life of Christ*, a commentary on the Gospels that borrowed deeply from the church fathers, proved particularly important to Ignatius's spiritual development. He discovered within himself a desire

In this engraving, the book held by Ignatius of Loyola, presumably his *Spiritual Exercises*, contains his motto: *AD MAJORAM DEI GLORIAM* ("For the greater glory of God"). This motto guides Jesuits still.

to be like Christ and emulate the heroic lives of the saints. In his autobiography, *A Pilgrim's Journey*, Ignatius describes the change from "having a vain and overpowering desire to gain renown" to feeling "loathsomeness for all his past life."[1]

In 1522, the recovered Ignatius made a pilgrimage to the Benedictine abbey in Montserrat, Spain. There he dropped "his sword and dagger at our Lady's altar

---

1. Ignatius of Loyola, *A Pilgrim's Journey*, nos. 1, 10. Translations from Ignatius of Loyola, *A Pilgrim's Journey: The Autobiography of Ignatius of Loyola*, trans. and commentary by Joseph Tylenda (Collegeville, MN: Michael Glazier, 1991), 16.

in the church."[2] He left the abbey as a poor pilgrim and went to live in a cave in Manresa where he prayed many hours a day. Ignatius also began formulating the Spiritual Exercises, a month-long retreat that stands at the heart of this spiritual path. Ignatius briefly traveled to the Holy Land, only to be rebuffed as a begging nuisance and ordered by Catholic Church authorities back to Europe. He decided that in order to help others, he needed a theological education, which he began at the University of Alcalá. He continued his studies in Paris where he met several students who also desired to live exclusively in service to God and the church. They would ultimately migrate to Rome and form the religious order *The Society of Jesus*, commonly known as the Jesuits.

The order, instituted in 1540, was committed to virtually anything the church needed; its mission was extremely open-ended. Ignatius and other Jesuits had guided many young men and some women through the Spiritual Exercises, which led to a rapid expansion of the order. By the time Ignatius died in 1556, over eight hundred Jesuits lived throughout Europe, with a few even engaged in missions in the Far East. However, few Jesuits actually knew much of what it meant to be a Jesuit. To be a Dominican was to be a learned preacher trained to give both clergy and laity an inspiring and intellectually compelling understanding of the gospel. To be a Carmelite was to be a monastic deeply engaged in the contemplative life. But what did it mean to be a Jesuit with such an open-ended mission?

In 1552, two of Ignatius's closest associates, Juan de Polanco and Jerónimo Nadal, asked Ignatius to dictate his autobiography. Nadal then traveled to all of the Jesuit houses in Europe to propagate both the order's revised constitution and Ignatius's story. Nadal believed that Ignatius's story was their story too; it was paradigmatic for the whole community. It was Nadal who coined the famous phrase "contemplation in action." This is who the Jesuits would become: they were to be more "Ignatiuses," who could discover God in the context of service. Among other things, Ignatius's autobiography describes a soul who has learned how to discern disordered desires, and so reject them, and has discovered how to encounter God in daily life. It also describes the quality of detachment or indifference. For Ignatian spirituality, being radically open to God's call, whatever it might be, requires cultivating a spacious, open heart and mind. Ignatius's autobiography focuses on helping souls and adopting the life of a pilgrim.

The Spiritual Exercises

Soon after Ignatius's conversion he developed the Spiritual Exercises, a month-long silent retreat designed to help in making an "election" or decision, or confirming on a deep level a decision one had already made. It served as a systematic

---

2. Ignatius of Loyola, *A Pilgrim's Journey*, no. 2.17.

way to come to a deep spiritual conversion. He begins the retreat director's manual with an explanation of his method:

> By the term *spiritual exercises* is meant every method of examination of conscience, of meditation, of contemplation, of vocal and mental prayer, and of other spiritual activities . . . every way of preparing and disposing the soul to rid itself of all inordinate attachments, and, after their removal, of seeking and finding the will of God in the disposition of our life for the salvation of our soul."[3]

Week One

The Exercises are divided into four periods, each lasting roughly one week. The entire Exercises are based on the principle that persons are created to love, praise, and serve God. Everything in the world, then, is only valuable insofar as it supports this end. The first week of the Spiritual Exercises commences with a meditation on the absolute love of God in creating human beings for the august end of living with him eternally. Once the soul clearly understands this, the rest of the week focuses on sin (universal and personal) and how the world and one's own life have resisted the divine plan. During one prayer period the retreatant focuses on Satan's rebellion and during another reflects on past sins.[4] By the end of the first week, one ought to see one's sins clearly and be repulsed by them as well as realize that one is loved and saved by Christ even as a sinner.

Week Two

If the purpose of the first week is to bring retreatants to a deep conviction of their personal sinfulness and God's overwhelming grace, the purpose of the second consists of eliciting a response to the question: Do you want to follow Christ? Week two's meditations help the retreatant to identify with the life of Christ and his ministry. One moves from meditations on the incarnation to his ministry and glorious entry into Jerusalem. Week one highlights personal impotence, while week two is about experiencing the liberating call of Jesus to be part of his saving project. Ignatius writes of the first meditation in week two: "This is to ask for what I desire. Here it is to ask for an intimate knowledge of our Lord, who has become man for me, that I may love him more and follow him more closely."[5]

---

3. *The Spiritual Exercises of St. Ignatius*, no. 1. Translations from Ignatius of Loyola, *The Spiritual Exercises*, trans. Louis Puhl (Chicago: University of Loyola Press, 1951), 1.

4. "I will weigh the gravity of my sins, and see the loathsomeness and malice which every mortal sin I have committed has in itself." Ibid., no. 57.

5. Ibid., no. 104.

Two of the most important meditations, which uncharacteristically are not biblically based, occur during the second week. In "The Call of an Earthly King" at the beginning of the second week, Ignatius has the retreatant imagine a holy, brave, and humble king who calls his subjects to join him in a holy crusade. This king promises that he will ride and sleep beside them, sharing the same food and drink and wearing similar clothing, and that they will share his victory. He writes, "Consider what the answer of good subjects ought to be to a king so generous and noble-minded."[6] Ignatius then has the retreatant imagine being called by Christ to fight for the kingdom of God under the same conditions and promises. Later in that second week, "A Meditation on Two Standards" has the retreatant consider that both Christ and Lucifer call the soul to themselves. Lucifer inspires horror and terror and summons his demons to destroy the world. They tempt with riches and the empty honors that go with the sin of pride. Christ, on the other hand, sends his followers throughout the world to preach the saving gospel. He attracts his followers with spiritual poverty, that is, humility. At this point the retreatant is called to clearly choose Christ.

Throughout the second week, the retreatant gets to know Christ, his values, and his ministry. This, Ignatius thought, is the Christ one must desire with all one's heart and serve with all one's strength. Retreatants also now ask for the grace to decide *how* to follow Christ, which could be in the married life, consecrated single life, or life of the religious orders. In Ignatius's own day, this was often the time young men decided to join the Jesuits.

Week Three

The third week of the Exercises is meant to confirm that decision—or, as Ignatius referred to it, election—by thinking about the consequences of that choice. This consists of a meditation on the Passion of Christ and an identification with Jesus, who suffers with and for the brokenness of the world. One meditates on every part of Jesus' final week in Jerusalem, including the Last Supper, his agony in the garden, his trials with the Sanhedrin and Pontius Pilate, and his crucifixion. The point here is that the decision to follow Christ and his victory must also be a decision to do so in and through his Passion. This is the cost of discipleship. While daunting, the cross becomes a meeting place of God's power, witness to the gospel, and deep forgiveness.

Week Four

In the third week, retreatants elect to join Christ through everything. They have fallen deeply in love with him, become convinced of his message and ministry,

---

6. Ibid., no. 94.

and are prepared to embrace a discipleship that includes a paschal movement of dying to themselves for his sake. During the fourth week, they meditate on his resurrected victory and share the glory of conquering evil. The retreatants experience Jesus alive, having surpassed all, and feel empowered to live in Jesus' unrestricted presence in the world. The mission and service of the gospel must be grounded in a lived experience of his victory.

The Suscipe and Anima Christi by Ignatius

Suscipe: Take, Lord, and receive all my liberty, my memory, my understanding and my entire will; all I have and call my own. You have given all to me. To you, Lord, I return it. Everything is yours; do with it what you will. Give me only your love and your grace. That is enough for me.

Anima Christi: Soul of Christ, sanctify me; Body of Christ, save me; Blood of Christ, inebriate me; Water from the side of Christ, wash me; Passion of Christ, strengthen me; Good Jesus, hear me; Within the wounds, shelter me from turning away; Keep me from the evil one; Protect me at the hour of my death; Call me into your presence; Lead me to praise you with all your saints forever and ever. Amen.[7]

Ignatian Prayer

Ignatian Contemplation

Central to the Exercises is Ignatian contemplation. Throughout the history of the church, biblical prayer has been important. From the patristic period on, lay people gathered daily in the church to chant the psalms and pray other biblical texts. Monks did this throughout the day and from the practice even developed a form of prayer called *lectio divina*, which involved reading the text prayerfully (*lectio*), probing the text for God's inspiration (*meditatio*), and responding prayerfully (*oratio*). Sometimes a sensed intimacy with God could even elicit a desire to remain, silent and still, in God's presence, having left behind the words of the text (*contemplatio*).

Ignatian contemplation follows something of this method, although it uses the term "contemplation" very differently. In Ignatian contemplation one does not simply read a text, but enters into the narrative as though actually present. Ignatius

---

7. See selected prayers of Ignatius of Loyola at *www.bc.edu/bc_org/prs/stign/prayers.html*.

encourages the "application of the senses," by which one imagines what every part of the scene feels like. For example, when meditating on Jesus' meeting and healing the blind man Bartimaeus in Mark 10:46–52, one might imaginatively enter into the scene where Jesus and his disciples leave Jericho. A blind man, Bartimaeus, calls out from among the large crowd, asking Jesus to have pity on him. The crowds try to silence him, but this only emboldens him. Jesus calls Bartimaeus over and asks him, "What do you want me to do for you?" Bartimaeus replies, "Master, I want to see." Jesus heals him, and Bartimaeus follows Jesus on the way.

Ignatian contemplation might have the meditator imagine what it would be like to be Bartimaeus and to suffer blindness or have some other malady. What difficulties and even persecutions would have been endured during those long years of illness? Then one might imagine the day: is it hot, cold? Is the sun out or is it cloudy? Are there trees and what do they look like? This could include a reflection on the smells of the day and the noise of the crowds or what kind of clothes everyone is wearing. The meditator might be emboldened by this opportunity to encounter the Messiah or even imagine being addressed by Jesus: "What do you want me to do for you?" Here one might consider one's deepest desires or deepest needs. For Ignatius, engaging one's deepest, most authentic desires also involves engaging God's Spirit, who infuses the soul with great desires. Retreatants might stay for a long time in this contemplation, asking God to reveal their deepest desires. This is what will ultimately be brought to Jesus.

Such a meditation might be done repeatedly, and each time one might encounter even deeper, more authentic desires or perhaps the same desire again and again—this itself is confirming. Alternately, a meditator might get stuck, unsure of this deepest, most authentic desire. It might take days or even weeks until that deepest desire becomes apparent. Typically, this meditation leads to insights into one's greatest spiritual thirst and leaves one with the understanding that Jesus wants to meet that thirst.

Colloquy: Talking to Jesus

A good deal of Ignatian prayer involves bringing up Jesus (or perhaps Mary or God the Father) and having a conversation, which Ignatius calls a "colloquy." This kind of prayer has many aims, one of which is simply intimacy. Ignatius speaks of talking to Jesus as a friend speaks to a friend. Ignatius argues that, although Jesus' words in such an imagined conversation come from one's own psyche, such a prayer provides opportunities for God to speak through one's mind and heart.

Two examples from James Martin's *A Jesuit Guide* show how this process might work. Martin describes two colloquies, both of which come from the exercises. In one, Ignatius has the retreatant imagine Christ upon the cross:

Imagine Christ our Lord present before you upon the cross, and begin to speak with him, asking how it is that though he is the Creator, he has stooped to become man and to pass from eternal life to death here in time, that thus he might die for our sins. I shall reflect upon myself and ask: "What have I done for Christ?" "What am I doing for Christ?" "What ought I do for Christ?" As I behold Christ in this plight, nailed to the cross, I shall ponder upon what presents itself to my mind.[8]

Martin makes this exercise more personal and speaks to the crucified Lord directly. "[I] started to grow angry. That anger was an obvious sign that something was happening deep down. 'I'm doing way too much!' I complained to Jesus in prayer, and then listed all the unnecessary projects that I should have declined. And I felt Jesus say to me, *'I'm not asking you to do all that.'*"[9]

Martin's second example recognizes Christ on the cross as someone who obviously understands suffering. Here he, like so many others, reflects with Jesus on his own suffering. "Seeing Jesus' suffering is a reminder that, for the Christian, we are accompanied by a God who, even if he does not—for whatever mysterious reason—take away our pain, understands it, since he lived as a human being. During the times of the worst anguish in my life it has been this prayer that has most consoled me: speaking with the Jesus who knows suffering."[10]

Consciousness Examen

Perhaps the most important spiritual practice in Ignatian spirituality is the "consciousness examen." This is not an examination of conscience, the practice of examining one's sins, often prior to the Sacrament of Penance. Rather, it is a spiritual exercise aimed at uncovering God's presence in one's life. It seeks to attune one's consciousness to the movements of the Spirit in one's life and how one has responded to those movements. Ignatius, who practiced this twice daily, considered this practice more important than any other spiritual exercise, a literal *must* for Jesuits on a daily basis. The examen has five steps: (1) recognizing one is in the presence of God; (2) giving thanks to God for the favors received; (3) asking for awareness of the Holy Spirit's aid; (4) recalling the specific events of the day; (5) offering gratitude, seeking forgiveness, and asking for continued growth in love.

Each of these steps deserves fuller consideration. The first step is not meant to be a quick intellectual acknowledgement of God, but a time to place oneself

---

8. Ibid., no. 53.

9. James Martin, *A Jesuit Guide to Almost Everything: A Spirituality for Real Life* (New York: HarperOne, 2010), 168.

10. Ibid., 298.

in God's presence quietly and lovingly. The context and ultimate aim of all prayer is this communion. Once settled in God's presence, one considers two kinds of favors: first, gifts given during that day, which involves noticing clues that guided one in living in God's love that day; and second, permanent favors, that is, gifts that comprise part of one's personality, vocation, and life in general. This second step entails reflecting on how those gifts have been experienced that particular day.

The third part of the examen is perhaps the most important. Here, in seeking the Spirit's aid, the individual asks the Spirit to guide one through the examen in wisdom as well as the freedom by God to look at oneself honestly and humbly. It is easy to take little or only partial responsibility for personal failings, so one seeks the grace for deep scrutiny. The examen aims to move one toward greater love and freedom for the future, so it requires looking at oneself without condemnation. Shame, for Ignatius, keeps people from God. Humble honesty allows for greater happiness and discipleship.

Ignatius's method involves recalling every event of the day. Thus one reviews the day hour-by-hour, noticing not only the particular events but also the *internal* responses to those events. Where was God there? Where was I inspired? Where was my heart divided? When did I act freely? One strives to see where Christ entered the decision-making process, even if implicitly. One reenters the experiences of the day, accepting them as the truth about oneself at that time. The freedom of the Spirit (third part) allows one to see both the beautiful and the ugly.

The final step of the examen is somewhat obvious. At this point, one has reviewed one's day, and to a certain extent one's life, and placed it before God. This last step, then, begins with gratitude. Even if the day seemed a failure, the examen helps reveal gifts received and perhaps participated in more than one would otherwise have realized. From this stance, one asks for forgiveness. There are literally thousands of small movements in one's heart throughout the day. To some, one responds expansively and in love and generosity; to others, one responds with tightness, reserve, and even outright sin. Ending the examen with the petition for greater freedom for growth and love logically completes the exercise. Engaging in self-scrutiny helps one recognize God's movements in one's life, moves one to seek God's forgiveness, and above all, offers one the opportunity for greater love.

Ignatian Discernment

The consciousness examen aims to help one grow in awareness of God's perpetual presence in one's life and heart. Where there is freedom and love, there is God's grace and a spirit of light. Where there is a disordered attachment, be it fear, greed, or any other dynamic that hinders the expression of authenticity, there is a dark spirit at work. The examen provides a way to constantly discern the movement of spirits, light and dark. It functions like Ignatian discernment writ small, a moment-to-moment, day-to-day practice of discipleship.

Ignatian spirituality also includes discernment on a much larger scale, as can be seen in the following scenario. Mary leaves college with two job offers—one to counsel underprivileged students in a Chicago high school and the second to counsel students in an upper-class private high school in Connecticut. Both could provide the opportunity for meaningful employment and service, but they would be decidedly different. Should Mary go to the underprivileged school, which has the greater need, or should she take the job in the upper-class school that, she presumes, educates future social leaders and where she thinks a witness to Christian values is particularly important? The first choice might appear more heroic, as it would require greater financial sacrifice on her part, but does this make it the most authentic choice for Mary? Ignatian discernment is about identifying God's will when faced with two good choices. Ignatius taught three ways or modes for determining God's will, which he called "elections."

First Mode: Clear and Unmistakable

The first mode is the easiest and requires virtually no real discernment. This consists of an unmistakable call from God, such as the risen Jesus calling Paul on the way to Damascus. Paul did not question the authenticity of his mystical experience. As noted in the chapter on mysticism, some experiences are so direct and profound that the soul simply cannot doubt that they came from God. They do not really require discerning God's will so much as simply obeying it—and given the extraordinary quality of the experience, one would have little problem doing so. If Mary heard an unmistakable voice from God telling her to go to Connecticut, her discernment would be done.

This mode of discernment, while appearing to be cut and dried, still involves asking questions, the first being whether it really is indubitable. Chapter 2 discussed the mystical experiences of a college student who later realized that his experiences were self-produced.

A second question considers whether such an experience aligns with scripture, church teaching, and reason. If it violates any of these, Ignatius believed it was highly doubtable. Finally, discernment entails distinguishing between the raw experience and one's interpretation of it. Often a dramatic experience from God is beyond words or concepts. Making sense of such experiences involves interpretation. While often necessary and not a liability, one must recognize it for what it is and ask, "How do I know my interpretation is accurate?" If, for example, Mary was considering both choices and, while thinking about the Chicago job became overwhelmed by God's direct presence in her soul, she might deem it proof that God wants her to take the Chicago job. Such an interpretation could indeed be sound, but it is just that, an interpretation. Mary would do well to consider whether God simply wanted to overwhelm her with his presence and she happened to be considering the Chicago option at the time.

Second Mode: Working with Desires and the Will

Ignatius believed that most Christians regularly wrestled with periods of consolation and desolation. For him, consolation refers to periods of being on fire for love of God. During such times virtue is easy and sin particularly distasteful. Consolation does not necessarily correspond to periods of emotional elation. For example, during the first week of the Spiritual Exercises retreatants pay particular attention to personal sinfulness. Sadness during this time actually reveals an experience of consolation, since one's experience directly connects to conversion. Typically, however, periods of consolation correlate to times of spiritual joy. God's grace feels warm, gentle, inspiring, and supportive. During such times, dark spirits, either from the psyche or supernaturally derived, would bring sorrow. Perhaps such dark spirits draw attention to difficulties associated with being faithful or elicit sadness for things missed.

Periods of desolation correspond to times of spiritual darkness, times when it seems hard to pray and temptations abound. These times are marked by thoughts of rebelliousness, selfishness, and even despair. During such times, dark spirits might feel artificially consoling because, although they cannot bring deep peace or actual delight, they can give an artificial sense of peace or delight. For instance, a college student might delight in planning for a spring break vacation that offers numerous opportunities for alcohol abuse and anonymous sex. This contributes to one's spiritual demise. During periods of desolation an authentic spirit of light would typically feel harsh, like a sting of conscience.

Honesty and self-knowledge are necessary in order to recognize dark spirits. Ignatius describes them as behaving like spoiled children who must be responded to quickly and dealt with firmly. He also characterizes such a spirit as a false lover who desires to keep the relationship secret. People do this with their sins, keeping them from others and even minimizing them to themselves. Finally, he suggests that a dark spirit can be like an army commander who will attack at the weakest point. One has to know one's weaknesses and where the dark spirits might likely attack.

The second mode of discernment involves listening to one's most authentic desires. Ignatius believed that God's will and the soul's will should align and that desires can be trusted when freed from any disorder. A happy, flourishing person reflects a Christian soul on the right path. The second mode, however, requires recognizing whether one is in a period of consolation or desolation. If in consolation, one can trust one's desires, as they are directed to God's glory. If in a period of desolation, one cannot trust one's desires, as one is struggling with disorders.

The Ignatian discernment strategy consists of four steps: (1) meditating on the life of Christ; (2) when in consolation, observing what God moves you to; (3) meditating on the alternatives of the choice and seeing how inspired you are with each alternative; (4) after a choice has been made, offering it back to God and asking for confirmation.

Meditating on the life of Christ brings one back to the logic of the Spiritual Exercises. The life of Christ serves as the model for Christian discipleship. One learns about Christ, his values, actions, teachings, and so on, and then strives to embody these. This first step could take many periods of prayer. Once grounded in Christ, one becomes aware of what one is being moved to. Ignatius says that often times a "counsel" comes to one's mind. In the case of Mary, it might be to take the Connecticut job. Even after experiencing such council, Mary might continue to hold both options in mind, perhaps even for many periods of prayer. Over such a lengthy period of discernment, one alternative ought to inspire Mary more than the other.

If perhaps Mary becomes convinced that God is drawing her to the Connecticut position, she might say to God something like, "I believe Connecticut is your will; now I set this aside and ask you to confirm it even more profoundly in my heart," as though it were not concluded. If it continues to feel right she may ask why that might be. Perhaps she is too attached to a cushy lifestyle or afraid of what her parents might think if she took the Chicago job. In the Ignatian model Mary would continue scrutinizing her inner life all through this. Ultimately, if it is the right decision, her fervor for God will increase.

Perhaps Mary finds herself in a period of desolation and cannot wait for a period of consolation because she has to make a decision immediately. In this case, given that her desires are in disorder, she might realize that the most attractive alternative is exactly the wrong decision. Dark spirits may be informing her desires and the spirit of light might feel distasteful. In a period of desolation Mary might find herself most attracted to the Connecticut position, and given that this attraction is likely disordered, she ought to choose Chicago.

Oftentimes, one part of the psyche is in consolation while another is in desolation. Mary might be in a place of fervor in general, finding prayer easy and sin unattractive, but yet still harbor a secret attachment to vanity and comfort. She knows that many among her family and friends would ridicule her if she chose the job in Chicago and this fills her with fear. She might choose Connecticut just to avoid confronting her fears and her attachments. She could question whether this decision is controlled by the part of her in consolation or the part in desolation. Discernment is complicated.

Third Mode: Reason

It could be the case that even if in a particularly strong consolation (or desolation), one might not recognize God's will for a particular discernment. In such a case Ignatius recommends using reason by applying the following method: (1) identify the decision to be made; (2) ask God to enlighten one's mind; (3) list the assets and liabilities of each alternative; (4) consider which option is more reasonable and which carries the weightier motivations; (5) after making a decision, return it to God and seek confirmation.

The first point of the method seems obvious enough: What is it I ought to decide? Yet, it may not be so obvious. For example, is Mary choosing a career path or perhaps simply a first job that she will have for only a couple of years before graduate school? What goes into being a counselor at each school? While the job titles seem equivalent, the actual jobs may be very different. Mary must ensure that she clearly understands each alternative. In asking God to enlighten her mind, Mary is not simply seeking rational sharpness to aid in her decision; she is asking for God's wisdom and consciously seeking God's will. Listing the alternatives, both pros and cons, means being mindful of her gifts and her professional strengths and weaknesses and considering how each job and the lifestyle that goes with it might affect her relationships and her spiritual life.

Presuming a complete and well-considered list, the next part of the discernment is the most important. Choosing one alternative over the other does not mean simply adding up the pros and subtracting the cons of each and finding which has the highest number. Thinking about which alternative is more reasonable is important. If Mary, for example, has always struggled with conflict, then the Chicago job could be a disaster, if it entailed dealing with conflicts. And what about weightier motivations? Mary might identify more pros with the Connecticut job and even fewer cons, but the chance to really make a difference in Chicago or the opportunity to confront her vanity might make the pros of the Chicago job carry more weight. This last point leads to a further Ignatian insight: one should consider which alternative would increase one's devotedness to God and which would challenge one's attachments most.

Ignatius suggests other ways to consider the third mode. If a friend in a similar circumstance asked which option she should choose, what would I recommend? A second suggestion involves considering the matter from an ultimate standpoint: what, at the moment of my death, would I have preferred choosing? When I look back at my life, which choice would I wish I had made? Finally, Ignatius suggests picturing oneself talking to Christ after death and asking oneself, which of the two choices would I most enjoy discussing with Christ?

This final counsel, and even the consideration at one's deathbed, might tempt one to think, "I would feel prouder to bring the harder choice to Christ." Ignatius is not advocating for the harder choice, but for the most *authentic* choice, the one that demonstrates the truest freedom and faithfulness to God. There is always a danger in "works righteousness," thinking that one merits something from God because of one's heroic actions. But a choice that ultimately boils down to "look at how great I was" is hardly authentic. Mary's life might be more heroic, at least romantically considered, if she took the Chicago job. It would be harder in some ways. She would have to live much more simply and she would be working directly with the poor. However, that may not be God's will for her—and finding God's will is the whole point.

Conclusion

Whereas Carmelite spirituality focuses on the interior life, Ignatian spirituality is a spirituality of doing.[11] John of the Cross argued that contemplative prayer does more for the universal church than any other spiritual work. Ignatian spirituality is about contemplation in action—that is, about discovering God's presence and activity in one's heart while still being active in the world. Ignatius said repeatedly that one must find God in all things. For Ignatius, discovering God means encountering God while engaged in the world. This is hardly easy, and it can be a cover for not praying at all. Ignatian spirituality proves daunting precisely because one is constantly at prayer, constantly creating a spacious mind and heart to listen to God in the midst of activity. The consciousness examen trains the heart to see where God was that day so as to be even more sensitive and solicitous to the divine presence the next day.

Because service dominates Ignatian spirituality, the kind of service one engages in is important. It would be typical for Jesuits to put at the front of virtually everything they write the phrase *ad majorem Dei gloriam* ("for the greater glory of God"). This is a hero's spirituality whereby one looks at all of one's pursuits and asks, How can I advance the greater glory of God? Jesuits regularly ask, What is the *magis* ("greater") possible here? What is the greater glory that can be advanced in this moment? A given situation might offer many excellent options for engagement, but for the better advancement of the kingdom of God, what is the *magis*?

The importance of Ignatian spirituality can hardly be overstated. Today, the vast majority of spiritual directors in the West, whether they be Catholic, Protestant, or evangelical, are trained principally through the Ignatian way. Ignatian style of biblical prayer is widely used throughout Christianity. Ignatian rules for discernment are by far the most utilized by pastors as well as spiritual directors. And the Ignatian emphasis of communing with God and discovering God's guidance in the midst of a busy world appeals to most Christians' circumstances.

---

11. In the Constitutions for the Society of Jesus, the phrase "service of God" occurs 140 times.

Questions for Review

1. How did the Jesuit Order develop from the time of Ignatius's conversion to the time of his death?
2. In what ways does Ignatian spirituality differ from and align with the other forms of Christian spirituality studied so far.
3. What are the main components of each week of the Spiritual Exercises?
4. What are the three "elections" or ways of discerning God's will in Ignatian discernment, and to what do they appeal?

Questions for Discussion

1. Ignatius found that stories of chivalry ultimately left him unsatisfied, while the Gospels and stories of saints inspired him. Have you ever had an experience where something that initially intrigued you left you feeling empty in the end? In contrast, have you found other influences that are continually life-giving for you?
2. Have you ever tried anything like Ignatian contemplation and put yourself deeply in a story? What are the possible benefits to doing this with scripture?
3. Is your decision-making process more like Ignatius's second mode of engaging deep authentic desires or third mode of using reason? What do you see as advantages to each?

Bibliography

Resources with annotations are highly recommended to students interested in further study.

Alphonso, Herbert. *Discovering Your Personal Vocation: The Search for Meaning through the Spiritual Exercises*. Mahwah, NJ: Paulist Press, 2001.

Egan, Harvey. *Ignatius the Mystic*. Wilmington, DE: Michael Glazier. 1987.

Egan, Harvey. *The Spiritual Exercises and the Ignatian Mystical Horizon*. St. Louis: Institute of Jesuit Sources, 1976.

Ewens, James, ed. *Accompaniment: The Integration of Faith, Prayer, and Daily Life*. Milwaukee: Ignatian Task Force Press, 1991.

Fleming, David. *The Spiritual Exercises of St. Ignatius: A Literal Translation and a Contemporary Reading*. Translated by Elder Mullan. St. Louis: Institute of Jesuit Sources, 1978.

Ignatius of Loyola. *Ignatius of Loyola: Spiritual Exercises and Selected Works.* Edited by George Ganss. Mahwah, NJ: Paulist Press, 1991.

Ignatius of Loyola. *A Pilgrim's Journey: The Autobiography of Ignatius of Loyola.* Translation and Commentary by Joseph Tylenda. Collegeville, MN: Michael Glazier, 1991.

Ignatius of Loyola. *The Spiritual Exercises.* Translated by Louis Puhl. Chicago: University of Loyola Press, 1951.

Martin, James. *The Jesuit Guide to Almost Everything: A Spirituality for Real Life.* New York: HarperOne, 2010.

This book popularizes the vast array of Ignatian insights in a way that is accessible and highly relevant.

Sheldrake, Philip. *Befriending Our Desires.* Rev. ed. London: Darton, Longman, and Todd, 2001.

This short book investigates how one ought to determine one's authentic desires and fruitfully engage them.

Toner, Jules. *Discerning God's Will: Ignatius of Loyola's Teaching on Christian Decision Making.* St. Louis: Institute of Jesuit Sources, 1991.

This book is arguably the strongest, most complete investigation of Ignatian discernment in English.

Internet Sources

Ignatian Spirituality. *www.ignatianspirituality.com/.*

This website offers a variety of resources for Ignatian spirituality.

Ignatian Spirituality Center. *www.ignatiancenter.org/ignatian-spirituality/.*

This website offers insights into Ignatian spirituality by topics and recommends books and other web resources for the study of Ignatian spirituality.

Muldoon, Tim. "Why Ignatian Spirituality Is Appealing for Young People." *www.youtube.com/watch?v=bQF8HhBUABs.*

(2 min.). Theologian Tim Muldoon briefly describes why Ignatian spirituality is particularly relevant today for young adults (2 min.).

Films

Black Robe. 1991.

This movie depicts a seventeenth-century Jesuit missionary traveling with Huron Indian guides to a remote mission.

11
Chapter

Spirituality of the Reformers

All human organizations find themselves regularly in need of renewal and reform, and the church is no exception. An early modern dictum expresses this well: *ecclesia reformata semper reformanda* ("the church is reformed and always reforming").

Even the apostolic church had reform movements. The church initially understood itself as a wholly Jewish expression of faith. Gentiles who wanted to join the movement had to become Jewish and follow the Jewish law (Torah). However, this came to be seen as an unnecessary burden, and the first great reform came when church leaders in Jerusalem decided that Gentiles were not required to follow Jewish law, save a few restrictions (Acts 15:22–29).[1]

The early church not only experienced reforms, it also experienced problems in leadership. At one point, Paul publically challenged Peter for acting hypocritically toward Gentiles (Gal. 2:4–14). Further, Paul believed that some preached for vain reasons (Phil. 1:15), and he described those whom he thought were perverting the gospel as "dogs" (Phil. 3:2).

The history of Christianity testifies to the ongoing need of reform. In the eleventh century, Pope Gregory VII worked to retake control of the Catholic Church from lay rulers and to reform the lives of bishops and priests. As mentioned in chapter 8, the Dominican and Franciscan orders arose in the twelfth century in order to revitalize the Church. During the fifteenth century the Council of Constance had to reconstitute the papacy itself. One could cite many other examples of reform within the Church. The sixteenth century bears witness to an extraordinary reform that broke Western Christianity apart. This chapter discusses the history of that reform and the spirituality of the three greatest leaders of the sixteenth century Protestant Reformation and their movements: Martin Luther, Ulrich Zwingli, and John Calvin.

---

1. Later Paul instituted a further reform that held that the Jewish law was no longer binding on any believer, whether Jewish or Gentile (Gal. 3:24–29). This, though, did not come without controversy and probably continued to be controversial for many years after Paul's death.

Historical Background

The fourteenth century was a disaster for the West. Economic growth, which had fueled the high middle ages, stagnated. In 1315–1317 famine struck Europe, and France was ravaged by war from 1337–1450. The Bubonic Plague ("Black Death") in 1348–1350 devastated many European cities and would reemerge periodically for decades. Peasants revolted against feudal lords, and the papacy itself moved to Avignon, France (1309–1378), thus losing much of its moral authority.

By 1500, a recovery was well under way. The population began rising by 1450, and between 1480 and 1530, a new prosperity began to emerge. This was the period of the Renaissance and a new cultural shift. The Renaissance represented an explosion of art, science, exploration, and a new kind of humanism. Renaissance humanism offered a new way of considering the human being and the very nature of human flourishing. No longer were virtue and wisdom learned through dry scholastic logic that moved from one deduction to another. Rather, one became imbued with the wisdom of the classics and thereby became a noble person. Many literate Christians took to reading the patristic masters rather than the abstract scholastic theology of the medieval period. While the writings of such giants as Augustine or John Chrysostom were far less systematic than Aquinas, they possessed a better rhetorical style and expressed a deep biblical imagination. Here the power of the word provided transforming spiritual and theological possibilities.

Perhaps the most famous Renaissance intellectual was Erasmus of Rotterdam. His works regularly challenged church and state, and he advocated for a simple piety based on the Bible. He invited the faithful to consider their daily lives as spirit-filled and potentially quite holy. His highly readable expression of the faith, *Enchiridion* (1510), was widely read and highly influential.

The Renaissance also created a greater sense of cultural democracy. The final two centuries of the medieval period saw the slow but progressive establishment of a literate middle class. The invention of the printing press in about 1439 made books widely available, and ideas could be quickly spread. It marked a time of personal empowerment. When Reformer Martin Luther proclaimed the priesthood of all believers, for example, he was not only making a theological point, he was also articulating the aspirations of an increasingly confident middle class.

One can observe this confidence in the growing body of grievance literature against the institutional Church that circulated throughout the early sixteenth century, particularly in Germany. The Church was in poor shape. Many priests were illiterate.[2]

---

2. The magical phrase "hocus pocus" comes from a bungled Latin phrase for the consecration at the Eucharist: *hoc est enim corpus meum* ("this is my very body"). Few people (priest and laity alike) knew Latin.

Demands for Church reform were widespread. King Ferdinand of Spain outlined a number of key reform steps, and he instructed the Spanish bishops attending the Fifth Lateran Council (1512–1517) to demand their implementation. Others at the council advocated for reforms to the papacy, the Roman curia (bureaucracy), and the episcopacy. The papacy was criticized for lavish excesses at the papal court; the curia, for the accumulation of offices and centralization of power; and the bishops, for suspect appointments and long absences from their dioceses. Bishops often purchased their offices and exercised their rule as a form of feudal right. Some were not equipped for the job, and many were not even residents of the dioceses they ran.[3]

Problems also affected the papacy. Candidates for the papacy were often members of powerful Italian noble families, who jockeyed for their favorite sons to occupy the papal throne. The three popes leading up to the Reformation offer a case in point. Pope Alexander VI (ruled 1492–1503), a member of the Borgias, a powerful Florentine banking family, was infamous for having bribed his way to the papacy despite having a number of mistresses and at least seven known illegitimate children. He was succeeded by Julius II (ruled 1503–1513), famous for his delight in military affairs and initiating the construction of Saint Peter's Basilica, paid in part by selling indulgences. Following Julius II was Leo X (ruled 1513–1521), another member of the Borgias.

Martin Luther (1483–1546)

Martin Luther was born in Eisleben of Saxony, a territorial state of the Holy Roman Empire (today northeast Germany). His father was a successful miner and eventually owned several mine shafts and copper smelters. Luther began his university education in Erfurt in 1501 where he studied law, but in July 1505, upon returning to the university after a family visit, he got caught in a thunderstorm. Terrified, he cried out, "Help me, Saint Anne! I will become a monk!" Popular biographies of Luther usually suggest that he regretted that vow, but thought it a mortal sin to break it. This may not be entirely the case. He had taken a leave of absence from his studies at the time, and, when his father urged him to return to law studies, he replied that he believed he could do more good as a monk than as a lawyer. Luther also embraced religious life with fervor.[4]

---

3. In France, for example, Antoine du Prat (1463–1535), the archbishop of Sens, entered his cathedral church only once, and that was as a corpse for his own funeral. In 1451, Duke Amadeus VIII of Savoy secured the appointment of his son as bishop of Geneva when the boy was only eight years old.

4. "I was a good monk," he reflected later, "and I kept the rule of my order so strictly that I may say that if ever a monk got to heaven by his monkery, it was I. All my brothers in the monastery who know me will bear me out." *Martin Luthers Werke, Kritische Gesamtausgab.* 69 vols. Weimarer Ausgabe Schriften (Wieimar: Bohlau, 1883–1929), 38:143.

In 1507, Luther was ordained a priest, and in 1512 he earned his doctor of divinity degree and began teaching biblical studies at the newly formed University of Wittenberg. During his early life as a professor he was troubled and perhaps even a bit neurotic. He exceeded his fellow monks in religious practice, even going to confession daily, but this gave him no peace or assurance. Was he a good enough Christian to be saved? Had he done enough?

Luther personally wrestled with a concern addressed in some sense in the early church, namely, what is the relationship between free will and grace? Pelagius, a fourth-century moral reformer, insisted that humans have free will, which allows them to follow God's commands. One would be judged on whether or not one had obeyed God. Augustine agreed with Pelagius that human beings had free will, but countered him on two fronts. First, he believed the soul was so devastated by sin that free will alone was insufficient to incline a person to resist evil and follow God. Second, he believed that God moved the soul to salvation by God's grace. Without that grace, human will was imprisoned. The Second Council of Orange (529) supported Augustine's view of the necessity of grace and that grace alone justifies a person. Furthermore, it taught that human beings needed a kind of predisposing grace even to be open to justification. However, the council also maintained that humans have the free will to accept or reject that grace, to engage and participate with it or neglect its movements in the soul.

The consensus in Luther's day held that individuals had a responsibility to cooperate with grace and choose to engage it throughout life. Lack of cooperation and ongoing engagement could result in losing one's justification. The dictum of the day was "God will not refuse grace to those who do what is within them" (*facerre quod in se est*). But how could individual Christians be sure that they had indeed done what they could to God's satisfaction? Could persons ever be sure of their salvation? The Church broadly taught that people could have a kind of moral certitude, which instills great confidence; still, the potential for self-deception in this regard was very real. Luther thought this possibility ultimately forced the soul to perpetually worry: "Have I done enough?"

Luther did not simply respond that Christians are justified by grace, as was broadly agreed. Rather, he believed that God's justification and even subsequent salvation was not dependent upon free will in any way. Human beings do not cooperate, and they play no part in God's justification. Luther identified three key components to justification: First, justification is *passive*, without any kind of cooperation or action on an individual's part. Second, it is *irresistible* in that God's grace literally takes over and transforms the soul. Finally, Luther believed that justification is an *alien righteousness*, that is, the righteousness a person gains is God's righteousness. God declares one just in light of his Son, and regards that person as though clothed in the cloak of Christ. Luther describes his epiphany:

> I greatly longed to understand Paul's Epistle to the Romans and nothing stood in the way but that one expression, "the justice of God," because

I took it to mean that justice whereby God is just and deals justly in punishing the unjust. My situation was that, although an impeccable monk, I stood before God as a sinner troubled in conscience, and I had no confidence that my merit would assuage him. Therefore I did not love a just and angry God, but rather hated and murmured against him. . . . I pondered until I saw the connection between the justice of God and the statement that "the just shall live by faith" [Rom 1:17]. Then I grasped that the justice of God is that righteousness by which through grace and sheer mercy God justifies us through faith. Thereupon I felt myself to be reborn and to have gone through open doors into paradise.[5]

The Indulgence Issue

Luther's position on justification contrasted with Roman Catholic teaching in several ways. Both parties agreed that it was grace that justified. But the Church, in contrast to Luther, taught that the soul had to cooperate somehow; it was not justified forcibly, nor was it utterly passive. Further, the Church taught that when God justified the soul, the soul was thereby changed and made to *be* righteous. This is to say, the first degree of sanctity or holiness is part of God's justifying grace. The soul's righteousness is real, and sanctification becomes part of one's experience of being saved. In proclaiming otherwise, Luther got the attention of Rome, which sanctioned him and demanded his silence on this issue. Although Luther's position on justification brought him into conflict with Rome, it was his objection to the practice of selling indulgences that drew him into public contention with the Catholic Church.

Early in Christianity the church practiced what would later be known as the Sacrament of Penance, or Confession. The church held that once Christians were baptized their moral lives had to evidence their new life in Christ. Christians, though, continued to wrestle with their moral lives. The church thought that individual Christians would work out minor sins with the aid of the conscience as they grew in the faith. But what about grave sins like adultery? The early church dealt with these through what they called the "Order of Penitents." Those who had committed a grave sin entered the order, confessed their sins to the bishop (who was the local pastor, in those days), and recommitted their lives to Christ. While in the Order of Penitents, however, they sat apart from others during the Eucharist and could not take communion. The faithful prayed for them and supported them during what was often a lengthy time of penance. When the bishop was satisfied with their penance, he proclaimed them absolved and allowed them to fully rejoin the life of the church.

---

5. Cited in Ronald Baiton, *Here I Stand: The Life of Martin Luther* (New York: Abington, 1950), 65.

As Christianity grew and spread, this practice changed rather dramatically. During the Middle Ages the Catholic Church taught that Christians needed to account for every sin and could do so with their parish priest. Priests relied on manuals that prescribed penances for certain sins. The Sacrament of Penance became a way of addressing both modest and serious sins. It involved four necessary aspects: (1) contrition—one had to be truly sorry for one's sins; (2) confession—one had to confess one's sins to a priest, who mediated both the community and God's forgiving word; (3) absolution—one was absolved of one's sins, that is, assured of God's forgiveness; and finally, (4) satisfaction—one underwent a necessary purging of the effects of those sins from one's soul. If the effects of sin were not purged in one's lifetime they had to be purged after death, in purgatory, thought of as a post-death experience of purification.

Typically, penances involved three traditional forms of renewal: prayer, fasting, and almsgiving. Penitents could give alms to the poor directly or to the Church. This opened up possibilities for corruption and abuse, such as paying money to the Church to be freed from suffering the consequences of one's sins in purgatory. Many challenged the practice of selling indulgences. Bohemian reformer John Hus (1369–1415) did so publically, leading to his trial and execution. The Church never taught that indulgences freed a person from sin, and it certainly insisted that one really needed full repentance to be forgiven. However, the indulgence program still looked to the faithful like a way to avoid the consequences of sin, and virtually everyone saw it as a way to enrich Rome.

In 1517 Pope Leo X authorized Archbishop Albrecht of Mainz to sell indulgences in northern Germany, the lion's share of which would finance the rebuilding of Saint Peter's Basilica. This constituted a financial strain for the German rulers, as disposable income would be diverted to Rome instead of the local economy. More to the point, it constituted a theological problem for Martin Luther.

The Ninety-Five Theses, Leipzig Debate, and Diet of Worms

According to the traditional story, Martin Luther posted ninety-five theses (statements) on the door of the Wittenberg chapel calling for a public debate, thus marking the beginning of the Reformation. This probably never happened. Luther wanted to address this issue more privately. On October 31, 1517, Luther wrote to Albrecht about his objections, enclosing the ninety-five theses. He waited for a response, which came relatively quickly: Rome cited him for teaching suspect doctrines about penance and papal authority.

In 1519, Luther and his colleague Andreas Karlstadt met with John Eck in Leipzig to debate the indulgence issue. Luther and Eck argued vigorously with a wealth of biblical and patristic material; Luther not only railed against indulgences but even the authority of popes and councils. Subsequently Eck

Martin Luther answers the summons of Emperor Charles V to appear at the Diet of Worms in this nineteenth-century engraving. By tradition, Luther is supposed to have uttered his "Here I stand" speech at Worms, but the story is unsubstantiated.

traveled to Rome with the debate's transcripts, and the universities of Louvain and Cologne condemned Luther. In 1520, a formal papal document (papal bull) demanded that Luther recant or be excommunicated. He publically burned the bull in Wittenberg.

During 1520 Luther wrote and published three great works. In his *Address to the Christian Nobility of the German Nation* he exhorted German princes to reform the Church if the hierarchy refused. In his *On the Babylonian Captivity of the Church* he argued that the gospel had become twisted by the institutional Church. He argued for only two sacraments, Baptism and Eucharist, and he rejected the teaching on transubstantiation of the Eucharist into the body and blood of Christ. He did not object to the real presence of Christ, but to the use of philosophical categories to explain it. Christ was "under" the bread, "with" the bread, and "in" the bread, but how he was there remained a mystery. Finally, he published *On Christian Liberty*, a book that described the nature of Christian discipleship.

Rulers in Germany argued before Holy Roman Emperor Charles V that Luther should not be condemned without a public hearing. When they met in Worms, Germany, for a formal *diet* or meeting, mostly to discuss the threat of the Ottoman Turks, Luther got his opportunity, although it was not much of a public hearing. Luther's books were stacked on a table and he was asked if he wrote them and what in them he now wanted to recant. Tradition has it that

Luther said, "Here I stand, I can do no other." What he actually said was less pithy but much richer:

> Unless I am convinced by the testimony of the Scriptures or by clear reason (for I do not trust either in the pope or in councils alone, since it is well known that they have often erred and contradicted themselves), I am bound by the Scriptures I have quoted and my conscience is captive to the Word of God. I cannot and will not retract anything, since it is neither safe nor right to go against conscience. May God help me! Amen![6]

Luther did not regard Church authority as absolute. He recognized the validity of a reasoned theological argument, but, for him, the Bible stood above all human authorities. He describes himself as "captive" to the word of God. Finally, in keeping with Renaissance culture, he embraced the principle of the primacy of the conscience. Faith was an intensely personal issue, one between the soul and the living God. He could not violate it.

Luther, burning the papal bull that excommunicated him, takes center stage in this nineteenth-century print of "heroes of the Reformation"—some of whom (note Wycliffe and Hus) actually predate the Reformation.

---

6. Martin Luther, *Luther's Works* (St. Louis: Concordia Publishing, 1955ff.), 32:112–13.

When Luther left Leipzig after his debate with Eck, Charles V declared him an outlaw and subject to capital punishment. In order to protect him, his prince, Frederick the Wise, arranged for Luther to be kidnapped. Luther spent the next ten months at Frederick's castle under the guise of a knight, adopting the name Junker Jörg (Sir George). During this time, he translated the New Testament into German for wide use among the people, and he eventually returned to Wittenberg a hero.

Lutheran Separation

Those who wanted to follow Luther's reform as an independent Christian communion initially had a difficult road to travel. In 1526, the First Diet of Speyer determined that each prince could decide how to address reform in his own land. The Second Diet of Speyer (1529) declared that Luther's reform would be tolerated only in those places where it could not be suppressed without violence. Further, those princes who accepted reform had to allow Roman Catholic Churches to co-exist. But in those principalities where the prince wanted to stay loyal to Rome, Lutheran Reformers had no rights. Six Lutheran princes protested against this arrangement and thus gained the name *Protestant*. In 1530, Emperor Charles V presided over the Diet of Augsburg. Luther, as an outlaw, was not permitted to attend, so his colleague Philip Melanchthon presented the formal Lutheran position, the *Augsburg Confession*, the foundational document of the Lutheran Church. Reformers from Germany and Switzerland rejected the Augsburg Confession and eventually submitted their own statements of faith. The *Peace of Augsburg* (1555) made it law in Germany that each principality could choose to either embrace Lutheranism or remain Roman Catholic. Those citizens who could not accept the decision of their principality were allowed to emigrate to lands aligned with their consciences. Southern Germany remained Catholic and northern Germany adopted Lutheranism.

Luther spent the remaining years of his life advancing the reform. He produced two catechisms, the *Large Catechism* for adults and the *Small Catechism* for children. He also revised the liturgy and produced a German hymnal. Luther's latter years as a pastor were not happy. Christians took seriously his challenge to Church authority, his insistence that works were entirely disconnected to salvation, and that one's own conscience trumped the laws of the Church. This resulted in a decrease in church attendance and a dramatic reduction in financial support. Ironically, over the next couple of centuries, Lutheran pastors increasingly preached sermons threatening divine retribution against members who openly disobeyed the disciplines of the Lutheran Church.

Luther's Spiritual Teachings

Luther did not think much of the human condition but he thought everything of God's grace: "If the word of God comes, it comes contrary to our thinking and our will. It does not allow our thinking to stand, even in those matters which are most sacred, but it destroys and eradicates and scatters everything."[7] For Luther, "One is at the same time both a sinner and a righteous person (*simul peccator et iustus*): a sinner in fact, but righteous by the sure imputation and promise of God. . . . And thus one is entirely healthy in hope, but is in fact still a sinner; but one has the beginning of righteousness, so that he continues more and more always to seek it, yet ever realizing he is unrighteous."[8]

While this seems a rather dour description of the human condition, Luther saw it as freeing. He believed this understanding would render irrelevant and harmless all questions about whether one has done enough, whether one is adequately cooperating with grace, and so on. For Luther, this position liberates one from the neurotic need to see if one is adequate; no one is! Now one can take one's eyes off the self and look only to Christ. The truly crucial problem, according to Luther, is taking one's eyes off of Christ.

The flip side of this passivity before God's grace is the proclamation of the utter effectiveness of God's activity in the soul: "The whole of a good action is wholly from God, since the will is simply enraptured, drawn, and moved by grace. Grace's drawing then resonates in the members and powers of the soul."[9] Thus, "Our works are then good when he alone is wholly their agent in us, so that no part of the work pertains to us."[10]

Does this mean that the will has no role in the Christian life, that the individual has no responsibility? The paradox for Luther is that, once freed from obsessing about oneself, once freed from the tyranny of "works righteousness," the Christian is now empowered to engage the Christian life vigorously. In this understanding, works become a response to grace and are driven by grace. Works are assumed, but not a condition for salvation. The Christian "acts out of an uncalculating, free, and spontaneous desire for pleasing God and promoting God's glory through these works, while in no way relying on the works themselves."[11] As Luther explained it, "The inner person, who by faith is created in the image of God, is both joyful and happy because of Christ in whom so many benefits are conferred on him; and therefore it is his one occupation to serve God joyfully and without thought of gain, in love that is not constrained."[12]

---

7. *Luther's Works*, 25:415.

8. Ibid., 25:260.

9. *Martin Luthers Werke*, 2:421.

10. Ibid., 5:169.

11. Ibid.

12. *Luther's Works*, 31:359.

Luther's Sacristy Prayer

Lord God, You have appointed me as a Bishop and Pastor of Your Church, but you see how unsuited I am to meet so great and difficult a task. If I had lacked Your help, I would have ruined everything long ago. Therefore, I call upon You: I wish to devote my mouth and my heart to you; I shall teach the people. I myself will learn and ponder diligently upon your Word. Use me as Your instrument—but do not forsake me, for if I should be on my own, I would easily wreck it all.[13]

Luther envisioned the Christian life as wholly joyful and free. Clearly he did not mean freedom to do whatever one wants. Luther was no libertine. In his *On Christian Liberty*, he challenges his reader: "Here a man cannot enjoy leisure; here he must indeed take care to discipline his body by fastings, watchings, labors, and other discipline and to subject it to the Spirit."[14] It is the same freedom preached by Paul: "For you were called for freedom, brothers. But do not use this freedom as an opportunity for the flesh; rather, serve one another through love" (Gal. 5:13). By looking only to Christ, one experiences the freedom of the children of God. This is an empowerment to love and serve. Having left behind an obsession with oneself, one finds Christ and only Christ, the true joy of the soul.

Ulrich Zwingli (1484–1531)

The first proponent of what would become the "Reformed tradition" was the Swiss Reformer Ulrich Zwingli.[15] Switzerland consisted of an association of largely independents states called cantons (the Confederation Helvetica). This structure proved important, as these cantons could more easily embrace the Reformation without the interference of the Holy Roman Emperor, and their major cities were free to act as they chose. Zwingli attended the University of Vienna (1498–1502) and then the University of Basel (1502–1506).[16] In 1506, he was ordained a priest and served in Garus, close to his hometown.

---

13. *www.iclnet.org/pub/resources/text/wittenberg/prayers/sacristy.txt.*

14. *Luther's Works*, 31:358.

15. The theology embraced by the Reformed tradition, however, was shaped primarily by Zwingli's younger contemporary, John Calvin (discussed below), who disagreed with Zwingli on many important points.

16. Both Basel and Vienna had been thoroughly influenced by Renaissance learning and Erasmus's writings, particularly those emphasizing the Bible as the great source of Christian inspiration and imagination.

In 1519 Zwingli came to Zurich as the principal preacher in the largest church in the city. By this time, he was convinced that every Christian belief and practice should be based on scripture, which he regularly contrasted to "merely human tradition." In Zurich he actively preached against many aspects of Catholicism, particularly those that had to do with the saints and icons (statues and paintings). As discussed in chapter 7, the issue of icons had been seemingly settled centuries earlier. Images of Christ and the saints were widely regarded as promoting devotion. The church, in both East and West, distinguished between veneration of the saints and worship of God. Zwingli, however, revisited this practice, now taking the part of the iconoclasts (icon-breakers). He saw in all icons blasphemy against the command against any graven images and considered them nothing but idols.

Zwingli's preaching alarmed the city council, which in 1523 arranged for a debate between him and a traditional Catholic representative. Zwingli won the debate decisively. This victory led the city fathers to announce separation from the Roman Catholic Church and the establishment of a reformed church based on scripture. By 1525, the council had replaced the Eucharist with a liturgy largely created by Zwingli himself. So focused on preaching the word, Zwingli would have liked to have dispensed with the Eucharist altogether and have the service exclusively devoted to the proclamation of the Bible and preaching the word. He did away with much church music and made the Eucharist a quarterly celebration.

Zwingli believed that the church should devote itself only to the practices found in the New Testament and that the Bible was clear on all important matters. If a given practice was not found in the New Testament, it was either optional (e.g., fasting), suspicious (e.g., tithing), or heretical (e.g., intercession of the saints). Given his iconoclasm, Zurich ordered in 1524 that all religious imagery be removed from every church and destroyed. Iconoclastic riots spread throughout the region, including in Bern (1528), Basel (1529), and Geneva (1535).

The Bible's Clarity

Could the Bible be interpreted so easily? Was it that clear? The Reformers embraced Luther's slogan *sola scriptura* ("scripture alone") and yet, Luther looked aghast at what happened in Switzerland. Luther was far less radical. While he believed that the institutional church could err and that some Roman Catholic practices were corrupt, he also honored the church's tradition at large. He thought iconography was proper, and he had a particular love for Mary, the mother of Jesus. While he challenged the idea of transubstantiation and the supposed scriptural basis for five of the seven sacraments, he also believed fully in the real presence of Christ in the Mass and embraced the practice of all seven rites. He thought confession was particularly valuable. Zwingli denounced all these views.

In 1529, Luther met with Zwingli and other Reformers in Marburg Castle at the request of the German prince Philipp I of Hesse. Philipp wanted to unite Protestant states in a political alliance and saw the need for religious harmony. The *Marburg Colloquy*, which spanned four days, was not a happy meeting. Luther left the meeting convinced that Zwingli was a heretic. The other Reformers in turn were not pleased with Luther either. For example, Luther's premier expression of "justification by faith alone" seemed problematic to Zwingli. All believed (as did Catholics) that Christians are justified by grace through faith. But faith *alone?* The New Testament did not use the term "alone" and the Epistle of James even explicitly states, "See how a person is justified by works and not by faith alone" (2:24). As for the Eucharist, Luther was convinced that the scriptures were clear about the real presence of Christ. Zwingli was equally convinced that the Bible taught that the Eucharist was merely a memorial meal. Whose interpretation was authoritative? For Lutherans, the answer was either decided by the Augsburg Confession or, on lesser issues, pastor by pastor. In Zwingli's view, because all Christians have the Holy Spirit who informs and guides their souls, every individual Christian's interpretation had a kind of self-authority.

Prayer of Ulrich Zwingli

Almighty, eternal and merciful God, whose Word is a lamp unto my feet and a light unto my path, open and illuminate our minds, that we may purely and perfectly understand thy Word and that our lives may be conformed to what we have rightly understood, that in nothing we may be displeasing unto thy majesty, through Jesus Christ our Lord. Amen.[17]

Zwingli's Spiritual Teachings

It proves difficult to elaborate Zwingli's spirituality. Above all, the Bible dominates his spiritual world. When the Bible is read and preached it becomes a sacrament of the presence of Christ himself, teaching and moving the soul. Zwingli writes that "I came at length to trust in no words [as] much as those [that] proceeded from the Bible."[18] There he experienced Christ most alive. The piety proclaimed by Zwingli was largely directed inward. While he conceded

---

17. *www.bybelwaarheid.com/index.php/en/the-prayers-of-the-church/item/279-the-prayers-of-the-church-prayer-of-ulrich-zwingli.html*.

18. Cited in Stephen Ozment, *The Age of Reform.* (New Haven: Yale University Press, 1980), 323.

that Christ's presence could be mediated in one's relationships and experience of the world, he actively deemphasized this in favor of the experience of the word, preached and heard in the heart. He did not want a purely anti-rational approach to the Bible, but even more so he did not want a purely rational one. The very point of the word of God was that it became an experience of the living Christ. It provided the content and served as the forum for personal transformation. The inner subjectivity of the word encountered had to be protected, indeed celebrated.

John Calvin (1509–1564)

John Calvin was born and raised in the town of Noyon, France, about seventy miles northeast of Paris. Although he wanted to follow his brothers into the priesthood, his father urged him to become a lawyer. After attaining his law degree at the University of Orleans, he went to Paris to study theology in 1531. Paris was a hotbed of theological controversy and decidedly hostile to Luther's reformation. Calvin, on the other hand, was sympathetic to Luther. He left Paris for Basel, Switzerland, and set out to write something similar to Luther's *Small Catechism*, which he entitled *Institutes of the Christian Religion*. This would become Calvin's masterpiece, and he continued to expand it for the next two decades, from six chapters to eighty. Calvin had no intention of becoming directly involved in the Reformation. He had planned to settle in Strasbourg, France, and spend the rest of his life studying and writing, but war made the road to the city impassible, and he ended up settling in Geneva, Switzerland. The city council had just evicted its bishop, and its leaders asked him to stay and help the cause.

All did not go well. His attempts to reform doctrine and practice proved controversial and were widely resisted, so much so that the city then evicted him and replaced him with a succession of weak ministers. Geneva seemed ripe for returning to Catholicism. French Cardinal Jacopo Sadoleto

INSTITVTIO CHRI-
ſtianæ religionis, in libros qua-
tuor nunc primùm digeſta, certiſque diſtincta capitibus, ad aptiſſimam
methodum: aucta etiam tam magna accesſione vt propemodum opus
nouum haberi poſſit.

IOHANNE CALVINO AVTHORE.

Oliua Roberti Stephani.

GENEVAE.
M. D. LIX.

Of the various Protestant traditions, Calvinism was the most theologically systematic right from the start. Calvin's major work, the *Institutes of the Christian Religion*, provided the foundation.

appealed to the Genevans to return to the Catholic fold. In his appeal he openly acknowledged the corruption in the Catholic Church and the need for internal reform, but argued that the Catholic Church was still the authentic church. Geneva's city council asked Calvin to respond, which he did in his famous *Reply to Sadoleto*. In it he argued that the Catholic Church had failed to continue the authentic tradition and had drifted too far from the ideal of a biblical church.

> You teach that all that has been approved for fifteen hundred years or more by the uniform consent of the faithful is, by our rashness torn up and destroyed. . . . [But] our agreement with antiquity is far closer than yours; all we have attempted has been to renew the ancient form of the Church which, at first distorted and stained by illiterate men of indifferent character, was afterwards criminally mangled and almost destroyed by the Roman pontiff and his faction.[19]

His response showed a belief in the church and solicitude for the tradition, but countered with the charge that Catholicism strayed too far from the tradition and distorted it. For Calvin, the church had two functions: preaching the biblical word and administering the sacraments. Elaborations that diverged from both the Bible and the apostolic church distorted the institution. Unlike Zwingli, Calvin believed that church life was central. His faith was a public faith, and he regarded any kind of privatized religion with suspicion. The scriptures were about truth—not each individual's personal appropriation of truth, but a public truth. Calvin recognized that the scriptures could be interpreted in a variety of ways, but insisted on the possibility of an authentic interpretation. In fact, much of his revisions to the *Institutes* consisted in a rigorously reasoned and defended interpretation of the Bible, showing how alternative interpretations were false.

In many ways, Calvinist theology represented a moderating voice between Luther's and Zwingli's. He supported belief in the real presence in the Eucharist because of its emphasis throughout the patristic era, but he showed more interest in its transforming effects than on what exactly constitutes it: "Our souls are fed by the flesh and blood of Christ in the same way that bread and wine keep and sustain physical life. . . . [This] cannot happen unless Christ truly grows into one with us, and refreshes us by the eating of his flesh and drinking of his blood."[20] Calvin also imagined a more democratic church, one that emphasized the priesthood of believers. For example, his system of church government involved synods of lay people. Geneva itself represented a church/state

---

19. *rels365fa10.pbworks.com/w/page/33320860/Calvin%27s%20%E2%80%9CReply%20to%20 Sadoleto%E2%80%9D*.

20. *Institutes of the Christian Religion* 4.17.7. Translation from John Calvin *Institutes of Christian Religion*, ed. John McNeill, trans. Ford Lewis Battles (Philadelphia: Westminster Press, 1960).

democracy, run by twelve members: four elected city officials, four pastors, and four lay elders of the congregation.

In another sense, Calvin's reform was rather extreme. He restricted public speech, dancing, and even the names one could give to one's children. Most severe was his understanding of the nature of the person before God. This included his teaching on "double predestination." Luther believed that souls had no free will regarding their election. God's grace worked within them passively and irresistibly. He did not consider faith itself as an act of the will, but the compelled response of a soul moved by God. Presuming that God did not save everyone, then Calvin's reasoning led to an obvious conclusion: God, from eternity, decided to create some for heaven and some for hell. Calvin saw this as a freeing message, one that allowed Christians to forget about themselves and focus on Christ and his redemption.

The doctrine of double predestination raises several questions: Is God then unjust in damning the vast majority of humans before they were born? What would motivate one to be good if the issue was out of one's hands? How could a person know that he or she was eternally elected? Regarding the first question, Calvin thought that double predestination demonstrated both God's justice and his mercy. Since all humans are sinners and deserve hell, God's damnation exemplifies his justice. And because no one deserves heaven, God's salvation demonstrates his mercy. As for motivation to be good, if any came from the soul's desire for salvation then that would constitute works righteousness, a failed plan. Rather, one does what is right simply because this is what a saved soul does. Finally, could an individual know that he or she was saved? Calvin thought, along with Luther, that the soul could know the presence of Christ within one's own heart.[21] The *Heidelberg Catechism* of 1563, created by Calvin's followers Casper Olevianus and Zacharius Usinus, said that the Holy Spirit, "assures me of eternal life, and makes me wholeheartedly willing and ready from now on to live for him."[22]

In contrast to the relatively privatized spirituality of Zwingli, the spirituality of Calvin's reformed movement was almost completely public and active. He was suspicious of any form of faith that withdrew from the world and especially from the public life of the church. Calvin himself said little about private prayer, but much about the church. The first chapter of his fourth book in the *Institutes* is entitled "The True Church with Which as Mother of All the Godly We Must Keep Unity." Calvin saw the medieval monastic system, which set some Christians apart, as a wrong-headed distinction between holiness and life in the world, and he would have none of it.

---

21. "Not only does Christ cleave to us by an indivisible bond of fellowship, but with a wonderful communion." *Institutes* 3.6.4.

22. Heidelberg Catechism, as cited by Howard Rice, *Reformed Spirituality: An Introduction for Believers* (Louisville: Westminster John Knox, 1991), 7.

T.U.L.I.P.

Although Calvin had much optimism for a holy faith thoroughly engaged in the world, he had little optimism for the state of the soul. Within a couple of decades Calvin's followers in Scotland produced the *Scots Confession* (1560), which proclaimed, "For by nature, we are so dead, blind, and perverse, that neither can we feel when we are pricked, see the light when it shines, nor assent to the will of God when it is revealed, unless the Spirit of the Lord Jesus quicken that which is dead . . . and bow our stubborn hearts to the obedience of his blessed will."[23] Within a century, the Calvinist Dutch Reformed Church held a national synod in Dordrecht, Netherlands (1618–1619). This included representatives from eight other European Calvinist churches. Their conclusions are sometimes termed the five points of Calvinism, given the acronym T.U.L.I.P.: Total depravity of the soul; Unconditional election; Limited atonement; Irresistable grace; and Perseverance of the saints. In short, souls are utterly sinful (and thus incapable of doing anything that would merit God's favor); God elects some without condition; Christ only atoned for those set apart from eternity; justification happens irresistibly (and is not dependent upon the individual's response to God's grace); and a person who is saved will remain in grace (as this was God's eternal plan—once saved, always saved).

Calvin and his followers could boast of a number of biblical verses to support each of these beliefs. Yet, they had to ignore other texts that did not work well in their worldview. For example, didn't Jesus save the entire world (John 3:16; 12:46)? Doesn't God desire mercy on all (Rom. 11:32)? Doesn't God will that all be saved (1 Tim. 2:4; 2 Pet. 3:9)? And didn't Jesus promise he would not reject any who would come to him (John 6:37)?

Calvinism, as it played out in practice, had a certain sense of circularity. In 1904, German sociologist Max Weber published *The Protestant Ethic and the Spirit of Capitalism*. In this study, Weber argued that many Calvinists worked very hard to be successful in the world in order to demonstrate that they were saved, as their lives showed fruit of God's election.

One problem in Calvinism is that many people, Catholic or Protestant, do not enjoy clear, palpable experiences of God in their lives. While the *Heidelberg Catechism* declared that "by his Holy Spirit, he also assures me of eternal life," many lacked this kind of clarity. John Updike's novel *In the Beauty of the Lilies* includes a telling conversation between Wilmot, a Calvinist pastor, and Orr, a dying parishioner. Orr was a simple man and serious about his faith, but he never had a palpable experience of Jesus Christ in his heart. In fact, in his conversation with Wilmot, he criticizes some members who seem to overshoot their religious experiences. Orr asks Wilmot about his chances of being saved. Wilmot assures him that they are very good. Orr demands to know on what basis Wilmot could

---

23. Cited in Rice, *Reformed Spirituality*, 21.

make such a claim. In reflecting on T.U.L.I.P. Orr argues that his salvation was something God decided from eternity and "There is nothing a poor body can do." God's election is both arbitrary and inscrutable. Maybe God chose Orr for heaven and maybe for hell; however, there is no way of cooperating with God's grace or affecting God's decision. Orr dies somewhat resigned as well as perfectly unnerved: he may be spending eternity in hell and there's "nothing a poor body can do."[24]

Prayer of John Calvin

Almighty God, since we are by nature so likely to make rash decisions, help us to learn to submit to You, and so to quietly rest in Your judgments so that we may patiently bear whatever chastisements that You may daily give us. . . . Help us to labor to mortify the flesh, so that by denying ourselves we may always declare You to be the only true God, and a just avenger, and our Father. Help us to renounce ourselves so that we may never depart from the purity of Your Word and so that we will be kept under Your yoke. Do this until we shall eventually attain that liberty which has been obtained for us by Your only-begotten Son. Amen.[25]

Calvin's Spiritual Teaching

Calvin's spirituality, like Zwingli's, is not easily categorized. On the one hand, it was relatively rational. Calvin's spirituality was certainly biblical, but he wanted to make sure that the Bible was intelligently interpreted, which resulted from theological argumentation. Faith was rational and could be defended. On the other hand, a robust sense of the living Christ within dominates the *Institutes*. The very point of the Eucharist, for example, was to *experience* the Lord's presence in one's heart and be transformed by that experience.

Further, Calvin's faith was utterly public. The church was central, and private prayer was valuable insofar as it led one to a deeper engagement in the church and world. Although not a "works righteousness" faith, it was decidedly a working righteousness one. The fruits of knowing the risen Lord within would be demonstrated by a life of skillful engagement in the community. The degree to which the kingdom of God was instantiated in this world depended

---

24. John Updike, *In the Beauty of the Lilies* (New York: Alfred A. Knopf, 1996), 43–48.

25. *misterrichardson.com/?p=313.*

on hard labor for the common good. While all Reformers would have agreed that "faith without works is dead" (James 2:26), Calvin's thought bears witness to this the most.

Conclusion

The Reformation created new ways of considering the Christian faith. No longer would the Reformers consider the church institution to have absolute authority. Rather, they put great emphasis on Christ and the soul, with the Bible being the centerpiece of spiritual and theological inspiration. As Lutheranism spread north through Scandinavia, various versions of Luther's theology and spirituality branched off, ranging from what is known as the *pietist* version of Lutheranism to what became known as the *orthodox* version. Those aligned to Zwingli's model spread as well, and it too took on various expressions, including the Disciples of Christ, the United Church of Christ, and many Baptist churches. Those aligned to Calvin became the Christian Reformed Church and Presbyterian Church, as well as other Baptist expressions.

Many Protestant churches and theologians now criticize the kind of biblicism that grounded the Reformation.[26] Most modern scholars talk about the Lutheran tradition of reading the Bible or the Reform tradition of interpreting the text. Even evangelical Christian scholars, who tend to be more conservative in such matters, generally recognize that the Reformers' views were, from a modern perspective, a bit naïve. Today they are more likely to speak of *prima scriptura* rather than *sola scriptura*.[27]

This in no way suggests that Protestant spirituality is inherently flawed. Protestants generally share a spirituality that looks to Christ above all. Being freed from the authority of the institution did not suggest being free from church discipline or public worship. Rather, it represented a refocusing on Christ, particularly in the written and preached word. Look at Christ, experience Christ within, and recognize that the assurance of salvation comes from knowing him: this was core to the Reformers' message, and it has remained so for many Christians. Additionally, Reformation spirituality challenges the potential elitism found in some forms of Roman Catholic spirituality. All believers have the same dignity before God and the same possibility to become holy, the Reformers

---

26. By biblicism is meant a confidence that the Bible provides the answer to every question, that it can be easily interpreted, and that such interpretation can be made without bringing the Bible into dialogue with theological principles not found within it.

27. As evangelical scholar Robert Johnson has said, "To argue that the Bible is authoritative, but to be unable to come to anything like agreement on what it says (even with those who share an evangelical commitment) is self-defeating." Robert Johnson, *Evangelicals at an Impasse: Biblical Authority in Practice* (Atlanta: John Knox Press, 1979), 6–7.

insisted. They challenged the Catholic priority of celibacy as more conducive to a holy life, and refocused attention on the holiness of day-to-day existence in society. They emphasized the priesthood of all believers and many Protestant communities today emphasize the unique authority of individual believers to interpret the word of God as the Holy Spirit moves their own soul. In short, Reformation spirituality is an empowered one.

Finally, from these Reformation greats Christianity received an inheritance of great hymnody, a return to a biblically oriented piety, and a way of thinking about the faith that grounds them in the world decisively. In the United States, the Protestant faith laid the foundation for slavery emancipation, as well as the temperance and women's suffrage movements. It contains true spiritual power.

Questions for Review

1. What socio-political factors facilitated the Reformation?
2. In what ways was the Catholic Church in need of reform just before the Reformation?
3. What role did Indulgences play in Catholic teaching and practice, and why did Luther object to them?
4. How did Luther understand freedom, and how was his position both the same as and different from that of the Catholic Church?
5. In what ways did Luther, Zwingli, and Calvin agree regarding Reformation theology and in what ways did they disagree?

Questions for Discussion

1. Both Luther and Calvin thought that church tradition was important, but that the Catholic Church, in their day, had strayed from the early church witness. Given what you know about the apostolic and patristic eras, do you think that they were fundamentally right or fundamentally wrong?
2. Both Luther and Calvin believed that human freedom played no role in the process of salvation, but that grace controlled everything. Does this argument seem compelling? What are the assets and liabilities of such a perspective?
3. What do you see as the major contributions of the Reformation for Christian spirituality? Are there any outcomes that seem to detract from spirituality?

Bibliography

Resources with annotations are highly recommended to students interested in further study.

Baiton, Ronald. *Here I Stand: The Life of Martin Luther.* New York: Abington, 1950.

This biography of Martin Luther is considered a classic.

Calvin, John. *Institutes of Christian Religion.* Edited by John McNeill. Translated by Ford Lewis Battles. Philadelphia: Westminster Press, 1960.

This is Calvin's masterpiece, and still serves as a foundational Protestant Reformed document.

Ford, Gerhard. *On Being a Theologian of the Cross: Reflections on Luther's Heidelberg Disputation, 1518.* Grand Rapids: Eerdmans, 1997.

Hendrix, Scott, ed. and trans. *Early Protestant Spirituality.* New York: Paulist Press, 2009.

Luther, Martin. *Luther's Works.* 54 vols. St. Louis: Concordia Publishing, 1955ff.

Luther, Martin. *Martin Luthers Werke, Kritische Gesamtausgabe.* Weimarer Ausgabe Schriften. 69 vols. Weimar: Bohlau, 1883–1929.

Luther, Martin. *On Christian Liberty.* Translated by W. A. Lambert. Minneapolis: Fortress Press, 2003.

Luther, Martin. *The Theologia Germanica of Martin Luther.* Translated by Bengt Hoffman. Mahwah, NJ: Paulist Press, 1980.

Marius, Richard. *Martin Luther: The Christian between God and Death.* Cambridge, MA: Harvard University Press, 1999.

This biography shows something of the personality of Martin Luther.

Ozment, Steven. *The Age of Reform.* New Haven: Yale, 1980.

Rice, Howard. *Reformed Spirituality: An Introduction for Believers.* Louisville: Westminster John Knox, 1991.

This may be the best short expression of modern Reformed spirituality in dialogue with its original tradition.

Rupp, E. Gordon, and Philip Watson, eds. *Luther and Erasmus: Free Will and Salvation.* Philadelphia: Westminster Press, 1969.

Senn, Frank, ed. *Protestant Spiritual Traditions.* Eugene, OR: Wipf and Stock, 2000.

Wicks, Jared. *Luther and His Spiritual Legacy.* Wilmington, DE: Michael Glazier. 1983.

Internet Sources

Episcopal Church. *www.episcopalchurch.org/.*

> Anglicanism, represented in the United States primarily by the Episcopal Church, embraced a less extreme break from Roman Catholicism than did the other Reformation churches. Anglicanism rejects the authority of the pope, but retains much of Catholic spirituality and worship.

Evangelical Lutheran Church in America. *www.elca.org/.*

> The Evangelical Lutheran Church in America is currently the largest Lutheran denomination in the United States.

Presbyterian Church (U. S. A.). *www.pcusa.org/.*

> Of the several denominations that have grown from the teachings of John Calvin, the PCUSA is the largest in the United States.

Southern Baptist Convention. *www.sbc.net.*

> The churches that are most closely aligned to the theology of Ulrich Zwingli tend either to be independent congregations or loosely affiliated in "conventions" rather than denominations. Of these, the Southern Baptist Convention is the largest in the United States.

Films

Luther. 2009.

> This biopic examines Martin Luther's personal battles and his transformation from a monk and teacher in a small German city into the leader of the Protestant movement.

12
Chapter

Evangelical Spirituality

Just under three-fourths of Americans identify themselves as Christian. Among them, about half claim to have been "born again," or to have accepted Jesus Christ as their personal Lord and Savior. Why just half? Wouldn't being Christian necessarily involve being born again or claiming to have Jesus as one's personal Lord? The term "born again" comes from John's Gospel in a dialogue Jesus has with the Pharisee Nicodemus. Jesus says, "Amen, amen, I say to you, no one can see the kingdom of God without being born from above" (John 3:3). The biblical phrase here is *gennēthē anōthen*, which can be translated "born from above" or "born again." Taking a new spiritual identity and accepting Jesus as Lord is central to Christian baptism and applies to all Christians. Why then did only half of American Christians respond positively to this identification? One answer might be that many self-identified Christians are merely culturally Christian and have not really appropriated their faith. Although perhaps true, it may have more to do with the way the phrases "born again" and "personal Lord" have become associated with the evangelical tradition. Such language can be a specific identifier for being an evangelical.

What makes a person an evangelical Christian is hard to define. For some, "evangelical" refers to belonging to a non-denominational Christian church. If one is not a Lutheran, Catholic, Presbyterian, and so on, then one is an evangelical. For others, it refers to both non-denominational churches (evangelical Free churches) as well as certain denominations that fall under a larger Evangelical umbrella, including Pentecostal denominations and the Southern Baptist Convention. For still others, it represents a way of being Christian that exists within a number of otherwise mainstream churches. All of these approaches are valid and each reflects something of the evangelical movement, from its beginnings to the present.

Initially, the term *evangelical* was used in the Reformation period to describe Christians who accepted the Reformers' insistence on a biblical faith, with an emphasis on the preached word. In the seventeenth century, it referred to the German Pietistic movement as well as forms of English Puritanism.

These emphasized personal conversion and a faith infused with heart. These movements advocated a life-transforming piety over a rational, rule-based Protestant faith. They showed little interest in dogma or liturgy, but great interest in an interpersonal life with Christ. These elements figure prominently among some Lutherans, Methodists, Congregationalists, Baptists, and Presbyterians, and more universally among Restorationist[1] churches such as the Church of Christ and Disciples of Christ. Today, it can also imply a particular theological framing of the faith. Generally speaking, evangelicals hold that the Bible is inerrant and verbally inspired; that is, they believe that the very words, not just the ideas, of the Bible are inspired by the Holy Spirit. They also believe that biblical interpretation is the job of the individual believer, rather than church authority. They tend to anticipate the near return of Jesus (the "second coming"), and they attach great importance to preaching. evangelicals observe the Lord's Supper and Baptism, but interpret them along Zwinglian lines, as symbols rather than sacraments. Historically, evangelicals have tended to be suspicious of Roman Catholicism. In general, their theology and spirituality draw heavily from Zwingli and Calvin.

In the modern period, evangelical Christianity has been wildly successful in terms of membership. John Vaughn, in *Church Growth Today*, reports that nine of the ten most rapidly growing non-Catholic churches in the United States, and 93 out of the top 100, self-identify as coming under the evangelical umbrella.[2]

Pietism and the Origins of Evangelical Christianity

By the late seventeenth century, many German Lutherans were unhappy with their state religion. They viewed Lutheran orthodoxy as austere and lacking warmth. After the Thirty-Years War (1618–1648) a revivalist movement known as Pietism emerged. It gained momentum when Philip Jakob Spener (1635–1705) published his *Pia Desideria* (Pious Desires) in 1675, which quickly became a sensation. This book challenged Lutheranism's obsession with theological orthodoxy and argued for a devotional life centered on a personal relationship with Christ. Later Nikolaus Ludwig von Zinzendorf (1700–1760) founded a Pietist community known as the "Herrnhuter," named after the village of Herrnhut in Saxony, Germany. This community stressed the importance of a religion of the heart, with a great emphasis on spiritual emotions. For Zinzendorf and his community, faith did not consist of mere acceptance of doctrine, nor even what Luther understood as absolute trust in Christ. Rather, it was about a personal, interior, transforming encounter with God.

---

1. Restorationism refers to efforts to restore the church to the supposedly pure state it enjoyed in the time of the apostles.

2. Mark Noll, *American Evangelical Christianity: An Introduction* (Oxford: Blackwell, 2001), 278.

In England, John Bunyan published *Pilgrim's Progress* just three years after Spener's *Pia Desideria*, in 1678. It too became an instant classic. Bunyan offered an allegory of the Christian struggle to overcome sin and find salvation. It succeeded in translating the truths of Protestant theology, particularly that of the Swiss Reformers, into the subjective experience of the pilgrim, the main character of the book, who represented every Christian. *Pilgrim's Progress* clearly communicated the message that doctrine and church institution mattered little, while one's individual relationship with God mattered completely. It told a story of inward repentance, assurance of Christ's forgiveness, and the grace-guided will to live a holy life. One can see in it something of the individualism that will mark evangelical Christianity. In contrast to Luther and Calvin's church-centered faith, this was an individual faith, with religion principally a private affair of the heart.

> Now I saw in my dream, that the highway up which Christian was to go, was fenced on either side with a Wall, and that Wall is called Salvation. Up this way therefore did burdened Christian run, but not without great difficulty, because of the load on his back.
>
> He ran thus till he came to a place somewhat ascending; and upon that place stood a Cross, and a little below in the bottom, a sepulchre. So I saw in my dream, that just as Christian came up with the Cross, his burden loosed from off his shoulders, and fell from off his back; and began to tumble, and so continued to do so till it came to the mouth of the sepulchre, where it fell in, and I saw it no more.
>
> Then was Christian glad and lightsome, and said with a merry heart, "He hath given me rest, by his sorrow, and life, by his death." Then he stood a while, to look and wonder; for it was very surprising to him that the sight of the Cross would thus ease him of his burden. He looked therefore, and asked again, even till the springs that were in his head sent the waters down his cheeks. . . . Then Christian gave three leaps for joy, and went on singing.[3]

This exemplifies a deeply heartfelt religious experience and illustrates an individualized expression of faith. The pilgrim walks the path of faith alone, personally scaling the wall of salvation, and finds that Christ's redemption eases his burden.

Methodism

Pietism marks the beginnings of a movement to relocate the essence of the Christian faith and revitalize the Protestant revolution. This collective agenda was furthered by the work of John Wesley (1703–1791), his brother Charles

---

3. John Bunyan, *The Pilgrim's Progress*, ed. Roger Sharrock (London: Penguin, 1987), 35–36.

(1707–1788), and George Whitefield (1714–1770), all of whom were members of the Church of England. All three bemoaned the prevailing religious culture, which they thought was geared to upper-class sensitivities and lacked transforming power. They gathered as students at Oxford University and founded a "Holy Club," where they met regularly and developed a rigorous schedule of spiritual disciplines. They came to be known as "Methodists" because of their methodical means for spiritual growth. John Wesley later would travel to Herrnhut to see how the German Pietist movement worked, and he came away both impressed and inspired to make this spirit part of his ministry.

Wesley describes his own profound conversion experience:

> In the evening I went very unwillingly to a society in Aldersgate Street [London], where one was reading Luther's Preface to the Epistle to the Romans. About a quarter before nine, while he was describing the change which God works in the heart through faith in Christ, I felt my heart strangely warmed. I felt I did trust Christ—Christ alone for salvation; and an assurance was given to me that He had taken away my sins, even mine, and saved me from the law of sin and death.[4]

Strikingly, Wesley was already a Christian, and a relatively serious one, but he describes this moment as his conversion. Conversion for him represents more than merely believing in the gospel or following the moral demands of his faith. Rather it served as a "second baptism" in which his heart _knew_ the Lord and experienced him powerfully within.

As the fledgling Methodist movement grew, members of the Church of England gathered during the week for prayer, Bible reading, and mutual support. Itinerant preachers would travel around the circuit of such groups to give additional support. Wesley preached throughout the English countryside. In contrast to more "high church" Anglicans, he sought out the laborers, particularly miners, and provided an appealing witness to an experiential form of Christian faith. Methodism's emphasis on experience raised criticisms among the press and upper class Christian culture. They called it "enthusiasm" and derided the sometimes dramatic religious fervor, such as "faintings and swoonings" that often accompanied conversions. Actually, Wesley was also suspicious of an overly emotional faith and had hoped to provide something of a middle ground between rigid orthodoxy and an excessively emotional faith. Wesley himself never left the Anglican Church. He had hoped to buttress it with authentic religious inner life, but ultimately after his death the movement he started evolved into a new denomination, the Methodist Church.

---

4. John Wesley, *Journal of John Wesley*, May 24, 1738, as cited in John and Charles Wesley, *John and Charles Wesley: Selected Prayers, Hymns, Journal Notes, Sermons, Letters and Treatises*, ed. Frank Whaling (Mahwah, NJ: Paulist Press, 1981), 107.

Evangelicalism in the United States
Early Revivals

The history of evangelicalism in the United States is marked by revivals and "awakenings." Between 1688 and 1763 Britain and France (and periodically Spain) fought a series of wars that regularly involved the North American colonies. These wars fueled fears among the colonists that the "Catholic powers" would overwhelm them. Religious revival served to return churches to true godliness and strengthened the colonists to face the perceived Catholic menace.

In the 1670s, Puritan leaders began calling for an outpouring of the Holy Spirit in order to reinvigorate church life. Samuel Torrey, pastor in Weymouth, Massachusetts, is seen by many as the first American evangelical.[5] Torrey thought that the church in the colonies was languishing, and he was certain that simply calling people to greater zeal would not achieve any substantive revitalization. The Holy Spirit had to revive them. By 1674 he was proclaiming to other pastors and congregations a need for a true Christian revival.

Among those who took on the call was Solomon Stoddard, pastor in Northampton, Massachusetts. He held five revivals, which he called "harvests" (1679, 1683, 1690, 1712, and 1718). A revival was typically a several-day gathering designed to reinvigorate the faith through singing, dramatic preaching, and calls for new (or renewed) conversions. Like Torrey, he believed that only God's grace could truly transform Christians. He also believed that powerful preaching was the principal means for God to work. He preached, and encouraged other pastors to preach, the very real threat of damnation and the beautiful hope of salvation. For him, the most effective part of the message was the dread of damnation. This would lead sinners to true "humiliation" or an utter sense of dread before God's holiness.

Revivals were held throughout New England. The first major event in Connecticut (1720) boasted hundreds of new conversions. Perhaps the greatest revival at the time came in 1727 in the aftermath of an earthquake that rocked New England. Seekers, utterly unnerved about the state of their souls, filled the churches. Pastors throughout the colonies responded to the earthquake with calls for repentance. In the 1720s and 1730s revivals spread to the middle colonies of New Jersey, Pennsylvania, and New York. As more clergy from the continent arrived, the Pietist "religion of the heart" took off full force.

Having one's own narrative of personal conversion, as seen in Wesley, was not new to American Protestantism. In Calvinsim, a palpable experience of the living Christ assured one of having been elected. In the seventeenth century, New England congregations typically only admitted to full membership those individuals who could detail such an experience. As the century progressed, fewer

---

5. A prominent figure, Torrey was twice offered the presidency of Harvard University, but declined both times.

and fewer could testify to such a conversion. As part of a compromise reached in 1662, many congregations began to accept "half-way" memberships, admitting Christians who, while not able to recount a dramatic conversion experience, did believe in the truths of Christianity and its morals. To a great extent these revivals aimed to provide the conditions conducive to such inner conversions.

Jonathan Edwards

Jonathan Edwards (1703–1758), Stoddard's grandson, led what was perhaps the greatest expression of revivalism, referred to as the *First Great Awakening*. Edwards held outdoor meetings that sometimes attracted as many as twenty thousand persons. The most important revival took place in 1734–1735 in Northampton, Massachusetts, where Edwards took over his grandfather's pulpit. Edwards's own account mentions thirty-two communities besides Northampton that experienced dramatic awakenings, often in response to threats of damnation. In this regard he followed his grandfather closely, as can be seen in this passage from his famous sermon *Sinners in the Hands of an Angry God*:

> The bow of God's wrath is bent, and the arrow made ready on the string, and justice bends the arrow at your heart, and strains the bow, and it is nothing but the mere pleasure of God, and that of an angry God, without any promise or obligation at all, that keeps the arrow one moment from being made drunk with your blood. . . . The God that holds you over the pit of hell, much as one holds a spider, or some loathsome insect over the fire, abhors you, and is dreadfully provoked: his wrath towards you burns like fire; he looks upon you as worthy of nothing else, but to be cast into the fire; he is of purer eyes than to bear to have you in his sight; you are ten thousand times more abominable in his eyes, than the most hateful venomous serpent is in ours. You have offended him infinitely more than ever a stubborn rebel did his prince; and yet it is nothing but his hand that holds you from falling into the fire every moment. It is to be ascribed to nothing else that you did not go to hell the last night; that you was suffered to awake again in this world, after you closed your eyes to sleep. And there is no other reason to be given why you have not dropped into hell since you arose in the morning, but that God's hand has held you up. There is no other reason to be given why you have not gone to hell, since you have sat here in the house of God, provoking his pure eyes by your sinful wicked manner of attending his solemn worship. Yea, there is nothing else that is to be given as a reason why you do not this very moment drop down into hell.[6]

---

6. Jonathan Edwards, "Sinners in the Hands of an Angry God," found at *voicesofdemocracy.umd.edu/edwards-sinners-in-the-hands-speech-text*.

This and other sermons had a great effect on their listeners, with some congregants fainting. Although this enthusiasm eventually waned, revivalism had become part of the American scene, due in large part to the publication of Edwards's memoirs, *Faithful Narrative*, which became a new literary genre: the conversion narrative.

George Whitefield

George Whitefield (1714–1770) was a friend of the Wesley brothers and certainly America's first religious celebrity. Although an Anglican priest, he worked with many different denominations. For him, and for the evangelical movement at large, religious loyalty had little to do with institutional membership and everything to do with new birth in the Spirit.

Whitefield grew up in England and became a deacon in the Anglican Church. After his diaconate ordination, he initiated an itinerant preaching mission, principally in London and Bristol. He became a sensation, and his published sermons were widely disseminated. Soon Whitefield was preaching to large crowds in open-air forums.[7]

In 1738, Whitefield received an invitation from the Wesley brothers, who had moved to the colonies to spread their Methodist style of faith. They had settled in the newly formed colony of Georgia and asked Whitefield to help with their mission. By the time he arrived, the Wesleys had already departed, their demanding morality having alienated many Georgian Christians.[8] After three months in Georgia, Whitefield returned briefly to England and was ordained a priest. There the Methodists warmly welcomed him and Whitefield, in turn, defended them against traditional Anglicans. Whitefield began to think that while he and his brother priests shared the same ordination, they did not share the same Christ. Theirs, he thought, was an outward Christ, believed in from a distance. He was convinced that one needed an inward Christ, a living Lord forming one's heart.

Whitefield returned to the colonies in 1739. Edwards had invited him to preach in his Northampton church, and Edwards later wrote that he was so struck by the elegance, grandeur, and deep faith of Whitefield that he wept throughout the entire sermon. From Northampton, Whitefield went on to Delaware and began his first major preaching tour of the colonies, including North Carolina, South Carolina, and Boston in 1740, and then back to England.

The Great Awakening brought dramatic changes. Denominations mattered little and dramatic interior faith meant much, so Christians began to

---

7. Ben Franklin once heard him preach in England and estimated that twenty-five thousand persons heard him that day.

8. John had also had an ugly public romance that scandalized the people of Savannah.

feel free to leave their established churches and form their own. This was profoundly threatening to established congregations. Connecticut even passed laws intended to stop itinerant preachers and the congregations they inadvertently created, but to little avail. Freedom of conscience, which the Protestant Reformers had celebrated, became central to the ethos of what was known as "radical evangelicalism." New England saw literally hundreds of new congregations spring up.

Many New Englanders believed these revivals were a prelude to the imminent second coming of Christ. Within twenty years, however, the colonists required another round of revivals. Interestingly, the leaders, while striving to instill personal faith, also appealed to rights of individual conscience. The evangelicals' emphasis on private judgment and freedom to separate from established powers unintentionally created a culture of populism and democratization in America, paving the way for the cause of independence from England.

Modern Evangelicalism in the United States

Second Great Awakening

1800–1830 saw a second great awakening, one that aligned with a ten-fold increase in church attendance, easily outstripping the population growth. The first revival happened in Rural Kentucky in 1801. It consisted of large camp meetings, the greatest being the "Cane Ridge" meeting, which lasted a week and was attended by over ten thousand persons. These are extraordinary numbers, given that Kentucky did not have the dense population of the New England states. Like previous revivals, this one appealed to people's emotions rather than their intellects and stressed an individual commitment to Christ over church membership. This second great awakening presaged the emergence of the "Bible Belt"—from Missouri, Kentucky, and North Carolina in the north to Texas through Georgia in the south—and formed the basis for the Southern Baptist Convention.

The Second Great Awakening differed from the first in that the second was decidedly more egalitarian, with little distinction made between the educated clergy and the uneducated laity. It stressed the spiritual impulses of ordinary people embracing a simple and enthusiastic faith; one they could define for themselves and witness to.

A pivotal figure in the Second Great Awakening was Charles Grandison Finney (1792–1875). One of his revival techniques was the "altar call," an invitation to come to the front of the congregation, publically accept the faith, and receive the "baptism of the Holy Spirit." The twentieth-century revivals would adopt this method. Finney also developed what he called the "anxious seat," where those considering becoming Christian would sit while others prayed over them. Like the Wesleys, Finney was known as a strict moralist. He believed that faith had to be expressed in an utterly new life, one free from sin. Finney also advocated for the abolition of slavery and championed the rights of women.

Developments in Evangelicalism in the United States

Dwight L. Moody (1837–1899) followed in Finney's footsteps. He not only continued revival meetings, but also started the Moody Bible Institute in Chicago. This and other "Bible colleges" were intended to prepare ministers for evangelization. Like Finney, he advocated for women to have leadership roles in the ministry, and his college regularly enrolled as many women as men. Moody applied business and advertising techniques to religious revivalism and held large interdenominational meetings, mostly in urban areas. Unlike the message of the brilliant and learned evangelicals of the eighteenth century, or even that of Finney, his was virtually anti-intellectual. He focused entirely on the love of God and a call to repentance. He viewed revivalism as a deeply emotional experience that led the sinner to God.

The Evangelical Alliance, formed in 1846, attempted to marshal Christian energy in the service of converting American society. Other similar societies spread the gospel message and inspired moral purity. They focused on the absolute authority of the Bible, human sinfulness, the desperate need for repentance, and the assurance of a saving, loving God. The evangelicals hoped to establish a Christian nation, and while perhaps laudable from the Christian perspective, they tended to identify "Christian civilization" (meaning "Protestant") with "American civilization." This has continued to haunt the evangelical movement, as many evangelical churches continue to conflate Christianity and the social, political, and economic interests of the United States.

While the Southern Baptist Convention, Assemblies of God, and the Christian Missionary Alliance grew rapidly in the early part of the twentieth century, evangelicalism slackened, partly due to the large-scale immigration of Catholics to the United States and partly due to a kind of fundamentalist battle with a more modern, more intellectual Christianity. The Scopes trial in 1925—one that pitted the theory of evolution against the literal reading of the biblical creation account—marked a watershed moment that made biblical literalism look intellectually unacceptable to the American public. By the 1940s Wheaton College near Chicago, Gordon College in Massachusetts, and Westmont College in California had ramped up their intellectual energies to try to bridge the intellectual-evangelical gap. One important figure of the time was Carl F. H. Henry (1913–2003), whose book *Uneasy Conscience of Modern Fundamentalism* (1947) proposed a more robustly intellectual evangelical message. He wanted evangelicalism to reconnect with mainstream American culture.

Billy Graham

William Franklin Graham, Jr., (b. 1918) is the most important figure in modern evangelicalism and indeed in modern American Christianity. In 1944, he became the first full-time employee of the Youth for Christ Movement, which was created to evangelize adolescents and young adults. He traveled widely and conducted tent crusades. In the summer of 1949, he planned a revival meeting in Los Angeles, anticipating that it would last about three weeks. The revival was a fantastic success, leading to the conversions of famous athletes and entertainers and even some reputed gangsters. The revival went on for three months, with crowds of six thousand jamming into his "canvas cathedral."

Graham is a product of American evangelicalism. He tended to align Christianity with the American nation, but also realized that evangelicalism needed to be grounded intellectually. The early Reformers and pioneer evangelicals—Luther, Calvin, and Zwingli—were classically trained and brilliant. The Wesley brothers, along with Whitefield, were Oxford-educated. Torrey was twice offered the presidency of Harvard, and Edwards, who trained at Yale, finished his career as the president of Princeton University. Finney too was a great intellectual, even as he proclaimed a faith easily appropriated by the masses. For fifteen years, he served as president of Oberlin College. Graham recognized the intellectual gap between evangelicalism and an intellectually rigorous faith. He co-founded *Christianity Today*, a magazine that aimed to bring intellectual

Photo By Eddie Boldizsar / Rex USA, Courtesy Everett Collection

Billy Graham preaches at the Crystal Palace in London in 1989. Graham would preach to live audiences of over two hundred million people in more than 185 countries before retiring in his mid-eighties.

respectability to evangelicals. He himself, however, was no scholar, nor did he pretend to be. His message was consistently simple: One needed to have faith in Christ. In 1957, he planned a major campaign in New York City and worked with mainstream Protestant churches in its execution. This marked a major turning point. Although criticized by more fundamentalist evangelicals, Graham gained popular support and was able to bridge wide divides among Christians.

On the one hand, Graham's Christianity looks a great deal like the evangelical Christianity already discussed. He appealed to the heart and focused on personal salvation. In addition, Graham's spirituality was highly individualistic, showing little concern for institutional religion or the theological divides between Christian denominations. On the other hand, he offered a rather bland Christianity. The Wesleys, Edwards, Whitefield, Finney, and others offered a strict Christianity that decisively challenged the moral lives of their listeners. Graham challenged sin, certainly, but in a relatively vague way: neglect of family, drunkenness, social instability. These challenges tended to be rather generic and unthreatening. In doing so, however, he retained a kind of broad acceptability that allowed him to preach widely, reminding people of their need for God's grace. His lack of specificity in preaching also allowed his ministry to be highly ecumenical, breaking the walls that separated many Christians.

Billy Graham's Altar Call

"You never know. To some of you who go out on the slick highways this afternoon, this may be the last sermon you will ever hear. . . . You may be a member of a choir. I don't know who you are or what you are, but you want to give your life to Christ on this opening Sunday afternoon. I'm going to ask you to do a hard thing, because coming to Christ is not easy. So many people have made it too easy. Jesus went to the cross and died in your place. Certainly you can come a few steps from where you are sitting and stand here, quietly and reverently, and with bowed head. And say, 'I need God; I need Christ. I want to be forgiven of my sins. I want a new life, and I want to start a new direction today.' You may be a rich man; you may be a poor man. You may be a man of great intellectual capacities and you have to come by faith. Because you'll never understand it intellectually. If you want to . . . come to the cross and give your life to Christ, I'm going to ask you to come."[9]

---

9. *www.jesuschristonly.com/sermons/billy-graham/christs-answer-to-the-world.html.*

Evangelicalism and the Religious Right

Jerry Falwell (1933–2007), a conservative Southern Baptist pastor, was initially critical of evangelical religion mixing with politics and, like Graham, shied away from any direct involvement. He even publically challenged more liberal Baptist ministers for taking part in the civil rights movement in the 60s, for he viewed their proper sphere of activity as ministering to the pastoral needs of their people. When the Supreme Court blocked prayers in school and legalized abortion in the 1970s, however, he had a change of heart. Falwell believed he was witnessing the secularization of a Christian nation. He, Timothy LaHaye, James Dobson, Pat Robertson, and many others created a new Religious Right, forming such lobbying groups as the Christian Coalition and the Moral Majority. They aligned with the Republican Party, which, from Ronald Reagan onward, promised a pro-life platform with traditional family values. In the 1960s, 57 percent of evangelicals in the North and 21 percent in the South were Republicans. By the 1980s, 72 percent of evangelicals in the North and 39 percent in the South were Republicans. This support of the Republican Party continued in the following decades, with evangelicals voting for Bob Dole by a three-to-one margin (1996). In the early twenty-first century evangelicals voted for George W. Bush by an 80 percent margin (2000, 2004), John McCain by a 71 percent margin (2008), and Mitt Romney—a Mormon versus a Protestant Christian—at 74 percent (2012).

Evangelical Christians of the late twentieth and early twenty-first century often continued to conflate Christianity and the United States. This represented a new kind of Manifest Destiny, with the United States somehow specially endowed as a Christian nation and carrying a heavy responsibility as such. This conversation on the 700 Club, a national evangelical television show, two days after the (9/11) terrorist attack on the World Trade Center and Pentagon underscores this point:

> **Jerry Falwell:** I've never sensed a togetherness, a burden, a broken heart as I do in the church today, and just 48 hours. I have a booklet I wrote ten years ago. I gave it away last night on the biblical position on fasting and prayer because I do believe that is what we've got to do right now—fast and pray. And I totally agree with you that the Lord has protected us so wonderfully these 225 years. And since 1812, this is the first time that we've been attacked on our soil, first time, and by far the worst results. And I fear, as Donald Rumsfeld, Secretary of Defense, said yesterday, that this is only the beginning. And with biological warfare available to these monsters; the Husseins, the Bin Ladens, the Arafats, what we saw on Tuesday, as terrible as it is, could be miniscule if in fact God continues to lift the curtain and allow the enemies of America to give us probably what we deserve.

Pat Robertson: Jerry, that's my feeling. I think we've seen the ante-chamber of terror. We haven't even begun to see what they can do to the major population.

Jerry Falwell: The ACLU's got to take a lot of blame for this.

Pat Robertson: Well, yes.

Jerry Falwell: And, I know I'll hear from them for this. But throwing God out successfully with the help of the federal court system, throwing God out of the public square, out of the schools. The abortionists have got to bear some burden for this because God will not be mocked. And when we destroy 40 million little innocent babies, we make God mad. I really believe that the pagans, and the abortionists, and the feminists, and the gays and the lesbians who are actively trying to make that an alternative lifestyle, the ACLU, People for the American Way, all of them who have tried to secularize America. I point my finger in their face and say, "You helped this happen."

Pat Robertson: Well, I totally concur, and the problem is that we have adopted that agenda at the highest levels of our government. And so we're responsible as a free society for what the top people do. And the top people, of course, is the court system.[10]

In this conversation Falwell and Robertson imagine that God had kept his providential and protective hand over America because it was special, but the increasing secularization of America had caused God to remove his protection. They do not claim that God was responsible for the attacks, but rather that God had been keeping the United States' enemies at bay until now. Missing from the conversation is any explanation of why culturally liberal movements necessarily violate God's laws. Many mainstream Protestants are pro-choice, and the ACLU is a non-profit organization designed to protect civil liberties. Court rulings separating church and state ironically were celebrated by many Baptists in the colonial period. Also absent from this discussion is any critique of the United States' past, including hundreds of years of human trafficking in the slave trade and a sordid history of racism. Would these not be more egregious violations of God's laws? One could also ask why Falwell and Robertson assumed that the United States is particularly important to God, when other countries have had to deal with terrorist groups for decades. While such assumptions about the United States and the politicizing of Christianity are still part of the evangelical landscape, some of the most prominent evangelical voices in recent years have taken strides to critique this religious/political collusion.[11]

---

10. Jerry Falwell, interview by Pat Robertson, *700 Club*, Christian Broadcasting Network, September 13, 2001.

11. These voices include Rick Warren, whom *Christianity Today* called "America's most influential pastor."

Conclusion

As noted at the beginning of this chapter, "evangelical" is not easy to define, as the term could refer to a grouping of non-denominational churches or denominations under a kind of historic umbrella or even a style of religious faith found with various intensity throughout Christianity. If one were to look at the three largest denominations that identify themselves as evangelical—Southern Baptist Convention, Church of God in Christ, and Assemblies of God—as well as with the general ethos found in the churches belonging to the National Association of Evangelicals (NAE) and para-church organizations such as the Billy Graham Evangelical Association (BGEA), Campus Crusade for Christ, and InterVarsity Christian Fellowship, one could identify some common characteristics. Some are assumed throughout Christianity, such as the Trinity, salvation through Christ via the cross and Resurrection, original sin, and so on. Others are more particular and include the following beliefs: (1) the Bible is the infallible, directly inspired word of God, providing the content for all doctrines; (2) the Holy Spirit dwells in believers and can be palpably known; (3) it is imperative to preach the gospel and win conversions for the sake of others' eternal life; (4) Christian life demands moral rectitude; (5) Christ will return visibly in the second coming and will institute a thousand year reign, which precedes the last judgment; and (6) Christian faith is primarily a personal and internal matter, in which one enters into a relationship with Christ and the soul becomes transformed by grace.

In evangelical spirituality denomination matters little, but the heart's conversion to a personal Lord matters mightily. The following two traditional evangelical hymns exemplify this aspect of the faith:

ROCK OF AGES, CLEFT FOR ME

Rock of Ages, cleft for me, let me hide myself in thee;
Let the water and the blood, from thy wounded side which flowed,
Be of sin the double cure; save from wrath and make me pure.

Not the labors of my hands can fulfill thy law's commands;
Could my zeal no respite know, could my tears forever flow,
All for sin could not atone; Thou must save, and thou alone.

Nothing in my hand I bring, simply to the cross I cling;
Naked, come to thee for dress; helpless, look to thee for grace;
Foul, I to the fountain fly; Wash me, Savior, or I die.

While I draw this fleeting breath, when mine eyes shall close in death,
When I soar to worlds unknown, see thee on thy judgment throne.
Rock of Ages, cleft for me, let me hide myself in thee.[12]

---

12. Augustus Toplady, *Rock of Ages, Cleft for Me* (1763), as cited in *www.hymnsite.com/lyrics /umh361.sht.*

BLESSED ASSURANCE

Blessed assurance, Jesus is mine! O what a foretaste of glory divine!
Heir of salvation, purchase of God, born of his Spirit, washed in his blood.
This is my story, this is my song, praising my Savior all the day long.

Perfect submission, perfect delight, visions of rapture now burst on my sight;
Angels descending bring from above, echoes of mercy, whispers of love.
This is my story, this is my song, praising my Savior all the day long.

Perfect submission, all is at rest, I in my Savior am happy and blest,
Watching and waiting, looking above, filled with His goodness, lost in his love.
This is my story, this is my song, praising my Savior all the day long.[13]

Such hymns express evangelical spirituality at its best—as the pursuit of a personal relationship with Jesus Christ, who offers salvation and who is known overwhelmingly in the heart. A person responds to this relationship with freedom, joy, gratitude, and praise. Evangelical spirituality is not a systematic plan, in the way that Carmelite spirituality is, for example. Nor is it an elitist spirituality requiring one to adopt a monastic life and live apart from the Christian laity. Rather, it is a popular (and popularist) celebration of a personal Lord who personally saves.

Questions for Review

1. In what different ways is the term *evangelical* used in this chapter?
2. What impact did the Pietists have on the development of evangelicalism in Europe and the British Colonies?
3. How did the seventeenth- and eighteenth-century revivals change the consciousness of the American colonists and pave the way for the American Revolutionary War?
4. What is the *religious right* and what is its association with Evangelicalism in the United States?

Questions for Discussion

1. Many evangelicals expect the imminent return of Christ; what role do you think this belief plays in the distinctively evangelical form of spirituality? Assuming that the second coming does not in fact occur soon, what impact do you think Christ's non-appearance will have upon evangelical spirituality?

---

13. Fanny Crosby, *Blessed Assurance* (1873), as cited in *www.hymnsite.com/lyrics/umh369.sht.*

2. Evangelicals emphasize personal interaction with God regardless of denominational lines. In what ways might this be a strength in the movement? How might it be a weakness?

3. Compare the individualistic, evangelical form of spirituality with other, more communal forms of spirituality that have been discussed in previous chapters. How do the two emphases—individual versus communal—reflect different understandings of what it means to be a Christian?

4. According to the chapter, Billy Graham adopted a basic, general presentation of the gospel. What are the assets and liabilities with this kind of Christian expression?

Bibliography

Resources with annotations are highly recommended to students interested in further study.

Bebbington, David. *Evangelicalism in Modern Britain*. London: Unwin Hyman, 1989.
    This historical survey investigates English and American evangelicalism especially in relationship to the larger culture.

Bunyan, John. *The Pilgrim's Progress*. Edited by Roger Sharrock. London: Penguin, 1987.

Collinson, Patrick. *The Birthpangs of Protestant England: Religious and Cultural Change in the Sixteenth and Seventeenth Centuries*. Basignstoke: Macmillan, 1986.

Hendrix, Scott, ed. and trans. *Early Protestant Spirituality*. New York: Paulist Press, 2009.

Kidd, Thomas. *The Great Awakening: The Roots of Christianity in Colonial America*. New Haven: Yale University Press, 2007.

Mardsen, George. *Understanding Fundamentalism and Evangelicalism*. Grand Rapids: Eerdmans, 1991.
    This is an excellent introduction to two related religious expressions.

Miller, Donald. *Reinventing American Protestantism: Christianity in the New Millennium*. Berkeley: University of California Press, 1997.

Noll, Mark. *American Evangelical Christianity: An Introduction*. Oxford: Blackwell, 2001.
    This is a good statistical overview of evangelical faith in the United States and how evangelicals engage such important issues as race and gender.

Whaling, Frank, ed. *John and Charles Wesley: Selected Prayers, Hymns, Journal Notes, Sermons, Letters and Treatises*. Mahwah, NJ: Paulist Press, 1981.

Internet Resources

"Billy Graham Crusade in Los Angeles, 1949." *www.youtube.com/watch?v=OEMdPTRdvEI.*

A video of Graham's preaching at the Los Angeles tent revival (3 min.).

Graham, Billy. "Who Is Jesus?" *www.youtube.com/watch?v=MIqRH1XBw5M.*

Graham preaches on the person and ministry of Christ in his own day and on the power of Christ's ministry in ours (41 min.).

Spirituality Shoppe: An Evangelical Center for the Study of Christian Spirituality. *spiritualityshoppe.org/.*

This website offers a variety of resources for evangelical spirituality.

Pentecostal Spirituality

W hen the time for Pentecost was fulfilled, they were all in one place together. And suddenly there came from the sky a noise like a strong driving wind, and it filled the entire house in which they were. Then there appeared to them tongues as of fire, which parted and came to rest on each one of them. And they were all filled with the holy Spirit and began to speak in different tongues, as the Spirit enabled them to proclaim. (Acts 2:1–4)

This account in Acts of the beginnings of the church contains themes that will recur as Pentecostalism emerges as a profoundly important Christian spirituality in the twentieth century. In a totally unpredictable and egalitarian way, the Holy Spirit appears to the disciples in the form of fire and anoints each one of them, empowering them to speak in many different languages, thus enabling them to proclaim the gospel. The narrative continues with witnesses questioning what it means. Peter explains: "This is what was spoken through the prophet Joel: 'It will come to pass in the last days,' God says, 'that I will pour out a portion of my spirit upon all flesh. Your sons and your daughters shall prophesy'" (Acts 2:16–18). Peter informs his listeners that the prophet Joel predicted this dramatic experience of the Holy Spirit as an eschatological sign, that is, evidence that the present age is ending and a new age is beginning.

The Bible reports that the early church was filled with gifts of the Holy Spirit, including the ability to speak prophetic words in foreign languages, heal, and expel demons. At one point the apostle Philip was in Samaria preaching, healing, and expelling unclean spirits. Simon the magician was so impressed that he asked to be baptized: "When Simon saw that the Spirit was conferred by the laying on of the apostles' hands, he offered them money and said, 'Give me this power too, so that anyone upon whom I lay my hands may receive the holy Spirit'" (Acts 8:18–19). Peter rebukes him, and Simon repents, which testifies to the impressive authority of the apostles. These gifts seem to have been given lavishly to many believers and not just the apostles. Paul writes to the church in Corinth, "I give thanks to my God always on your account for the grace of God bestowed on you in Christ Jesus, that in him you were enriched in every way . . . so that you are not lacking in any spiritual gift" (1 Cor. 1:4–7). Later in the same letter he describes these gifts:

> To each individual the manifestation of the Spirit is given for some benefit. To one is given through the Spirit the expression of wisdom; to another the expression of knowledge according to the same Spirit; to another faith by the same Spirit; to another gifts of healing by the one Spirit; to another mighty deeds; to another prophecy; to another discernment of spirits; to another varieties of tongues; to another inter-pretation of tongues." (1 Cor. 12:7–10)

Paul goes on to rank these gifts: "first apostles; second, prophets; third, teachers; then, mighty deeds; then, gifts of healing, assistance, administration, and variet-ies of tongues" (1 Cor. 12:28).

The early church could be called *charismatic* (from the Greek word for "gift") because it apparently was endowed with a great number of spiritual gifts. While these did not entirely fade from the church, they were in subsequent times not as regularly expressed. The church has always had persons who exercise the gifts of teaching and administration, for example. The more traditional and hierarchical denominations, such as the Catholic Church, believe that bishops carry on the apostolic gift. Prophets and visionaries, though rare, have emerged throughout the history of the church. The gift of tongues, however, apparently dropped out of the church's expression quickly, certainly by the latter part of the first century.

Pentecostalism celebrates the resurgence of all of these gifts, particularly the gift of tongues, in the grand way both Acts and Paul describe them. For Pen-tecostals, this modern era represents a new Pentecost, a renewal of these gifts of the Spirit and, with it, a renewed eschatological fervor, anticipating the sec-ond coming of Christ. Today, Pentecostals, together with charismatic Christians in mainstream churches, number perhaps half a billion worldwide. There are as many as thirty-eight thousand denominations of Pentecostal churches. The movement spread so quickly that within ten years of its emergence, its mes-sage reached over fifty different nations. This chapter will sketch the history and spirituality of this movement.

Background to Pentecostalism

As noted in the last chapter, evangelical Christianity swept across the United States, Europe, and indeed other parts of the world, through the Pietist and Methodist movements. These movements emphasized the importance of the heart and emotions. Further, the great revivalists insisted that a hallmark of true Christian faith was a dramatic experience of God transforming one's soul, thereby removing sin and invigorating one with the life of the Spirit. By the 1840s, the Methodist revival dominated the American Protestant scene. At that time, for every six Baptists there were ten Methodists, and they outnumbered Presbyterians, Congregationalists, Episcopalians, Lutherans, and Calvinist Reform church members combined.

Through the nineteenth century, however, Methodism became more staid and far less evangelical, a circumstance that precipitated the revivals discussed in the last chapter. Some Christians left Methodism and formed "holiness churches," small denominations that linked dramatic experiences of God with radical holiness. For these communities, once one was truly baptized in the Spirit, one became perfectly holy.[1]

Many American Protestants, particularly those in the holiness churches, embraced what has been called the "fullness gospel," the "fourfold gospel," or the "foursquare gospel." This "fullness gospel" centers on Jesus as (1) Savior; (2) baptizer in the Holy Spirit; (3) healer; and (4) soon-coming King. Holiness preachers, such as A. B. Simpson (1843–1919), who founded the Christian and Missionary Alliance, were followed by other notable preachers, such as Charles Cullis and Carrie Judd Montgomery. Notably, they all claimed that Christ promised that the gifts of healing would be widely available to the church. They took certain passages in the Bible as their warrant: "Amen, amen, I say to you, whoever believes in me will do the works that I do, and will do greater ones than these, because I am going to the father. And whatever you ask in my name, I will do, so that the Father may be glorified in the Son. If you ask anything of me in my name, I will do it" (John 14:12–14); and, "Is there anyone among you sick? He should summon the presbyters [elders] of the church, and they should pray over him and anoint him with oil in the name of the Lord, and the prayer of faith will save the sick person" (James 5:14–15).

One of the great revivalists of the nineteenth century was John Nelson Darby (1800–1882), an Irish minister who traveled widely in Ireland, Britain, Switzerland, the United States, and even Australia and New Zealand. Darby argued that Christ would soon return and "rapture" true believers (that is, draw them up to heaven), leaving the rest of humanity to face the terrors of the Antichrist. The Jewish people, he said, would undergo purifying suffering until Christ returned again, but many would convert. Then Christ would return gloriously and lead a fight against the antichrist, which would culminate in a decisive battle at Armageddon. After the defeat of the Antichrist, Christ would establish his *millennial* ("thousand-year") reign leading up to the final judgment. The belief that Christ will return to earth to establish the millennial kingdom is known as premillennialism. "Dispensational" theology embraced the premillenialist position, and helped to popularize it. Dispensationalism asserts that

---

1. These churches include the Church of God (1886), the Christian and Missionary Alliance (1887), Church of the Nazarene (1895), and Pilgrim Holiness Church (1897).

God's dealings with humanity over time have taken the form of a series of dispensations. Humanity is now on the verge of the final dispensation, awaiting the thousand-year reign of Christ. D. L. Moody (1837–1899) took up Darby's interpretation of scripture and made it central to the theological training in his Moody Bible Institute. He was not alone. Other revivalists embraced this biblical interpretation, and it was reinforced by the wildly popular Scofield Reference Bible (1909), which had a built-in commentary that helped popularize dispensational theology and, with it, premillennialism.

Many of these movements go together. The early revivals introduced a less intellectual and highly emotional Protestant religiosity that emphasized the heart and the transformative possibilities of the indwelling presence of God. Revival meetings often facilitated dramatic experiences of God and equally dramatic numbers of conversions. From this starting point emerged various expressions of evangelical Christianity, each convinced that Christ's Spirit empowered their healing ministries to flourish. Finally, many believed that they were literally living in the last days before the second coming. Virtually all Christian communities recognize the contemporary age as the "last days" in the sense that Christ's salvation established the final covenant. However, the holiness movement, and the charismatic movement that arose from it, believed in the *imminent* coming of Christ. The full flourishing of the Holy Spirit's gifts was tantamount to God's guarantee of this imminent coming.

The Origins of the Pentecostal Movement

In 1855 in Russia and Armenia, evangelical revivals brought about speaking in tongues and dramatic healing ministries. In 1905–1906, many Christians throughout southern and central India began receiving visions and speaking in tongues. In 1906, at a revival in Los Angeles, hundreds of participants started speaking in tongues. In 1930, in Glasgow, Scotland, speaking in tongues broke out in a parish church. Some of these occurrences appear to have happened independently from the others. The seeds of Pentecostalism had arrived.

In 1895, Pandita Sarasvati Ramabai (1858–1922), an evangelical Christian with ties to the holiness movement, started a Christian mission in Kedgaon, India, to serve the needs of destitute adolescents and young women. They called it the "Mukti Mission," from the Hindi word meaning "salvation." By 1900, the Mukti Mission housed two thousand residents. In 1906, a number of the young women residing there began spreading the gospel to local Hindus. These women engaged in a kind of internal revival that lasted sixteen months, with many of the women experiencing ecstatic phenomena, something that had happened the year earlier elsewhere in India. The Mukti Mission became the main Pentecostal center of India. In 1907, the mission started publishing a newsletter, *The Mukti Prayer-Bell*, that described its experiences and missionary pursuits.

Similar experiences occurred on the other side of the globe in Azusa Street, Los Angeles. William J. Seymour (1870–1922) came to Los Angeles after spending six weeks at a Bible school in Houston run by Charles Fox Parham (1873–1929). Parham had made the connection between baptism in the Holy Spirit and speaking in tongues. Speaking in tongues became the necessary sign, Parham taught, of a true Spirit baptism. Seymour had come to Los Angeles in 1906 to be a pastor at a holiness congregation. In April a revival broke out, including speaking in tongues. Those leading the revival, including Seymour, relocated to 312 Azusa Street, a two-story building that once served as an African Methodist Episcopal Church. During the long-lasting revival, an earthquake occurred in San Francisco. The revivalists interpreted this as an eschatological sign that the world would come to an end soon. The mission ran around the clock, with fifteen hundred persons a day from all over the city, then the country, and then the world, coming to receive their own Pentecostal baptism. Seymour started a monthly newspaper, *The Apostolic Faith*, which had fifty thousand subscribers at its height. Within two years of the Azusa Street revival, associated missionaries went to twenty-five countries. Within ten years, they had spread the message to fifty countries.

In 1906 one of Ramabai's fellow missionaries, Minnie Abrams, published a booklet, *The Baptism of the Holy Spirit and Fire*, which sold thirty-thousand copies. She visited her friend May Louise Hoover in Valparaiso, Chile, and they disseminated the booklet there. In 1909, Methodist churches in Valparaiso and Santiago began Pentecostal revivals. At the same time, Korea too experienced a Pentecostal revival. At a convention in Pyongyang led by Sun Ju Kil, a premillennial dispensationalist preacher, many in the audience began speaking in tongues. In 1908 in Gansu, Western China, a Chinese preacher, Brother Yong, experienced Spirit baptism and started to speak in tongues and, reportedly, to heal, prophesy, and cast out demons.[2] In 1914–1915 William Wade Harris from Cape Palmas, Liberia, led a revival that included widespread speaking in tongues; it boasted of 120,000 conversions in a single year.

These early, dramatic expressions of early Pentecostalism demonstrate that the movement did not begin as an organized outgrowth of existing Protestant churches, but rather as more of a missionary enthusiasm of Christians with a common experience of Spirit baptism. Soon, however, denominations were set up, and theological lines were drawn. Some argued for the necessity of a three-stage conversion: conversion and baptism; Spirit baptism, with the gifts of the Holy Spirit; and full sanctification or radical holiness (complete sinlessness). Others advocated a "finished work" program, a two-stage process consisting of regular conversion and then Spirit baptism that also included full sanctification. Others even proclaimed a "oneness gospel," which argued that Jesus was the incarnation of the Trinity, a singular God who was experienced in three different

---

2. This happened a full four years before Western Pentecostals brought missions to China.

modes. This latter group today consists of about ten percent of all Pentecostals denominations. The largest group of Pentecostals adheres to the "finished work" theology and includes the Church of God in Christ and the Assemblies of God. Some counts put today's Assembly of God membership at forty million.

The Charismatic Renewal Movement

For decades, Pentecostal Christians isolated themselves from the rest of mainstream Christianity for several reasons. The holiness churches, many of whose members later became Pentecostals, believed that Spirit baptism meant they were utterly sinless and thus distinct from the larger society and even other Christians. Pentecostals also typically believed that tongues and other gifts from the Holy Spirit comprised a necessary part of being a bona fide Christian—if one did not speak in tongues, one was not anointed by the Spirit and thus was not Christian. Pentecostals, along with some other evangelicals, were also premillennial dispensationalists who expected the imminent coming of Christ. They devoted their energies, therefore, toward making converts, as those who had not converted would be damned; conversely, since the end was imminent, they saw no need to involve themselves in culture or in political or social events. In fact, many Pentecostals were conscientious objectors during the First World War, for they saw the war as the great sign preceding the second coming.

By the middle of the twentieth century, however, the Pentecostal movement had changed its position on social and political participation. Many denominations joined the National Association of Evangelicals in 1943, thereby becoming more mainstream. Oral Roberts brought the Pentecostal subculture into the homes of Americans through his weekly television program and his magazine *Abundant Life*, which had a circulation of over one million at its height. In 1963, he began Oral Roberts University and shocked the Pentecostal world by becoming an ordained Methodist minister in 1968. Earlier in 1960 Roberts had joined Pat Robertson to begin the Christian Broadcasting Network. Robertson, too, would form his own university, initially called the CBN University and now named Regent University, which today is the most influential Pentecostal university in the nation.

Another factor that brought Pentecostalism into the mainstream of the religious culture of the United States is that, in the 1950s, some members of mainstream Protestant denominations began to experience Spirit baptism and to receive the gifts of the Spirit. Many remained inside their traditions as a kind of sub-group, additionally meeting outside regular church gatherings for Pentecostal prayer. They are typically called "charismatic Christians."

The Catholic charismatic movement began in 1967 at Duquesne University in Pittsburgh. Two lay theology professors had received Spirit baptism and passed this on to about thirty students during a retreat, who then formed the Catholic Charismatic Renewal (CCR). The CCR spread from there to the University of

Notre Dame and Michigan State University and by 1976 had grown to three hundred thousand Catholics. The CCR movement reached its peak in Kansas City at a conference that included fifty thousand Charismatic Christians from all denominations. The conference's chairman, Kevin Ranaghan, described it as the most ecumenical mass gathering of Christians in 800 years. By 2010 there were over 120 million Catholic Charismatics in 220 countries, particularly in South America.

The Pentecostal movement still tends to follow the fullness gospel and most Pentecostals still await the imminent second coming, a view often shared by evangelicals. However, Pentecostalism has become a much tamer movement overall, with Pentecostals less likely to focus on the second coming and far more likely to see something of the kingdom of God realized here and now in the forms of health, happiness, and financial prosperity. Most strikingly, given the origins of the movement, a sizeable minority of Pentecostals do not speak in tongues.

Michelle's Witness

"When I went to seminary, I became friends with a few Pentecostal students who had come to a Baptist seminary instead of one in their own tradition. At about the same time, my younger sister married a man who had come from a Pentecostal church. My new brother-in-law was very nice. But he insisted that salvation was followed by 'baptism in the Holy Spirit' and this was demonstrated by tongue-speaking. . . . Well, I was not convinced. . . . Then several years later, I was a visiting professor at a university. . . . I was smart enough to seek counsel from a colleague at the seminary whom I trusted [who] explained that intellectual and analytical types like him and me were very prone to overthinking. . . . There is a place for critical analysis even of sermons and hymns—but while one is trying to worship is probably not the right time! . . . A light bulb went on in my head. I finally knew a practical purpose for glossolalia. I went back to my office and prayed very simply to receive the gift of tongues, not really believing anything would happen. It came with a rush as real as the wind at the first Pentecost. Suddenly, I was speaking in sounds or words that I did not know as fast as a babbling brook! Just as suddenly, the presence of God was real and palpable in a way that I had not known in over three years. Tears streamed down my cheeks. I felt loved by Love Himself."[3]

---

3. Paul Alexander, *Signs and Wonders: Why Pentecostalism Is the World's Fastest Growing Faith* (San Francisco: Jossey-Bass, 2009), 42–44.

Characteristics of Pentecostal Spirituality
Worship

Pentecostal Spirituality is most clearly evident in a revivalist kind of worship that is highly emotional. Such worship services are meant to offer great freedom in the Spirit to speak and sing in tongues, proclaim a prophecy, and actively respond to the preached word. A worship service might be filled with drums, electric guitars, tambourines, clapping hands, dancing, and hugging. While more traditional Christians might view it as a kind of liturgical chaos, it is an organized chaos. The first part of the service includes loud music and jubilant singing, interspersed with prayer (sometimes in tongues and sometimes in the vernacular). After about an hour, the frenetic quality gives way to a quieter atmosphere with softer, more relaxed singing and music. This provides an opportunity for the minister to preach. There is no set lectionary, so the minister preaches from any biblical text. Then there is an altar call for those seeking prayers, with gentle music in the background.

Pentecostals refer to two kinds of speaking in tongues. First, there is the gift of tongues typically received in Spirit baptism. This form typically consists of repetitive sentences or phrases and is understood as a personal gift of prayer from God for interior edification. Pentecostals base this understanding of tongues on such texts as Romans 8:26–27: "In the same way, the Spirit too comes to the aid of our weakness; for we do not know how to pray as we ought, but the Spirit itself intercedes with inexpressible groanings. And the one who searches hearts knows what is the intention of the Spirit, because it intercedes for the holy ones according to God's will." Such tongues might be expressed during community prayer, but only during times when congregants are engaged in personal prayer.

The second gift of tongues involves a form of prophecy in which God is understood to speak through someone for the building up of the community. Paul explains: "Pursue love, but strive eagerly for the spiritual gifts, above all that you may prophesy. For one who speaks in a tongue does not speak to human beings but to God, for no one listens; he utters mysteries in the spirit. On the other hand, one who prophecies does speak to human beings, for their building up, encouragement, and solace" (1 Cor. 14:1–3). Someone with the gift of interpretation is needed to decipher the message. Frequently, yet another member of the congregation participates by confirming the interpretation.

In *Signs and Wonders*, Pentecostal theologian Paul Alexander explains that those who pray in tongues find it to be a highly intimate expression of prayer. It allows for and encourages an emotional interaction with God. He also argues that many, especially those on the margins of society, experience it as emotionally purging and even socially empowering. Finally, it opens Christians up to a spiritual space where the sacred and mundane can meet, where amazing things can happen and are expected to happen.

Miracles

Pentecostal spirituality expects miracles; many Pentecostals tell miraculous stories of healing and divine intervention. This happens in family gatherings, church services, and even the most casual conversations on the sidewalk. Two believers could be sitting in a restaurant talking about their lives, when one mentions a personal struggle or a challenge in a loved one's life. It would not be unusual for them to begin praying for a healing or miracle right then and there.[4]

Prophecy

Most Pentecostals believe that God speaks to them regularly through prophecy, dreams, visions, and spiritual intuitions. They are much more likely to report having received a direct revelation from God than are other Christians. They also know that such experiences can be psychosomatic, so as a rule they seek confirmation of these spiritual phenomena from other members of the community.

The story of Heidi Baker offers a striking example. She had just returned from a mission in Mozambique with her husband Rolland, and was feeling depressed about the lackluster outcome of their ministry there. She was attending a Pentecostal service in Toronto in the mid-1990s led by Randy Clark when he asked her, "Do you want the nation of Mozambique?" He then proclaimed, "The blind will see. The crippled will walk. The deaf will hear. The dead will be raised, and the poor will hear the good news." Heidi cried out, "Yes," after which she felt the power of God flowing through her body like electricity. Clark then proclaimed, "You'll have hundreds of churches!" She laughed—it had taken her and Rolland eighteen years to plant four small churches in Hong Kong—but later admitted, "I knew I heard the Lord."

Heidi was not a newcomer to Pentecostalism or to prophecy. She reports that, as an adolescent in 1976, she had heard God's voice saying, "You are called to be a minister and a missionary, to go to Africa, Asia, and England." At another time she had heard God tell her that she would marry Rolland Baker, a man she had never heard of. After she met Rolland and ultimately married him, they went together as missionaries to Hong Kong for fourteen years. They then began a mission in London for the homeless while also studying at Kings College. From there, they moved to Mozambique in 1995.

After a year, they saw many of their missionary attempts sabotaged and found themselves in Toronto, emotionally exhausted. After Heidi's experience there with Clark, her family returned to Mozambique. Things did not go well at first, but they remained undeterred because they believed in the prophecy.

---

4. In a ten-country survey, most Pentecostals attested to personally experiencing or witnessing the healing of an injury or illness. See Pew Forum on Religion and Public Life, *Spirit and Power: A 10-Country Survey of Pentecostals* (Washington, DC: Pew Forum on Religion and Public Life, 2006), 4.

The ministry she and Rolland started in 1980, now called Iris Global, has since founded eleven thousand churches worldwide, has built schools, children's centers, and medical care facilities, and has established feeding centers, healing ministries, and well-drilling programs.

The Bible and Storytelling

Pentecostalism, like evangelicalism, tends towards biblical fundamentalism. "Believing in the Bible" constitutes a regular theme. Generally speaking, they consider the Bible verbally and directly inspired by the Holy Spirit and therefore inerrant. While evangelical and Pentecostal scholars are typically aware of and often open to modern biblical scholarship, a critical understanding of scripture has not made its way into the culture of Pentecostalism. Sermons are often interspersed with "the Bible says," which for congregation members essentially translates to "God says."

What distinguishes Pentecostals is that the Bible works less like a set of propositions, as it does in evangelical Christianity, and more like a resource for storytelling. They use the Bible to explain how the Holy Spirit works in their lives and in the church, particularly regarding healing and prophecy. It serves as a narrative resource into which they can interject their own lives. God dramatically intervened for King David in a battle, and now does so in the life of a believer against the enemy of alcoholism or family strife. An angel frees the imprisoned Peter from Herod's clutches and now God sends an angel to free and guide the believer during a challenging time. The Bible becomes a supernatural sourcebook where one can see how God worked scripturally and imagine how God is working in one's life.

Personal stories of God's intervention in life are not only part of Pentecostal spirituality, they also play a role in the liturgy. It is not unusual for someone from the congregation to stand up in the middle of a worship service and tell a personal story to the community. Stories—whether biblical, personal, or a combination of the two—help one think like a Christian and provide a context for one's hope for conversion or success. Pentecostal stories are almost always about hope and victory.

These stories also often deal with spiritual power and warfare. Many cultures in the developing world believe (as does the New Testament) that the world is crowded with demons and angels. Pentecostal spirituality, of all the Christian spiritualities, is the most suited to integrating this belief and interpreting personal and social events accordingly. Just as the Gospels contain numerous accounts of exorcism, exorcisms comprise a regular part of Pentecostal practice in Africa, Asia, and South America. Pentecostal spirituality accepts such a worldview, and claims to show how Christ (and the power of his name) can conquer these malevolent spirits.

Prosperity Preaching

One of the leading early Pentecostal revivalists, Smith Wigglesworth (1859–1947), taught the controversial "positive confession," whereby one could claim a gift from God and, if one had faith, God would bestow it. His ministry focused on biblical passages such as: "The Lord will affirm the blessings upon you, on your barns and on all your undertakings; he will bless you in the land that the Lord is giving to you" (Deut. 28:8); "Give and gifts will be given to you; a good measure, packed together, shaken down, and overflowing, will be poured into your lap" (Luke 6:38); "I came so that they may have life and have it more abundantly" (John 10:10); and "Beloved, I hope you are prospering in every respect and are in good health, just as your soul is prospering" (3 John 2). With these and other passages seeming to promise earthly rewards for believers, Wigglesworth and those who followed a positive confession form of Pentecostalism propagated what is now known as "prosperity preaching."

In its most modest form, this kind of message promotes a sort of holistic spirituality. Christians generally agree that Christ's salvation most importantly involves eternal salvation, that is, union with God for eternity. Does this mean, however, that Christ does not want his followers to enjoy healthy, wholesome lives here on earth? No, Pentecostalism argues, Christ wants that too. The healing ministry central to Pentecostalism imagines that Christ came to save the whole person, and indeed Jesus' ministry on earth involved numerous healings. Healing was a sign of the kingdom of God he came to proclaim. Oral Roberts's ministry led the way in the United States for a more robust version of this vision whereby Christian faith involved physical health, moral rectitude, and financial success.

By the 1980s, prosperity preaching had moved to a new level and had become central to Pentecostal preaching throughout the United States, Africa, Asia, and Latin America. Gloria Copeland and her husband Kenneth are among the foremost prosperity preachers in the United States. She promises that if you give $1 for the gospel's sake, God will make sure you get $100 return. $10 gets you $1,000, and $1,000 ensures you $100,000. She and her televangelist husband own a six million dollar mansion and a twenty million dollar jet. "Receive your miracle," she tells her listeners. "If you have a need, plant a seed."

The spiritual principle is simply this: God wants Christians to claim wealth. "Just claim it every day" comprises the first step. The second consists of thanking God in advance for already granting it and waiting until it comes to full fruition in one's bank account. Success stories abound among prosperity preachers. One person, down on his luck, gives his last $10 to the ministry, and soon after finds out that he has inherited a fortune. Another going through business bankruptcy gives money to the ministry and subsequently discovers that an almost unimaginably large order has come in that has not only saved the business but has also made him a millionaire.

Robert Tilton, an American prosperity preacher with a televangelistic info-mercial called *Success-N-Life*, testified in court to making $800,000 a month. Astounding as this figure is, ABC's *Prime Time Live* in 1991 reported that it was actually far more. Tilton regularly asks for a "seed faith gift" of $200. Sim-ilarly, Bruce Wilkenson's book, *The Prayer of Jabez*, promises Christians wealth if only they pray and have enough faith. It has sold over twenty million copies to date.

Prosperity preaching has exploded all over the globe. Over 90 percent of Pentecostals in Nigeria, South Africa, India, and the Philippines believe in pros-perity preaching. It is the cornerstone of Brazil's Universal Church of God's Kingdom, which reports over ten million members and owns banks, numerous radio stations, and Brazil's third largest television network.

Some Pentecostal Christians have fired back at this form of their faith. The Assemblies of God church, for example, has formally repudiated the pos-itive confession formula. Other Pentecostals, such as Ron Sider, author of *Rich Christians in an Age of Hunger*, have challenged first-world Pentecostals to focus less on accumulating wealth; he advocates working for political change as the authentic Christian response to hunger and poverty. Despite these efforts, Pen-tecostal Christianity in general does not emphasize political or social activism as a means to deal with material inequities in their communities or worldwide.

Concerns with a Pentecostal Spirituality

This chapter has focused on the inspiring and explosive spiritual force of Pen-tecostalism in the twentieth century. However, some concerns about Pente-costalism have also been raised, often by scholars within their own ranks. The first concern, mentioned above, is the strong tendency toward biblical funda-mentalism. Few Pentecostal scholars are biblical literalists. They recognize var-ious and even competing theologies in the Bible and wrestle with these, as all biblical scholars do. The same holds true of evangelical scholars. For the vast majority of biblical scholars the phrase "word of God" is understood in a subtle and nuanced manner. They point out that language itself is a human phenom-enon rooted in corporeality and discursive thought. This cannot be predicated on God who is pure spirit. Nor can one literally attribute language (as humans understand it) to God, because of the limited character of language and the transcendence of God. Scholars also see obvious contradictions in the text, and narratives that do not line up with decided historical facts; one must ask, if the very words of scripture are inspired, why did God inspire contradictions and errors? There also exists a necessary relationship between scripture and tradi-tion, which Christian scholars of all types recognize, but which many evangel-ical and Pentecostal pastors and their flocks discount completely. Evangelical theologian Kenton Sparks writes,

Recall that among committed inerrantists we will find those who believe in "predestination" and "free will," in "premillennial" and "postmillennial" eschatology, in "infant baptism" and "believer's baptism," in the "elder rule" and "congregational rule." On almost every important interpretive question in every biblical book, we find a wide variety of "inerrantist" readings. . . . It is hardly conceivable that evangelicals could assent to so many differing and contradictory viewpoints if the Bible spoke as clearly and univocally as we are wont to suppose."[5]

Premillennial dispensationalism approaches the book of Revelation as a future history book, with relatively easy-to-interpret markers of the end time. This is an interpretive error made by those who lack a sense of literary genre (apocalyptic in this case), a mistake few biblical scholars would make. Prosperity preaching focuses on texts that appear to support this theological agenda, but simply ignores others that contradict it, such as "Woe to you who are rich, for you have received your consolation" (Luke 6:24); "How hard it is for those who have wealth to enter the kingdom of God" (Mark 10:23); and "Those who want to be rich are falling into temptation and into a trap and into may foolish and harmful desires, which plunge them into ruin and destruction" (1 Tim. 6:9).

Pentecostal spirituality also must wrestle with the dark side of faith in God's miraculous workings. As Pentecostals themselves sometimes reflect, they rarely tell stories about the times when miracles did not happen, when prayers were not answered, and when people were not healed. These seem to be forgotten or explained away by such platitudes as "God said no, and God knows best," or "It isn't God's timing *yet.*" The healing stories themselves often seem exaggerated, with further scrutiny revealing the lack of clarity about whether a real miracle actually occurred. One could feel healed of, say, chronic pain, only to find that the pain has reemerged later, after the adrenalin has worn off. A potential danger of this spirituality is an over-emphasis on wishful thinking or even faith in faith itself.

Finally, while Pentecostal spirituality exudes an upbeat and hope-filled spirit, it often deals badly with negative emotions such as sadness or anger. These can get buried under the cheery façade of "just having faith," or "waiting for my miracle." It can lead to a kind of life-long giddiness that everything is excellent and blessed when that may not really be the case. When prayers go unanswered, it is even possible to blame the victim; since God gives health and prosperity to those who have the faith to claim these blessings, then those who lack these things are at fault—they did not have sufficient faith.

---

5. Kenton Sparks, *God's Word in Human Words* (Grand Rapids: Baker Academic, 2008), 257–258, 327.

Conclusion

Pentecostalism is easily the most vibrant and growing Christian spiritual movement in the world. It seeks to celebrate and facilitate dramatic experiences of the indwelling Spirit. The very openness to the Spirit enables believers to have further encounters. It is also an everyday spirituality, where common experiences take on religious weight and importance. This spirituality is lively and emotionally powerful, with engaging worship and explosive experiences of God. It is also wholly democratic, where the priesthood of all believers is not only preached but lived out. This empowers women, and opens up opportunities for ministry without first requiring people to undergo lengthy, expensive training. It easily engages indigenous cultures, especially those with a spiritual worldview aligned to Pentecostal assumptions about good and evil spirits and the spiritual warfare facing the church. Finally, Pentecostalism (along with evangelicalism) is committed to conversions. Mainstream Protestants and Catholics do not evangelize like Pentecostals. Mainstream Christians see God's saving grace as extending outside of the borders of a Christian confession. More conservative versions of Christianity view conversion as imperative, as the mission statement of the Bakers's Iris Global makes clear:

> What began as a ragged band of young beggars, thieves and delinquents has developed by the power of the Holy Spirit into a closely-knit national family of thousands of churches and a broad ministry encompassing Bible schools, children's centers, church-based orphan care, primary education, medical clinics, constant evangelistic and healing outreaches, farming, well drilling and much else. Our vision in the Lord is constantly increasing. But most of all we proclaim Jesus. He is our salvation, our prize, our reward, our inheritance, our destination, our motivation, our joy, wisdom and sanctification—and absolutely everything else we need, now and forever. All His grace and power flow to us through the Cross and no other way. We are glad to be known as social workers and humanitarians, and to have a reputation for doing good. But all is in vain if we do not bring to the people faith in our God and Savior Jesus Christ. We want to be known by His Name, first and foremost. And we do not expect fruitfulness to come out of anything but intimacy with Him.[6]

Questions for Review

1. What biblical passages do Pentecostals invoke to support the gift of tongues?
2. What are the foundations of Pentecostalism in the world and in the United States?
3. How did the Pentecostal church develop into the global force it is today?

---

6. *www.irisglobal.org/home.*

4. What features of Pentecostalism distinguish it from evangelical Christianity at large?
5. What impact does biblical literalism have upon the everyday life of Pentecostals?

Questions for Discussion

1. What do you make of the origins of Pentecostalism through essentially simultaneous but seemingly independent movements worldwide? If one concludes that these developments were divinely directed, must one also conclude that God wants contemporary Christians to embrace this form of spirituality? Why or why not?
2. To what do you attribute the phenomenon of speaking in tongues: divine inspiration, a self-induced altered state of consciousness, or something else? What role do you think it can play in Christian spirituality?
3. Prosperity preaching exists in many quarters of the Pentecostal Church. Do you feel that there is a legitimate place for it in Christian thought and practice, given your understanding of Christianity? Does it matter that this is a relatively new expression of Christian spirituality?
4. Although Pentecostal scholars generally approach the Bible with the tools of modern scholarship, most Pentecostal pastors and their community members take the Bible quite literally. How do you account for this? Is it problematic for a major segment of the church to be so disengaged from academic study?

Bibliography

Resources with annotations are highly recommended to students interested in further study.

Alexander, Paul. *Signs and Wonders: Why Pentecostalism Is the World's Fastest Growing Faith.* San Francisco: Jossey-Bass, 2009.
   This short book expresses the ideals, theology, and experiences of Pentecostalism in a sympathetic and balanced manner.

Anderson, Allan. *An Introduction to Pentecostalism.* Cambridge: Cambridge University Press, 2004.

Anderson, Allan. *To the Ends of the Earth: Pentecostalism and the Transformation of World Christianity.* Oxford: Oxford University Press, 2013.
   This book details the history and theology of the Pentecostal movement throughout the world, and how it has affected Christianity worldwide.

Armstrong, Karen. *The Battle for God: A History of Fundamentalism*. New York: Random House, 2001.

Coleman, Simon. *The Globalisation of Christianity: Spreading the Gospel of Prosperity*. Cambridge: Cambridge University Press, 2000.

Kay, William. *Pentecostalism: A Very Short Introduction*. Oxford: Oxford University Press, 2011.

This very short book, part of the Oxford Introduction series, provides a great deal of information about the origins and dynamics of Pentecostalism.

Miller, Donald, Kimon Sargeant, and Richard Flory, eds. *Spirit and Power: The Growth and Global Impact of Pentecostalism*. Oxford: Oxford University Press, 2013.

This edited work by nineteen scholars examines the various ways Pentecostalism has transformed and often competed with mainstream Christianity.

Pew Forum on Religion and Public Life. *Spirit and Power: A 10-Country Survey of Pentecostals*. Washington, DC: Pew Forum on Religion and Public Life, 2006.

Ruthven, Malise. *Fundamentalism: A Very Short Introduction*. Oxford: Oxford University Press, 2004.

Smith, Christian. *The Bible Made Impossible: Why Biblicism Is Not a Truly Evangelical Reading of Scripture*. Grand Rapids: Brazos Press, 2011.

Sparks, Kenton. *God's Word in Human Words*. Grand Rapids: Baker Academic, 2008.

Internet Resources

"ABC Report on Tongues." Reported by Diane Sawyer. ABC. 2013. *www.you tube.com/watch?v=s9Ep0WHAsIY*.

This report investigates the practice of speaking in tongues (17 min.).

Christianity Today. "Pentecostalism." *www.christianitytoday.com/ct/topics/p/pentecostalism/*.

This site is provided by the evangelical magazine *Christianity Today* as a resource for essays on Pentecostalism.

"A Look at Snake-Handling Churches in Appalachia." Reported by Anderson Cooper. CNN. 2012. *www.youtube.com/watch?v=cwBVcsWYJd8*.

Pentecostals & Charismatics for Peace & Justice. *pcpj.org/*.

This site is dedicated to social justice efforts in the Pentecostal community.

Pew Research Center: Religion & Public Life. "Spirit and Power: A 10-Country Survey of Pentecostals." *www.pewforum.org/2006/10/05/spirit-and-power/*.

This site provides a massive amount of data about the Pentecostal movement.

14

Liberation Spirituality

The emergence of any spirituality is intrinsically connected with history and culture, grounded in lived experience. The patristic church's spirituality developed in the context of increasing Gentile membership and persecution by the state. Monastic spirituality developed, in part, as a critique of normative Christianity and a settled institution. The patristic greats discussed in chapter 5 were highly influenced by the philosophical assumptions of the day, particularly Platonism. In fact, the historical situation conditioned every one of the spiritualities explored so far. Moreover, spirituality must be experienced as relevant to the time. Authentic spirituality is not static, but a dynamic experience of life in the Spirit in a given moment. A classic expression of spirituality is not limited only to one culture or period of history, but can speak relevantly throughout history. And yet, spiritualities do move and change as historical conditions themselves change. Without such development, they would merely be interesting historical artifacts.

Having an authentic Christian spirituality involves recognizing one's own past as well as the classic resources from the tradition, particularly scripture. However, being relevant also entails appropriating these resources to an ever-new moment. Gustavo Gutiérrez, a pioneer in liberation theology writes, "A spirituality is a concrete manner, inspired by the Spirit, of the living Gospel; it is a definite way of living 'before the Lord,' in solidarity with all human beings, 'with the Lord,' and before humanity."[1] Gutiérrez insists that spirituality is a definite, specific way of living the gospel in a given time and that it must align with the imperatives of the moment. He also makes it clear that spirituality has to be associated with the human condition; it is a way of being before the Lord in solidarity with other persons.

Liberation spirituality is a modern movement that attempts to be faithful to the gospel in the context of the real historical situation here and now. It is grounded in many of the virtues already identified and with a clear biblical vision,

---

1. Gustavo Gutiérrez, *A Theology of Liberation: History, Politics, and Salvation*, trans. Caridad Indra and John Eagleson, rev. ed. (Maryknoll, NY: Orbis Books, 1988), 204.

principally in the witness of the prophets and ministry of Jesus. It marshals these resources to address the suffering of the poor and marginalized in societies with a vast divide between the small number of "haves" and the overwhelming majority of the suffering "have nots." Gutiérrez observes, "Everywhere we look, we see death. . . . We are confronted with a reality contrary to the reign of life that the Lord proclaims."[2]

Some have accused liberation theologians of being religiously dressed "leftists" in a culture war between socialism and free market capitalism. Liberation theologians reply that they merely take the witness of Jesus in the Bible, particularly his preaching on the kingdom of God, and apply it to the real life situation of widespread poverty in the countries where they live.

The Kingdom of God

Biblical discussion of the reign of God reaches back to the monarchical period (eleventh to sixth centuries BCE), and refers to God's rule over creation and history. As this theme developed biblically, God's mighty rule came to be envisioned as an eschatological or end-time reality. On that day God's rule will be fully manifested: "How beautiful upon the mountains are the feet of him who brings glad tidings, announcing peace, bearing good news, announcing salvation, and saying to Zion, 'Your God is King!'" (Isa. 52:7). Beginning around 165 BCE, many Jews began to think of the reign of God apocalyptically: they expected that the world as we now experience it would be replaced by a radically different age to come. The kingdom of God was also Jesus' central theme. It functions as a kind of master symbol in his ministry, appearing fifty-six times in Matthew's Gospel alone. Jesus preached that the kingdom was at hand (Matt. 3:2; Mark 1:15) and even upon us (Matt. 12:28; Luke 11:20), while also something to anticipate in its fullness (Matt. 6:10). Although Jesus did not seem to have a utopian political order in mind, the kingdom was something to learn about, seek, and make part of one's life. It represented a new era where good will triumph over evil, and peace, harmony, and justice will prevail.

In preaching the kingdom, Jesus constantly upset the social and religious standards of his day. For him, the kingdom showed a preference for the outcasts and the poor. At one point, when religious authorities challenged him, he replied, "Amen, I say to you, tax collectors and prostitutes are entering the kingdom before you" (Matt. 21:31). In the most famous sermon of Luke's Gospel, Jesus proclaimed, "Blessed are you who are poor, for the kingdom of God is yours" (6:20). Indeed many of his parables contrasted rich and poor, with God favoring the poor while castigating the rich for having little consideration for those who are less well off: "There was a rich man who dressed in purple garments and fine linen and dined

---

2. Gustavo Gutiérrez, *We Drink from Our Own Wells: The Spiritual Journey of a People*, trans. Matthew O'Connell (Maryknoll, NY: Orbis Books, 1984), 10.

sumptuously each day. And lying at his door was a poor man named Lazarus, covered with sores" (Luke 16:19–20). Jesus goes on to say that the poor man was taken to Abraham's bosom while the rich man entered the flames of hell.

Was Jesus a revolutionary, trying to undermine the political order? The short answer is that Jesus was not a political messiah. A nuanced answer, however, would acknowledge that Jesus regularly challenged every one of society's conventions that allowed suffering and injustice. He struggled mightily against any form of the anti-kingdom, which included the powerful people of his day. This conflict with power acts as a unifying thread throughout the Gospels. The author of Mark's Gospel writes that early in his public ministry, "The Pharisees went out and immediately took counsel with the Herodians against him to put him to death" (3:6). Significantly, both religious leaders and political leaders (the Herodians) felt unnerved by him and his message.

Jesus' message was not limited to good news about heaven; he also taught his disciples to pray, "Your kingdom come, your will be done *on earth* as it is in heaven" (Mark 6:10, emphasis added). This kingdom is good news for the poor, the outcast, and the marginalized. Jesus' gospel also challenged those who neglected the poor: "Woe to you who are rich" (Luke 6:24). The kingdom, clearly, was for everyone, but not everyone would embrace it in the same way. While the poor heard about God's lavish graciousness and compassion, the rich learned that the kingdom demanded that they take on the plight of the poor and conform their lives to the demands of justice. Many considered Jesus a dangerous man, and he was condemned by Pilate as a political agitator. Does this mean that Jesus was a political revolutionary? No. But he was a prophet whose message challenged every level of power. That made him a dangerous man with formidable enemies.

Jesus' call for a kingdom of justice echoed a central theme in the prophetic tradition of the Old Testament, as touched on in chapter 1. Many of the prophets linked authentic worship of God to a just society. In Isaiah's inaugural sermon, he prophesied that justice was the true fasting God desired (1:3–17). Later, Isaiah identified justice as the only condition that would prevent Israel's destruction (58:1–9).

> Is this not, rather, the fast that I choose: releasing those bound unjustly, untying the thongs of the yoke; setting free the oppressed, breaking off every yoke? Is it not sharing your bread with the hungry, bringing the afflicted and the homeless into your house; clothing the naked when you see them, and not turning your back on your own flesh? Then your light shall break forth like the dawn, and your wound shall quickly be healed. Your vindication shall go before you, and the glory of the Lord shall be your rear guard (Isa. 58:6–8).

Jeremiah preached that the temple would only be holy if oppression was reversed (7:3–11), a prophecy that almost got him killed. More heatedly, Amos taught that Israel's sacrificial offerings to God in the temple actually became blasphemous when justice was not administered to the people (4:4–5). Hosea equated injustice with ignorance of God (4:1–2), and Micah believed that a life of justice and mercy constituted the true sacrifice that was acceptable to God (6:8). The list could go on. According to Luke's Gospel, Jesus begins his ministry by quoting Isaiah 61:1–2: "'The Spirit of the Lord is upon me, because he has anointed me to bring glad tidings to the poor. He has sent me to proclaim liberty to captives and recovery of sight to the blind, and to let the oppressed go free, and to proclaim a year acceptable to the Lord.' . . . Today this scripture is fulfilled in your hearing" (Luke 4:18–21). According to the Gospels, Jesus saw his ministry through Isaiah's prophetic lens: in the kingdom the poor, captives, blind, and oppressed will be freed. Clearly, the kingdom of God embraces more than just questions of economic inequities. Jesus preached against sin and about the need for interior purification. Ultimately, discipleship would require renouncing one's life of self-advancement for the gospel. Following Jesus would necessarily involve a kind of dying to one's old self and realizing a new life in God: "For whoever wishes to save his life will lose it, but whoever loses his life for my sake and that of the gospel will save it" (Mark 8:35). Even here, though, living no longer for oneself and living for God means taking on God's priorities in the world.

Sermon by St. John Chrysostom

Do you really wish to pay homage to Christ's body? Then do not neglect him when he is naked. At the same time that you honor him here with hangings made of silk, do not ignore him outside when he perishes from cold and nakedness. For the One who said, "This is my body" . . . also said, "When I was hungry you gave me nothing to eat." . . . For is there any point in his table being laden with golden cups while he himself is perishing from hunger? First fill him when he is hungry and then set his table with lavish ornaments. Are you making a golden cup for him at this very moment when you refuse to give him a cup of cold water? Do you decorate his table with cloths flecked with gold while at the same time neglect to give him what is necessary for him to cover himself? . . . The conclusion is: Don't neglect your brother in his distress while you decorate his house. Your brother is more truly his temple than any church building.[3]

3. John Chrysostom, *On Matthew: Homily* 50.4; quoted in *The Faith That Does Justice*, ed. John Haughey (Mahwah, NJ: Paulist Press, 1977), 131.

History of Latin America and the Liberation Movement

How does the theme of justice, so prominent in the prophets, relate to today's historical situation? According to the World Bank, twenty-five thousand children die of starvation each day and more than a billion persons live on less than a dollar a day. Is justice served by merely encouraging the rich to be more charitable to the poor and the poor to accept their dismal circumstances? Or is the kingdom now reduced to "going to heaven" with no relevance to questions of justice? For liberation theologians, assuaging the poor with the hope of a future eternal life while they suffer oppression in the present is tantamount to gutting the gospel message and twisting the very meaning of the kingdom of God.

Social and Economic History of Latin America

Central and South America include countries with excellent natural resources, though these countries have historically lacked the social and economic infrastructure to take advantage of them. In the 1950s, companies from industrialized countries, such as the United States, made deals with governments and land owners to utilize these resources in the production of consumer goods. These companies vigorously exported Latin American resources, such as wood, coffee beans, and fruits like bananas. It was billed as advancement for these countries, which would now be able to participate more fully in world markets and develop economically. By the 1960s, however, that this arrangement simply exploited these resources for the enrichment of already developed countries had become clear.

Economists, once hopeful about the possibilities of development in Latin America, realized that powerful economies had actually become more powerful while developing economies grew weaker and more impoverished. Some economists utilized tools from Marxism to analyze the situation. In the middle to late nineteenth century, economic theorists Karl Marx and Friedrich Engels argued that economics fundamentally controlled structures of culture, including class, morality, religion, and politics. Marx claimed that "religion is the opiate of the people." By this he meant that religion unwittingly supported systems that exploited the masses and condemned them to a grueling life of poverty while offering a kind of moral support to keep them going. Religion also offered the possibility of an afterlife, so long as one behaved docilely and accepted one's place in society. Marx believed that religion, in effect, colluded with economic power to keep the masses in line. Marx's political followers created socialist and communist states to reverse the exploitation of workers by controlling economies and dismantling capitalism. Marxism served not only as a denunciation of the free market, but also as a challenge to religion.

As noted in chapter 8, when economies dramatically change, they cause extraordinary disparities between the wealthy and the poor. Economists recognized that just as a capitalist economic structure created an underclass of poor workers within a given country, so now it created a division between wealthy and underclass countries. Latin America was being exploited, because of its economic vulnerability, to the enrichment of the United States and, to a lesser degree, Europe.

From the 1960s through the 1980s, countries in Latin America went through a series of violent revolutions that were often brutally suppressed by dictators and the military they controlled. Many Latin Americans saw these revolutions as a fight for economic justice and a contest between northern and southern hemispheres. The United States saw these revolutions as parts of a larger political fight between East and West, between democracy and communism. Cuba, which had experienced a revolution in the 1950s, was the first country to successfully liberate from its dictatorship; it allied with the communist Soviet Union. While the United States tried, rather successfully, to isolate Cuba, it also supported Latin American governments who opposed any socialist agenda, even if they did so brutally.

The contest between political ideologies was not even always a contest between democracy and communism. In 1984, socialist Daniel Ortega won the presidency of Nicaragua with 67 percent of the vote in what international monitors concluded was a fair election. However, because he aligned himself with other socialists in Latin America, including Fidel Castro of Cuba, the Reagan administration armed resistance fighters, the Contras, to overthrow the government. This created the conditions for a vicious civil war that lasted until 1990.

The Catholic Church and Liberation Theologians

The Catholic Church was the largest Christian denomination in many parts of the world that experienced social upheaval during this period, and the Church did not remain silent. On the one hand, it resisted the socialist political agenda because of its clear anti-religious stance. Indeed, in countries where communism took root, a loss of civil rights and a suppression of religion often followed. The Church also objected to framing the human condition in terms of capital and labor, seeing this reduction of human beings as potentially leading to abuse and violence. Indeed, numerous communist governments have been guilty of massacring their own citizens: Stalin's Soviet government killed twenty-five million, Mao's Chinese government killed thirty-five million, and the Khmer Rouge's Cambodian government killed two million.

On the other hand, the Church favored the cause of the people, who in this case were clearly brutalized by abject poverty. In 1955, the bishops of the Latin American Bishops Conference (CELAM) began to take a prophetic stance against economic injustice in their land. In 1968, CELAM met in Medellin, Columbia, and called for a "preferential option for the poor." In this, they reflected Jesus' preaching about the kingdom of God as human flourishing, particularly for the poor. In so doing, they also echoed Jesus' denunciation of what they called "structural sin," economic structures that inherently abuse, manipulate, or exploit others: "To us, the Pastors of the Church, belongs the duty . . . to denounce everything which, opposing justice, destroys peace."[4]

CELAM also met in Puebla, Mexico in 1979, Santo Domingo, Dominican Republic in 1992 and finally in Aparecida, Brazil in 2007 to reiterate the imperative for liberating the peoples of Latin America. The bishops of CELAM were bolstered by a new theological enterprise occurring in Latin America called "liberation theology," in which theologians reflected on the plight of the poor, the structures of sin, and Jesus' message in order to empower them to seek justice.

Social Justice Encyclicals of the Twentieth Century

The following are Social Justice Encyclicals from popes throughout the twentieth century: Pius XI's 1931 *Quadregesimo Anno* (*After Forty Years*) strongly critiqued unrestrained capitalism. John XXIII's 1961 *Mater et Magistra* (*Mother and Teacher*) argued that Christians have a responsibility to eliminate excessive inequities, particularly among richer and poorer nations. Paul VI's 1967 *Populorum Progressio* (*On the Development of Peoples*) argued for the universal destination of goods, just wages, security of employment, and fair working conditions. John Paul II's 1981 *Laborum Exercens* (*On Human Work*) examined the problem of capitalism's failure to fairly compensate those who contribute to labor. John Paul II's 1987 *Sollicitudo Rei Socialis* (*On Social Concern*) surveyed the structures of sin in developing nations. John Paul II's 1991 *Centesimus Annus* (*The Hundredth Year*) emphasized the problems between rich and poor nations, environmental degradation due to unrestrained consumerism, and the relationship between the right to private property and the demand for equitable distribution.

---

4. CELAM, *Peace*, no. 20, in *Renewing the Earth: Catholic Documents on Peace, Justice and Liberation*, ed. David Obrien and Thomas Shannon (New York: Doubleday, 1977), 569.

The Church informally adopted liberation theology, but continued to have grave concerns about it. Liberation theology follows a long line of formal social justice teachings in the modern Catholic Church. These started in 1891 with Leo XIII's encyclical *Rerum Novarum* (*On the Condition of Labor*), which argued for the rights of workers, their freedom to form unions, and the necessity of the government to ensure an equitable distribution of wealth. Other encyclicals followed.

From Paul VI on, these encyclicals assert that socialism is not the answer, but also that structures of injustice must be analyzed and countered. Further, while maintaining the right to private property, the Church considered this a subsidiary right, one that needed to be balanced with the common good and the health of society. As John Paul II wrote in *Sollicitudo Rei Socialis*, "The goods of the world are equally meant for all. The right to private property is valid and necessary, but it does not nullify the value of this principle. Private property, in fact, is under a social mortgage."[5]

Some bishops even spoke and acted like liberation theologians, prophetically challenging the status quo. Oscar Romero, archbishop of San Salvador, El Salvador, placed himself on the front line of social conflict on behalf of his people. Shortly after Romero was named archbishop, his friend Father Rutilio Grande was assassinated for creating self-reliant groups among the poor campasinos. Romero reflected, "When I looked at Rutilio lying there dead I thought, 'If they have killed him for doing what he did, then I too have to walk the same path.'"[6] Romero spoke out against the widespread poverty, systematic injustice, and the torture and murders of citizens who spoke up. He urged American president Jimmy Carter to stop arming the Salvadoran government. During his three years as archbishop, more than fifty priests had been attacked and six assassinated. In February of 1980, the University of Louvain awarded Romero an honorary doctorate for his prophetic call for peace and justice. During his acceptance speech, he said,

> But it is important to note why [the Church] has been persecuted. Not any and every priest has been persecuted, not any and every institution has been attacked. That part of the church has been attacked and persecuted that put itself on the side of the people and went to the people's defense. Here again we find the same key to understanding the persecution of the church: the poor. . . . Now we realize what sin is. We realize that offences against God bring death to human beings. We realize that sin is truly death-dealing; not only does it bring the interior death of the one who commits it; it also produces objective death. We

---

5. *Sollicitudo Rei Socialis*, no. 42.

6. Michael Hays and David Tombs, eds., *Truth and Memory: The Church and Human Rights in El Salvador and Guatemala* (Leominster, UK: Gracewing Publishing, 2001), 4.

OSCAR RIVERA/EPA /LANDOV

Oscar Romero, hailed by many as "Saint Romero of the Americas" for his advocacy of the poor, was beatified in 2015 in this ceremony in San Salvador, El Salvador.

are thus reminded of a basic truth of our Christian faith. Sin caused the death of the Son of God; sin continues to cause the death of the children of God.[7]

Romero was assassinated on March 24, 1980 while celebrating Mass, just one day after ordering Salvadoran Christians to disobey any order that violated human rights.

Nonetheless, both Pope John Paul II and Cardinal Ratzinger, who headed the Vatican's office for doctrine and later became Pope Benedict XVI, had problems with liberation theology. Many liberation theologians used Marxist tools of social analysis to identify problems in Latin American economies, particularly in regard to the ways capitalism dominated class systems and exploited workers. While Pope Paul VI's *Populorum Progressio* allowed for some Marxist analysis, the question remains, just how Marxist should such an analysis be? Further, liberation theology decidedly challenged the governments and policies in Latin America. Their work provided some of the grounding ideology of revolutionaries. Should the Church support violent overthrows of existing governments? Finally, some criticized liberation theology for being too concerned with economic justice, while neglecting other central themes of the gospel. These critics alleged that liberation theologians presented Jesus as a virtual revolutionary. In his opening address to the bishops of CELAM at Puebla, John Paul II said,

> We find "re-readings" of the Gospel that are the product of theoretical speculations rather than of authentic meditation on the word of God as a genuine evangelical commitment. In some cases people are silent about Christ's divinity, or else they indulge in types of interpretation

---

7. See *Signos de vida y fidelidad: Testimonios de la Iglasia en América latina, 1978–1982* (Lima: CEP, 1983), 2.

that are at variance with the Church's faith. Christ is alleged to be only a "prophet," a proclaimer of God's Kingdom. . . . In other cases people purport to depict Jesus as a political activist, a fighter against Roman domination and the authorities, and even as someone involved in class struggle. This conception of Christ as a political figure, a revolutionary, a subversive of Nazareth, does not tally with the Church's catechesis.[8]

In 1984, the Vatican issued a document entitled "Instruction on Certain Aspects of the Theology of Liberation," which affirmed liberation theology in so far as it addressed the kind of liberation from injustice imperative in many developing countries. It also, however, challenged the overuse of Marxist analysis, which it feared reduced the faith to matters of economic fairness. Despite these problems, the Catholic Church eventually came to accept liberation theology as a standard and venerable project. In 1986, Pope John Paul II addressed a letter to the bishops of Brazil that took a clearly positive interpretation of liberation theology's aims. In it he spoke of the rare gift of liberation theology's commitment to justice. In 2012, Pope Benedict XVI appointed Gerhard Müller as Prefect of the Congregation for the Doctrine of the Faith (the Vatican's doctrinal center). A decade earlier, Müller had coauthored a book with Gustavo Gutiérrez entitled *On the Side of the Poor: Liberation Theology, Theology of the Church.* Furthermore, on September 3, 2013, Pope Francis I spent an entire day with Gutiérrez discussing theology. *L'Osservatore Romano,* the Vatican's semi-official newspaper, published an essay on the event that said, "Liberation theology can no longer remain in the shadows to which it has been relegated for some years, at least in Europe."

Liberation Spirituality
Challenge to Inadequacies in the Tradition

Christian spirituality, particularly in the Catholic Church, can tend toward individualism, as though the Christian message dealt exclusively with the soul and one's private relationship to God, with little interest paid to the state of the world's affairs.[9] It is a wholly interior spirituality, accessible only to a fortunate minority for whom the necessities of life are guaranteed, allowing them to pray at length. Most Christians do not share this life, but are immersed in families, hard work, and the challenges of living their faith in the midst of society.

As noted earlier, spirituality is about lived experience, which, to be sure, involves one's own experience. The challenge of liberation spirituality lies in

---

8. No. I. 4. See *www.ewtn.com/library/PAPALDOC/JP791228.htm.*

9. In Carmelite spirituality, for example, the dominant preoccupation of Teresa of Ávila and John of the Cross was the development of prayer and spiritual purification.

connecting one's spirituality to the lived experience of the mass of humanity, to their concrete situation. Liberation spirituality considers any spirituality that does not do so a failed project.

The liberation movement believes that spirituality requires a creative tension among values. It needs to balance transcendence and immanence, for God is found both beyond this world and immanently in the lives of people. It needs to balance the spiritual with the material, which are not separate spheres of existence or concern, but represent the very nature of living in the world. To be concerned about the soul but not the body is to split the human person. Spirituality needs to balance contemplation and action. While cultivating a deep interior life is crucial, if the transformative action of the Spirit does not imply engagement with others, it suggests that no real transformation has taken place. And finally, it needs to balance the personal and social dimensions of human life. Spirituality involves the transformation of both the soul and socially constituted relationships. Further, liberationists argue, this cannot be limited to responding to others' needs, but must also seek just structures that produce life and countering unjust structures that guarantee mass suffering.

Realized Eschatology

The term *eschatology* refers to the end times. Broadly, Christians believe that they are in the final stage of salvation history and that the covenant that Christ proclaimed is God's final and complete covenant. The Incarnation, which bridged the divide between God and humanity decisively, the cross as a conclusive sacrificial atonement for sin, and the Resurrection conquering death are collectively understood as God's definitive program for salvation. Thus Christianity understands itself as a religion of the end times. What this means concretely is more complicated. For example, does this mean that Christ will return imminently? The first Christians surely thought so.[10] Many evangelical and Pentecostal Christians also believe that Christ will return in their lifetime.

Another way to talk about eschatology is to envision it as referring to the final covenant, inaugurated by Jesus and to be concluded at his second coming. In this sense, the kingdom is already here and embraced in part, but is not yet fully realized. Theologians refer to the "eschatological tension" between the kingdom as both "already" here and "not yet" completely accomplished. In such a framework, one experiences grace and salvation even as one continues to struggle with sin. Further, the very call of Christ is to advance or "build the kingdom." Liberation spirituality focuses on this eschatological tension. It reflects the relationship between salvation history and the liberation of the poor, and believes that engaging in liberation is central to advancing the kingdom of God. Christ

---

10. At one point, Paul even imagined that he would still be alive at the second coming (1 Thess. 4:14).

is the redeemer who has achieved salvation for the world, and a spirituality of liberation involves realizing that vision of justice.

Liberation spirituality entails radical conversion to God and commitment to Christ. Participating in Christ's redeeming work provides the context of this conversion. Liberation spirituality calls individuals to step out of their comfort zone and confront every power of the anti-kingdom, everything that undermines human dignity. Conversion does not merely consist of professing God's existence and striving to avoid sin. Rather, it involves communion with God and aligning one's heart, soul, and strength to God's kingdom. Deep faith, liberation spirituality insists, demands a loving attitude toward all human beings, because they are God's own and share in God's love. Thus a Christian's response to others constitutes his or her response to God. Theologian Roger Haight writes,

> To worship God is to surrender the whole of one's life to the will of God. And that will as far as we know is totally and absolutely for or in favor of human life, for people who are God's own people. God's will for human existence in this world is for justice being extended to all of God's people. And thus God's will extends especially out to those who have nothing, or nothing but God. If to know God is to do justice, then to worship God is to surrender to God's will by service to the neighbor most in need.[11]

Solidarity

Fundamental to liberation spirituality is solidarity with the poor. It consists not merely of sympathy for those who suffer, but of taking on their lives as one's own. CELAM explicitly adopted this posture of solidarity when the bishops took up the image of the Good Samaritan in their 2007 meeting in Aparacida, Brazil. The image comes from one of Jesus' parables, which tells the story of a man who was robbed, brutally beaten, and left for dead. Two passersby, one a priest and the other a Levite, see the man's body and continue on the road to Jerusalem:

> "But a Samaritan traveler who came upon him was moved with compassion at the sight. He approached the victim, poured oil and wine over his wounds and bandaged them. Then he lifted him on his own animal, took him to an inn and cared for him. The next day he took out two silver coins and gave them to the innkeeper with the instruction, 'Take care of him. If you spend more than what I have given you, I shall repay you on my way back.' Which of these three, in your opinion, was

---

11. Roger Haight, *An Alternative Vision: An Interpretation of Liberation Theology* (New York: Paulist Press, 1985), 250.

neighbor to the robbers' victim?" He [a scholar of the law] answered, "The one who treated him with mercy." Jesus said to him, "Go and do likewise." (Luke 10:33–37)

The bishops of CELAM proclaimed, "Illuminated by Christ, the suffering, the injustice, and the cross [of our people] call us to live like a Samaritan Church" (no. 27). They felt compelled to follow the practice of Jesus and make themselves neighbors, especially to those who suffer, so that they can help create a society where no one is marginalized (no. 135). They called for all Christians to take up the task of "making ourselves neighbors . . . going as good Samaritans to meet the needs of the poor and those who suffer, and creating the just structures that are the condition without which a just social order is not possible so that the continent might become our common home" (no. 537).

Evangelical spirituality emphasizes the cross, for it is on the cross that Christ frees one from sin and makes it possible for one to become a child of God. Few Christians would disagree with this. For liberation spirituality, the cross means not only this, but also committing oneself to building a world of love, peace, fraternity, and self-surrender to God. It means suffering with and for the poor as a result of that commitment. And it means solidarity with the disinherited. The cross represents victory, certainly, but it also functions as a symbol of the devastating consequences of sin. The brutalized and disfigured body of Christ is what sin looks like; it represents what sin does to the soul and to the human condition. The church as the body of Christ suffers the same disfigurement. To blithely accept this, to live without solidarity, is to fail to recognize this central insight into the cross.

Encountering the Lord

The First Letter of John opens by asserting that discipleship starts with experiencing God's transforming love, and from that the possibility to live a new life:

> What was from the beginning, what we have heard, what we have seen with our eyes, what we looked upon and touched with our hands concerns the Word of life. . . . Now this is the message that we have heard from him and proclaim to you: God is light, and in him there is no darkness at all. If we say, "We have fellowship with him," while we continue to walk in darkness, we lie and do not act in truth. But if we walk in the light as he is in the light, then we have fellowship with one another, and the blood of his Son Jesus cleanses us from all sin (1 John 1:1–7).

The author of this passage says that he has seen and heard the Lord, and from that experience testifies that others too might have fellowship with God, leaving the darkness and entering the light. If liberation spirituality is about working towards an authentic experience of life and light and rejecting the darkness of sin and oppression, it is also about proclaiming, first and foremost, that such an agenda is based on an initial experience of God's gratuitous love. Grace precedes everything, and to know the Lord is to first encounter the Lord.

In the context of extreme poverty, new, real, and authentic experiences of God emerge. Liberation theologians argue that the poor experience Christ's love profoundly. Poverty, although deplorable, also holds within it the potential for an experience of dignity. There is something in the condition of the poor that creates the posture of a radical dependence on and openness to God. Gutiérrez writes,

> Beyond any possible doubt, the life of the poor is one of hunger and exploitation, inadequate health care and lack of suitable housing, difficulty in obtaining an education, inadequate wages and unemployment, struggles for their rights, and repression. *But that is not all. Being poor is also a way of feeling, knowing, reasoning, making friends, loving, believing, suffering, celebrating, and praying.*[12]

Liberation spirituality aims to make visible here and now the victory over death that the poor believe Christ has already won for them and which they already experience in a real sense in their lives. To live in the barrios is to encounter people of deep faith, a community that shares with one another generously, and persons who gladly walk with each other in their mutual struggles.

Freedom

One of the most important themes in the New Testament is freedom. Paul writes about freedom from the law: "For freedom Christ set us free" (Gal. 5:1). This is not the freedom of a libertine, freedom to do whatever one wants, but freedom for service: "For you were called for freedom, brothers. But do not use this freedom as an opportunity for the flesh; rather, serve one another through love" (Gal. 5:13). James refers to loving service as living under "the law of liberty" (2:12). This freedom, while clearly a freedom from sin and selfishness, is also a freedom for love, communion, and service.

Liberation theologians talk about a kind of interior freedom that poor people experience—a freedom from the human addiction for comfort and self-protection and a freedom that unleashes a bold witness to a faith in action. This is the freedom Romero proclaimed. His love for God, and his experience of God's overwhelming love for him, empowered him to stand up for his people against every form of darkness and violence. It enabled him to submit to martyrdom as he took on the forces of that anti-kingdom.

---

12. Gutiérrez, *We Drink from Our Own Wells*, 125 (emphasis added).

Hope and Joy

Christian spirituality is a life of hope. Indeed, it upholds the ultimate hope of life after death. At the end of the day, Christians believe that eternal life is the fruit borne of faith while on earth. Christian spirituality also offers hope in the eternal meaning of life. Belief in the resurrection undergirds the conviction that life will have the last word, even in the midst of death. Hope refers to both the present and the future. If it were merely a hope in the future, then it would have no experiential grounding. If it were a hope grounded only in the present, then it would not be complete, for life is not complete. Rather, for liberation spirituality, hope is only possible for a kingdom that can be realized here and now as it moves to its fullness in eternal life. It is here that Christian hope joins with an active love of the neighbor.

The very desire to change reality is an expression of this hope. Gutiérrez writes, "There is a kind of paradoxical 'resignation' to joy that is nothing else than the recognition of the strengthening presence of God and the community—a recognition in which our fears, doubts, and discouragement . . . are routed by the power of the Lord's love."[13]

Spiritual Childhood

Gutiérrez describes liberation spirituality as a kind of spiritual childhood. For him, it represents a deep trust and intimacy with the divine. Spiritual strength comes from a radical, childlike dependence on God. Material poverty even helps to condition this, as the poor have little temptation to rely on anything else. Christian spirituality, he argues, can never be triumphalistic, but only a ready disposition of the soul that hopes for everything from the Lord. It is an attitude of radical openness to God.

Conclusion

The focus of this chapter has been liberation spirituality as it is being expressed in Latin America, the place where it originated as a particular theology and spiritual expression. But Christian liberation movements are certainly not limited to this geography or Latin America's particular need. As theologian and philosopher Dorothee Soelle writes, "This theology was taken up in many parts of the Third World, in South Africa as in Southeast Asia, and by blacks in the United States and by Christian women all over the world."[14] It is a spirituality that

---

13. Ibid., 119.

14. Dorothee Soelle, *The Silent Cry: Mysticism and Resistance*, trans. Barbara and Martin Rumscheidt (Minneapolis: Fortress Press, 2001), 283.

inclines to any state of marginalization; one that seeks both to learn from those whom society has disenfranchised and walk in solidarity with them toward recreating structures that bear the justice of the kingdom of God. The liberation movement in Latin America has an analogue with a feminist critique of Christian patriarchy. One also finds this same dynamic in "black theology." James Cone, one of the great articulators of this theological movement, writes, "The task of black theology, then, is to analyze the nature of the gospel of Jesus Christ in light of oppressed blacks so that they will see the gospel as inseparable from their humiliated condition and as bestowing upon them the necessary power to break the chains of oppression."[15]

Liberation spirituality makes an extraordinary case for itself. It carries with it many of the values seen in other spiritualities. It is a spirituality of deep faith and dependence on God, one that demands daunting inner purification (loving one's enemies), and that is filled with Christian virtues and practices. It retrieves the original message of Jesus in ways that appear extraordinarily faithful to the Gospels. In addition, it takes seriously the conditions of the world. Not many readers of this book probably have firsthand experience with poverty, much less abject poverty. Liberation spirituality demands a response to the question: How can one be faithful to the gospel and not see the disconnect between a comfortable middle-class existence, which statistically few in the world enjoy, and the gross suffering of the majority of human beings? To make matters worse, those who enjoy a middle-class existence are complicit in that suffering. The low cost of the clothes that they wear and the food that they eat is partly due to the economically exploitative international system that provides these goods. International corporations get cheap resources from vulnerable societies made by companies that pay grossly inadequate wages. There is a moral, theological, and spiritual shadow over the developed world. Liberation spirituality calls for all humans to step out of this shadow and enter the light of authentic solidarity.

This is also a spirituality that has encountered resistance particularly in the United States, perhaps because it challenges a whole lifestyle, which many find unnerving. In addition, it is difficult to imagine how one might live liberation spirituality in the United States; but it can be done. Many Christians volunteer to work with and for others who have real need. Soup kitchens, homeless shelters, and so on, provide venues for authentic service for the gospel. Further, many support social and governmental policies that make a "preferential option for the poor." Most deeply, liberation spirituality calls for a bona fide solidarity with the poor and taking on their plight as one's own. John Markey argues in *Moses in Pharaoh's House* that a liberation spirituality in North America is not only possible, but crucial. Markey sees in it the resources to break down walls of individualism, greed (and its counterpart, envy), and a distorted understanding of human flourishing. He also sees in it possibilities for deep conversion of heart and mind.

---

15. James Cone, *A Black Theology of Revelation* (Maryknoll, NY: Orbis Books, 1986), 5.

Questions for Review

1. What are some Old Testament precedents for Jesus' approach to issues of social justice, as depicted in the Gospels. How does liberation theology utilize these Old Testament precedents?
2. What social, political, and economic developments led to the rise of liberation theology?
3. In what ways did the institutional Catholic Church support liberation theology and in what ways did the Church critique it?
4. How does liberation theology challenge individuals and institutions?

Questions for Discussion

1. Many historians and economists conclude that the developed economies, such as those of Europe and the United States, became wealthier and more stable at the expense of developing countries, whose citizens suffered and continue to suffer widespread poverty. Assuming this to be correct, how should this conclusion affect your life specifically?
2. Do you think liberation theology and spirituality is a legitimate option for those in developed countries like the United States? If so, how would it work? If not, what problems might emerge in the process of adopting it?
3. Liberation spirituality claims that poverty can enhance a person's experience of God in some ways. What do you make of this claim?
4. In your opinion, what does liberation spirituality demand of middle-class Americans in their daily lives?

Bibliography

Resources with annotations are highly recommended to students interested in further study.

Boff, Leonardo. *Saint Francis: A Model for Human Liberation*. Translated by John Dierchsmeier. New York: Crossroad, 1982.

Boff, Leonardo, and Clodovis Boff. *Introducing Liberation Theology*. Maryknoll, NY: Orbis Books, 1986.

    This is an excellent introductory text outlining wide-ranging themes in liberation theology.

Conn, Joann Wolski, ed. *Women's Spirituality: Resources for Christian Development*. Mahwah, NJ: Paulist Press, 1986.

Fredriksen, Paula. *From Jesus to Christ: The Origins of the New Testament Images of Jesus*. New Haven: Yale University Press, 1988.

Gutiérrez, Gustavo. *A Theology of Liberation: History, Politics, and Salvation*. Translated by Caridad Inda and John Eagleson. Rev. ed. Maryknoll, NY: Orbis Books, 1988.

This premier expression of liberation theology introduced the movement to the world.

Gutiérrez, Gustavo. *We Drink from Our Own Wells: The Spiritual Journey of a People*. Translated by Matthew O'Connell. Maryknoll, NY: Orbis Books, 1984.

This is Gutierrez's reflection on how liberation theology is also a biblically grounded spirituality.

Haight, Roger. *An Alternative Vision: An Interpretation of Liberation Theology*. New York: Paulist Press, 1985.

Hays, Michael, and David Tombs, eds. *Truth and Memory: The Church and Human Rights in El Salvador and Guatemala*. Leominster, UK: Gracewing Publishing, 2001.

Johnson, Elizabeth. *Quest for the Living God: Mapping Frontiers in the Theology of God*. New York: Continuum, 2008.

This book describes various experiences of God, particularly from points of view that are otherwise marginalized.

Johnson, Elizabeth. *She Who Is: The Mystery of God in Feminist Theological Discourse*. New York: Crossroad, 1995.

Lassalle-Klein, Robert, ed. *Jesus of Galilee: Contextual Christology for the Twenty-First Century*. Maryknoll, NY: Orbis Books, 2011.

Light, Aimée Upjohn. *God at the Margins: Making Theological Sense of Religious Plurality*. Winona, MN: Anselm Academic, 2014.

Markey, John. *Moses in Pharaoh's House: A Liberation Spirituality for North America*. Winona, MN: Anselm Academic, 2014.

Ruffing, Janet, ed. *Mysticism and Social Transformation*. Syracuse: Syracuse University Press, 2001.

Segundo, Juan Luis. *The Historical Jesus of the Synoptics*. Translated by John Drury. Maryknoll, NY: Orbis Books, 1985.

Segundo, Juan Luis. *The Liberation of Theology*. Maryknoll, NY: Orbis Books, 1976.

Signos de vida y fidelidad: Testimonios de la Iglasia en América latina 1978–1982. Lima: CEP, 1983.

Sobrino, Jon. *Christology at the Crossroads: A Latin American Approach*. Maryknoll, NY: Orbis Books, 1978.

Sobrino, Jon. *Jesus the Liberator: A Historical Theological Reading of Jesus of Nazareth*. Translated by Paul Burns and Francis McDonagh. Maryknoll, NY: Orbis Books, 1993.

This book argues powerfully that Christology has been co-opted by the academy in ways that do not represent either the historical Jesus or the experience of most humans.

Soelle, Dorothee. *The Silent Cry: Mysticism and Resistance*. Translated by Barbara and Martin Rumscheidt. Minneapolis: Fortress Press, 2001.

Internet Resources

Adams, Samuel. "What Is Liberation Theology?" 2014. *www.bing.com/videos/search?q=liberation+theology&FORM=VIRE1#view=detail&mid=97BF20ABC37A54B8439797BF20ABC37A54B84397*.

A brief lecture on the foundation of liberation theology by a Mennonite minister (4 min.).

Liberation Theologies: Resources, Library, and Online Bookstore. *liberationtheology.org/*.

This site is a resource center for liberation theology and spirituality.

Films

Romero. 1989.

Film depicting Archbishop Oscar Romero's emerging support of the poor and oppressed of El Salvador, which led to his martyrdom in 1980.

15

Comparative Spirituality

What should a Christian think about other religions? Are they sincere human ways to imagine God, but not actual revelations of God? Are they valuable, but limited, expressions of God's grace, while Christianity has the absolute and fullest revelation? Are they uniquely valid articulations of religious truth, different but equally worthwhile? Are they akin to different paths up the mountain, providing different means to the same summit?

Some Christians view other religious traditions negatively as, at best, worthy expressions of the moral life, but not salvific. Because such Christians consider Christianity the only means of salvation, they deem non-Christian religions to be necessarily failed projects from the start. These Christians are sometimes referred to as "exclusivists." While not necessarily arrogant or self-righteous, the exclusivist position expresses a fundamental belief that there is no salvation outside of a Christian confession.[1] Exclusivists in general are most often found in evangelical and Pentecostal communities.

Other Christians believe that God's grace extends beyond the borders of Christianity. They consider Christ the absolute savior, but believe that his saving grace operates in and through the souls of all people and that their implicit but real participation in that grace allows them to be saved, even without an explicit Christian confession. Often called "inclusivists," they affirm the priority of Christianity, believing God's revelation is most clearly expressed there. Inclusivists also argue that other religions are authentic responses to God, infused in some way by Christ's grace. They contend that not only can the soul of a non-Christian cooperate with grace, but various non-Christian religions can as well. They would affirm the above-mentioned scriptural citations, since they do consider Christ the savior of all, but they would also draw on other texts, such as "Whoever loves a brother or sister lives in the light" (1 John 2:10) and "God is

---

1. The exclusivist position draws on such biblical warrants as "I am the way, the truth, and the life; no one comes to the Father except through me" (John 14:16) and "Only in him [Jesus] is there salvation; for of all the names in the world given to men, this is the only one by which we can be saved" (Acts 4:11–12).

love, and those who abide in love abide in God, and God abides in them" (1 John 4:16) and "God . . . wills everyone to be saved" (1 Tim. 2:4). Inclusivists are more likely to be found in mainstream Protestant churches as well as the Roman Catholic and Eastern Orthodox traditions.

A third Christian response to the religious other is called "pluralism." Pluralist Christians believe that God transcends all boundaries, categories, and conceptualizations, making any articulation of belief, by its very nature, relative to human considerations. Pluralists see the many religions as addressing God variously, but believe it is the same God, the same Absolute Reality, being known through different religious paradigms or models. Some pluralists focus on different religions as the means for the same salvation, while others highlight the same fundamental religious experiences that they see expressed in different traditions. These Christians believe in the Bible, but think that the exclusive claims in the Bible were meant to inculcate an absolute faith in Jesus. They are convinced that Jesus really does save, but that belief does not, in their opinion, preclude the possibility of other avenues of salvation as well. Although few Christian churches formally embrace the pluralist position, a number of individual Christians would consider themselves pluralists.

A final position that has taken hold in recent years is "mutualism." Christians taking this stance believe that religions differ so greatly from each other, and each represents such a unique expression, that they cannot be compared. They argue against attempts to make comparisons across the traditions, such as correlating heaven with nirvana or God with Daoism's eternal *dao*. Rather, they argue for allowing the religious other to be truly other, as an expression of a unique version of reality, articulating their own understanding of Ultimate Reality. The mutualist stance has taken hold among some scholars, though their numbers are few.

Among scholars, even evangelical scholars, the exclusivist position has the fewest adherents. It closes off the possibility of salvation to whole swaths of people who in many cases had no realistic chance to become Christian. Moreover, its understanding of grace seems restrictive, and it does not seem to look at the phenomena of religious experience or religious transformation objectively. Most scholars acknowledge that the same kinds of religious experience that Christians have are also available in other traditions. The vast majority of Christians and Christian scholars take the inclusivist position, which they see as faithful to the absolute salvation proclaimed in Christianity while still respectful of authentic practice in other religions.

Spirituality and Interreligious Dialogue

In 1984, the Vatican's Pontifical Council for Interreligious Dialogue published *The Attitude of the Church towards the Followers of Other Religions*. It provides a good template for any Christian interested in other religions. In it, the Catholic

Church, which is doctrinally committed to the inclusivist position, discusses ways of engaging the religious other. It assumes that true dialogue involves mutual learning and enrichment; in order for true dialogue to occur, one must believe that the religious other has something to bring to the encounter that one's own religious outlook could find helpful. The document explores several forms of dialogue, each with its own agenda: a dialogue of life, which concentrates on how each religion uniquely expresses our common humanity; dialogue of deed and collaboration, which focuses on how different religions can cooperate toward the common good; theological dialogue, which seeks better understanding of the religious other, and oneself, in the context of dialogue; and finally, a dialogue of religious experience, which involves sharing one's spiritual life and even the possibility for corporate religious experience, such as prayer.

Many scholars in interreligious work focus on the last two types of dialogue. Among other things, they believe that encountering the religious other may help them understand their own faith better. This discipline is called "comparative theology." In comparative theology, scholars try to enter into the religious worldview of another religion and use this engagement as a means to encounter their own religion in different ways. They think of the process in terms of "passing over" and "coming back." One passes over into the texts and religious imagination of other faiths and returns to one's own, asking new questions or bringing new insights into one's theological horizon. The point of this kind of comparative work is not to create new theological truths, and certainly not to suggest a new religious narrative by merging insights from other religious traditions. Rather, by reflecting on insights from other traditions, one sees one's own faith from a different perspective, perhaps even asking new questions of one's own tradition.

Interreligious encounters can also offer a person new insights, perhaps even insights from God. Pope John Paul II touched on the possibility of new religious learning in his reflection on the interreligious experience of the 1986 Assisi Day of Prayer, which brought together representatives from many religious traditions. He said, "There are undeniably differences [in religions] that reflect the genius and spiritual 'riches' that God has given to the peoples."[2]

This chapter looks at three religious traditions and, using excerpts from their classic texts, takes up the task of comparative theology by exploring how a Christian spirituality might be enlarged by these encounters. It will highlight Theravada Buddhism, in particular a small part of the classic text the Dhammapada. It will then explore the more enigmatic religious horizon of Zen, whose uniqueness provides a very different invitation to a Christian re-imagining of the spiritual life, by engaging classic stories and sayings from this tradition. Finally, the chapter will enter into a Daoist religious horizon, particularly through the Dao-De-Jing and the Zhuangzi. It will consider how artful attention to

---

2. John Paul II, "The Meaning of the Assisi Day of Prayer," *Origins* 16, no. 31 (1987): 561–63, at 562.

Pope John Paul II gathered representatives of twelve world religions to the World Day of Prayer for Peace in 1986. At the time, it was the largest gathering of diverse religious leaders in history.

emerging energies might invite a reassessment of a Christian worldview, one that may overcome limitations discovered in it. Although the chapter does not present an exhaustive investigation into any of these religious horizons, it aims to show how comparative work can strengthen a Christian spirituality.

Buddhism and the Dhammapada

The Dhammapada[3] is an anthology of the Buddha's teachings in the form of aphorisms collated under twenty-six themes as chapters. It is the most revered and quoted part of the canon. Theravada Buddhist monks typically memorize the entire 423 verse text as part of their formal training, and they chant many of its verses daily. Part of the Dhammapada's value is that it acts as a kind of canon within the canon, referencing every essential part of Buddhism, from the eight-fold path to the complexity of Buddhist anthropology. Thus it does not serve merely as a compendium or Buddhist catechism, but lies at the very heart of the Buddhist ethos.

It begins with this famous verse: "All phenomena are preceded by the mind, created by the mind, and have the mind as their master. If one speaks or acts from a corrupted mind, suffering follows as a cart-wheel follows the ox's foot."

---

3. The following translations of the Dhammapada are the author's.

Verse two is its counterpart: "All phenomena are preceded by the mind, created by the mind, and have the mind as their master. If one speaks or acts with a pure mind, happiness follows as a never-departing shadow." These set out a foundational supposition in Buddhism. Individual experience—and subsequent happiness or suffering—is grounded in the quality of the mind. Chapter 1 of the Dhammapada, "Pairs," offers different versions of that contrast. The chapters that follow it flesh out these two mental postures and show in detail how the fool and wise one variously engage life in light of this foundational teaching. The Dhammapada aims to reveal the true path as attractive and promising and to demonstrate that the path most travel actually brings affliction.

This text is also rich in metaphor and metaphoric relations, which can be seen in its very title. *Dhamma* (or *dharma* in Sanskrit) can mean "truth," "law," or "teaching," and *pada* means "foot" or "footstep." The title creates an image of movement. One is on a journey, and this text both describes the right path as well as presents itself as a companion along the way. It includes frequent images of walking, journeying, running, navigating, arriving, and leaving. Even those first two celebrated verses consider life through the image of travel, either with the drudgery of a heavy yoke or with the happy lightness of a shadow.

Even as action expresses skillful Buddhist practice, the Dhammapada's primary intention is to encourage tranquility. Over half the verses incorporate images of calm or equanimity, such as being a rock or an island. The Dhammapada characterizes authentic religious life as one of action and stillness, as the following verses regarding action make clear:

29. Vigilant among the negligent, wide awake among the sleeping, the deeply wise one goes forth, like a swift horse who leaves the nag behind.

31. The monk, devoted to vigilance, and seeing the danger in negligence, goes forth like a fire burning every fetter, gross and subtle.

46. Knowing this body to be like foam, realizing its mirage-like nature, cutting off the flowers of Māra, one may go unseen by the King of Death.

60. Long is the night for the wakeful, long is a trek for the weary, long is samsara for fools who do not understand the true Dharma.

91. Those who are mindful depart; they do not delight in a house. They leave behind every home, like geese who abandon a pond.

Consider some verses about stillness:

25. Through effort, vigilance, restraint, and self-control, the wise one makes himself an island that a flood could not overwhelm.

28. When the wise one expels negligence by vigilance, having ascended to the stronghold of wisdom, and free from sorrow; he

observes the sorrowing crowd, as a sage standing on a mountain observes fools on the plain.

81. Just as a solid rock is unmoved by the wind, so the wise are unmoved by blame or praise.

82. Just as a deep lake is clear and undisturbed, so the wise become clear, having heard the teachings.

94. One whose senses are as calm as horses well-tamed by a charioteer, who has abandoned pride and is free from toxins, is envied even by the gods.

Christian Reflection on Buddhism and the Dhammapada

Can Buddhism and the Dhammapada challenge the way that Christians think about or engage their religious concerns? That is, if a Christian were to pass over into its worldview, how might it speak to Christian spirituality?

Most authentic spiritualities have an ultimate horizon that guides and inspires the aspirant. Buddhists understand their ultimate horizon as nirvana, while for Christians it is heaven. A danger in focusing on such a horizon is becoming overly concerned with the ultimate end and missing the importance of the path and the quality of the moment. Considerations of heaven and hell dominate biblical texts. Although the Bible recognizes the importance of life in the Spirit, it regularly describes the presence of the Spirit in conjunction to ultimate salvation.

> We ourselves, who have the first fruits of the Spirit, we also groan within ourselves as we wait for adoption, the redemption of our bodies. (Rom. 8:23)

> Now the one who has prepared us for this very thing [salvation] is God, who has given us the Spirit as his first installment. (2 Cor. 5:5)

> [You] were sealed with the promised holy Spirit, which is the first installment of our inheritance toward redemption as God's possession. (Eph. 1:12–13)

The New Testament also couches many exhortations to virtue and holiness in terms of salvation or damnation.[4] Even Paul's long exhortation to holiness at the end of Romans encouraging purity of mind and body, unity among members, and love for all, ends with, "each one of us shall give an account of himself to God" (Rom. 12:1–14:12).

---

4. "Do you not know that the unjust will not inherit the kingdom of God?" (1 Cor. 6:9); "For anyone who eats and drinks [the Lord's Supper] without discerning the body, eats and drinks judgment on himself" (1 Cor. 11:29).

While the Dhammapada mentions nirvana (the ultimate goal), the quality of life here and now comprises its dominant theme. Further, it is far less concerned with the nature of experience than with the quality of the mind and its relationship to whatever is experienced. The first noble truth in Buddhism is that life is suffering. The second explains that life is suffering because of craving. The third asserts that bringing an end to craving would result in freedom from suffering. The fourth provides an eightfold path as the means to attain this freedom. People crave gratifying experiences; they crave security. They want to protect and advance the ego. The Buddha's fundamental message is this: see suffering, expose its cause, and be free. Here is where either liberty or imprisonment exists. Craving, or lack thereof, determines whether life is filled with suffering or embraced in joy.

Taking this Buddhist posture seriously does not require the rejection of any Christian presuppositions. It may, however, cause one to see them differently. The Christian tradition, for example, points out the tragedy of sin and the inevitability of God's judgment, while Buddhism emphasizes the suffering that comes from a toxic mental state. This shift in emphasis may affect how one encounters a text such as the Jesus' parable of the Pharisee:

> "Two people went up to the temple area to pray; one was a Pharisee and the other was a tax collector. The Pharisee took up his position and spoke this prayer to himself, 'O God, I thank you that I am not like the rest of humanity—greedy, dishonest, adulterous—or even like this tax collector. I fast twice a week, and I pay tithes on my whole income.' But the tax collector stood off at a distance and would not even raise his eyes to heaven but beat his breast and prayed, 'O God, be merciful to me a sinner.' I tell you, the latter went home justified, not the former; for everyone who exalts himself will be humbled, and the one who humbles himself will be exalted." (Luke 18:10–14)

Jesus contrasts the posture of pride with that of humility and challenges his hearers to the latter. A Buddhist sensibility invites an additional analysis: a recognition that the Pharisee is suffering. Not only will his ego-inflated pride condition a wretched afterlife, it also creates suffering in the moment. The Pharisee's delusion, the fact that he does not realize his situation, makes it all the more tragic. In short, the Pharisee *craves* superiority, and this keeps him from being spiritually free. As is written in the Dhammapada: "Whatever an enemy would do to an enemy, a hater to one hated, worse still, the harm a wrongly-directed mind can do to itself" (no. 42).

Buddhist cultivation of awareness of the toxic mind does not stop here. Without the deep self-awareness that Buddhism fosters, a reader can easily and unwittingly take on the very mental state of the Pharisee by judging him. One can proudly imagine oneself superior for not being like the judgmental Pharisee.

Buddhist wisdom constantly returns to the quality of the mind and the relationship one has with one's experiences. In this case, it asks readers, "What is your mental state as you appropriate the insights of the parable?"

Buddhist wisdom even helps in dealing with these toxic thoughts. The Dhammapada offers many suggestions, from investigating their source to countering them with wholesome thoughts to cultivating a repugnance for the harm that they do (nos. 5, 7, 8, 223, 224). Given, however, that Buddhists believe all phenomenal reality lacks absolute substance and permanency, it also offers the strategy of simply watching these thoughts arise and dissipate on their own. One need not identify with them: "For those who are always awake . . . the toxins disappear" (no. 226). Buddhism invites Christians to embrace the parable more fully and to cultivate compassion toward all who suffer delusion—Pharisee, publican, and oneself alike. Could Buddhism help Christians understand Jesus better?

Zen and Its Classics

While the Dhammapada represents fundamental precepts embraced by most Buddhists, it directly reflects the Theravada school. Zen, an expression of the Buddhist Mahayana school, reinterprets it most interestingly. Zen has no official canon, but the excerpts used here come from some of its most important thinkers and represent some of the most beloved texts in the Zen tradition.

Nagarjuna (150–250 CE) is widely considered the intellectual founder of Mahayana Buddhism. Among other things, he argued that the necessary conclusion to the Buddha's teaching on no-self and impermanence was that even nirvana is empty. Further, he contended that emptiness itself cannot be maintained as an absolute metaphysical principle. Regarding everything, including nirvana, Nagarjuna taught that "form is emptiness and emptiness is form." How could nirvana be empty of itself and also include form? The Theravada tradition holds that nirvana was neither empty nor a relative truth, but something ultimate and beyond the phenomenal world. Nirvana, in fact, represented freedom from the conditioned life, which is called *samsara*. For Nagarjuna, nirvana and samsara interpenetrate and even collapse into each other.

> There is no difference at all between nirvana and samsara. There is no difference at all between samsara and nirvana. . . . What is identity, and what is difference? What is eternity, what non-eternity? What do eternity and non-eternity together mean? What does negation of both issues mean? Bliss consists in the cessation of all thought, in the quiescence of plurality. No separate reality was preached at all, nowhere and none by Buddha![5]

---

5. E. A. Burtt, ed. *The Teachings of the Compassionate Buddha: Early Discourses, the Dhammapada and Later Basic Writings* (New York: New American Library, 2000), 152–53 (trans. slightly adjusted).

What does it mean to say that samsara and nirvana are identical? It remains unclear whether Nagarjuna meant that they were exactly the same reality or that they referenced different experiences of the same reality. He may not have intended a metaphysical claim at all, but rather used this identification between the two as a way to free the mind from dualistic thinking, so as to see reality directly. A favorite Zen story in the Mahayana canon is about one of the Buddha's sermons where he simply held up a lotus flower. His followers imagined it a metaphor. The lotus was a popular symbol in Indian spirituality because, although often found in muddy waters, the flower's texture ensures that slime does not stick to it. It highlights the idea that a person ought to remain pure in a filthy world. Only one present, Mahakashyapa, understood the sermon and became immediately enlightened. The lesson consisted simply of seeing the flower, no more, no less. Mahakashyapa did this; he engaged the everyday, ordinary experience of life, directly and immediately. This is the "ordinary mind" of Zen.

Stories like this abound in Zen. A disciple asks the master, "What is enlightenment?" And the master responds, "I chop wood. I carry water. What joy! What bliss!" Another involves two aspirants boasting about their masters. One describes his master's ability to bilocate and walk on water, while the other responds that his master is more advanced: "When he is tired, he just rests; when he is hungry, he just eats; and his mind is ever at peace." The great master Huang–po (d. 850) described enlightenment simply and elegantly: "Enlightenment is not something to be attained. If right now you bring forth this non-attaining mind, steadfastly not obtaining anything, then this is enlightened mind. Enlightenment is not a place to reside. For this reason there is nothing attainable."[6] Simply chopping wood, just eating, or bringing forth a non-attaining mind requires extraordinary spiritual discipline and mental cultivation.

Dogen (1200–1253) writes: "To study the Buddha Way is to study the self. To study the self is to forget the self. To forget the self is to be actualized by myriad things. When actualized by myriad things, your body and mind as well as the bodies and minds of others drop away. No trace of enlightenment remains, and this no-trace continues endlessly."[7] In this famous and somewhat enigmatic teaching, one hears echoes of the historical Buddha's insistence on looking at oneself in order to realize that there is no eternal self at all. Thus, paying attention to the self reveals no-self, allowing one to stop identifying with one's experience and, thus, to stop craving. One can also detect Nagarjuna's insistence that form drops into emptiness. Still, it contains something new: "No trace of enlightenment remains, and this no-trace continues endlessly." For Dogen, enlightenment is right there, simply waiting to be realized. To imagine enlightenment as

---

6. Dogen, *Moon in a Dewdrop: Writings of Zen Master Dogen*, Kazuaki Tanahashi, ed. and trans. Robert Aitken et al. (San Francisco: North Point Press, 1985), 70.

7. Cited in Stephen Addis et al., eds. *Zen Sourcebook: Traditional Documents from China, Korea, and Japan* (Indianapolis: Hackett Publishing, 2008), 152.

anything other than attending to the continuous flow of reality—something that has a trace—is to fail to understand its very nature.

While Dogen represents the Soto school of Zen, the Rinzai school advocated a kind of pressure cooker approach in which an enlightenment experience eventually explodes in the mind. One of the most well-known techniques of this school is the *koan*, an impossible question or puzzling dialogue such as, "What is your original face before your parents were born?" Or, "If you meet the Buddha, kill him." Perhaps the most famous koan is this: "Two hands clap, and there is a sound. What is the sound of one hand?" The disciple can only penetrate this *koan* by moving beyond linear, subject-object thinking, by using the mind to transcend the mind. The great master Keizann Jokin (1268–1325) writes.

> Apply yourself wholeheartedly to the task of holding on to your *koan*, never letting it go off the center of your consciousness, whether you are sitting or lying, walking or standing still. . . . The time will most assuredly come . . . when the distinction of subject and object is utterly obliterated, when the inquiring and inquired are fused into the one perfect identity . . . that brings peace to all your inquiries and searchings.[8]

With intense practice, one starts living inside the *koan* and the two hands become one. There is no difference between two hands clapping (oppositional thinking) and one hand clapping (unitive thinking), for subject and object distinctions have dissolved.

Famous Zen Koans

- What is your original face before your parents were born?
- If you meet the Buddha, kill him.
- Master: I don't like to hear the word *Buddha*. Disciple: Do you help people or not? Master: Buddha, Buddha!
- Disciple: In the day, there is sunlight; at night, there is firelight. What is *divine light?* Master: Sunlight, firelight.
- Disciple: Who is the Buddha? Master: Three pounds of flax.
- Disciple: What is the meaning of the first patriarch's visit to China? Master: The cypress tree in the front courtyard.
- Disciple: What are honest words? Master: Eat an iron stick!

---

8. Ibid., 141–42.

Christian Reflection on Zen and Its Classics

How does encountering these classical Zen references challenge a Christian consciousness? Interestingly, Zen's emphasis on paradoxical language and non-linear thinking highlights the very same characteristic in the Christian tradition. The theme of the kingdom of God, for example, not only emerges regularly in Jesus' preaching, it also dominates Christian discourse. Like Zen enlightenment, it stands before (Rom. 14:17), among (Luke 17:21), and even upon Christians (Matt. 12:28; Luke 11:20). It is also something to anticipate, something to be realized in the future (Matt. 6:10). Christian preaching tends to bandy the term around quite casually, as if its meaning is clear to all and could even be equated with social justice. Zen sensitivities can help Christians read the scriptures and speak about the kingdom with greater care, recognizing it for the mystery it really is (Luke 17:20). Jesus could provoke the Christian imagination to engage the kingdom in some way, even as it could not be directly addressed. A famous axiom in Zen cautions not to confuse the finger pointing to the moon with the moon itself. Zen's "beginner's mind," one that seeks a fresh openness to and direct engagement with the moment, has everything to do with receiving the kingdom like children (Matt. 18:3–4; Mark 10:15; Luke 18:16–17).

An additional interesting parallel between the gospel and Zen is the paschal mystery: "For whoever wishes to save his life will lose it, but whoever loses his life for my sake will save it" (Luke 9:24). Such a saying works like a *koan*. If a person ultimately wants to save one's life, then that person has to lose it. However, if the intention is to preserve one's life *by* losing it, then has one really given it away? One could easily imagine a Zen master saying to a disciple: "Living is dying; dying is living." John's Gospel highlights this paradox by identifying the cross as the place of glory. It is the very self-emptying offering of Christ that draws all to him (12:32), reveals his glory (17:1), and expresses the divine nature (8:28).

The foregoing observations are not meant simply to point out that both Zen and Christianity have paradoxes, nor to equate Zen enlightenment with the cross. Rather, they suggest that the wisdom of the Zen tradition can help in rethinking one's approach to Christian paradoxes. Zen challenges Christians to enter into their transformational possibilities rather than try to figure them out, that is, to live or become one with the paradox. Embracing the paradox of radical self-renunciation and attaining the Absolute, and thus self-realization, is discussed throughout the Christian mystical tradition. Saint Bonaventure writes, "For by transcending yourself and all things, by the immeasurable and absolute ecstasy of pure mind, leaving beyond all things, and freed from all things, you will ascend to the superessential ray of darkness."[9] Meister Eckhart makes the same sort of challenge:

---

9. Bonaventure, *The Soul's Journey into God* 7.5, in *The Soul's Journey into God; The Tree of Life; The Life of St. Francis*, trans. Ewert Cousins (Mahwah, NJ: Paulist Press, 1978), 115.

Men's last and highest parting occurs when, for God's sake, he takes leave of God. St. Paul took leave of God for God's sake and gave up all that he might get from God. . . . In parting from these, he parted with God for God's sake and yet God remained in him as God is in his own nature . . . but more as an "is-ness," as God really is. Then he neither gave to God nor received anything from him, for he and God were a unit, that is, pure unity.[10]

Perhaps the most daunting example appears in the writings of Saint John of the Cross, who imagined coming to union with God as ascending Mount Carmel. Interestingly, John not only describes the path itself as "nothing," but also characterizes the goal as attaining nothing: "The path of Mount Carmel, the perfect spirit: nothing, nothing, nothing, nothing, nothing, nothing, and, even on the Mount, nothing."[11] The very same nothing is simultaneously everything: "As soon as natural things are driven out of the enamored soul, the divine is naturally and supernaturally infused, since there can be no void in nature."[12] When Zen masters say that "emptiness is fullness and fullness is emptiness," perhaps a legitimate Christian parallel could be "emptiness is divinization and divinization is emptiness."

One of Zen's great gifts is its insistence on being radically engaged at every moment in a posture of "nonattaining." Similarly, the Christian mystical traditions consider nonattaining the only posture by which to unite with God, as Saint Thérèse of Lisieux's famous "little way" clearly shows. Every moment was an offering, a self-emptying in love. She writes, "Yes, my Beloved, this is how my life will be consumed. I have no other means of proving my love for you than that of strewing flowers, that is, not allowing one little sacrifice to escape, not one look, one word, profiting by all the smallest things and doing them through love."[13] Thérèse makes it clear how spiritual poverty actually works toward the richest kind of life:

Living on Love is giving without limit

Without claiming any wages here below.

Ah! I give without counting, truly sure

That when one loves, one does not keep count! . . .

---

10. Meister Eckhart, *Meister Eckhart: A Modern Translation*, trans. Raymond Blakney (New York: Harper Torchbook, 1957), 204.

11. John of the Cross, *Sketch of Mount Carmel*, in *The Collected Works of St. John of the Cross*, trans. Kieren Kavanaught and Otilio Rodriguez (Washington, DC: Institute of Carmelite Studies, 1991), 111.

12. John of the Cross, *The Ascent of Mount Carmel* 2.15, in *The Collected Works of St. John of the Cross*, 199.

13. Thérèse of Lisieux, *Story of a Soul: The Autobiography of Thérèse of Lisieux*, trans. John Clarke, 2nd ed. (Washington, DC: Institute of Carmelite Studies, 1976), 196.

Overflowing with tenderness, I have given everything
To his Divine Heart . . . lightly I run.
I have nothing left but my only wealth:
Living on Love.[14]

Zen's understanding of such things as the unity of the absolute and the relative, nirvana and samsara, do not exactly correlate to the relationship between nature and grace or humanity and divinity. Nonetheless, perhaps the conversation with Zen can help Christians re-appropriate the spiritual wisdom of the tradition in a new way. The Divine is everywhere and nowhere, and union with God proves elusive until one stops grasping for it.

Daoism, the Dao De Jing, and the Zhuangzi

The foremost representatives of the Daoist religious horizon are Laozi [Lao Tzu] (6th century) and Zhuangzi [Chuang Tzu] (369–286 BCE), who wrote the classic texts Dao De Jing and Zhuangzi respectively. These texts and their spiritual worldview open onto another horizon from which to reconsider one's religious suppositions.

Many translations of these works have co-opted the uniqueness of Daoism's horizon in an attempt to bring Daoist intelligibility to the West:

> The *Dao* that can be told is not the eternal *Dao*. The name that can be named is not the eternal name. The nameless is the beginning of heaven and earth. The named is the mother of ten thousand things. Ever desireless, one can see the mystery. Ever desiring, one can see the manifestations. These two spring from the same source but differ in name; this appears as darkness. Darkness within darkness. The gate to all mystery.[15]

This translation sounds quite mystical. One can even imagine theistic themes and detect principles aligned with Christian spirituality. The eternal *Dao* could easily correspond to God the Father as absolute mystery and the *Dao* that can be named as Christ/*Logos*, through whom the universe was created. The text also seems to invite readers to approach divine realities with the detachment and emptiness recommended by John of the Cross. One might even imagine a description of how both the apophatic and kataphatic authentically witness to

---

14. Thérèse of Lisieux, *The Poetry of Thérèse of Lisieux*, trans. Donald Kinney (Washington, DC: Institute of Carmelite Studies, 1966), 90.

15. Lao Tzu [Laozi], *Tao Te Ching*, trans. Gia-Fu Feng and Jane English (New York: Vintage Books, 1972), no. 1.

the same divine mystery (the same source) but also differ. Knowing God in this creative tension, one enters the gate of divine mystery.

Such an approach presumes that Chinese metaphysics correspond to Western assumptions about the universe. Traditionally, the Western mind thinks of the universe as divinely governed by unchanging natural and moral laws. From God (*theos*) comes an underlying creative organizing principle (*logos*) that reflects divine order and law (*nomos*). In contrast, the Chinese Daoist point of view is virtually acosmic, with no concept of a coherent single-ordered world. The closest Chinese word for cosmos is *yuzchou*, which expresses the interdependence between time and space. Further, there is no permanent reality or eternal substratum behind appearances; there is just the ceaseless flow of life. Even created realities are more like events that are intrinsically related to other events. The shape of things and what they do are real, but they are interdependent, mutually determining realities expressed in a wide-ranging flow. This approach is found in Mahayana Buddhism as well, and Zen Buddhism is particularly influenced by Daoist principles.

This alternative translation tries to respect this acosmic perspective:

> Way-making (*dao*) that can be put into words is not really way-making, and naming that can assign fixed reference to things is not really naming. The nameless is the fetal beginnings of everything that is happening, while that which is named is their mother. Thus, to be really objectless in one's desires is how one observes the mysteries of all things, while really having desires is how one observes their boundaries. These two—the nameless and what is named—emerge from the same source yet they are referred to differently. Together they are called obscure. The obscurest of the obscure, they are the swinging gateway of the manifold mysteries.[16]

Here, instead of presenting *dao* as a Chinese version of God, the text describes *dao* as emergence. It invites readers to see mystery in life, although this can happen only by not dictating what it should look like. To be objectless in one's desire is to stop trying to manipulate reality and instead allow it to unfold. At the same time, having some kind of intention can prove valuable in properly engaging that same reality. The challenge is to balance knowing and unknowing, conceptualizing and recognizing that reality is beyond the limits of concepts. *Dao* is intimately associated with *yin* and *yang*. They have a dynamic relationship with each other, as seen in the Daoist symbol:

---

16. Lao Tzu [Laozi], *Dao De Jing: Making This Life Significant: A Philosophical Translation*, trans. and com. by Roger Ames and David Hall (New York: Ballantine Books, 2003), no. 1.

At the top of the symbol, *yang* is prominent, and the *yin* gives way, while the opposite can be seen at the bottom of the symbol. Within each energy exists a small circle or presence of the other. The relationship between *yin* and *yang* is one of harmony, and adapting that harmony—knowing which energy is called for at a given moment—involves careful practice. Collectively, *yin* represents such things as female, darkness, earth, winter, silence, receptivity, and stability; *yang* represents male, light, heaven, summer, sound, assertion, and dynamism.

© Babii Nadiia / Shutterstock.com

Chinese tradition sees the world in terms of the subtle interplay between *yin* and *yang*. Together they constitute the balanced flow of all nature, and thus both are necessary.

Directly associated with the principles of *yin* and *yang* are the *wu*-forms. *Wu* in Chinese represents negation. Daoism regularly calls for a *wu*-posture. *Wu-wei*, for example, literally translates "no-action." However, it is not mere passivity, but instead acting in a non-imposing manner. One does not force something, but learns to work with the energies emerging. *Wu-wei* goes hand in hand with *ziran* (what-is-spontaneously-so). Practicing *wu-wei* becomes the condition of possibility for spontaneity. An enlightened ruler provides a good example of the interrelationship between *wu-wei* and *ziran*:

> With the most excellent rulers, their subjects only know that they are there. The next best are the rulers they love and praise. Next are rulers they hold in awe. And the worst are the rulers they disparage. Where there is a lack of credibility, there is a lack of trust. Vigilant, they are careful in what they say. With all things accomplished and the work complete, the common people say, "We are spontaneously like this."[17]

Excellent rulers are vigilant, that is, mindful and prudent. They are not lax or unengaged, but because their activity is *wu-wei* their creative moral presence is not even noticed. It aligns with the energy around them and works with that energy optimally. Thus the people's flourishing seems—and is—utterly natural to them.

The *wu*-forms allow aspirants to work with the energy before them harmoniously. To do so, they must be free from any artificial concepts, a value expressed by the concept of *wu-zhi*. Typically translated as "no-knowing," *wu-zhi* can also be translated as "non-static knowing" It is the principle of dropping all artificial mental constructs in order to free oneself for the uniqueness of the moment, for what is unfolding. With *wu-zhi*, not only would one serve the truth better, that is, serve the ever-changing emerging reality, one would also experience

---

17. Ibid., no. 17.

great enjoyment in life. Clinging to a false, static reality is bound to frustrate and exhaust the human spirit. *Wu-zhi* aligns with *wu-yu* (no-desire), which represents objectless desire or the freedom from needing to define, possess, or control the moment. A Daoist worldview clearly desires happiness and flourishing, but highlights the idea that one can only attain these desires by letting go of the neurotic need to control the moment or mentally ossify reality. Aligned with Zen's belief in the world as constantly unfolding, Daoism also insists that the only way to engage it skillfully is by respecting this using the practice of *wu*.

Daoism offers a daunting challenge to cultivate the mental and spiritual habits of letting go, being attentive, and wisely engaging the world in its mystery. It seeks to optimize creative possibilities precisely by letting go of the ego's agenda. Zhuangzi writes,

> Let your mind wander in simplicity, blend your spirit in the vastness, follow along with things the way they are, and make no room for personal views—then the world will be governed. . . . I take inaction [*wu-wei*] to be true happiness, but ordinary people think it is a bitter thing. . . . The inaction of Heaven is its purity, the inaction of earth is its peace. So the two inactions combine and all things are transformed and brought to birth. . . . I say, Heaven and earth do nothing and there is nothing that is not done. Among men, who can get hold of this inaction?[18]

Daoism challenges its adherents to empty themselves of the need to control, hoard, exert ambition, and inflate their egos. The result is a spacious mind and heart that works harmoniously with the flowering energy of *yang* and the receptive energy of *yin*.

Christian Reflection on Daoism, the Dao De Jing, and the Zhuangzi

Daoism sensibilities differ greatly from Christian ones. For example, Christianity is convinced of a loving, personal God, while the *dao* is utterly impersonal and certainly not God as traditional theism imagines. Most Christians also think of the universe as imbued with a moral law, called the natural law or divine law, that comes from God and reflects God. They believe that this law should not be violated, since that would transgress God's goodness and work against the very moral foundations of God's creation. In one sense, Daoism upholds a clearly contrasting understanding of both the universe and morality. While natural

---

18. Chuang Tzu [Zhuangzi], *The Complete Works of Chuang Tzu*, trans. Burton Watson (New York: Columbia University Press, 1968), 91, 112–13.

law advocates argue that the natural law protects personal and social integrity, Daoism imagines that such a framing violates *wu-zhi* (non-static knowing) and, when taken as an absolute, even compromises human dignity and flourishing. Daoism insists that a one-size-fits-all moral code wrongly presupposes a static universe. Rather, being moral means employing the art of virtue according to the energies and uniqueness of the emerging moment.

That Daoism advocates a different moral framework, one that cannot be reconciled to standard Christian moral thought, does not mean that it merely represents a competing vision. It may be possible to appreciate its impulses to stretch Christian understandings of how the universe operates and indeed how to understand the very nature of things. For example, some Christians, particularly from evangelical and Roman Catholic traditions, embrace a strict understanding of the natural law on issues such as women's nature and role. Pope John Paul II, for example, regularly contrasted women and men, much like Daoism does, though in a more absolute way. For him, the *genius* of women involves receptivity, watchfulness, contemplation, and nurturance, and he frequently warned against blurring sexual distinctions: "'Masculinity' and 'femininity' are distinct, yet at the same time they complete and explain each other;" women have essentially different resources and a "female personality." This, he claimed, Christ himself recognized by excluding women from the "priestly service of the Apostles."[19]

Daoist sensibilities also distinguish women and men, femininity and masculinity, but not in such an unqualified way. A Daoist religious imagination involves negotiating complementary energies, particularly as it refers to the dynamics of *yin* and *yang*. Without care, the principles of *yin* and *yang* can lead to stereotypical associations. *Yin*, for example is feminine and receptive, while *yang* is masculine and active. These distinctions, however, are not meant to be absolute. Even in *yin's* strongest position, it holds a circle of *yang* while *yang* likewise contains *yin* within itself. Further, *yin* energy in everyone and everything moves toward *yang*, which itself recedes to reveal *yin*. Men also express themselves with *yin* and women with *yang*. Such a complementary anthropology may help these Christians better negotiate the dual natures of feminine and masculine. They can still recognize distinctions and emphases between genders without making them absolute.

The predominance of the *wu*-forms in the Daoist art of living can help in recovering a proper sense of what the early monastic tradition called "discretion" or "discrimination" (*diakrisis*). Discretion is the cultivated capacity and spiritual gift that allows the serious aspirant to recognize true and false spirits, proper asceticism, the most propitious way to pray, act, and so on. Without it,

---

19. Pope John Paul II, *On the Dignity of Women* (*Mulieris Dignitatem*), nos. 10, 17, 25, 26, 37–38, 61–62, trans. Vatican (Boston: Daughters of St. Paul, 1988).

even though something might be good in itself, it could be harmful to the soul. Before acting, one has to practice watching and listening, trying to discern the movements of the Spirit and what would be the most appropriate response in that particular moment.

Because of the human condition, those who have an agenda regularly commit blunders in pastoral ministry. Even while applying good pastoral principles, ministers can be out of sync with individuals or congregations in need. In a crisis, ministers may be so caught up in their own discomfort with the pain and ambiguity before them that they lack an authentic healing presence. The principle of *wu-yu* (objectless desire) frees them from any set agenda and allows the true need of the one seeking help to emerge organically. Without the need to fix the situation or answer unasked questions, one can simply engage with the energies present.

Conclusion

Authentic Christian spirituality involves the interplay among scripture, tradition, and experience. The current historical situation, the modern experience, can invite Christians to factor in other traditions. As venerable expressions of the spiritual life they can make a kind of claim on Christians as wisdom traditions of great power and insight. Negotiating their claims need not undermine Christian faith commitments; rather, they offer different worlds into which one may pass, enlarging both the Christian sense of self and of home. Drinking from their wells, Christians find not only a different kind of refreshment, but also fascinating new opportunities to be nourished and sustained by their own wells. The brief examples discussed in this chapter hint at the possibilities of such passing over. Yet even such a brief foray highlights how Christians can develop greater sensitivity to the nature of the mind and its proper object of focus. Christians might find themselves reconsidering how religious paradox provides transformational possibilities and how divine encounters can happen in ordinary experiences. Finally, they can discover additional sensitivities to the actual nature of reality as ever-evolving.

Questions for Review

1. What is the difference between comparative theology and comparative religion?
2. How does Buddhist spirituality help in understanding certain Christian ideas?
3. How could Zen help Christians rethink the way Jesus preached?
4. How might the principles of Daoism enrich a Christian spirituality?

Questions for Discussion

1. In your opinion, which is the most reasonable and faithful Christian theology of religions: exclusivism, inclusivism, pluralism, or mutualism? How would you defend your choice?

2. Do you see any overlap between a Buddhist understanding of the spiritual life and that of monastic or patristic thinkers?

3. Are there areas of your life that might be helped by implementing the Daoist principles of *wu-wei* (non-impositional action) and *wu-zhi* (non-static knowing)?

4. What similarities do you see among the religions discussed in this chapter? How might a Christian understand or make sense of the aspects of those religions that are strikingly different from Christianity?

Bibliography

Resources with annotations are highly recommended to students interested in further study.

Addis, Stephen, et al., eds. *Zen Sourcebook: Traditional Documents from China, Korea, and Japan.* Indianapolis: Hackett Publishing, 2008.
This is a fine collection of Zen classical material and scholarly commentary.

Bonaventure. *The Soul's Journey into God: The Tree of Life: The Life of St. Francis.* Translated by Ewert Cousins. Mahwah, NJ: Paulist Press, 1978.

Burtt, E. A., ed. *The Teachings of the Compassionate Buddha: Early Discourses, the Dhammapada and Later Basic Writings.* New York: New American Library, 2000.

Chuang Tzu [Zhuangzi]. *The Complete Works of Chuang Tzu.* Translated by Burton Watson. New York: Columbia University Press, 1968.

Clooney, Francis X. *Comparative Theology: Deep Learning across Religious Borders.* Chichester, UK: Wiley-Blackwell, 2010.
This describes the aims and possibilities of interreligious work as explained by its foremost scholar.

Eckhart, Meister. *Meister Eckhart: A Modern Translation.* Translated by Raymond Blakney. New York: Harper Torchbook, 1957.

Feldmeier, Peter. *Encounters in Faith: Christianity in Interreligious Dialogue.* Winona, MN: Anselm Academic, 2011.

Fredericks, James. *Buddhists and Christians: Through Comparative Theology to Solidarity.* Maryknoll, NY: Orbis Books, 2004.

John of the Cross. *The Collected Works of St. John of the Cross.* Translated by Kieren Kavanaught and Otilio Rodriguez. Washington, DC: Institute of Carmelite Studies, 1991.

John Paul II. "The Meaning of the Assisi Day of Prayer." *Origins* 16, no. 31 (1987): 561–63.

John Paul II. *On the Dignity of Women (Mulieris Dignitatem).* Translated by the Vatican. Boston: Daughters of St. Paul, 1988.

Lao Tzu [Laozi]. *Dao De Jing: Making This Life Significant: A Philosophical Translation.* Translation and Commentary by Roger Ames and David Hall. New York: Ballantine Books, 2003.

   Ames and Hall reinterpret the Dao De Jing based on a deep understanding of the Chinese language within the ancient Chinese worldview.

Lao Tzu [Laozi]. *Tao Te Ching.* Translated by Gia-Fu Feng and Jane English. New York: Vintage Books, 1972.

   This is the most famous classic text and the basis of Daoism.

Race, Alan. *Christians and Religious Pluralism: Patterns in the Christian Theology of Religions.* Maryknoll, NY: Orbis Books, 1983.

   This classic analysis of Christian approaches to other religions provides the standard categories and analyses through which other works respond.

Suzuki, D. T. *The Essentials of Zen Buddhism.* Edited by Bernard Phillips. Westport, CT: Greenwood Press, 1962.

Thérèse of Lisieux. *The Poetry of Thérèse of Lisieux.* Translated by Donald Kinney. Washington, DC: Institute of Carmelite Studies, 1966.

Thérèse of Lisieux. *Story of a Soul: The Autobiography of St. Thérèse of Lisieux.* Translated by John Clarke. 2nd ed. Washington, DC: Institute of Carmelite Studies, 1976.

Yashinori, Takeuchi, ed. *Buddhist Spirituality: Indian, Southeast Asian, Tibetan, Early Chinese.* New York: Crossroads, 1995.

Internet Resources

Patel, Eboo, and Skye Jethani. "Interfaith Dialogue." 2011. *www.youtube.com /watch?v=jiatHzkKymw.*

   Daniel Pawlus leads a conversation about interreligious dialogue with a Muslim and Christian leader who were boyhood friends. The participants discuss how to engage each other skillfully for ongoing cooperation and authentic witnessing to their respective faiths (14 min.).

Films

Jesus and Buddha: Practicing across Traditions. 2012.

This documentary focuses on three Christian theologians with deep experience in Buddhism discussing the interconnections between the two religions and the possibilities of mutual belonging uniting both.

Three Modern Witnesses

The first chapter of this book noted that Christian spirituality is neither just a lived extrapolation of doctrine, nor a prescriptive "one-size-fits-all" program. Rather, there are many different Christian spiritualities, each describing a different expression of faith. Further, scholars widely agree that authentic Christian spirituality ought to approach discipleship holistically by addressing a range of issues, including the body, relationships, work, and community. Christian spirituality also involves a creative interplay of sources, including personal and communal experience, scripture, and theology. It has recurrent elements, such as grace, life in the Spirit, imitation of Christ, and prayer.

This chapter explores the lived spirituality of three Christians who differ from each other in experience, personality, and theology. Two are Roman Catholics: a lay woman and a monk. The third is an evangelical pastor of a megachurch in California.

Dorothy Day (1897–1980): Christ's Prophet

Dorothy Day was born in Brooklyn, New York, and raised in San Francisco and Chicago. Her father was a sports writer in San Francisco, but when the 1906 earthquake destroyed the newspaper's facilities and he lost his job, they moved to Chicago. Day had been something of a religious child. While her parents were, at best, nominal Christians, she regularly attended the Episcopal church near her house in Chicago. She was taken by the liturgy, loved the psalms, and felt the desire to pray. "All my life I've been haunted by God," Dorothy Day writes.[1] In fact, once in the company of playwright Eugene O'Neil, she heard him recite Francis Thompson's poem "The Hound of Heaven," and it preoccupied her heart for years. Nonetheless, by the time she was seventeen and a college student at the University of Illinois, she considered herself an agnostic, perhaps even an atheist. Already, Day had become politically active. She joined the Socialist Party

---

1. Dorothy Day, *The Long Loneliness* (New York: HarperCollins, 1997), 11.

at the University of Illinois and was particularly concerned about the rights of workers. Day observed that religion seemed to be exactly contrary to what the world needed. Christianity preached "peace and meekness and joy" while the world needed social revolutionaries. Joy was the last thing she wanted.[2]

After two years of college, Day moved to New York, where she took a politically radical turn. She worked on socialist publications and was engaged in issues of fair wages, anti-war issues, and women's rights. She lived a bohemian life. Day was briefly married to Berkeley Tobey and became pregnant. Not wanting children, she had an abortion, an experience she later wrote about in a semi-autographical novel entitled *The Eleventh Virgin*.

As a young woman, Day was arrested at a protest supporting women's voting rights. Appalled at the treatment some prisoners—including fellow suffragists—received, she went on a hunger strike with other prisoners. She was given a Bible in prison and clung to the words. Day tried to convince herself that she read it merely to pass the time, "But the words kept echoing in my heart."[3] This echoing of truth forced her to recognize her shallowness and the shallowness of the socialist movement she supported.[4]

In the mid-1920s, Day entered into a kind of common law marriage with Forster Batterham, a fellow socialist. They lived in a small cottage along the beach on Staten Island and were happy in many ways. They loved each other, enjoyed the then uncorrupted natural beauty of Staten Island, and had many friends, including prominent literary figures. However, Day became increasingly interested in religion, a topic Batterham was not even willing to discuss. Day began to recite the rosary daily and attend Sunday Mass at a nearby church. She also found herself drawn to Christian classics, such as *The Imitation of Christ*, and the writings of Augustine, Teresa of Ávila, and John of the Cross. Soon, she discovered that she was pregnant. Although Batterham had not wanted a child, he found himself, along with Day, joyfully anticipating the birth. When their daughter Tamar Teresa was born, they were both elated. At this point, however, Day's growing spiritual sensibilities took a serious turn. Day had decided to become Catholic, a decision that brought on two related crises. As a Catholic, she could no longer live with a common law husband; they would have to be married in church. Further, she insisted on baptizing Tamar Teresa and raising her in the Catholic faith, and Forster wanted no part of it.[5] Because of her religious convictions she had to leave Forster.

---

2. "I was unhappy and rejoiced in my unhappiness." Ibid., 42.

3. Ibid., 81.

4. "I was a petty creature, filled with self-deception, self-importance, unreal, false, and so, rightly scorned and punished. I was willing not only to say two and two were five, but to think it. . . . We helped others, it is true, but we did not deprive ourselves in order to help others." Ibid., 79, 87.

5. "I could not become a Catholic and continue living with him, because he was averse to any ceremony before officials of either Church or state. He was an anarchist and an atheist, and he did not intend to be a liar or a hypocrite. . . . I loved him. It was killing me to think of leaving him." Ibid., 147–48.

Day became a Catholic in 1927 when she was thirty years old. The first year was difficult for her, and her inner life seemed dry and restless. Only after her Confirmation a year later did she experience a deep sense of peace.[6] Her spiritual growth and deepening faith continued for the next several years, although she still struggled to integrate her faith with her commitment to alleviate human suffering.

In 1932, five years after her baptism and just as the Great Depression was getting under way, Peter Maurin arrived in New York City. Born in France in 1877, he later settled in Canada. He lived in Canada as a kind of modern Saint Francis, embracing poverty for the love of the gospel. He worked during the day as a simple laborer and spent his nights sleeping in skid-row shelters. He was taken by Pope Leo

Dorothy Day's spirituality entailed activism on many fronts. At the time this photograph was taken, at age sixty-three, she was deeply involved in protests against nuclear warfare.

XIII's social encyclical *Rerum Novarum* (1881), particularly the claim, "Once the demands of necessity and propriety have been met, the rest belongs to the poor" (no. 22).

When Day and Maurin met, she remembers that he spoke to her about the social gospel for seven straight hours uninterrupted. He told her that the social revolution had to be a spiritual and physical revolution together. Day later reflected: "Worldly justice and unworldly [spiritual] justice are quite different things. The supernatural approach when understood is to turn the other cheek, to give up what one has, willingly, gladly, with no spirit of martyrdom, to rejoice in being the least, to be unrecognized, the slighted."[7]

Together, Day and Maurin started a newspaper, *The Catholic Worker*, which reflected Catholic social teaching as it related to the justice and peace issues of the day. They also established *Houses of Hospitality* where the poor would be welcomed. These centers provided food for the hungry, addressed their spiritual

---

6. "It was only then that the feeling of uncertainty left me, never again to return, praise God." Dorothy Day, *From Union Square to Rome* (Maryknoll, NY: Orbis Books, 2006), 142.

7. Day, *The Long Loneliness*, 59.

needs, and also provided a gathering place for the community. On May 1, 1933, Day went to Washington Square Park in Greenwich Village and distributed the first edition of *The Catholic Worker*. She sold it for a penny, which remains its price even today.

Seeing Christ in Self and Others

Peter Maurin was Day's most important mentor. He helped her realize the intrinsic dignity in herself and others, to see Christ everywhere. She writes,

> Peter made you feel a sense of his mission as soon as you met him. He did not begin by tearing down, or by painting so intense a picture of misery and injustice that you burned to change the world. Instead, he arose in you a sense of your own capacities for work, for accomplishment. He made you feel that you and all men had great and generous hearts with which to love God. . . . But it was seeing Christ in others, loving the Christ you saw in others. Greater than this, it was having faith in the Christ in others without being able to see Him.[8]

Benedict's rule instructed the monks to regard all as Christ, particularly the visitor and the stranger. Benedict did not consider this a mere imaginative exercise; it reflected a deeply sacramental worldview, one where God recreates the universe in his passionate mercy, where God's love and presence really exists everywhere, and where all persons are claimed by Christ and moved by his grace. In his view, the universe is "Christified." The Catholic Worker movement embraced such a sacramental vision. Sometimes it was not easy to see. Once, a volunteer at a House of Hospitality asked Day about the poor, and she replied, "You will learn two things about the homeless: they smell and rarely thank you." This, for her was not meant to disparage the poor, but to serve as a wakeup call from any idyllic notion of service: It is often not pleasant and it can never be about you.

Communion

In her many articles and talks Day spoke eloquently about the Catholic doctrine of the mystical body of Christ, that is, the belief that all Christians—for her, all humans—are interconnected to God with one another.[9] In Catholicism, the Eucharist represents both communion with the body of the risen Lord and simultaneously communion with one another in him (1 Cor. 10:16ff). For Day, this is a profound mystery. This communion of the body, she believed, is founded on love:

---

8. Ibid., 171.

9. Paul reflected on this several times in his letters (Rom. 12:4ff; 1 Cor. 6:15ff; 12:12ff).

But the final word is love. At times it has been in the words of Father Zossima [Dostoyevsky's *Brothers Karamazov*], a harsh and dreadful thing, and our very faith has been tried through fire. We cannot love God unless we love each other, and to love we must know each other. We know him in the breaking of the bread and we know each other in the breaking of the bread, and we are not alone anymore. Heaven is a banquet and life is a banquet too, even with a crust, where there is companionship.[10]

Prayer

Perhaps the most essential part of Day's spirituality was prayer. How does a person whose life consisted of long hours of service and single motherhood live a life of prayer? Day rose early for private prayer before Tamar Teresa awoke. She also devoted herself to daily Mass, despite having to pass the long bread lines. For her, this grounded the service she would then provide throughout the day. For the most part, however, prayer was a constant part of her daily life: "Because I am a woman involved in practical cares, I cannot give the first half of the day to these things, but must meditate when I can, early in the morning and on the fly during the day. . . . At the kitchen table, on the train, on the ferry, on the way to and from appointments and even while making supper or putting Teresa to bed."[11]

Day on Prayer

I do believe in a personal God. I have had too many prayers answered in a direct personal way. Also I believe in praying to the saints, our friends, for help. I believe in the resurrection of the body (a gloried body) and life everlasting. That is in the Creed. I'm going to pray to the Little Flower [St. Therese of Lisieux] to send you a rose some time just to confound you, so that you will begin to think there is something in this personal business. They are as personal as you and I. Also our Lord Jesus Christ, who is God too, a most personal God, who fed the hungry, healed the sick and shared the fish on the shore with Peter. Keep praying for me, my dear. (To Ammon Hennacy, July 19, 1950)[12]

---

10. Day, *The Long Loneliness*, 285.

11. Dorothy Day, *House of Hospitality* (New York: Sheed & Ward, 1939), 2–3.

12. *ncronline.org/blogs/road-peace/dorothy-days-letters-show-heartache-faith.*

In addition to private prayer, the Houses of Hospitality had communal prayer. They prayed the rosary at noon and Vespers in the evening. Catholic Worker members also regularly took retreats, which Day organized, as well as solitary days of reflection. Without these more sustained periods of prayer, she was convinced that workers would burn out. She identified this need not just in the other workers, but in herself. [13]

She once reflected after a difficult period:

> And after the effects of last night's and this morning's heavy praying have been peace and joy and strength and thanksgiving, and a great deal of humility too. . . . I should know by this time that just because I *feel* that everything is useless and going to pieces and badly done and futile, it is not really that way at all. Everything is all right. It is in the hands of God. Let us abandon everything to Divine Providence. [14]

Thomas Merton (1915–1968): A Modern Mystic

Thomas Merton was arguably the most influential writer of Christian spirituality in the twentieth century. In his short life he published over sixty books and reintroduced the contemplative and mystical life to the modern Christian world. Like Dorothy Day, his early life would not have suggested anything of the kind. Merton was born in southern France in 1915, the son of a New Zealander father and American mother who met at art school in Paris just before the outbreak of the First World War. Merton's mother died when he was six, and he followed his painter father throughout parts of the United States, Europe, and even Bermuda. He lived a kind of vagabond life. Merton's father sent him to a boarding school in Oakham, England, when he was 16. That same year his father died. Although a friend of his father's became his formal guardian, Merton was mostly on his own. At eighteen he enrolled at Cambridge University, but only spent a year there. Instead of devoting himself to his studies, this bright and precocious young man spent that year partying and carousing. One of his several girlfriends became pregnant, and his guardian, after making arrangements for the young woman and her son, sent Merton to New York and Columbia University. In 1940, his former girlfriend and son died in the Nazi blitz of London.

Merton settled down somewhat at Columbia and became a relatively diligent student, although his fondness for drinking and frequenting jazz clubs continued. He embraced the student life fully, joining student organizations and becoming the arts and humor editor for *The Jester*, a Columbia student literary

---

13. "It is because I too am hungry and thirst for the bread of the strong. I too must nourish myself to do the work I have undertaken; I too must drink at these springs so that I may not be an empty cistern and unable to help others." Day, *Long Loneliness*, 263.

14. Day, *House of Hospitality*, 97–98.

publication. He also met and spent time with some of the most intellectually lively students and professors at Columbia. He was widely liked and considered very bright, funny, musical, and quick witted. Among his closest friends were Robert Lax, who later became a famous poet, and Robert Giroux, who would rise to prominence as a famous publisher. Merton describes his greatest influence at the time as Professor Mark Van Doren, a Shakespeare scholar, who helped him with his writing and even planted the seeds of his vocation.

In the spring of 1938, while walking down Fifth Avenue, Merton saw displayed in a store window a book by the French philosopher Etienne Gilson, *The Spirit of Medieval Philosophy*. He was taking a course in medieval poetry and thought it might

Merton sought solitude at Gethsemani Monastery, where he was photographed late in life. His inner, contemplative life led him to engage the problems of the larger world, including race relations, world peace, and Christianity's relationship to other faiths.

help. He describes sitting on a bus and paging through this newly bought book only to realize, much to his chagrin, that it was something of an apologetics of Catholic thought, a philosophical examination on the nature of God. He almost threw it out the window. Instead, however, he decided to read it. Merton was, at the time, dismissive of religion and assumed, like many of his urbane colleagues, that God was "a noisy mythological figure" and that religion was little more than "neuroses and projections." In Gilson's book, Merton discovered a clear, sophisticated, and intellectually rigorous understanding of God. He quickly realized that he wanted to know the God that Gilson had described.

Responding to his newfound religious hunger, Merton began attending various church services, though they did not make an impact. Then one Sunday, he woke up with a strong desire to go to Mass, so he visited the Church of Corpus Christi, the Catholic church associated with Columbia. He was taken with the experience. Though he did not understand much of the liturgy, which was in Latin, he was overwhelmed by the intensity of prayer he found in the people there. He left Mass and went to breakfast at a local diner. Everything seemed different. Even the diner seemed different. He felt like he was "sitting in the

Elysian Fields." Soon after that, Merton sought formal instruction to enter the Catholic faith.

Merton and Monastic Life

One day, not long after his conversion, his best friend Robert Lax, a deeply spiritual person, asked him, "Tom, what do you want out of life." Merton replied, "Well, I suppose I want to be a good Catholic." Lax responded, "No, no, that's not enough. You should want to be a saint."[15] This both unnerved and deeply inspired Merton, and he decided to become serious about his spiritual life. Soon after, he explored the possibility of becoming a priest. He sought out the Franciscan Order, and initially all seemed to go well. When he came clean to the Franciscans about his past in Cambridge, however, they rejected his application. After leaving Columbia with a Masters degree in English, Merton took a job at St. Bonaventure's, a Franciscan college in upstate New York. He decided that if he could not become a priest formally, he would live the lifestyle of one. So he started praying the Divine Office of scriptural prayer seven times a day and going to daily Mass.

While on a semester break, Merton went to New York, where he visited his friend Dan Walsh, an adjunct professor of medieval philosophy at Columbia. Walsh told him that he thought the most inspiring Catholic order was the Trappist Order, a strict group of monks who lived in silence, slept on straw, and only bathed once a week. He encouraged Merton to make a Holy Week retreat at the Trappist monastery of Our Lady of Gethsemani outside of Louisville, Kentucky. Merton later wrote that he immediately experienced Gethsemani as "the still point around which the whole country revolves without knowing it."[16]

Merton wanted in, and he was relieved that the Trappists did not balk at his checkered past, but accepted him fully. By the next December (1941), he entered the abbey as a postulant, the first step of initiation. With a few exceptions, such as periodic medical care in Louisville, Merton remained inside the confines of Gethsemani for the next twenty-seven years. It was at Gethsemani that Merton experienced, for the first time in his life, a profound sense of wholeness and peace. He also discovered a depth of union with God that would overwhelm his soul and redefine his self-understanding.

Merton's religious superiors quickly recognized that he was extraordinarily gifted, with a deep interior life, an engaging personality, and an ability to communicate the essence of Christian communion with God. The abbot made him the Master of Scholastics from 1951–1955 and a Novice Master from 1955–1965. The former position made him the foremost educator of monks seeking

---

15. Thomas Merton, *The Seven Story Mountain* (Orlando, FL: Harcourt Brace Jovanovich, 1948), 264.

16. Ibid., 363.

further education to become ordained as priests, and the latter position made him the principal formation instructor in the monastic life. He also started to write, and this avocation dominated much of his working life in the monastery.

Merton gained public fame when he published his autobiography, *The Seven Storey Mountain*. In it, he describes his life, his hunger for God, and the effects of entering the monastery. It became an instant best seller. Merton tapped into the spiritual hunger of many modern Americans. In this and subsequent books, he showed people how God could be calling in the depths of their souls. He also detailed how preoccupations could frustrate the soul's deepest needs. Finally, he described the deepest dynamics of the interior life, that is, what God looks and feels like, and how one might come to a deeper communion with God.

Despite the strictness and isolation of the monastic life, Merton ironically became one of the great social voices of the fifties and sixties. He wrote on poverty, the nuclear arms race, and the evils of racism. For him, these were not outside of the purview of the interior life or even the life of the monastery. Rather, he saw his increased social awareness as a result of his deep interior life with God. Merton also began correspondences with representatives from other religious traditions, particularly Islam, Daoism, and Buddhism. In many ways, he was a dilettante. He had not studied these religions deeply and made assumptions that scholars today would deem uncritical. On the other hand, due to his own mystical life, his intelligence, and his deep spiritual intuitions, Merton made many of these seemingly exotic traditions intelligible to his readers. Without blurring them with Christianity, he wrote about their many profound insights into the nature of the human condition and about God's presence through these various religious traditions. He was one of the great pioneers in interreligious dialogue.

The last three years of Merton's life, beginning in 1965, he became a virtual hermit. According to the Rule of Benedict (Trappists are part of the Benedictine monastic family), after having been grounded in the community life, one could seek permission to pursue an even more radical life of solitude and prayer. It was during this time that he had something of a monastic crisis. While receiving medical care at a hospital in Louisville, he bonded with and fell in love with a nurse. Their romance was brief, lasting only from April to September 1966. They met infrequently, because of his situation, including a few clandestine visits, a picnic in Louisville after a doctor's appointment, and at least two meetings on the monastery grounds.

In his journals Merton details the upheaval this affair occasioned within him. On May 27, 1966, he writes, "There is no question that I *cannot* let this become a sexual affair, it would be disastrous for us both. . . . We have agreed again that our love has to be chaste and I know she means it and wants it, so do I, but we are not safe with each other."[17] However, it did become sexual,

---

17. Thomas Merton, *Learning to Love: Exploring Solitude and Freedom*, vol. 6 of *The Journals of Thomas Merton*, ed. Christine Bochan (New York: HarperSanFrancisco, 1997), 70.

which both excited him and traumatized his psyche. He writes, "The one thing that troubles me most in it all—I see my instability and a certain *dishonesty*. . . . Those weeks in May were much more troubled even than I realized—and I did suffer a lot."[18] The affair left him humbled and humiliated. Despite his acclaim as America's foremost spiritual voice, Merton made no pretense to being anyone significant before God, as can be seen in this self-evaluation: "The overall impression: awareness of my own fantastic instability, complexity, frailty. . . . There was no longer anything to pride myself in, least of all *being a monk* or being anything—a writer or anything."[19]

What did this affair mean? Was it simply a mid-life crisis, or did his isolation as a hermit facilitate not only a depth of interior solitude but also a depth of loneliness that made him vulnerable? How could someone be so close to God and so spiritually transformed and still break his vows? Perhaps Merton's brief affair exemplifies the complexity of the psyche and the power of human love, particularly sexual love. His affair, although morally compromising, need not invalidate his holiness. Rather, it shows human fragility and the intricacies and shadows of the human condition. One finds authentically and deeply spiritual people who, surprisingly, are overly sensitive or vain in one area of their lives, but that does not negate the real spiritual depth that they have. Humans are complicated.

Prayer: Finding What Is Already There

For Merton, prayer was an intentional expression and action. One simply has to cultivate the discipline to pray, and slowly one moves from more active prayer to more contemplative prayer. The chapters on the patristic fathers and Carmelite spirituality show this as well. "If you want a life of prayer," Merton writes, "the way to get it is by praying."[20] On the other hand, Merton was convinced that prayer should be the center of all activity, a kind of inner quality of communion that imbued everything one did: "Contemplation is inseparable from life and from the dynamism of life—which includes work, creation, production, fruitfulness, and above all *love*. Contemplation is not to be thought of as a separate department of life. . . . It is the very fullness of a fully integrated life."[21]

Merton writes: "Whatever I may have written, I think it all can be reduced in the end to this one truth: that God calls human persons to union with Himself and with one another in Christ. . . . If I have written about interracial justice, or thermonuclear weapons, it is because these issues are terribly relevant to

---

18. Ibid., 123.

19. Ibid., 124–25.

20. Patrick Hart, ed. *Thomas Merton, Monk: A Monastic Tribute* (New York: Sheed & Ward, 1974), 79.

21. Thomas McDonnell, ed., *A Thomas Merton Reader*, rev. ed. (New York: Image Books, 1974), 400.

Merton's Prayer

MY LORD GOD, I have no idea where I am going. I do not see the road ahead of me. I cannot know for certain where it will end. Nor do I really know myself, and the fact that I think I am following your will does not mean that I am actually doing so. But I believe that the desire to please you does in fact please you. And I hope I have that desire in all that I am doing. I hope that I will never do anything apart from that desire. And I know that if I do this you will lead me by the right road though I may know nothing about it. Therefore I trust you always though I may seem to be lost and in the shadow of death. I will not fear, for you are ever with me, and you will never leave me to face my perils alone.[22]

one great truth: that man is called to live as a Son of God."[23] Merton believed and experienced an indwelling presence of God that represented something of the core of his soul. Like Teresa of Avila in her *Interior Castle*, Merton believed that God dwells in the center of one's very being and is the cause of all that is good and true about oneself: "The identification which we seek . . . is therefore a *conscious realization of the union that is already truly effected between our souls and God by grace. . . .*"[24]

In prayer, Merton taught, "we discover what we already have. . . . We already have everything but we don't know it and don't experience it. . . . All we need is to experience what we already possess."[25] The greatest problem in experiencing this divine core is the advancement of what Merton often called the "false self," the sense of one's identity separate and independent from God. As discussed in the chapters on mysticism, the desert fathers, the patristic greats, and the Carmelites, a deep mystical life holds a kind of creative tension between seeing God as distinct from the soul, a Being to love and be loved by, and as a Being one identifies with (divinization). Merton saw the not-fully-realized soul as one that still clings to this separation, this lack of identification. The false self strives to advance and protect itself, while the true self realizes its identity in and

---

22. Thomas Merton, *Thoughts in Solitude* (New York: Farrar, Straus, and Cudahy, 1958), 83.

23. Alfred Horrigan et al., eds., *Thomas Merton Studies Center* (Santa Barbara, CA: Unicorn Press, 1971), 14–15.

24. Thomas Merton, *Spiritual Direction and Meditation* (Collegeville, MN: Liturgical Press, 1960), 45.

25. Hart, *Thomas Merton, Monk*, 80.

through God. Ultimately, the contemplative life consists of dismantling this false self and entering communion where God is both loved and seen as one's essence, indeed the core of oneself: "What happens is that the separate identity that is *you* apparently disappears and nothing seems to be left but a pure freedom indistinguishable from the infinite Freedom, love identified with Love . . . He is the *I* who acts there. He is the one Who loves and knows and rejoices."[26]

Rick Warren (b. 1954): America's Pastor

In 2002, *Christianity Today* declared Rick Warren "America's most influential pastor." Since that time, Warren's ministry has grown and developed to such an extent that this title does not adequately reflect his current ministerial stature. Today his ministry and his reputation make him legitimately America's Pastor. In 2005, to mark the twenty-fifth anniversary of Warren's ministry, his Saddleback church booked Angel Stadium in Anaheim, California. The 45,000 seat stadium was nearly filled. During the course of the celebration, itself a kind of revival, Warren introduced the president of Rwanda, Paul Kagame. A few years before, Kagame invited Warren to work with churches in Rwanda, a country devastated by poverty and genocide, so that he might help this struggling country become the first "purpose-driven nation."

During the celebration Warren announced his latest and most ambitious project to date. His church, Saddleback Valley Community Church, would lead a campaign to address the problems of poverty, disease, lack of education, and spiritual emptiness around the world. His P.E.A.C.E. plan consisted of Planting churches, Equipping servant-leaders, Assisting the poor, Caring for the sick, and Educating the next generation. At the end of the service, instead of a Billy Graham-style altar call for non-believers to claim Christ as their Savior, he called on everyone present to commit themselves to this vision. They resoundingly cheered.

Rick Warren was born in 1954 to Dorothy (Dot) and Jimmy Warren, a Baptist minister. They had met in church in 1943, dated for two months and married after only a three-week engagement. Jimmy was then sent off to the South Pacific during World War II. When he came home, he and his wife began a ministry that would ultimately support the start of 150 churches worldwide. Much of Warren's young life was spent in the community of Redwood Valley of Mendocino County, California. There he, his sister, and his brother were raised as devout Baptists, a regimen that included daily quiet time for prayer, Sunday school, church services, and a midweek Bible study. Warren, a popular and religiously devout young man, was Ukiah High School senior class president and founder of a Christian high school youth club.

---

26. Thomas Merton, *New Seeds of Contemplation* (New York: New Directions, 1961), 283, 287.

Warren's Prayer at Obama's Inauguration

Almighty God, our Father, everything we see, and everything we can't see, exists because of you alone. It all comes from you, it all belongs to you, it all exists for your glory. History is your story. The Scripture tells us, "Hear, O Israel, the Lord is our God, the Lord is one." And you are

Rick Warren, in 2008 in New York City, speaking at the Clinton Global Initiative to politicians, philanthropists, and business leaders on global issues. Warren stands out as an evangelical who is deeply concerned with social issues.

the compassionate and merciful one. And you are loving to everyone you have made. Now today, we rejoice not only in America's peaceful transfer of power for the 44th time, we celebrate a hinge point of history with the inauguration of our first African-American president of the United States. We are so grateful to live in this land, a land of unequaled possibility, where the son of an African immigrant can rise to the highest level of our leadership. And we know today that Dr. King and a great cloud of witnesses are shouting in heaven. Give to our new president, Barack Obama, the wisdom to lead us with humility, the courage to lead us with integrity, the compassion to lead us with generosity. Bless and protect him, his family, Vice President Biden, the Cabinet and every one of our freely elected leaders. Help us, O God, to remember that we are Americans, united not by race or religion or blood, but to our commitment to freedom and justice for all. When we focus on ourselves, when we fight each other, when

Continued

Warren's Prayer at Obama's Inauguration Continued

we forget you, forgive us. When we presume that our greatness and our prosperity is ours alone, forgive us. When we fail to treat our fellow human beings and all the earth with the respect they deserve, forgive us. And as we face these difficult days ahead, may we have a new birth of clarity in our aims, responsibility in our actions, humility in our approaches and civility in our attitudes—even when we differ. Help us to share, to serve and to seek the common good of all. May all people of good will today join together to work for a more just, a more healthy, a more prosperous nation and a peaceful planet. And may we never forget that one day, all nations, and all peoples, will stand accountable before you. We now commit our new president and his wife, Michelle, and his daughters Malia and Sasha, into your loving care. I humbly ask this in the name of the one who changed my life—Yesua, Isa, Jesus [Spanish pronunciation], Jesus—who taught us to pray: Our Father, who art in heaven, hallowed by Thy name. Thy kingdom come, Thy will be done, on earth as it is in heaven. Give us this day our daily bread. And forgive us our trespasses, as we forgive those who trespass against us. And lead us not into temptation, but deliver us from evil, for Thine is the kingdom and the power and the glory forever. Amen.[27]

Warren graduated in 1972 and attended California Baptist University. He had already built a name for himself in high school, preaching as a teenager to other teens at youth revivals. As a college student, he paid most of his expenses with honoraria from speaking engagements. In fact, during college he spoke at over 120 youth retreats and revivals. Warren knew he wanted to be a pastor and even considered missionary work. The faculty at California Baptist was so impressed with him that during his senior year they invited him to teach a course on evangelism.

During his college years, Warren met S. A. Criswell, the former president of the Southern Baptist Convention and the pastor of the largest church in America at the time—comprised of 15,000 members. Criswell was speaking in San Francisco, and Warren and a friend cut classes to drive 350 miles north to hear him. After his sermon, Warren and many others stood in line to meet him. While shaking Warren's hand, Criswell said, "Young man, I feel led to lay hands

---

27. *www.christianstogether.net/Articles/137547/Christians_Together_in/Christian_Life/Christians _and_Politics/Rick_Warrens_prayer.aspx.*

on you and pray for you!" He placed his hands on Warren's head and prayed, "Father, I ask you that you give this young preacher a double portion of your Spirit. May the church he pastors grow to twice the size of the Dallas church [Criswell's]. Bless him greatly, O Lord."[28]

During Warren's sophomore year he met Elizabeth Kay Lewis, the daughter of a Baptist pastor. Kay first saw Warren during their freshman year at a campus meeting; he was on stage doing an impression of Billy Graham. At the time, she was not at all taken with him. Shortly thereafter she started dating one of his close friends. The summer after their freshman year, Warren was invited to speak at Kay's father's First Baptist Church in Fresno. Kay played the piano at the evening program. Warren remembers, "I looked right over at her right before I got up to speak, and God said just as clearly as I'm talking to you, 'You're going to marry that girl.' Now I immediately doubted it for two or three reasons—first, I didn't love her; second, God had never before or ever since talked to me that clearly in my life; and number three, she was madly in love with my best friend."[29] So Warren stayed away. Soon after, Kay's boyfriend broke up with her and within weeks Warren began to spend time with her casually. He finally asked her out for ice cream. This was their first date. The second date was a Christian service off campus. After the event, they walked back to campus and out of his mouth came the words, "Will you marry me?" Kay was still in love with Warren's best friend, although by now it was clearly unrequited. Kay recalls, "I instantly said to God, 'Okay, God, I don't love him. I'm in love with his best friend. What in the world do I say to this guy who has asked me to marry him?' And God clearly said to me, 'Say yes, and I'll bring the feelings.' So I said yes." This would mark the first time they kissed.[30]

At the end of his junior year, at the age of 21, Warren was ordained a Baptist minister on May 27, 1975. Less than a month later, he and Kay married. She was still waiting for the feelings to arrive, and they assuredly came early in their marriage. After graduating, Rick and Kay moved to Fort Worth as he pursued seminary training at the Southwestern Baptist Theological Seminary. There, he continued to preach at revivals and even co-wrote two small books with ministers Billie Hanks, Jr., and Wayne Watts, *The Victory Scripture Memory Series* and *Twelve Dynamic Bible Study Methods for Laity*. During a weekend of pastor training at Hanks's ranch, Hanks asked Warren to teach the day's class. Warren walked up to the blackboard and drew a baseball diamond. He described first base as "Membership," committing to Christ and the church; second base was "Maturity," committing to daily prayer and tithing; third base represented "Ministry," representing Christian service; home plate was "Mission," evangelizing

---

28. Jeffery Sheler, *Prophet of Purpose: The Life of Rick Warren* (New York: Doubleday, 2009), 77.

29. Ibid., 74.

30. Ibid., 75.

others; and the pitcher's mound was "Magnification," or worship of the triune God, which tied all the bases together. This baseball diamond program became the foundation of Warren's massively successful Saddleback church and the basis of his book, *The Purpose Driven Church.*

Before graduating from seminary, Warren wrote to the hundred largest churches in America, asking them how they grew and how they remained healthy. Among other things, he realized that in virtually every case the pastor had been there twenty years or longer. Pastoral longevity would become a fundamental commitment for him. He had Kay put up a map of the United States on the wall of their apartment in Fort Worth, and they zeroed in on four possible places where they believed people were most unchurched: Seattle, San Francisco, Orange County, and San Diego. Orange County was particularly interesting for them, as it was one of the fastest growing areas in the country.

Warren wrote a letter to Rev. Herman Wooten, a Baptist minister in Saddleback Valley: "Dear Mr. Wooten, I'm thinking about coming to Saddleback Valley to start a church. I'm not asking for money. I'm not asking for support. I just want to know what you think about the area. Does it need churches?" That letter crossed in the mail with a letter that Wooten had simultaneously written to Warren: "Dear Mr. Warren, I understand you're thinking about starting a new church. Have you ever considered California? Have you ever considered starting a church in Saddleback Valley?"[31]

In January 1980, Warren, his wife, and toddler daughter moved to Saddleback Valley. They were virtually paupers at the time. They decided on a condominium because their realtor, Don Dale, who became their first parishioner, assured them that the first month's rent would be free. Then Bill Grady, a pastor from Fullerton who had heard he was starting a church, called to promise him two month's rent. They had breathing room.

For the next twelve weeks, Warren went door-to-door to over two thousand homes asking people four questions: Why do you think most people don't attend church? If you were looking for a church, what would you look for? What advice would you give me as a pastor of a new church that really wants to be a benefit to the community? How can I, as a pastor, help you? Over and over he heard that services were boring, communities were not friendly, and there was no adequate child care. With the support of five churches, Warren and a few new parishioners who met in his condominium sent out fifteen thousand letters inviting people to church.

Saddleback grew exponentially, so much so that it frequently had to change venues to accommodate its congregation. By the time the church acquired property in 1990 it had three thousand members. Within a year it grew to four

---

31. Richard Abanes, *Rick Warren and the Purpose That Drives Him* (Eugene, OR: Harvest House, 2005), 44.

thousand. Even before it had a permanent church, Saddleback was sponsoring conferences to train other pastors in the best practices. These evolved into week-long seminars that to date have trained four hundred thousand pastors from 162 different countries.

In 1994, the Christian publishing company Zondervan approached Warren with a two-book deal: the first would be a church-growth guide for pastors and the second would discuss lay discipleship. Warren got an advance of $150,000, which he pledged to the church in a fund-raising campaign. Zondervan had great hopes for the first book, expecting it to sell about thirty-five thousand copies. Within the first year *The Purpose Driven Church* sold one hundred thousand copies; by 1996 it had sold over a million.

Warren was supposed to have the follow-up book, *The Purpose-Driven Life*, written by 1997, but he kept putting it off. He finally sequestered himself for seven months and produced the text in 2002. Divided into forty relatively short chapters filled with Bible quotations, the book was meant to be a kind of forty-day retreat or spiritual journey. The first part of the book deals with the question: What on earth am I here for? The following parts of the book respond to this pivotal question with various answers for the reader to reflect upon. The first answer is: You were planned for God's pleasure. This discusses the necessity of prayer and biblical meditation. The second answer is: You were formed for God's family. This discusses the necessity of becoming baptized and part of the church. The third answer is: You were created to become like Christ. Here Warren discusses how to create godly habits and take on the mind or spirit of Christ. The fourth answer is: You were shaped for serving God. This is about ministry and how to find the kind of service that corresponds to one's personality, piety, and convictions. The final answer is: You were made for mission. It is imperative to evangelize.

Zondervan wanted to aggressively market the book, but Warren offered his own plan. First, Zondervan would make copies available to Saddleback members for only seven dollars, a third of the book's retail price. Second, Zondervan would provide 225,000 copies, also at seven dollars, to other churches participating in the first wave of the *Forty Days of Purpose* campaigns. These churches promised to engage in their own kind of retreat with their own parishioners, using Warren's book. Zondervan was uneasy. "You don't understand," Warren told them, "this book is not going to sell a million. It's going to sell *tens* of millions."[32] By September 2004, *The Purpose-Driven Life* had sold twenty million copies and remained on the New York Times best seller list for advice books for the next 188 weeks. To date, it has sold over thirty million copies.

Warren was already famous; now he was extremely wealthy. He and Kay responded to their new situation by making four decisions. First, they committed themselves not to change their lifestyle. They remained in the house they

---

32. Sheler, *Prophet of Purpose*, 179.

bought in 1992 and continued to drive the Ford they then owned. Warren also stopped taking a salary and repaid Saddleback the salary he had earned over the past twenty-five years of ministry. Then they committed themselves to *reverse tithing* whereby they gave to the church 90 percent of their income and kept only 10 percent for themselves. And finally, they started three foundations: one to train pastors, the second to work on missions following the P.E.A.C.E. plan, and the third to address the AIDS and orphan crisis in Africa.

Kay's particular contributions were AIDS relief, and the "A" and "C" aspects of the P.E.A.C.E. plan: Assist the poor and Care for the sick. For decades, part of Saddleback Church's self-understanding had involved serving the community, but it had not been actively involved in working with the poor. Warren describes the change:

> God had led me to Psalm 72. That is Solomon's prayer for more influence. It can sound like a selfish prayer. But then he says, so that the king may care for the widow and orphan, support the oppressed, defend the defenseless, care about the prisoner, help the foreigner, and so on—it's all the marginalized of society. And God said to me, *The purpose of influence is to speak up for those who have no influence.* That changed my life. I had to repent. I said, 'God, I can't think of the last time I thought about widows and orphans. They're not on my agenda. I'm building a big church in a very affluent area with gated communities.' You know, there aren't any homeless people on the streets here. . . . And I said, 'I'm sorry, God. How did I miss those 2000 verses on the poor in the Bible? How did I miss that with all my training, doctrine, and education? How did I miss that?' . . . Six months prior to my finding Psalm 72, Kay had read a *Time* magazine article about AIDS in Africa. . . . She shared that with me before I saw Psalm 72 and told me how she was supposed to be a spokesperson for AIDS.[33]

Reshaping the Mega-Church Phenomenon

The Mega-Church Movement began in the 1970s. In 1979, there were ten mega-churches in the United States. In 1980, the year Saddleback began, there were fifty. This number grew to three hundred in 1990 and five hundred by the early 2000s. In the mega-church, the church itself is often less what draws people in than the pastor. Such is the case with Warren and Saddleback, although he tries to ensure that the Christian message and not the messenger remains the focus. Still, there is a market-driven quality to this trend, and Saddleback is part of that.

---

33. Abanes, *Rick Warren and the Purpose That Drives Him*, 21.

Warren was ordained a minister in the Southern Baptist Convention, the most prominent denomination of the evangelical community and also a decidedly specific denomination. Saddleback, however, has removed virtually all Baptist identifiers, which is part of its appeal. In fact, when Warren began his church he conducted several focus groups and discovered that the term "Baptist" did not sit well with them. This led him to relinquish the Baptist connection. Both Warren's best-selling books are clearly market-savvy. Regarding *The Purpose-Driven Life*, Rich Karlgaard, publisher of *Forbes* magazine, called it "the best book in entrepreneurship, business, and investment in a long time. . . . Identify a consumer need—the religious consumer need—and fill it."[34]

Warren would probably wholeheartedly agree with that characterization. He considers it a good thing to intelligently and thoughtfully give people the kind of church that they want. His critics contend that he creates little more than a "feel-good" version of Christianity. He has countered that joy is the hallmark of Christianity and that in no way does Saddleback lose the content of the Christian message even as it updates the mechanism for providing it. Much in his ministry supports that defense. While everyone is welcome to worship there, members of Saddleback must commit themselves explicitly to the principles of the baseball diamond he drew back in his seminary days: daily prayer and tithing, belonging to small faith-sharing groups, being part of one of dozens of ministries ministries of the church, and committing oneself to sharing the Christian message. For the twenty thousand formal members of Saddleback, this hardly looks like "Christianity-lite."

Warren has also helped to reinvent the evangelical tradition. As chapter 12 discussed, American evangelical Christianity can often tend toward right-wing politics with a particular penchant for Manifest Destiny. In addition, the largest churches often have not been socially conscious except for their role in culture-war controversies such as abortion and same-sex marriage. Warren's theology is decidedly conservative in such matters, but not narrowly so. He and other like-minded pastors have been at the forefront of concern for global warming, poverty, and social justice. He describes it as a middle way between liberal mainline churches that have a social gospel and those churches that focus solely on salvation. "It's time to bring these back together. I am calling for a return to nineteenth-century Evangelicalism."[35]

In 2007, Warren got a call from Israeli Prime Minister Benjamin Netanyahu, who expressed gratitude for evangelical support of the State of Israel,

---

34. George Mair, *A Life with Purpose: Reverend Rick Warren: The Most Inspiring Pastor of Our Time* (New York: Berkley Books: 2005), 82. University of Southern California's religion professor, Donald Miller, sees the same thing in the church itself: "Saddleback attends to the consumer demand by fine-tuning their worship and organizational style to today's culture, not the cultures of the past." Ibid., 125.

35. Abanes, *Rick Warren and the Purpose That Drives Him*, 25.

but noted that it seemed to be waning. As mentioned in chapters 12 and 13, much of this support for Israel was connected to dispensationalist theology that considered the State of Israel as a forerunner to the apocalypse. Warren reports that he told the Prime Minister,

> First, you need to understand that there is a new wind blowing in evangelicalism in relationship to Israel. . . . The days of "Israel can do no wrong, and everybody else can do no right" are over. . . . People now are looking for a just settlement. They want human rights. Yes, we want to protect Israel's sovereignty, but, yes, we also believe that Palestinians cannot just be dominated indefinitely and left in a state of transition and tension.[36]

A Final Word

Rick Warren has been a famous pastor of one of the largest churches in the United States for over twenty-five years. He also, unwittingly, became wealthy. Fame and money represent clear temptations to any public figure, religious or otherwise. What America has found in Warren is simply a pastor. He remains friendly and accessible. He's not a hand-shaker; he's a hugger. In his sermons, he regularly witnesses about his own Christian walk, including how he has dealt with the tragic death of his son in 2013 and the counseling he and Kay have undergone to care for their marriage. In short, he has made himself vulnerable and transparent. His ministry is a world-wide operation that fosters church growth and supports international responses to poverty and illness. He has given away the vast majority of his income and lives a simple middle-class life. There is one more fact about Rick Warren that may offer some insight into this man. From his college days on, Warren has suffered from a rare brain disorder that cannot process adrenaline. Virtually every time he preaches he experiences headaches, dizziness, and blurred vision. In response to a question he receives periodically about the possibilities of getting self-absorbed by his celebrity, he said, "You have no idea. I'm saying, 'God get me through this.' It creates a sense of dependency, a sense of humility—what Paul would call a thorn in the flesh [2 Cor. 12:7]. It's been a governor on my life that keeps me focused on God rather than focusing on the crowds."[37] Perhaps his greatest strategy is this: realizing his vulnerability and focusing on God.

---

36. Sheler, *Prophet of Purpose*, 244.

37. Ibid., 174.

Conclusion

All three of the individuals discussed in this chapter are, arguably, great Christians who exemplify both their specific religious traditions and their own particular Christian walks. Dorothy Day looks, acts, and speaks like a member of the Catholic Worker movement, searching and finding Christ in the least among us and advocating for their well-being and dignity. Thomas Merton speaks the resonant message of monasticism. His life of deep prayer gave him insights that many Christians with an interior bent recognize as true to themselves. And Rick Warren represents the theology and spirituality of the evangelical tradition. They are all deeply Christian, but their spiritualities are markedly different. They might question parts each other's theologies, and they certainly would not personally embrace each other's ministries as their own. Yet it is likely that they would see in each other a profound expression of the Christian faith, one that has transformed them personally and inspired multitudes of other Christians.

From the lived example of these three witnesses one can glean several insights about Christian spirituality. First, there is simply no single Christian spirituality. The Christian tradition is large enough and varied enough to contain these and a host of other spiritualities. The spirituality of each represents a larger tradition. In this sense, they serve as exemplars of families of Christian spirituality, with one focused on works of mercy, another on contemplative prayer, and another on evangelization. Further, although Day and Merton look like Catholics and Warren looks like an evangelical, they are not merely representative figures. They exemplify the fact that, in the end, there are as many Christian spiritualities as there are Christians. Some are more profound or comprehensive than others. Some are more laudable, while others more vulnerable to critique. Even these three are not beyond question.

Second, they exemplify the cost of deep discipleship, and the necessary faith that accompanies it. Day's regular life was hard, as the title of her most famous autobiography, *The Long Loneliness*, indicates. To find and love Christ in the poor, the homeless, the drug addicted, is a challenging task; it requires everything that one has. The reality of the daily grind of advocating for them, befriending them, and serving them soon strips away any romantic notions of service. Merton's deep mystical life was essentially a deconstruction of the very self he brought to the monastery. The conditions of Gethsemani, particularly during the time he lived there as a monk, were rugged and challenging. To flourish there, as he did, meant giving up everything for the singular, radical pursuit of finding God. The inscription on the gates of Gethsemani monastery is telling: GOD ALONE. Finally, Warren found himself marrying a woman he believed God had commanded him to marry and going where God sent him with no money or personal experience building a church. Trust in God's providence dominated his ministry from the start. While some contemporaries have made their mega-church empires virtual fiefdoms of self-interest, he has remained focused on his community and on supporting other ministers. His talent for preaching has come at the cost of great and regular suffering, and he has witnessed to a life of humility and transparency, all the while making the message about Christ and not about himself.

Finally, these three show just how much Christian spirituality is a journey. Both Day and Merton began their young adulthoods as morally compromised non-believers. Yet they followed their spiritual hunger to find God. Even as they did, they imagined their lives as an ongoing journey. Day strove to integrate her passion for justice and her Catholic faith in a way that was comprehensible to her and that allowed for a profound ministry to emerge, while she continued to look for and find God in the most unlikely places. Merton might have been a poster child for the dictum "God draws straight with crooked lines." Even in the monastery, he saw himself less an accomplished Christian and more an ongoing journeyman of the soul. His autobiography, *The Seven Storey Mountain*, which chronicles his early life up to becoming a monk, ends as follows: *sit finis libri, non finis quaerendi* ("Let it be the end of the book, but not the end of searching"). Warren has continued to keep his heart open. He was twenty years into his ministry when both Psalm 72 and his wife Kay convicted him with the imperative to serve the poor and ill. It would have been easy for a widely popular and influential pastor to think that he had "made it," but in his own words, "I had to repent." This opened a new chapter in his ministry, and his journey continues.

Questions for Review

1. What role did prayer play in Dorothy Day's spirituality? In what forms of prayer did she typically engage?
2. What were Thomas Merton's main contributions to Christian spirituality?
3. How did Rick Warren handle the tremendous success of his ministry and publications?
4. In what way do these three figures represent similar spiritualities? What are the clearest differences among them?

Questions for Discussion

1. Do you think it is possible to recognize the person of Jesus in everyone, particularly those who are poor, illiterate, and socially limited, as Dorothy Day attempted to do? How would one go about doing this?
2. Merton's brief love affair with the nurse humbled him and helped him to recognize his fragility. How can failings or sin lead someone to become a

better person? Is it possible to be glad about such failures, after the fact, or must they always occasion only regret?

3. Do you think it is appropriate to use market analysis and business strategy in Christian discipleship making? What are the assets and liabilities of such an approach?

4. Of the three witnesses in this chapter, whose spirituality do you most identify with and why?

Bibliography

Resources with annotations are highly recommended to students interested in further study.

Abanes, Richard. *Rick Warren and the Purpose That Drives Him*. Eugene, OR: Harvest House, 2005.
> This is a bit of an apologetics for Warren, given the criticisms of him made in some quarters of the evangelical community. Its greatest value is that it works like an extended interview with Warren himself.

Day, Dorothy. *From Union Square to Rome*. Maryknoll, NY: Orbis Books, 2006.

Day, Dorothy. *House of Hospitality*. New York: Sheed & Ward, 1939.

Day, Dorothy. *The Long Loneliness*. New York: HarperCollins, 1997.
> This is Day's most famous autobiography—a classic.

Day, Dorothy. *On Pilgrimage*. Grand Rapids: Eerdmans, 1999.

Hart, Patrick, ed. *Thomas Merton, Monk: A Monastic Tribute*. New York: Sheed & Ward, 1974.

Horrigan, Alfred, et al., eds. *Thomas Merton Studies Center*. Santa Barbara, CA: Unicorn Press, 1971.

Mair, George. *A Life with Purpose: Reverend Rick Warren: The Most Inspiring Pastor of Our Time*. New York: Berkley Books, 2005.
> This is a sympathetic, but fair and analytical, study of Warren and his ministry.

McDonnell, Thomas, ed. *A Thomas Merton Reader*. Rev. ed. New York: Image Books, 1974.

Merton, Thomas. *Contemplative Prayer*. New York: Image Books, 1996.
> This is one of Merton's small but invaluable books on the nature of prayer.

Merton, Thomas. *Learning to Love: Exploring Solitude and Freedom*. Vol 6 of *The Journals of Thomas Merton*. Edited by Christine Bochan. New York: HarperSanFrancisco, 1997.

Merton, Thomas. *Mystics and Zen Masters*. New York: Delta, 1961.

Merton, Thomas. *New Seeds of Contemplation*. New York: New Directions, 1961.
This represents perhaps Merton's best collection of reflections on the interior life and its relationship with living every day.

Merton, Thomas. *No Man Is an Island*. New York: Image Books, 1967.

Merton, Thomas. *The Seven Storey Mountain*. Orlando, FL: Harcourt Brace Jovanovich, 1948.
Merton's famous autobiography, it chronicles his early life up to the time he entered Gethsemani monastery.

Merton, Thomas. *Spiritual Direction and Meditation*. Collegeville, MN: Liturgical Press, 1960.

Merton, Thomas. *The Way of Chuang Tzu*. New York: New Directions, 1965.

Merton, Thomas. *Zen and the Birds of Appetite*. New York: New Directions, 1968.

Mott, Michael. *The Seven Mountains of Thomas Merton*. Rev. ed. New York: Harcourt Brace, 1984.
This is perhaps the best biography of Merton available.

Sheler, Jeffery. *Prophet of Purpose: The Life of Rick Warren*. New York: Doubleday, 2009.
This is a sound biography of Warren.

Internet Resources

Barron, Robert. "Thomas Merton, Spiritual Master." 2015. *www.youtube.com /watch?v=5X8fp2CvQmA*.
Barron describes the person and impact of Thomas Merton (9 min.).

Daily Hope with Rick Warren. *rickwarren.org/*.
This is Rick Warren's own website that provides ministerial resources for Christians.

"Dorothy Day 1977." *www.youtube.com/watch?v=oDkv2ULYSXA*.
A brief interview with Dorothy Day (5 min.).

Dorothy Day Collection. *dorothyday.catholicworker.org/*.
This site offers copious primary source materials about Dorothy Day and the Catholic Worker movement.

"Dorothy Day Documentary: Don't Call Me a Saint." 2008. *www.youtube.com /watch?v=RKiLCDaCAOU*.
Documentary on Day (3 min.).

Martin, James. "Dorothy Day." "Who Cares about the Saints?" 2012. *www.you tube.com/watch?v=SIknaD0qtOU*.

This is James Martin describes the life and spirituality of Dorothy Day (9 min.).

Thomas Merton Center: Pittsburgh's Peace and Justice Center. *thomasmerton center.org/*.

This is the primary research center for Thomas Merton Studies.

Warren, Rick. "Learning My True Identity in Christ." *www.youtube.com/watch?v=VGu51dQksB4*.

This is a sermon by Warren on discovering one's identity in Christ (106 min.).

Films

Entertaining Angels: The Story of Dorothy Day. 1996.

This film tells the story of Dorothy Day from her activism in the 1920s and 1930s to her ministry throughout her life.

Glossary

Ambrose of Milan (340–397) Bishop and theologian who influenced Augustine's understanding of philosophy, theology, and church life.

anamnēsis The process where, in liturgy, one re-enters into the original saving events of Christ.

anchoritism The first form of monasticism, whereby solitary monks lived lives of asceticism and prayer.

Antony of Egypt (251–356) An Egyptian anchoritic monk and monastic master whose biography by Athanasius, *The Life of Antony*, served as a model for the monastic way.

apatheia A term used by both some Greek philosophical schools and the church fathers to describe a state of mind and heart characterized by freedom from inordinate desires or passions.

apophatic Greek for "negative" and pertaining to mystical experiences that transcend human concepts. In mysticism, apophatic experiences are direct experiences of God that are beyond the human ability to understand.

apostolic church The period of church history starting with the apostles and ending in the early second century.

asceticism Refers to a practice or lifestyle of discipline, restraint, and control of the passions and bodily pleasures.

Augustine of Hippo (354–430) Bishop and the most influential Christian theologian in Western Christianity. He developed a deeply ecclesial conception of the experience of God and the activity of the Spirit.

authority From the Latin *auctoritas* (origination or source) and related to *auctorare* (to bind). Theologically, it pertains to what grounds one's theology and spirituality.

Basil the Great (330–379) Bishop of Caesarea in Cappadocia (modern Turkey) and one of the most influential theologians of the early church. His rule became the dominant expression of monasticism in Eastern Christianity.

Beguines Movement of lay women who lived together and managed their own spiritual and apostolic lives outside of traditional women's religious orders.

Benedict of Nursia (480–547) Leading figure in Western monasticism whose rule eventually became the standard for the West.

biblical inerrancy A belief that the Bible is inspired by the Holy Spirit in such a way as to be free of errors. While not all groups that accept the inerrancy of the Bible read it in a literalistic manner, many do.

Calvin, John (1509–1564) Swiss reformer known for his new catechism, *Institutes for Christian Life*, democratic view of the church, and strict understanding of predestination known as double predestination. The Reformed tradition of Protestantism derives its origins primarily from Calvin.

Carmelites Monastic order originating in Palestine in the early thirteenth century and moving to Europe by the end of the thirteenth century. Its major representatives, Teresa of Ávila and John of the Cross, are particularly known for their contributions to understanding the stages of spiritual growth and their mystical doctrine.

Carthusians Order of semi-hermits started in 1084 by Saint Bruno of Cologne, who reacted to standard Medieval monastic life.

Cathars Preaching movement in the Medieval period that taught a kind of dualism of matter and spirit and ultimately divorced itself from the church.

Catherine of Siena (1348–1380) Italian lay woman and mystic, whose spiritual life gave her insights into theology and whose spiritual authority played a role in Italian political and church life.

CELAM Synod of Latin American Catholic bishops formed in 1955 to address the Catholic Church in Latin America.

cenobitism The community form of monasticism. A monk or nun who belongs to a group in a monastery is a cenobite.

consciousness examen Daily step-by-step process of recognizing God's permanent gifts and ongoing presence in one's life.

covenant A binding together of two or more parties in a relationship of mutual trust and responsibility.

dao Literally means "way" or "way-making" and references the underlying reality behind the created world.

Dei Verbum (Dogmatic Constitution on Divine Revelation) The formal teaching document of the Catholic Church's Second Vatican Council (1962–1965) on the nature of divine revelation, particularly the relationship between scripture and tradition, and the role of Jesus as the absolute revelation of God.

Dhammapada Canonical anthology of the Buddha's sayings that present major aspects of his teachings.

dispensationalism View that God has dealt with humanity in a series of dispensations (similar to covenants) over time. Dispensationalists believe that the last dispensation, in which Christ will return to institute a thousand-year reign, is imminent.

divinization The process by which the human person becomes so transformed by God as to fully live God's life within oneself. Ultimately, it represents radically participating in God's life in heaven.

doctor of the Church A Roman Catholic title honoring those who have made contributions to the intellectual and spiritual doctrines of the Church that it considers perennially important.

Dogen (1200–1253) One of the most influential teachers of Soto Zen Buddhism.

Dominic Guzman (1170–1221) Spanish priest who started the Dominican Order, which focused on apostolic simplicity and preaching the gospel. One of its main aims was teaching illiterate church members and checking the growing unorthodox movements, such as the Cathars.

double predestination The view that God chose people to be damned or saved from the beginning of time, and that they have no ability to alter that election.

ecclesial Literally "regarding the assembly," from the Greek *ekklēsia*. Refers to that which is associated with the church.

Edwards, Jonathan (1703–1758) Eighteenth-century New England minister who was responsible for beginning the first American revival movement, the First Great Awakening.

eros The Greek word for love that entails a drive for union. While often used to refer to sexual union, it can also refer to the loving drive for union with God.

eschatological Pertaining to the "end times" or near end of the present age.

Evagrius of Pontus (345–399) One of the great intellectual and spiritual synthesizers of monastic life, whose work explores such ideas as the spiritual progress of the soul, temptations and how to address them, and levels of prayer.

exclusivism View in the theology of religions that one's religion is the only access to God or salvation.

fourfold method of interpretation Patristic approach to interpreting the Bible, where texts were understood as addressing either the literal (historical), moral, analogical, or anagogical realities of the faith, or some combination of the four.

Francis of Assisi (1181–1226) Perhaps the most popular saint in Western Christianity besides Mary, Saint Francis created a religious order that focused on preaching the gospel, caring for the poorest of the poor, and living a highly ascetical life of poverty.

gift economy   A feudal cultural and economic expression where goods were exchanged to enhance the giver's status as well as form bonds between people.

grace   God's unmerited favor and gift of saving love.

Graham, Billy (b. 1918)   Most famous evangelical preacher in the second half of the twentieth century.

Gregory of Nyssa (335–295)   Bishop and influential patristic thinker on Christian doctrine and the progress of the mystical path.

Hildegard of Bingen (1098–1179)   Benedictine nun whose mystical visions led to her becoming a theological authority and preacher.

Humiliati   Group of priests and laymen who traveled throughout Italy preaching apostolic simplicity and serving the poor.

iconoclasm   The position that icons or images, especially of Christ, violate the commandment not to make graven images of God.

iconodulism   The position that icons or images of Christ and the saints spiritually represent the meaning of Christ and the presence of the saints and offer possibilities for meditation.

icons   Images of important Christian figures, including Christ and the saints, thought to mediate in some way the spiritual presence of those portrayed.

Ignatius of Loyola (1491–1556)   Saint who, with several others, began the Society of Jesus. Ignatius's spirituality grounds the order and focuses on radical availability to God in everyday life as well as learning to discern God's presence in the midst of life.

inclusivism   View in the theology of religions that one's religion is the primary or best expression of God and that access to God or salvation comes implicitly through one's own religious understanding.

indulgence   The remission of temporal punishment for sin.

Jesus Prayer   A repetitive prayer ("Lord Jesus Christ, have mercy on me") that facilitates contemplation of Christ and the practice of unceasing prayer.

John Cassian (360–435)   Eastern deacon who introduced a systematic form of Eastern monasticism to the West.

John of the Cross (1542–1591)   Saint and doctor of the Catholic Church, arguably the greatest articulator of Catholic mysticism.

kataphatic   Greek for "positive" and pertaining to mystical experiences that utilize one's senses or ability to conceptualize.

Logos   Greek term meaning reason or word. Plato spoke of the Logos as God's creative power, emanating order and reason. In John's Gospel, Logos designates the second person of the Trinity, the Son.

Luther, Martin (1483–1546)   German Reformer who ignited the Protestant Reformation. He is known for his objection to indulgences, for the ninety-five theses, and for a stringent view of human free will.

Marx, Karl (1818–1883)   Philosopher and economic theorist who argued that the structures of society, including religion, were fundamentally controlled by economics.

Methodism   Originally a movement and eventually a Protestant denomination inspired by John Wesley, Charles Wesley, and George Whitefield, emphasizing personal experience and regular methods for spiritual growth.

mystical union   The experience of absolute union with God.

Nagarjuna (150–250)   Most important early intellectual force for Mahayana Buddhism, particularly with regard to his concepts of universal emptiness and "suchness" in all things.

ninety-five theses   A series of theological points of disputation against Catholic Church teaching, penned by Martin Luther, challenging in particular the use of indulgences.

Origen (185–254)   The most influential patristic theologian in the East, he is known for his heavy reliance on Platonic themes in service of Christian theology and mysticism.

Pachomius (290–346)   Leading figure in cenobitic monasticism who helped establish early models of community life.

patristic church   The period of church history starting in the second century and ending in the sixth.

penthos   Compunction or sorrow for one's sins.

perennialism   View that mysticism is pan-religious and that mystics from a wide variety of religions have the same experience of the divine.

Peter Damian (1007–1072)   A monk who lead the West's anchoritic movement and advocated radical poverty and detachment from society.

Pietism   German movement that sought to refocus Lutheranism on a vibrant inner life in reaction to the perceived dryness of the Lutheran Church. It served as a foundation for the American evangelical movement.

Platonism   The philosophy of Plato (428–348 BCE) and later Plotinus (205–270) that understood the universe as created through a series of emanations representing truth, goodness, and beauty. This philosophy influenced the patristic church.

pluralism   View in the theology of religions that one's religion is only one way among other ways to consider God or salvation, both of which exceed all religions.

pneuma The Greek word for spirit. The related term, *pneumatikos* ("spiritual"), is used in the New Testament to refer to someone who is guided by the Holy Spirit or has become a renewed spiritual person.

positive confession View that God offers gifts in the forms of wealth, health, or other goods to persons who have the faith to claim them in advance.

postmodern mutualism View in the theology of religions that religions are unique and that their respective understandings of such things as ultimate reality or paths to holiness cannot be aligned to other religions.

premillennialism Belief that Christ will return to earth and establish a kingdom lasting a thousand years (see Rev. 20:1–6).

Premonstratensians Order of parish priests, started by Saint Norbert in 1120, who served local parish communities and whose members lived an austere common life.

prosperity preaching Form of Pentecostalism that emphasizes earthly success and wealth as part of the gifts God desires to give to his disciples. Prosperity preaching asserts that if one has faith and claims God's good gifts, God will in fact grant those gifts.

The Protestant Ethic and the Spirit of Capitalism Influential book by sociologist of religion, Max Weber. He argued that Protestants, while theologically imagining themselves free from any works righteousness, actually worked very hard to succeed, as this success would be evidence of God's election.

Pseudo-Dionysius (fifth or sixth century) Patristic thinker who aligned Christian truths and mysticism with the created order and expressions of church life.

purgation, illumination, and union These three stages traditionally used to describe the Christian path, with purgation representing the moral ordering of one's life, along with long-practiced mental prayer; illumination representing the focus on God's indwelling within the soul; and union representing the soul's absolute communion with God.

Rabbinic Judaism Form of Judaism that arose after the destruction of the Second Temple in 70 CE. It grew out of the Pharisaic tradition and became the dominant form of Judaism to the present day.

Romero, Oscar (1917–1980) Salvadoran archbishop who spoke up for the poor and opposed the Salvadorian power structure that oppressed them. He was assassinated while presiding at the Eucharist.

sacraments Established rituals intended to deepen and enhance the practice of one's faith. While the early church did not have a set number of sacraments, the most important ones were baptism and Eucharist.

Spiritual Exercises A month-long retreat whereby one learns how to identify with the life and mission of Jesus especially for the purpose of discerning God's will in one's life.

stigmata The wounds of Christ miraculously appearing and remaining on the bodies of some Christians, particularly those whose spiritualities focused on the Passion of Christ. Saint Francis of Assisi was the first to receive the stigmata.

Teresa of Ávila (1515–1582) Saint and doctor of the Catholic Church, known for her presentation of spiritual stages of the interior life.

theōsis The Greek word for divinization, it means being transformed by God and participating in God's life.

Torah Hebrew for law, direction, or instruction. It can refer to the first five books of the Old Testament, the many commandments of God in the Old Testament, or the revelation of God in the Old Testament. Jews distinguish between written Torah, the biblical texts, and oral Torah, which represents applications of these texts in the life of Judaism.

tradition Refers to the whole of the life of the church, including the witness of the apostles, experience of the church, prayer, liturgy, and developing theological commitments.

Trinity The Christian understanding of the one God who has three dynamic inner relations (or persons) as Father, Son, and Holy Spirit.

T.U.L.I.P. Acronym for the five points of Calvinism as developed by the Reformed Church in the early seventeenth century. These are: **t**otal depravity; **u**nconditional election; **l**imited atonement; **i**rresistible grace; and **p**erseverance of the saints.

Waldensians French group of laymen and women, organized in 1170, who challenged the worldliness of the institutional church.

Wesley, Charles (1707–1788) Anglican priest and prolific hymn writer who helped his brother John spread the spirituality that would become Methodism.

Wesley, John (1703–1791) Anglican priest and itinerant preacher responsible for developing the ideas that eventually resulted in the Methodist Church.

Whitefield, George (1714–1770) Anglican priest and friend of the Wesleys, known for his popular preaching that focused on the individual and the need for personal conversion.

wu-**forms** Principles of Daoism that refer to approaching experiences and their emerging energies in ways that do not try to manipulate them.

yin/yang These refer to complimentary energies or characteristics, such as feminine/masculine, dark/light, and receptivity/activity.

Zwingli, Ulrich (1484–1531) A Swiss reformer and first contributor to the Reformed tradition of Protestantism, he is known for his iconoclasm and radical rejection of Catholic tradition.

Index

Note: The abbreviations *cap*, *i*, *s*, or *n* that follow page numbers, indicate captions, illustrations, sidebars, or footnotes, respectively.

A

abbas, 97, 100, 100*n*6, 104, 106, 109, 110
abbots, 110, 111–12
Abraham, 46
Abrams, Minnie, 233
Abulafia, Abraham, 28
Abundant Life (magazine), 234
acedia (listlessness), 107–8
action and works. *see also* service
   Aurelius on, 76
   Buddhism and, 268
   Daoism and, 278–79
   discretion and, 105, 109
   faith *versus*, 202, 208
   Ignatian spirituality and, 174, 176, 187
   Jesus and, 185
   liberation spirituality and, 58, 255
   liturgy and, 123
   Luther on, 199
   Merton on, 294
   Origen on, 82
   prayer and, 294
   righteousness and, 187, 316
   Warren on, 294
Acts of the Apostles (Luke), 11, 12*i*, 54, 59, 91, 229
Adam and Eve, 125, 149
addiction, 8–9
Address to the Christian Nobility of the German Nation (Luther), 196
ad majorem Dei gloriam ("for the greater glory of God"), 187
Aelred of Reivaulx, 148
After Forty Years (*Quadregesimo Anno*) (Pius XI), 251*s*
AIDS relief, 302
Albert the Great, 139
Albrecht of Mainz, 195
Alcoholics Anonymous, 8–9

Alexander, Paul, 236
Alexander VI, 192
allegories, 77–78, 84, 85–86, 214
Altenstaig, Johannes, 12
Amadeus VIII of Savoy, 192*n*3
Ambrose of Milan, 70, 87, 108, 311
ammas, 101, 104, 150
Ammonas, 100*n*6
Amos, 18, 247–48
anagogical meaning, 84, 313
anamnēsis, 123, 125, 126, 311
anchorites. *see* hermits
angels, 81, 91, 128*n*15, 143–44, 162, 165, 238
Anselm of Canterbury, 148
Anthony, 97
antiphon, 65
Antony of Egypt, 102–3, 311
apatheia, 65–66, 69, 76, 82, 88, 107, 146, 147, 311. *see also* detachment; passions; virginity (celibacy)
apathy, 66*n*18
apocalypticism, 60–61, 60*i*, 241. *see also* eschatology; kingdom of God
apokatastasis, 81
apophatic mysticism
   Augustine and, 90
   authenticity and, 34
   bodies and, 120
   Carmelites and, 159
   Daoism and, 276–77
   defined, 29, 311
   Gregory of Nyssa on, 86
   intellect and, 140
   materialism and, 121
   medieval, 146
   monasticism and, 114
   Pseudo-Dionysius and, 93
   rarity of, 158
   scholars and, 32

Teresa of Ávila and, 161–62
union with God and, 75
apostles, 59, 67, 67*n*19, 229. *see also* Peter
and other apostles
apostolates, 141
apostolic church, 58–60, 71–72, 190, 311.
see also early church; patristic era
Apostolic Faith, The (newspaper), 233
Aquinas, Thomas, 12, 26, 91, 139, 140
Aristotle, 79*s*
Armageddon, 231
artists, 22, 122*s*, 132
asceticism. *see also* moral rigor; passions
anchoritism and, 311
Augustine and, 88
Carmelites and, 160, 166
early church and, 65–66, 68–69
Francis of Assisi and, 141, 142, 145,
313
John of the Cross on, 167
monasticism and, 102, 103, 106, 146
patristic era and, 97
Plotinus and, 79
prevalence of, 158
Assemblies of God, 220, 225, 234, 240
Assisi Day of Prayer (1986), 266
astrology, 87*n*18
Athanasius, 80, 102, 102*n*9, 311
*Attitude of the Church towards the Followers
of Other Religions, The* (Pontifical
Council for Interreligious Dialogue),
265–67
Augsburg Confession, 198, 202
Augustine of Hippo
Antony of Egypt and, 102
background, 87–88
Christocentrism and, 16
fasting, on, 146
free will, on, 193
John of the Cross and, 169
monasticism and, 108
mysticism and, 26, 88–91
ordination of, 64–65, 88
overview, 311
Renaissance and, 191
resurrection of body, on, 70
saints, on, 69–70
theology and, 311

Trinity, on, 17
women, on, 147
Aurelius, Marcus, 76, 76*n*1
authenticity, 54, 186–87, 245, 264
authority. *see also* freedom
apostles and, 229
Bible and, 44–45, 220
bishops and, 63
defined, 311
doctors of the church and, 158
evangelicals and, 213, 220
individuals and, 202, 208
Jesus and, 49
Judaism and, 68
Luther and, 195, 197, 198
monasticism and, 100, 105, 166
mystical experiences and, 33
papal, 191, 195
women and, 69, 101, 111*cap*, 150–54
awakenings, 216–17, 218–20, 313
Aztecs, 35–37

B

Baker, Heidi, 237–38, 242
baptism
apostolic era and, 62
Augustine and, 88
early church and, 316
Eastern Orthodoxy and, 123–24, 133
evangelicals and, 213, 241
identity and, 125, 212
Luther on, 196
Patristic Era and, 65
Red Sea crossing and, 86
saints and, 71*s*
Baptism of the Holy Spirit and Fire, The
(booklet), 233
Baptists, 208, 212, 213, 223, 224, 296. *see
also* Southern Baptist Convention
Bartimaeus, 180
Bartolomeo de'Dominici, 152
Basilica of San Francesco d'Assisi, 144*i*
Basil the Great, 80, 83, 105–6, 106*n*14,
107, 311
Batterham, Forster, 286
beggars, 138, 139, 141
Beguines, the, 153–54, 311

Benedictines, 137, 146, 150–51, 288. *see also* Bernard of Clairvaux; Trappist Order
Benedict of Nursia, 110–11, 110–14, 111*i*, 112*s*, 288, 311
Benedict XVI, 253, 254
Bernard of Clairvaux, 22, 148–49, 149–50, 151
Bernini, Lorenzo, 162
Bible, the (Scriptures). *see also* New Testament; Old Testament (Hebrew Bible); Word of God
    authority of, 44–45, 56
    Calvinism and, 206
    Calvin on, 204, 207
    contemplative prayer and, 178–79
    diversity and, 55
    Erasmus and, 200*n*16
    eroticism and, 83
    evangelicals and, 208, 208*n*27, 213, 225, 240–41
    exclusivism and, 264*n*1
    Gregory of Nyssa and, 84, 93–94
    holiness and, 47–55, 47*n*7
    liberation spirituality and, 245–49
    Luther on, 197
    modern interpretations, 94
    mysticism and, 26
    Origen on, 93–94
    overview, 47, 55
    patristic era and, 313
    Pentecostals and, 229–30, 239, 240
    pluralism and, 265
    Reformers and, 208, 212
    Renaissance and, 191
    revelation and, 12, 42–44
    Scopes trial and, 220
    spirituality and, 47, 55
    storytelling and, 238
    themes, 45–47
    U.S. evangelicalism and, 220
    vernacular, 154
    Warren and, 301
    Zwingli on, 201–3, 202–3
"Bible Belt," 219
"Bible colleges," 220
biblical inerrancy, 213, 238, 241, 312
biblicism, 208, 208*n*26

Billy Graham Evangelical Association (BGEA), 225
bishops, 63, 92, 136, 138, 192, 230. *see also* Romero, Oscar
black theology, 260
Blessed Assurance (hymn), 226
bodies. *see also* asceticism; health, biological; sexuality; virginity (celibacy)
    Augustine on, 88, 89
    Buddhism and, 272
    Cathars and, 138
    evil and, 138
    grace and, 146
    John of Damascus on, 120*n*1
    medieval piety and, 155
    monasticism and, 105
    Origen on, 81
    Paul on, 81*n*10
    Plato on, 78, 120
    resurrection of, 69, 70, 80, 81, 81*n*10, 259, 289*s*
Bonaventure, 274
Bonhoeffer, Dietrich, 21
Book of Divine Works (Hildegard of Bingen), 152
Book of Kells, 48*i*
Book of Life's Merits (Liber vitae meritorum) (Hildegard of Bingen), 151
Book of Psalms, The (Cravin), 47*n*7
"born again," 212
bride metaphors, 61, 86, 129, 147, 149, 149*n*16, 155. *see also* nuptial metaphors
Brown, Peter, 71
Bruno of Cologne, 137–38
Bruno of Olmutz, 154
Buddhaghosa, 8, 293
Buddhism, 7, 30, 266, 267–76, 273*s*. *see also* Buddhaghosa
Bum nulla, 160
Bunyan, John, 214
Bush, George W., 223

C

"Call of an Earthly King, The" (Ignatius of Loyola), 178
Calvin, John and Calvinism. *see also* Reformers; T.U.L.I.P

Eucharist and, 64s
evangelicals and, 213
overview, 203–8, 213, 238, 241, 312
prayer of, 207s
revivals and, 216–17
spiritual teaching of, 207–8
writings of, 203i
Zwingli and, 200n15
Campus Crusade for Christ, 225
"Canticle of the Creatures, The" (Francis of Assisi), 142s–143s
capitalism, 13, 137, 140, 206, 246, 250, 251s, 253, 316
Carmelites, 158, 160, 162, 166, 170–71, 176, 294, 312. see also John of the Cross; Teresa of Ávila
Carthusians, 137–38, 312
Cases, Bartolome de las, 35
Casey, Michael, 112s
Cassian, John, 109–10, 314
Cathars, 138, 153, 312
Catherine of Siena, 22, 32, 147, 152–53, 166, 312
Catholic Charismatic Renewal (CCR), 234–35s
Catholic Church. see also community; Latin Church; sacraments
  Calvin on, 204
  inclusivism and, 265
  interreligious dialogue and, 265–66
  liberation theologians and, 250–54
  Luther and, 194, 197, 198
  Revelation and, 42–43
  saints and, 71s
  sins and, 195
  U.S. evangelicalism and, 216
  women and, 280
Catholic Worker, The (newspaper), 287, 288
Causes and Cures (Causae et curae) (Hildegard of Bingen), 151
cave, allegory of, 77–78
CBN University, 234
Celestial Hierarchy (Pseudo-Dionysius), 91, 92
celibacy (virginity), 66–69, 67i, 69, 72, 88, 97, 115, 152, 209. see also marriage; sexuality

cenobitism, 103, 105, 312. see also Pachomius
Centesimus Annus (The Hundredth Year) (John Paul II), 251s
Cesaria, 109
Cesarius, 109
charism, 160
Charismatics, 32, 230, 234–35s
Charles V, 196, 196cap, 198
childhood, spiritual, 259, 274
China, 233, 233n2
Chrismation, 124–25
Christian and Missionary Alliance, 220, 231, 231n1
Christian Broadcasting Network, 234
Christian Coalition, 223
Christianity Today (magazine), 221–22, 224n11
Christian Reformed and Presbyterian Church, 208
Christocentrism, 15–16, 21
Chrysostom, John, 109, 127, 191, 248s
Chuang Tzu (Zhangzi), 276
Church of Christ, 213
Church of God, 231n1
Church of God in Christ, 225, 234
Church of the Nazarene, 231n1
Cicero, 87
circumcision, 46
City of God (Augustine), 70
Clare of Assisi, 37
Clement of Alexandria, 26, 76
Clement of Rome, 72n31
Climacus, John, 21–22, 130–31
"colloquy," 180
commandments, 174
Commentary on Song of Songs (Gregory of Nyssa), 86
Commentary on Song of Songs (Origen), 83
community. see also individualism
  Beguines and, 153–54
  Benedict on, 112–13, 112s
  biblical themes and, 47
  Calvin on, 205, 207–8
  Carmelites and, 160
  characterized, 17
  Day and, 290
  discipleship and, 62–63

early church and, 72, 72n31
Holy Spirit and, 12
liberation spirituality and, 255
monasticism and, 103, 104, 105, 146
patristic era and, 64–65
Paul on, 17, 288n9
speaking in tongues and, 236
Warren and, 306
comparative spirituality. *see also* Buddhism;
Daoism; diversity
exclusivism/inclusivism, 264–65
interreligious dialogue and, 265–67,
281
pluralism and, 265
compline, 113
concepts. *see also* intellect (rationality)
(reason); minds
Benedict on, 113–14
Buddhism and, 271
contemplation and, 161
Daoism and, 277, 278–79
Dionysius on, 120
Evagrius on, 108
Gregory of Nyssa on, 86
mysticism and, 26, 28, 29, 75
pluralism and, 265
Pseudo-Dionysius on, 92, 93
Teresa of Ávila on, 164
universality and, 27, 30
Cone, James, 260
Conferences (Cassian), 109
Confession (Sacrament of Penance),
194–95
Confessions (Augustine), 69–70, 89–90,
129n16
Confirmation, Eastern Orthodox, 124
Confucianism, 28
Congregationalism, 213
conscience, 197, 198
consciousness examen, 181–83, 187, 312
consolation, 184–86
Constantine, 98
constructive interpretation, 14
contemplatio, 114, 179
contemplation. *see also* meditation;
mysticism; prayer; Spiritual Exercises
action, in, 174, 176
apatheia and, 66

Benedictine, 114
Cassian on, 110
Eastern Orthodoxy and, 130–31
Evagrius on, 107, 108
icons and, 120
Ignatian spirituality and, 174, 179–82
imagination and, 180–81
John of the Cross on, 167, 168, 169
Merton and, 290
Origen on, 81, 82
Plotinus on, 79
prayer and, 18
Pseudo-Dionysius and, 93
union with God and, 80
Contras, 250
conversion. *see also* Whitefield, George
Augustine and, 73, 87–88, 129n16
baptism and, 62
evangelicals and, 213, 215, 216, 218,
221, 225
Francis of Assisi and, 141
Ignatius of Loyola, 38, 176, 177
liberation spirituality and, 256, 260
Merton and, 291–92
Pentecostals and, 233, 238, 242
repentance and, 100
revivals and, 217, 232
three-fold pattern and, 21
women and, 117
conversion narrative, 218
Copeland, Gloria and Kenneth, 239
Corinthian church, 72n31
Corinthians 1, 67–68, 67n19, 72n31
Cost of Discipleship, The (Bonhoeffer), 21
Council of Constance, 190
Cousins, Ewert, 8
covenants
defined, 45, 312
Jesus as, 49, 58, 68, 72, 126
law and, 59
relationship and, 46
second coming and, 255
Cravin, Toni, 47n7
creation (natural world)
Augustine on, 87, 89
Daoism and, 279
Dionysius on, 91–92, 94
Eastern Orthodoxy and, 125, 133

evolution *versus*, 220
feminine sexual mysticism and, 149
Hildegard of Bingen and, 149, 151, 152
Judaism and, 68
kingdom of God and, 246
Nicaea II on, 122
Origen on, 81, 82
spirituality themes and, 45, 46
Teresa of Ávila on, 163
Criswell, S. A., 298–99
critical analysis, 14
cross, the, 16, 53, 257, 274
Cross and Crown (*Spirituality Today*), 12
crucifixion, the, 53, 54
Cuauhtlatzin, Juan Diego, 35–37, 36*cap*
Cuba, 250
Cullis, Charles, 231
cultural and historical contexts. *see also*
    early church; patriarchal culture;
    patristic era *and other eras*
    Beguines and, 153–54
    Bible and, 44–45
    historical models and, 12–13
    Jesus and, 54, 56
    liberation spirituality and, 345–46
    Marx on, 249
    medieval piety and, 136–37
    modern Christian spirituality and, 13–14
    mystical experiences and, 30, 34–37
    overview, 245
    patristic era, 75–77
    poverty and, 258
    Reformers and, 191–92
    Renaissance and, 191
Cyril of Jerusalem, 125

D

Damian, Peter, 137, 315
Dao De Jing (Laozi), 266, 276, 279–81
Daoism, 28, 266, 276–81, 283, 293, 312, 317
Darby, John Nelson, 231–32
Dark Night, The (John of the Cross), 159*s*
David, King, 46, 238
Day, Dorothy, 285–90, 287*i*, 305, 306

day-to-day life, 174, 182, 187, 191, 209, 242. *see also* here-and-now; Ignatius of Loyola and Ignatian spirituality
decisiveness, 53
Decius, 80
Decretum Gelasianum, 71*n*30
Dei Verbum (Word of God) (Vatican II), 42–44, 312
Demetrius, 80
demons, 68, 81, 98, 102, 107–8, 178, 229, 233, 238
De Scandalis Ecclesiae (*On the Scandal of the Church*) (Gilbert of Tournai), 154
desires, trusting, 184–85
desolation, 184–86
detachment, 169, 174, 176, 177, 315. *see also apatheia*
Deuteronomy, Book of, 55
"devotion," 12
Dhammapada, 266, 267–71, 312
Dialogue (Catherine of Siena), 152
Dialogues (Gregory), 110
Dictionaire de spiritualité, 12–13
Didache (*Teaching*) *of the Twelve Apostles*, 20, 61–62
Diet of Augsburg, 198
Diet of Worms, 196–97, 196*i*
dignity, 258, 280, 288
Dionysius the Areopagite, 91–93, 94, 120
discernment, 182–87, 281
disciples, 125
discipleship
    characterized, 20–21
    early church and, 63
    Eastern Orthodoxy and, 133
    Ignatius of Loyola on, 178–79, 182, 183, 185
    Luther on, 196
    modern witnesses and, 185, 301, 305
    New Testament on, 50, 50*n*9, 53, 54, 248, 257
    Paul on, 19
Disciples of Christ, 208, 213
discretion, 105, 109–10, 280–81
dispensationalism, 231–32, 234, 241, 312–13
dispensational theology, 233
diversity, Christian, 55, 242, 267*cap*

Divine Names, The (Pseudo-Dionysius), 91
Divine Office (Liturgy of the Hours), 65, 113, 115, 160
divine reading (*lectio divina*), 113–14, 179
divinization (*theōsis*)
    apatheia and, 66
    Augustine and, 90
    defined, 313, 317
    Eastern Orthodoxy and, 119
    John of the Cross on, 170
    John on, 166
    mysticism and, 295
    suffering and, 166
    Ultimate Horizon, as, 18–19
    Zen Buddhism and, 176, 275
Dobson, James, 223
doctors of the church, 158, 313
Dogen, 272–73, 313
Dole, Bob, 223
Dominic, 138–39
Dominicans (Order of Preachers), 138–40, 152, 160, 176, 190
double predestination, 205, 313
douleia (veneration), 121
Dumitru, Nicusor, 122s
Dutch Reformed Church, 206

E

early church. *see also* apostolic church; New Testament; patristic era
    apocalypticism and, 60–61
    Apostolic Church and, 58–60
    asceticism and *apatheia* and, 65–66, 68–69
    center of life, as, 64–65
    communal identity and, 62–64, 72
    Dionysius on, 120
    Eucharist and, 62–63
    free will and, 193
    Gospels and, 42
    Holy Spirit and, 229
    Judaism and, 58–59, 68, 190
    moral rigor and, 61–62, 65–69
    overview, 71–72
    patristic era and, 64–65
    sacraments and, 316
    saints and, 69–71s

spiritualite and, 12
    virginity and, 66–69
Eastern Orthodoxy
    Eucharist and, 126–29
    icons and, 119–23, 121n3, 122s, 126, 127i, 129i, 132
    inclusivism and, 265
    liturgical prayer and, 123–25
    monastic model and, 115
    Origen and, 80
    overview, 119
    prayer and, 130–32
    prayer and contemplation and, 130–32, 133
    sacraments and, 132–33
    saints and, 71s
    Virgin Mary and, 129–30, 133
ecclesial, 313
Ecclesiastical Hierarchy, The (Pseudo-Dionysius), 91, 92
Eck, John, 195–96
Eckhart, Meister, 274–75
economic factors, 136–37, 140, 191, 195, 249–50. *see also* capitalism; gift economy; Marx, Karl and Marxism; poverty and the poor; socialism; wealth
    Latin America and, 250
Ecstasy of Teresa, The (Bernini), 162
ecstatic experiences
    Catherine of Siena and, 152, 153
    example of, 33
    Origen on, 83
    Pentecostals and, 232
    perennialism and, 29
    Pilgrim's Progress and, 132
    Plotinus on, 79
    Teresa of Ávila and, 161, 162
    Zen enlightenment and, 274–75
education, 137, 138–39, 191, 219
Edwards, Jonathan, 217–18, 221, 313
Egan, Robert, 37
Egypt, 97, 103
eikōn (icons), 119–23, 121n3, 122s, 129i, 132
ekklēsia, 313
"elections," 178, 183
Eleventh Virgin, The (Day), 286
El Greco, 12i

elitism, 158, 208–9
emotional faith
  gender and, 146–48, 155
  icons and, 120
  Methodism and, 215
  Pentecostals and, 230, 236, 242
  Pietism and, 213
  revivals and, 219, 220, 232
  Wesley, J. and, 215
emotions, 131, 132, 184, 241
emptiness, 271–72, 275, 279
Enchiridion (Erasmus), 191
Endres, John, 47*n*7
engagement, 49
Engels, Friedrich, 249
enlightenment, 272–73, 274
Entry of the Theotokos, 129–30
Epistle of Barnabas, 20
Erasmus of Rotterdam, 191, 200*n*16
eremitical monasticism, 109
eros, 82–83, 313. *see also* sexuality
eschatology, 72, 143*s*, 230, 241, 255–56,
  313. *see also* apocalypticism; kingdom
  of God
Essenes, 58*n*1
eternal life, 249, 259. *see also* resurrection
  of bodies
Eucharist. *see also* Lord's Supper
  Calvin on, 204, 207
  Day on, 288–89
  defined, 128
  Didache and, 62
  early church and, 62–63, 316
  Eastern Orthodox, 120, 124, 126–29,
    126*n*13
  "hocus pocus" and, 191*n*2
  Luther on, 196, 202
  monks and, 100
  mysticism and, 26
  Order of Penitents and, 194
  Pseudo-Dionysius on, 92
  real presence and, 64*s*
  Zwingli and, 201, 202
Eugenius III, 151
Eunapius of Sardis, 70
Eusebius of Caesarea, 80*n*8, 82
Evagrius of Pontus, 106–8, 108*n*20, 110,
  313

Evangelical Alliance, 220
evangelical counsels, 174
evangelicalism
  intellect and, 220–22, 222*s*
evangelicals. *see also* Southern Baptist
  Convention; Warren, Rick *and others*
  Bible, on, 208, 208*n*27, 213, 225,
    240–41
  characterized, 212–13
  common characteristics, 225, 242
  cross and, 257
  Eucharist and, 64*s*
  exclusivism and, 265
  Jesus as revelation and, 42
  Methodism and, 214–15
  Pietism and, 213–14
  "piety" and, 12
  second coming and, 255
  United States and, 216–24
  Warren and, 298, 303
Eve, 125, 130, 149
evil, 49–51, 60–61, 71–72, 86, 87, 138
exclusivism, 264, 264*n*1, 313
Exodus story, 83, 84, 85–86
experience, spiritual. *see also* ecstatic
  experiences; mysticism
  apostles and, 12
  biblical themes and, 47
  Calvinism and, 206–7
  Carmelites and, 171
  discernment and, 183–84
  Gilson and, 291
  Gregory of Nyssa on, 86
  "holiness churches" and, 231
  John of the Cross on, 167
  liberation spirituality and, 257–58
  Merton on, 295
  Paul of Tarsus and, 47*n*7
  scholars and, 9–10, 11
  union with God and, 167

F

faith, Christian. *see also* action and
  works; Catholic Church; discipleship;
  diversity; martyrdom; saints
  baptism and, 124
  Bible and, 47*n*7

church and, 120
community and, 17, 204, 205, 207
cross and, 16
day-to-day life and, 191
decisiveness and, 53
eternal life and, 259
evangelicals and, 212, 215, 218,
    219–20, 222, 225
free will and, 205
Holy Spirit and, 13, 54, 230
icons and, 121, 122s
individuals and, 7
intellect and, 140, 207
interreligious dialogue and, 266, 281
Jesus, in, 59, 222, 265, 288
John of the Cross on, 169, 170
Judaism and, 68, 85, 190
justice and, 18
liberation spirituality and, 245, 253,
    254, 256, 258, 260
love and, 289
Paul on, 14–15, 230
Pentecostals and, 230, 239, 240, 241,
    242, 316
Pietiests and, 213, 214
poor and, 52, 258
Reformers on, 194, 197, 202, 207
suffering and, 51, 61, 184, 287
virtue, as, 169, 170
wealth and, 239, 240
works *versus*, 202, 208
Faithful Narrative (Edwards), 218
Falwell, Jerry, 223–24
fasting, 174
father metaphor, 43s
feast days, 71
Felicity, 70
feminine piety, 146, 155, 278, 280
feminine sexual mysticism, 149–50
feminism, 260
Ferdinand of Spain, 192
feudalism, 136, 137, 191
Fifth Lateran Council, 192
find God in all things, 174, 187
"finished work" theology, 234
Finney, Charles Grandison, 219–20, 221
First Council of Constantinople, 83
First Diet of Speyer, 198

First Great Awakening, 217, 218–19, 313
Flowering of the Godhead, The (Mechtild of
    Magdeburg), 154
"for the greater glory of God" (*ad majorem
    Dei gloriam*), 187
Forty Days of Purpose campaigns, 301
fourfold method of interpretation, 84, 94,
    114, 313
Franciscans, 141–42, 142s–143s, 144i,
    145–46, 154, 190, 292, 313. *see also*
    Gilbert of Tournai
Francis I, 254
Francis of Assisi, 12–13, 37, 140–46,
    140n4, 142s–143s, 166, 313, 317
Franklin, Benjamin, 218n7
Frederick the Wise, 198
freedom (liberation). *see also* authority;
    Exodus story
    apatheia and, 66
    Benedict's steps and, 112s
    Buddhism and, 270, 271
    Calvin on, 205
    celibacy and, 67
    Ignatian spirituality and, 182
    Ignatius of Loyola on, 177
    John of the Cross on, 168
    liberation spirituality and, 258
    Luke's Gospel and, 52
    Luther on, 199–200
    moral rigor and, 72
    mystical experiences and, 37
    Origen on, 81
    Protestantism and, 208
    Protestant Reformers and, 219
    purgation and, 21
    sin and, 14–15
free will, 193, 205, 241
Friars Minor ("Little Brothers"), 140n4
fullness gospel, 231, 235

G

Galatians, Letter to, 14–15, 59
Garrigou-Lagrange, Reginald, 170–71
Gentiles, 59–60, 190
Germanus, 109
Germany, 198
gift economy, 136, 137, 314

gifts of the Spirit, 229–30, 231, 234, 239, 316. *see also* speaking in tongues

Gilbert of Tournai, 154

Gilson, Etienne, 291

Gloriam Virginalem (Gregory IX), 153

God. *see also* concepts; knowledge of God; Ultimate Reality; union with God (unitive way)
    becoming, 18–19
    Daoism and, 276
    human face of, 52–53
    image of, 122, 133
    impersonal, 90
    Logos and, 77
    love and, 15, 43s, 90–91
    Mary of Egypt story and, 99
    Origen on, 82–83
    Pietism and, 213
    Pseudo-Dionysius on, 91, 92–93
    suffering and, 16
    will of, 256

Good Samaritan, 256–57

Gospel of Mark: A Commentary, The (Maloney), 50n10

Gospels. *see also* John's Gospel *and other gospels*
    early church and, 42
    Eastern Orthodox liturgy and, 128
    examples spirituality and, 48–54
    icons and, 122s
    liberation spirituality and, 253–54
    Ludolph's commentary on, 175
    Luther on, 196

grace. *see also* sin
    Benedict on, 112–13, 288
    bodies and, 146
    Calvin on, 205
    defined, 314
    diversity and, 264–65
    evangelicalism and, 216
    exclusivism and, 265
    free will and, 193
    Gregory of Nyssa on, 86
    hope and, 169
    Ignatius of Loyola on, 178
    law and, 46
    liberation spirituality and, 258
    Luther on, 193–94, 199

monasticism and, 100, 102, 102n9, 103, 113

Paul on, 14, 229–30

Pentecostals and, 242

purgation and, 21

sacraments and, 64–65, 123

saints and, 71, 71n30

Teresa of Ávila on, 163–64

theology and, 12, 13n8

Updike on, 207

Graham, Billy, 221–22, 221i, 222s, 314

Grande, Rutilio, 252

greed, 61, 137, 182, 260, 270. *see also* wealth

Greek philosophers, 68, 77–80, 79s, 87. *see also* Plato and Platonic school

Greeks, 123

Greeley, Andrew, 25

Gregory (pope), 110

Gregory IX, 154

Gregory of Nazianzus, 80, 107

Gregory of Nyssa
    fasting, on, 146
    knowledge, on, 86, 86n16
    life of, 83
    Moses, on, 83–86
    mysticism and, 26, 29, 314
    Origen and, 80
    Pseudo-Dionysius and, 91
    relics, on, 70
    women, on, 147

Gregory of Palamas, 91

Gregory the Great, 68–69

Gregory VII, 190

Gregory XI, 153

Guerric of Igny, 148

Guide to Living the Truth (Casey), 112s

Guigo II, 114

Gutiérrez, Gustavo, 245, 254, 258, 259

Guzman, Dominic, 138, 313

H

Hadewijch of Antwerp, 150

Hagia Sophia, 126n13, 129i

Haight, Roger, 256

Hanks, Jr., Billie, 299

Harris, William Wade, 233

health, biological, 7, 239
heaven, 19, 32, 86, 126, 126n13, 269
Heidelberg Catechism (Olevianus and
    Usinus), 205
Henry, Carl F. H., 220
here-and-now, 245–46, 254–55, 270. *see
    also* day-to-day life
hermits (anchorites), 103, 104, 105,
    106–8, 109, 137–38, 293, 294, 311.
    see also Antony of Egypt; Carmelites;
    Carthusians; Cassian, John; Catherine
    of Siena; Damian, Peter; Merton,
    Thomas; Theophan the Recluse
"Hernnhuter," 213, 215
hierarchies, 92
Hilary of Poitiers, 108
Hildegard of Bingen, 150–52, 151i, 314
Hinduism, 28, 30. *see also Prasna
    Upanishad*
historical models, 12–13. *see also* cultural
    and historical contexts
"hocus pocus," 191n2
holiness. *see also* monasticism
    Antony of Egypt and, 103
    Bible and, 45, 47–55, 47n7
    celibacy and, 69
    Eastern Orthodoxy and, 133
    engagement and, 49
    "holiness churches" and, 231
    law and, 59
    life *versus*, 205
    Merton and, 294
    monastic model and, 115
    morality and, 61–62
    Reformers on, 208–9
    saints' graves and, 70
    Teresa of Ávila on, 163
    universality and, 171
holiness churches, 231, 231n1, 232, 234
Holy Spirit. *see also* gifts of the Spirit;
    pneuma (spiritualitas); speaking in
    tongues
    Acts, in, 11, 12i, 54, 229–30
    allegories and, 86
    Augustine on, 88, 311
    Calvin on, 205, 206
    community and, 62
    evangelicals and, 213

faith and, 13, 54, 230
    "holiness churches" and, 231
    Ignatian spirituality and, 174, 181–82
    love and, 15
    Luke's Gospel and, 52
    Parham on, 233
    Paul on, 15
    Pentecostals and, 229, 234, 238
    Puritanism and, 216
    salvation and, 269
    Second Great Awakening and, 219
    Zwingli on, 202
Homily on Psalm 99 (Augustine), 90
Hoover, May Louise, 233
hope. *see also* salvation and redemption
    anagogical meaning and, 84
    eternal life and, 259
    John of the Cross on, 169, 170
    liberation spirituality and, 259
    Luther on, 199
    Moses and, 85
    Pentecostals and, 238, 241
    Theophan on, 131
Hortensius (Cicero), 87
Hosea, 248
Houses of Hospitality, 287–88, 290
Huang-po, 272
human growth and flourishing
    Augustine on, 90
    Bible and, 45
    Daoism and, 278–79, 280
    interreligious dialogue and, 266
    John of the Cross on, 170
    liberation spirituality and, 260
    Origen on, 82
    Plato on, 77
    Renaissance and, 191
    scholars on, 10
human nature and condition. *see also*
    sexual stereotypes; sin; suffering
    Christ and, 155
    divinity and, 16
    liberation spirituality and, 245, 250
    Luther on, 199
    Merton on, 293–94
    Origen on, 82
    Plato on, 77–78
    scholars on, 8

twelve-step spirituality and, 9
wu-yu and, 281
Humbert of Romans, 139
Humiliati, 138, 153, 314
humiliation, 216, 260, 294
humility
    Day and, 290
    Francis of Assisi and, 143, 144, 145
    Ignatian spirituality and, 178
    medieval spirituality and, 155
    Pachomius on, 104
    parable of Pharisee and, 270
    Teresa of Ávila and, 163, 165
    twelve steps of, 111–12*s*
    Warren on, 297*s*–298*s*, 304, 306
Hundredth Year, The (*Centesimus Annus*)
    (John Paul II), 251*s*
Hus, John, 195, 197*cap*
hymnody, 209

I

iconoclasm, 121, 201, 314, 317
iconodulism, 121, 314
icons (*eikōn*), 119–23, 121*n*3, 122*s*, 126,
    127*i*, 129*i*, 132, 201, 314
identity
    baptism and, 125, 212
    biblical themes and, 47
    early church and, 62–64, 72
    Eastern Orthodoxy and, 132–33
    Judaism and, 59
    Merton on, 295–96
Ignatius of Antioch, 63, 63*n*14, 72, 98,
    98*n*1
Ignatius of Loyola and Ignatian spiritual-
    ity. *see also* Spiritual Exercises
    contemplative prayer, on, 179–83
    day-to-day and, 174, 314
    discernment, on, 182–87
    exercises and, 176–79
    Jesuits and, 175*cap*
    life of, 175–76
    modern Christian spirituality and,
        187–88
    service and, 174, 176, 183, 187
    Suscipe and Anima Christi, 179*s*
    union with God and, 38

ignorance, 108, 108*n*20
illumination, 21, 75, 316
image of God (divine likeness), 86
imagination, 180–81
Incarnation of Christ, 16, 119–20, 122,
    147
inclusivism, 264–65, 266, 314
indigenous cultures, 242
individualism. *see also* community; identity
    evangelicals and, 213
    faith and, 7
    inadequacy of, 254
    monasticism and, 100
    mysticism and, 31, 37
    North American and, 260
    Pietism and, 213, 214
    Plato on, 78*i*
    Reformers and, 199, 202, 208, 209
    U.S. evangelism and, 219, 222
indulgences, 192, 194–95, 314
Innocent III, 141
Innocent IV, 160
Institutes (Cassian), 109
Institutes of the Christian Religion (Calvin),
    203, 203*s*, 204, 207
Institution of the First Monks, The, 160
"Instruction on Certain Aspects of the
    Theology of Liberation" (Vatican), 254
intellect (rationality) (reason). *see also*
    concepts; emotional faith; minds
    Aquinas on, 12
    Calvinism and, 207
    Dominicans and, 138–39, 140
    evangelicalism and, 220–22, 222*s*
    Gregory of Nyssa on, 86
    Ignatius of Loyola on, 186–87
    John of the Cross on, 168, 169
    Luther on, 197
    monasticism and, 106–7, 158
    Moody and, 220
    Pentecostals, 235*s*
    Reformers and, 221
interdisciplinary factors, 10
Interior Castle (Teresa of Ávila), 22,
    162–63, 295
interreligious dialogue, 265–67, 281, 293
InterVarsity Christian Fellowship, 225
In the Beauty of the Lilies (Updike), 206–7

Iris Global, 238, 242
Isaac (abba), 110
Isaac of Stella, 148
Isaiah, 18, 247, 248
Islam and Muslims, 28, 30, 118, 293
Israel, 45, 46, 48, 49, 55, 303–4. *see also*
    Judaism

J

James, Letter of, 18, 258
Jeremiah, 18, 247
Jerome, 12, 44, 55, 70
Jesuit Guide, A (Martin), 180–81
Jesuits (Society of Jesus), 38, 175*cap*, 176,
    178, 181
Jesus (Christ). *see also* cross, the; New
    Testament
    action and works and, 185
    baptism of, 125
    Bible and, 43–44
    celibacy, on, 69
    Christocentrism and, 16
    covenant, as, 49, 58, 68, 72, 126
    Daoism and, 276
    faith in, 59, 222, 265, 288
    feminine qualities of, 147–49
    Gospels and, 48–54
    historical, 54, 56
    Ignatius of Loyola on, 178–79
    imitation of, 138*n*1, 144, 178
    Incarnation of, 16, 119–20, 122, 147
    John's Gospel and, 53
    kingdom of God, on, 246–48
    liberation spirituality and, 253–54
    love, on, 15
    monophysite controversy and, 91
    mysticism and, 25
    Origen on, 82
    Pentecostals and, 242
    politics and, 247, 254
    Resurrection of, 16, 50*n*9, 53, 57, 125,
        126, 179, 225, 255
    revelation, as, 42
    self and others, in, 288
    spirituality and, 11
    suffering and, 53, 53*n*13, 178
    talking with, 180–81, 186

Way and, 20
    Word of God and, 43–44
Jesus Prayer, 131–32, 314
Jewish mystics, 30
Jewish War (66-73), 50*n*10, 58–59
Joel, 229
John, First Letter of, 19, 187, 257–58
John of Damascus, 120*n*1
John of the Cross. *see also* Carmelites
    Buddhism and, 275
    Daoism and, 276
    Dark Night, The, 159*s*
    Ignatian spirituality *versus*, 174
    individuality and, 254*n*9
    life of, 166
    mysticism and, 26, 28, 30, 312
    perennialists and, 30
    Schneiders's categories and, 8
    Teresa of Ávila and, 160, 166
    union with God and, 167–70
John Paul II, 251*s*, 252, 253–54, 266, 266*i*,
    280
John Scotus Erugena, 91
John's Gospel. *see also* Gospels
    "born again" and, 212
    Buddhism and, 274
    faith, on, 54
    Logos and, 76, 314
    love and, 15, 53
    Pharisees and, 59
    spirituality of, 11, 52–53
    Word of God and, 42
Johnson, Robert, 208*n*27
John the Baptist, 52
John XXIII, 251*s*
Jokin, Keizann, 273
Jordan of Saxony, 139
joy
    action and works and, 199
    confession and, 100
    consolation and, 184
    contemplation and, 81
    Day on, 286, 290
    evangelicals and, 226
    Francis of Assisi and, 145
    freedom and, 200
    Holy Spirit and, 15
    humility and, 112*s*

Ignatius of Loyola and, 175
liberation spirituality and, 259
Matthew's Gospel on, 54
Pentecostals and, 242
Pilgrim's Progress and, 214
prayer and, 132
sexual metaphors and, 149
Syncletica on, 101*s*
Warren on, 303
wives and, 68
Zen Buddhism and, 272
Judaism. *see also* Israel; Old Testament
apocalypticism and, 246
covenants and, 46–47
Darby on, 231
early church and, 58–59, 68, 190
image of God and, 86
Justin and, 76*n*3
Matthew's Gospel and, 49, 58
Rabbinic, 59, 316
Romans and, 59–60
sanctuaries and, 127
judging, 270–71
Julian of Norwich, 32, 148
Julius II, 192
justice
biblical themes and, 46
characterized, 18
Day and, 306
Day on, 287
encyclicals and, 251*s*–252
God's, 193–94, 205
Isaiah and, 247
Israel/Palestinians and, 304
kingdom of God and, 247–49
Latin America and, 250, 252
liberation spirituality and, 254, 256
Luke's Gospel and, 54
patristic era and, 75
preaching and, 274
Justin, 76, 76*n*3

K

Kagame, Paul, 296
Kallistos of Diokleia, 133
Karlgaard, Rich, 303
Karlstadt, Andreas, 195–96

kataphatic mysticism
Augustine and, 90
authentic, 33–35
Carmelites and, 159
case study, 35–37
characterized, 29, 314
Daoism and, 276–77
examples of, 30, 32–33
perennialism and, 30
Pseudo-Dionysius and, 93
rarity of, 158
Teresa of Ávila and, 162, 165
Katz, Stephen, 30, 31
Kil, Sun Ju, 233
kingdom of God. *see also* apocalypticism;
eschatology
Buddhism and, 274
celibacy and, 69, 72
children and, 62–63
community and, 205, 207–8
eschatological tension and, 255
Gospels and, 49, 51–52
justice and, 247–49
liberation spirituality and, 255–56
mysticism and, 25
Old Testament and, 58
Pentecostals and, 235, 241
politics and, 50
kisses, spiritual, 22, 149
knowledge of God, 89–90, 93, 105, 107, 170,
277. *see also* concepts; union with God
koans, 273, 273*s*, 274

L

Laborum Exercens (*On Human Work*)
(John Paul II), 251*s*
Ladder of Divine Ascent, The (Climacus),
21–22
Ladder of Spiritual Love (Rusbroeck), 22
LaHaye, Timothy, 223
language, 43*s*, 75, 240
Laozi (Lao Tzu), 276
Large Catechism (Luther), 198
Last Supper, 126
Latin America, 249–54, 260
Latin American Bishops Conference
(CELAM), 250–51, 256–57, 312

Latin Church, 129
latreia (worship), 121
lauds (*prime*) (Psalms), 113
law, the, 46, 49, 59, 83, 190, 279, 280. *see also* Torah
Lax, Robert, 291, 292
Lazarus, 247
lectio divina (divine reading), 113–14, 179
leftists, 246
Leipzig debate, 195–96
leitourgia (liturgy), 123
Leo X, 192, 195
Leo XIII, 252, 287
Letter of Barnabas, 61
Letter on Religious Life (Humbert), 139
Leviticus, Book of, 55
Lewis, Elizabeth Kay, 299, 304, 306
liberation spirituality. *see also* Chrysostom, John; freedom (liberation); Gutiérrez, Gustavo
    Bible and, 245–49
    Catholic Church and, 250–54
    characteristics of, 260
    eschatology and, 255–56
    freedom and, 258
    global, 259–60
    here-and-now and, 245–46
    hope and joy and, 259
    kingdom of God and, 246–48, 255–56
    Latin America and, 249–50
    poor, the and, 256–58, 260
    spiritual childhood and, 259
    tradition and, 245–46, 254–55
    United States and, 260
Liber vitae meritorum (*Book of Life's Merits*) (Hildegard of Bingen), 151
Life of Antony, The (Athanasius), 102, 102n9, 106–8, 107, 311
Life of Christ, The (Ludolph of Saxony), 175
Life of Moses, The (Gregory of Nyssa), 26, 83, 84
light metaphor
    allegory of cave and, 77
    Antony of Egypt and, 102
    Augustine and, 89–90
    Buddhism and, 273
    Calvin and, 206
    Dionysius and, 92

early church and, 65
Eastern Orthodoxy and, 121, 124, 125, 128, 130
Francis of Assisi and, 142s–143s
Gregory of Nyssa and, 86
Ignatian discernment and, 182–83, 184, 185
Israel and, 48
John, First Letter of and, 257–58, 264
John of the Cross and, 159s
John's Gospel and, 52, 53
Origen and, 86n16
prophecy and, 247
way of, 20, 61
yin/yang and, 278, 317
Zen koan and, 273s
Zwingli's prayer and, 202s
listlessness (*acedia*), 107–8
literary genres, 44
Little Brothers (Friars Minor), 140n4
little way, 275–76
liturgical prayer, 123–25, 127–28
liturgies, 91, 92, 198, 238. *see also* baptism *and other liturgies*
Liturgy of the Hours (*Divine Office*), 65, 113, 115, 160
Lives of the Desert Fathers (*Vitae Patrum*), 101n7
Living Flame of Love, The (John of the Cross), 174
Logos, 76, 77, 79s, 81, 82, 276, 277, 314
Longer Rules (Basil), 106n14
Long Loneliness, The (Day), 305
Lord's Supper, 62i, 63, 213. *see also* Eucharist
love
    apatheia and, 66
    Aquinas on, 140
    Augustine on, 90–91
    Day on, 288–89
    Evagrius on, 107
    God and, 15, 43s, 90–91
    Holy Spirit and, 15
    Ignatius of Loyola on, 178–79
    John of the Cross on, 169, 170
    John's Gospel and, 15, 53
    knowledge and, 90
    Origen on, 83

Teresa of Ávila on, 164
Trinity and, 17
wound of, 165
Ludolph of Saxony, 175
Luke's Gospel, 11, 51–52, 54, 246–47, 248.
   see also Gospels
Luther, Martin. *see also* ninety-five theses;
   Reformers
   Calvin and, 203
   Eucharist and, 64s, 196
   freedom, on, 15
   grace, on, 193–94, 199
   independent communion and, 198
   indulgences and, 194–95
   life of, 192–93, 192n4
   middle class and, 191
   overview, 315
   reform activities of, 195–98, 197i
   spiritual teachings of, 199–200s
   Zwingli *versus*, 201–2
Lutheranism, 208, 213, 315

M

Macrina, 83, 105
Mahayana Buddhism, 271–72, 277
Mamaea, Julia, 80
Manicheism, 87, 87n18
Marburg Colloquy, 202
Margaret, 67i
Markey, John, 260
Mark's Gospel, 49–51, 50nn9,10, 54, 247.
   see also Gospels
marriage, 67–68, 67n19, 68–69, 101. *see
   also* nuptial metaphors; patriarchal
   culture; virginity (celibacy)
Martha and Martha story, 110
Martin, James, 180–81
Martin of Tours, 108–9
martyrdom, 60, 61, 70, 76n1, 80, 98, 258,
   287
Marx, Karl and Marxism, 249, 253, 254,
   315
Mary, Virgin, 32, 35–37, 36i, 51, 128,
   129–30, 133
Mary of Egypt, 98–99, 100
Mater et Magistra (*Mother and Teacher*)
   (John XXIII), 251s

material world, 121–22, 138, 255, 312
Matēr Theou, 129i
Matoes, Abba, 100
Matthew's Gospel, 48–49, 51, 54, 58. *see
   also* Gospels
Maurin, Peter, 287, 288
Maximus the Confessor, 66, 91
McCain, John, 223
McGinn, Bernard, 30–31, 32
Mcquarrie, John, 7
Mechtild of Magdeburg, 154
medieval piety, Western
   cultural context and, 136–37
   Dominican spirituality, 138–40
   feminine affective piety and, 146–50
   feudalism and, 136
   Franciscan spirituality, 140–46,
      142s–143s, 144i
   hermits and heretics and, 137–38
   patristic era and, 155
   women and, 150–54
meditatio, 114, 179
meditation, 18, 20, 168, 289–90, 289s. *see
   also* contemplation; Spiritual Exercises
   (Ignatius of Loyola)
"Meditation on Two Standards, A"
   (Ignatius of Loyola), 178
Meditations (Aurelius), 76
Mega-Church Movement, 302–4, 306
Melanchthon, Philip, 198
mendicants, 138, 139
Merton, Thomas, 290–96, 291i, 305, 306
Messages of Biblical Spirituality (Osiek,
   ed.), 47n7
messiah, 25, 46, 59, 180, 247
metaphors, 43s, 83, 112–13, 148–49,
   268–69
Methodism, 213, 214–15, 230–31, 233,
   234, 315, 317
Micah, 248
Milan, 87
Miller, Donald, 303n34
minds, 268–69, 270–71, 272, 273,
   274, 279. *see also* concepts; intellect
   (rationality) (reason)
miracles, 35–36i, 70, 237, 237n4, 241
modern Christian spirituality. *see also*
   Day, Dorothy; evangelicals *and others*;

Mega-Church Movement; Merton,
   Thomas; Warren, Rick
   Benedict's steps and, 112s
   biblical interpretation and, 44
   Carmelites and, 170–71
   cultural and historical contexts and, 13
   Ignatius of Loyola and, 187–88
   marriage and, 69
   saints and, 71s
   three witnesses and, 305–6
   U.S. evangelicalism and, 219–24
Moloney, Francis, 50n10
monachos, 97
monarchical period, 246
monarchy, 45
monastery at Cassino, 111
monastery of St. Catherine, 104i
monasticism. see also Carmelites and other
   orders; cenobitism; Mary of Egypt and
   other monks; prayers
   Augustine and, 88
   Basil the Great and, 311
   Benedict of Nursia and, 311
   Calvin on, 205
   capitalism and, 137
   Daoism and, 280–81
   early, 97–98
   Gilson and, 292–94
   Gregory of Nyssa and, 83
   harlots of the desert and, 98–101s
   intellect and, 106, 107
   Merton and, 305
   model, as, 100, 114–15
   Origen and, 80
   path and, 22
   Plato and, 146
   Pseudo-Dionysius on, 92
   repentance and, 99, 100
   western, 108–14
Monica, 69–70, 87, 89
monophysite controversy, 91
Montgomery, Carrie Judd, 231
Moody, Dwight L., 220, 232
morality, 137, 279–80
Moral Majority, 223
moral rigor. see also asceticism; passions
   apatheia and, 66
   Bible and, 84

early church and, 61–62, 65–69
   Finney and, 220
   Francis of Assisi and, 142
   Origen on, 82
   Patristic Era and, 65
   U.S. evangelicalism and, 222
   Whitefield and, 218, 218n8
Moses, 26, 46, 48, 49, 83–86, 101s, 140
Moses in Pharaoh's House (Markey), 260
Mother and Teacher (Mater et Magistra)
   (John XXIII), 251s
Mother Teresa of Calcutta, 54n14
Mukti Mission (India), 232
Müller, Gerhard, 254
mutualism, 265, 316
mysteries. see Incarnation of Christ and
   other mysteries; mysticism
mystērion, 25
Mystical Theology (Pseudo-Dionysius), 91
mysticism. see also apophatic mysticism;
   contemplation; kataphatic experiences;
   perennialism; Teresa of Ávila and other
   mystics; union with God (unitive way)
   Augustine of Hippo and, 88–91
   authenticity and, 34
   Buddhism and, 274
   Carmelite, 171, 312
   Cassian and, 110
   characterized, 25–31
   church life and, 316
   Daoism and, 276
   examples, 27–28, 37–38, 78–79
   Gregory of Nyssa and, 84–86, 314
   Merton and, 290, 305
   monasticism and, 113–14
   Origen and, 81–83
   overview, 37–38
   patristic era and, 75
   Spanish, 160
   union with God and, 26, 27–28, 31, 38,
      75, 295
   universality and, 27–37, 31s
Mysticism (Underhill), 29

N

Nadal, Jerónimo, 176
Nagarjuna, 271–72, 315

National Association of Evangelicals (NAE), 225
Native American spiritualities, 9, 30
natural law, 280
natural world, 278*cap. see also* creation
Neoplatonism, 91–92, 107
Nero, 50, 60
Netanyahu, Benjamin, 303–4
Netherlands, 206
new creation, 125
New Testament. *see also* early church; Gospels; Jesus (Christ); Paul of Tarsus; Revelation, Book of *and other books*
    angels and, 238
    biblical themes and, 45
    covenants and, 46
    Luther's translation of, 198
    Pseudo-Dionysius and, 92
    salvation and, 269, 269*n*4
    Zwingli and, 201
Nicaea II (Seventh Ecumenical Council), 121–22, 121*n*3
Nicaragua, 250
Nicodemus, 212
night of the senses/spirit, 167–70
9/11 attacks, 223–24
Ninety-Five Theses, 195–98, 315
nirvana, 270, 271–72
Noffke, Suzanne, 152–53
non-Christian religions, 264
none, 113
Norbert, 138, 316
numerology, 60
nuptial metaphors, 149–50, 149*n*18, 152, 158, 159*s*, 164, 165, 166, 170. *see also* bride metaphors

O

Obama, Barack, 297*s*–298*s*
obedience, 146, 174
O'Connor, Kathleen, 47*n*7
Old Testament (Hebrew Bible). *see also* prophecy and prophets; Torah
    Christian spirituality and, 45–47
    early church and, 68
    icons and, 120, 120*n*2
    John's Gospel and, 52–53

Judaism and, 42
    kingdom of God and, 58
    liturgy and, 123
    love and, 15
    nuptial metaphors and, 149, 149*n*18
    path and, 22
Olevianus, Casper, 205
On Christian Liberty (Luther), 15, 196, 200
"oneness gospel," 233–34
On Human Work (*Laborum Exercens*) (John Paul II), 251*s*
On Seeing God (Augustine), 89
On Social Concern (*Sollicitudo Rei Socialis*) (John Paul II), 251*s*, 252
On the Babylonian Captivity of the Church (Luther), 196
On the Condition of Labor (*Rerum Novarum*) (Leo XII), 252, 287
On the Development of Peoples (*Populorum Progressio*) (Paul VI), 251*s*, 253
On the Scandal of the Church (*De Scandalis Ecclesiae*) (Gilbert of Tournai), 154
On the Side of the Poor: Liberation Theology, Theology of the Church (Gutiérrez and Müller), 254
ora et labora, 113
Oral Roberts University, 234
oratio, 114, 179
Order of Penitents, 65, 194
Order of Preachers (Dominicans), 138–40, 152, 160, 176, 190
Origen
    background, 80–81
    Bible, on, 93–94
    Evagrius and, 107
    light and, 86*n*16
    martyrdom of father and, 80, 80*n*8
    material world and, 121
    mysticism and, 81–83, 315
    Plato and, 81, 315
    prayer, on, 18
    sins, on, 100
Ortega, Danial, 250

P

Pace of Augsburg, 198
Pachomius, 104–5, 315. *see also* cenobitism

paganism, 85, 120
Palemon, 104
Palladius of Galatia, 101
pantocratōr, 126
papal bull, Luther's burning of, 196, 197*i*
parables, 51–52
Parham, Charles Fox, 233
paschal mystery, 274
passions. *see also apatheia;* asceticism;
    moral rigor; suffering; virginity
    (celibacy)
    ammas in the desert and, 101*s*
    asceticism and, 65–66
    Augustine and, 88
    Gregory of Nyssa on, 86
    Mary of Egypt and, 99
    monasticism and, 22
    mysticism and, 120
    Origen on, 82
    Plato on, 78
    Stoics on, 79*s*
    suffering and, 65*n*17
path, 21–22
patriarchal culture, 44, 69, 97, 260. *see also*
    marriage; women, authoritative
patriarchs, 22
patristic era. *see also* Augustine of
    Hippo; Gregory of Nyssa; Origen;
    Pseudo-Dionysius
    Bible and, 313
    community and, 64–65
    contemplative prayer and, 294
    defined, 58, 315
    icons and, 120
    intellectual life and, 75–77
    legacy of, 93–94
    Luther and, 195
    medieval world and, 155
    monasticism and, 106
    moral rigor and, 72
    overviews, 75, 97
    Plato and, 94, 315
    Pseudo-Dionysius and, 91
    Renaissance and, 191
    saints and, 70–71
    souls, on, 80
    Virgin Mary and, 130
    women and, 146

patristic period, 75–96, 146
patrons, 70–71
patterns of life, 47
Paul of Tarsus. *see also* Galatians, Letter to
    and other letters
    Augustine and, 88
    baptism, on, 125
    bodies, on, 81*n*10
    celibacy, on, 66–68, 67*n*1
    Christocentrism and, 15–16
    community, on, 17, 288*n*9
    discernment and, 183
    divinization, on, 19
    experiences of, 47*n*7
    faith, on, 14–15
    freedom, on, 200, 258
    grace and, 14
    Holy Spirit, on, 229–30
    intellect and, 140
    Judaism and, 58
    law and, 59, 190*n*1
    Luther and, 193–94
    martyrdom of, 50
    mysticism, on, 26
    nuptial metaphors and, 149
    Peter and, 190
    prayers, on, 130
    Pseudo-Dionysius and, 91
    salvation, on, 269
    second coming, on, 255*n*10
    speaking in tongues, on, 236
    spirituality, on, 11
    thorn in the flesh and, 304
    virtues, on, 169
Paul VI, 251*s*, 252, 253
P.E.A.C.E. plan, 296, 302
Pelagius, 193
penances, 195
Pentecostals
    Bible and, 229–30
    characteristics of, 235, 236–40, 242
    charismatic renewal and, 234–35*s*
    concerns and, 240–41
    cultural and historical context, 230–32
    evangelicalism and, 212
    gifts and, 230
    kataphatic experience and, 32
    origins of, 232–34

prosperity preaching and, 239–40, 241,
316
second coming and, 255
penthos, 100, 315
perennialism, 29, 30–32, 315
"perfection," 12
Perpetua, 70
personal and communal engagement, 47
Peter, 50, 67*n*19, 190, 229, 238
Peter, Second Letter of, 19, 50
petitionary prayer, 18
Pharisees, 58–59, 212, 270–71, 316
Philippians, letter to, 16
Philipp I of Hesse, 202
Philip the apostle, 229
physikē, 107
Pia Desideria (Pious Desires) (Spener),
213
Pietism, 212–14, 230, 315
evangelicalism and, 216
piety, 12. *see also* medieval piety, Western
Pilgrim Holiness Church, 231*n*1
Pilgrim's Journey, A (Ignatius of Loyola),
175, 176
Pilgrim's Progress (Bunyan), 214
Pious Desires (*Pia Desideria*) (Spener),
213
Pius XI, 251*s*
Plato and Platonic school
Augustine and, 87, 89–90
God, on, 90
icons and, 121
Incarnation and, 119–20
monasticism and, 146
Origen and, 81, 315
overview, 76–80, 79*s*
patristic legacy and, 94, 315
Pseudo-Dionysius and, 91–92
pleasure, 68–69
Plotinus, 27, 78–79, 82
pluralism, 265, 315
pneuma (*spiritualitas*), 11, 12, 316
poets, 22
Polanco, Juan de, 176
politics
apostolic church and, 71
Catherine of Siena and, 153
Catholic Church and, 250–51

Daoism and, 278
Day and, 185–86, 287*cap*
evangelicals and, 220–21, 223–24, 303–4
Jesus and, 247, 254
kingdom of God and, 50
Latin American, 250
Merton and, 293, 294–95
Pentecostals and, 240
Revelation and, 60
Pontifical Council for Interreligious
Dialogue, 265–67
poor, the. *see* poverty and the poor
popes and Rome, 153, 166, 190, 191, 192,
194, 195, 198. *see also* Francis I *and
other popes*
Populorum Progressio (*On the Development
of Peoples*) (Paul VI), 251*s*, 253
Porete, Marguerite, 37–38
positive confession, 239, 316
postmodern mutualism, 265, 316
poverty and the poor. *see also* evangelical
counsels; justice; service; solidarity;
wealth
Augustine and, 88, 108
Beguines and, 153
Catherine of Siena and, 152
challenge of, 305
Chrysostom and, 109
Damian and, 315
Day and, 287–88
Dominicans and, 138
Francis of Assisi and, 13, 141, 142, 144,
145–46, 313
freedom and, 258
Isaiah on, 18
kingdom of God and, 246–47
liberation spirituality and, 246, 249,
250, 252, 256–58, 259, 260
Luke's Gospel and, 51–52
medieval period and, 137, 138, 155
patristic era and, 75
Pentecostals and, 240
preferential option for, 251
Romero and, 252–53, 253*cap*, 316
Warren and, 296, 302, 303, 304
practice, Christian, 19–22
praktikē, 107
Prasna Upanishad, 28

Prat, Antoine du, 192*n*3
prayer. *see also* contemplation; liturgical
prayer; mysticism
    Antony of Egypt and, 102, 103
    Augustine and, 89
    biblical themes and, 46
    Calvin's, 207*s*
    Cassian on, 110
    "centering," 171
    Day and, 289–90, 289*s*
    Dominicans and, 140
    Eastern Orthodox, 128*n*15, 130–31,
      132, 133
    Evagrius on, 107, 108
    Francis of Assisi's, 142*s*–143*s*
    Gilson and, 291
    icons and, 123
    Ignatian spirituality and, 185
    Ignatius of Loyola on, 179–82
    Luther's Sacristy, 200*s*
    mental, 164, 168
    Merton and, 292, 293, 294–96, *295*s
    monasticism and, 113–14
    mysticism and, 28
    Origen on, 82
    overview, 18
    path and, 22
    patristic era and, 97
    Pentecostals and, 241
    purgation and, 21
    quiet, of, 164
    recollection, of, 164
    Syncletica on, 101*s*
    Teresa of Ávila on, 163
    union, of, 164
    Warren's, 297*s*–298*s*
    Zwingli's, 202*s*
Prayer of Jabez, The (Wilkenson), 241
preaching
    criticisms of, 190
    Dominicans and, 139
    evangelicals and, 213, 216
    Franciscans and, 141–42
    Hildegard of Bingen and, 152
    justice and, 274
    Pentecostals and, 236
    prosperity, 239–40, 241, 316
    Zwingli and, 201

predestination. *see* double predestination;
    free will
preferential option for the poor, 251, 260
premillennialism, 231–32, 233, 234, 241,
    316
Premonstratensians, 138, 316
Presbyterians, 213
pride, 104, 105, 107, 124, 137, 178, 269,
    270, 294. *see also* humility
prime (lauds) (Psalms), 113
printer press, 191
"proficient," 168
prophecy and prophets, 45, 46, 149, 230,
    236, 237, 238, 247. *see also* Amos *and*
    other prophets
prosperity preaching, 239–40, 241, 316
Protestant Ethic and the Spirit of Capital-
    ism, The (Weber), 206, 316
Protestantism, 64*s*, 71*s*, 129, 216, 224, 231,
    234, 265. *see also* Methodism *and other*
    sects; Reformers
Proverbs, Book of, 55
psalms, 106, 107, 113, 115, 302, 306
Psalms *(prime) (lauds)*, 113
Pseudo-Dionysius, 91–93, 94, 316
psychology, 107–8, 171
purgation, 21, 75, 316
Puritanism, 212, 216
Purpose Driven Church, The (Warren), 300,
    301
Purpose-Driven Life, The (Warren), 301, 303

Q

Quadregesimo Anno (After Forty Years)
    (Pius XI), 251*s*

R

Rabbinic Judaism, 59, 316
Ramabai, Pandita Sarasvati, 232
Ranaghan, Kevin, 235
Raply to Sadoleto (Calvin), 204
rapture, 162
rationality. *see* intellect
Reagan, Ronald, 223, 250
reality, 37, 77–78, 271, 272, 273, 277,
    278–79

real presence, 64s

reason. *see* intellect

redemption. *see* salvation and redemption

Reformed tradition, 200–203, 200n15, 202s, 317

Reformers. *see also* Calvin, John; Luther, Martin; Protestantism; Zwingli, Ulrich
historical background and, 190–92
intellect and, 221
Protestant spirituality and, 208–9
works, on, 208

Regent University, 234

Regula Magistri (*Rule of the Master*), 110

relevancy, 245

relics, 70

Religious Right, 223–25

Renaissance, 191, 200n16

repentance, 98, 99, 100

Republic, The (Plato), 77

Republican Party, 223

Rerum Novarum (*On the Condition of Labor*) (Leo XII), 252, 287

Restorationism, 213, 213n1

resurrection of bodies, 69, 70, 80, 81, 81n10, 259, 289s

Resurrection of Christ, 16, 50n9, 53, 57, 125, 126, 179, 225, 255

revelation, 12, 42–44, 132, 151, 169, 237, 312

Revelation, Book of, 48i, 60–61, 241

revivals, 216–17, 221, 230–31, 232, 233, 296, 299, 313

Révue d'ascétique et de mystique (*Révue d'histoire de la spiritualité*), 12

Richard of Saint Victor, 22

Rich Christians in an Age of Hunger (Sider), 240

righteousness, 187

Rinzai school of Zen, 273

Roberts, Oral, 234, 239

Robertson, Pat, 223, 224, 234

Rock of Ages, Cleft for Me (hymn), 225

Romanian, 87

Romans, Letter to, 236

Rome and papacy, 153, 166, 190, 191, 192, 194, 195, 198. *see also* Francis I *and other popes*

Rome and Romans, 50, 58, 59–60, 70–71, 75–77, 80, 80n8, 87. *see also* Nero *and other Romans*

Romero, Oscar, 252–53, 252i, 258, 316

Romney, Mitt, 223

Rublev, Andrei, 17i

Rule of Benedict, The (Benedict), 111–14

Rule of the Master (*Regula Magistri*), 110

Rumi, Jalāl ad-Dīn Muhammad, 28

Rusbroeck, John, 22

Russians, 126n13, 131–32, 232

Rwanda, 296

S

Sacrament of Penance (Confession), 194–95

sacraments, 64–65, 91, 120, 123, 146, 196, 316. *see also* Eucharist *and other sacraments*

sacrifice, 45, 46, 59–60, 126, 131, 183, 248, 275

Saddleback church, 296, 300–301, 302–3, 303n34

Sadduccees, 58n1

Sadoleto, Jacopo, 203–4

Saint Peter's Basilica, 192, 195

saints, 69–71, 71n30, 71s, 129, 146, 175, 201. *see also* Teresa of Ávila *and other saints*

salvation and redemption. *see also* grace; sin
Calvin on, 205
defined, 45
early church and, 72
exclusivism and, 264, 265
free will and, 193
God's program for, 255
grace, on, 14
Holy Spirit and, 269
Luke's Gospel and, 51
Origen on, 80–81, 82
Pentecostals and, 239
Pietism and, 214
Reformers and, 208
sin and, 65

samsara, 271–72

San Domiano chapel, 140n4

Sarah, 101
Sayings of the Desert Fathers, The, 101
Schneiders, Sandra, 8, 9–10, 11. *see also* ultimate horizon
scholars of spirituality, 7–11, 11*s*, 22, 94, 171, 240, 265
Scholastica, 111, 111*i*
science, 22, 45
Scofield Reference Bible, 232
Scopes trial, 220
Scots Confession, 206
second coming, 213, 219, 230, 231, 232, 235
Second Council of Constantinople, 80
Second Council of Orange, 193
Second Diet of Speyer, 198
Second Great Awakening, 219–20
second sight, 105
Second Vatican Council, 17, 42–44, 312
self, the, 272, 295–96
Septuagint, 123
service
    Antony of Egypt and, 103
    apatheia and, 82
    Basil and, 105
    Beguines and, 153
    Carmelites and, 158
    Day and, 287–88, 289, 305
    Francis of Assisi and, 37, 141–42
    holiness and, 49
    Ignatian spirituality and, 174, 176, 183, 187
    monasticism and, 108, 113
    Teresa of Ávila and, 163, 166
    union with God and, 75
    virginity and, 66
    Warren and, 299, 301
700 Club (TV show), 223
Seven Storey Mountain, The (Merton), 293, 306
Seventh Ecumenical Council (Nicaea II), 121–22, 121*n*3
sext, 113
sexuality, 68–69, 82, 149–50, 155, 184, 293–94. *see also* feminine sexual mysticism; nuptial metaphors; virginity (celibacy)
sexual stereotypes, 146–47

Seymour, William J., 233
shame, 182
Sheldrake, Philip, 154
Shepherd of Hermas, 61
Shintoism, 30
Shorter Rules (Basil), 106*n*14
Sider, Ron, 240
Signs and Wonders (Alexander), 236
Simon Peter, 25–26
Simon the magician, 229
Simplicianus, 87, 102
Simpson, A. B., 231
sin. *see also* grace
    allegories and, 84
    asceticism and, 68
    Augustine on, 88
    biblical themes and, 45
    Buddhism and, 270
    Calvinism and, 206
    defined, 45
    early church and, 72
    Eastern Orthodoxy and, 125, 128
    freedom and, 14–15
    free will and, 193
    God's justice and, 205
    Graham on, 222
    holiness churches and, 234
    human condition and, 54, 257
    Ignatius of Loyola on, 177, 177*n*4
    kingdom of God and, 248
    Luther on, 199
    marriage and, 67, 68
    Middle Ages and, 195
    monks and, 98, 100
    Order of Penitents and, 194
    Origen on, 80–81
    original, 88
    Patristic Era and, 65
    Pentecostals and, 233
    Romero on, 252–53
    seven deadly, 137
    Teresa of Ávila on, 163, 165
Sinners in the Hands of an Angry God (Edwards), 217–18
slavery, 15, 44, 86, 209, 224
Small Catechism (Luther), 198, 203
socialism, 246, 249, 250, 252, 286, 286*n*4
Social Justice Encyclicals, 251*s*–252

Society of Jesus (Jesuits), 38, 175*cap*, 176, 178, 181

Soelle, Dorothee, 37, 259

solidarity, 52, 256–57, 260

Sollicitudo Rei Socialis (*On Social Concern*) (John Paul II), 251*s*, 252

Song of Songs, 149

sortes apostolicae, 140*n*4

Soto school of Zen, 273

souls. *see also* contemplation; union with God
  allegories and, 83
  Cassian on, 110
  early American engraving of, 78*i*
  Evagrius on, 107
  Francis of Assisi on, 146
  Greek philosophers on, 78–79, 79*s*
  Gregory of Nyssa on, 86
  Origen on, 80–81, 82
  patristic era and, 80
  prayer and, 130
  Teresa of Ávila and, 162–63, 165–66

Southern Baptist Convention, 212, 220, 225, 303. *see also* Warren, Rick

Spain, 160, 166, 192

Sparks, Kenton, 240–41

speaking in tongues, 232, 233, 234, 235, 235*s*, 236

Spener, Philip Jakob, 213

Spirit of Medieval Philosophy, The (Gilson), 291

"spiritual but not religious," 9

spiritual core, 8

Spiritual Exercises (Ignatius of Loyola), 175*i*, 176–79, 184, 185, 316

spiritualitas (*pneuma*), 11, 12, 316

spiritualite, 12

spirituality, Christian. *see also* Bible, the; modern Christian spirituality; mysticism
  defined, 7–11
  essential characteristics of, 14–19
  field of study, as, 11–14
  overviews, 22–23, 285
  religion and, 9*s*
  themes, recurrent, 20–22
  variability and, 305

Spirituality of Paul, The (Tobin), 47*n*7

Stephen, 70

stigmata, 143–45, 317

stillness, 268–69, 292

Stoddard, Solomon, 216, 217

Stoicism, 76, 79*s*

storytelling, 238

Success-N-Life, 240

suffering. *see also* passions; poverty and the poor
  Buddhism and, 270
  consolation and, 181, 184
  crucifixion and, 53
  feminine piety and, 147
  God and, 16
  Gospels on, 51, 53, 54
  Jesus and, 53, 53*n*13, 178
  John of the Cross on, 170
  justice and, 18
  liberation spirituality and, 255
  passions and, 65*n*17
  sexuality and, 294
  Teresa of Ávila and, 165–66

super-sensible realities, 7

Suscipe and Anima Christi, 179*s*

Switzerland, 200–203, 202*s*, 203–4, 204–5, 214

symbols, 123, 213

Symmacus, 87

Syncletica, 101

Syria, 97, 103

T

Talmud, 68

Teaching (*Didache*) *of the Twelve Apostles*, 20

tears, spiritual, 22, 100, 100*n*6, 101*s*, 147

televangelists, 240

Temple, Monarchy and Word of God (Endres), 47*n*7

Temple in Jerusalem, 58–59, 316

Teresa of Ávila, 26, 32, 160–66, 165–66, 254*n*9, 312, 317. *see also* Carmelites; *Interior Castle*

Teresa of Calcutta, 54*n*14

terse, 113

Tertullian, 68

Theodore the Studite, 122

theologia, 107

theology, 12, 171, 231–32, 260, 266, 311
Theophan the Recluse, 130
theōsis. see divinization
Theravada Buddhism, 266, 271–73*s*
Thérèse of Lisieux, 275–76, 289*s*
thick description, 14
Three Ages of the Interior Life, The
    (Garrigou-Lagrange), 170–71
three-fold pattern, 21
Tilton, Robert, 240
Timothy 2, 44
Tobey, Berkeley, 286
Tobin, Thomas, 47*n*7
"tonsure," 125
Torah, 49, 50, 190, 317. *see also* law, the
Torrey, Samuel, 216, 221
tradition, 42, 42*n*1, 240–41, 245–46,
    254–55, 317
Trappist Order, 292, 293
Trier Synod, 151
Trinity
    art and, 17*i*
    characterized, 16–17, 317
    Eastern Orthodoxy and, 128, 128*n*15,
        130
    evangelicals and, 225
    feminine qualities of, 148
    Logos and, 314
    mystical experiences and, 30
    Pentecostals and, 233–34
    prayers and, 128, 128*n*15
    Teresa of Ávila and, 165
Tugwell, Simon, 139
T.U.L.I.P, 206–7, 317
Twelve Dynamic Bible Study Methods for
    Laity (Hanks, Warren and Watts), 299
twelve-step spiritualities, 8–9

U

ultimate horizon, 8, 18–19
Ultimate Reality, 27, 265. *see also*
    mysticism
Underhill, Evelyn, 29–30, 31, 32
Uneasy Conscience of Modern Fundamental-
    ism (Henry), 220
union with God (unitive way). *see also*
    divinization (*theōsis*); mysticism

apophatic mysticism and, 75
Augustine on, 89, 90–91
Buddhism and, 275, 276
Carmelites and, 158, 159*s*
Cassian on, 110
Christian path and, 316
contemplation and, 80
Diego and, 26
Eucharist and, 126
Francis of Assisi on, 143*s*
Gregory of Nyssa and, 84
heaven and, 19
John of the Cross on, 167–70, 168*i*
Merton and, 292, 293, 294–95, 296
Origen on, 82–83
path and, 22
Plotinus on, 78–79
Pseudo-Dionysius on, 91–92, 93
Revelation, Book of, and, 61
sexual metaphors and, 149–50
Spanish piety and, 160
Teresa of Ávila and, 162, 164–65,
    164*n*4
three-fold pattern and, 21–22
United Church of Christ, 208
United States and Americans. *see also*
    Edwards, Jonathan *and other Americans*
    born again Christians and, 212
    evangelicals and, 216–24, 220–21,
        223–24, 303–4
    Latin America and, 249, 250
    liberation spirituality and, 260
    mystical experiences and, 25
    prosperity preaching and, 239–40
    Protestantism and, 209
unity of church, 63, 205
unity of God, 265
Universal Church of God's Kingdom, 241
universality, 10, 14, 27–37, 31*s*, 55, 171. *see*
    also diversity; unity of church
Updike, John, 206–7
Usinus, Zacharius, 205

V

Vatican II, 17, 42–44, 312
veneration (*douleia*), 121
vespers, 113

Victory Scripture Memory Series (Hanks, Warren and Watts), 299
virginity (celibacy), 66–69, 67*i*, 69, 72, 88, 97, 115, 152, 209. *see also* evangelical counsels; marriage; sexuality
Virgin Mary, 32, 35–37, 36*i*, 51, 128, 129–30, 133
virtues, 22, 107, 110, 169. *see also* justice *and other virtues;* morality
Vladimir of Kiev, 126*n*13
Vocabulary of Theology (Altenstaig), 12
Vulgate, the, 11–12
vulnerability, 145, 147, 155, 250, 260, 294, 304

W

Wakefield, Gordon, 7
Waldensians, 138, 153, 317
Walsh, Dan, 292
Ward, Benedicta, 98, 98*n*2
Warren, Rick, 224*n*11, 296–304, 297*s*–298*s*, 305
Watts, Wayne, 299
Way, the, 20
Way of the Pilgrim, The (anonymous), 131–32
wealth. *see also* economic factors; greed; indulgences; poverty and the poor
    Antony of Egypt and, 102
    Beguines and, 154
    Humiliati/Waldensians and, 138
    kingdom of God and, 246–47
    Latin America and, 249–50
    Leo XIII on, 252
    Mary of Egypt and, 98
    positive confession and, 239, 316
    prosperity preaching and, 239–40, 241, 316
    Social Justice Encyclicals and, 251*s*
    solidarity and, 260
    Teresa of Ávila and, 163
    Warren and, 301–2, 304
Weber, Max, 206, 316
Wesley, Charles, 214–15, 218, 221, 317
Wesley, John, 214–15, 218, 221
Whitefield, George, 215, 218–19, 218*nn*7–8, 221, 317
Wigglesworth, Smith, 239

Wilkenson, Bruce, 240
William of St. Thierry, 148
Williams, Rowan, 7
wisdom, 45–46, 52–53, 55, 60, 85, 87, 92, 109, 158
Wisdom Literature, The (O'Connor), 47*n*7
wives, 44, 68. *see also* marriage
women. *see also* ammas; Beguines, the; feminine piety, sexual stereotypes; marriage; Mary of Egypt *and other women;* virginity (celibacy)
    authoritative, 150–54
    conversion and, 117
    Daoism and, 280
    monasticism and, 98–101, 101*n*7, 105, 109, 111, 111*i*, 160
    patristic period and, 146
    Pentecostals and, 242
    Protestantism and, 209
    Roman Catholicism and, 280
    virginity and, 69, 97
    Waldensians and, 138
Wooten, Herman, 300
Word of God, 42, 43*s*, 52–53, 86, 113, 129, 197, 240. *see also* Bible, the (Scriptures)
Word of God (*Dei Verbum*) (Vatican II), 42–44, 312
works. *see* action and works
World Day of Prayer for Peace (1986), 266*cap*
World Spirituality: An Encyclopedic History of the Religious Quest (Cousins), 8
worship (*latreia*), 121, 236
wu-forms, 278–79, 280–81, 317
wu-yu, 281
Wycliffe, 197*cap*

Y

Yan Hui, 28
yin and *yang*, 277–78*i*, 280, 317
Yong, Brother, 233
yuzchou, 277

Z

Zealots, 58*n*1
Zen Buddhism, 266, 271–76, 273*s*, 277

Zhangzi (Chuang Tzu), 276
Zhuangzi, 266, 279
Zhuangzi (Chuang Tzu), 276
Zinzendorf, Nikolaus Ludwig von, 213

ziran, 278
Zondervan, 301
Zwingli, Ulrich, 64s, 129, 200–203, 202s, 208, 213, 317. see also Reformers